BROKEN COVENANT:
Signs of a Shattered Communion

By Parker T. Williamson

REFORMATION PRESS

Broken Covenant:

Signs of a Shattered Communion

Reformation Press books, monographs and other resources are available at special discounts in bulk purchases for educational and ministry use. For more details, contact:

Director of Publications
Reformation Press
P.O. Box 2210
136 Tremont Park Drive
Lenoir, North Carolina 28645
Call us at 1-800-368-0110

Or visit PLC Publications on the Web at www.resourcecatalog.org

Cover Design: Joel McClure/HeuleGordon, Inc.; Grand Rapids, Michigan

ISBN 9781934453025

PRINTED IN THE UNITED STATES OF AMERICA

For Patty

Table of Contents

PREFACE

"Bloody Sunday," March 7, 1965, was an eviction decree. The sight of billy clubs cracking African American heads on a blood-spattered Alabama bridge catapulted me from seminary seclusion to follow the Rev. Dr. Martin Luther King, Jr. along a strip of asphalt that stretched from Selma to Montgomery.

As we marched toward the citadel of Southern segregation, our prophet/leader spoke of having been to the mountain, of seeing humanity through its Creator's eyes, of discovering that our oneness is to be found in submission to the One who made us.

TRAVELING IN TWO DIRECTIONS

Some of us who walked that highway followed Martin Luther King. Others used him. To the untrained ear, their demand for autonomy, wrapped in the language of entitlement, may have sounded like King's defiance of injustice, but our themes were as different as night and day. Traversing one pavement, we marched in distinctly different directions.

When King defied a law, he did so in obedience to a higher law – that eternal, moral law that Southern segregationists had abridged. King had no patience with those who placed themselves above the law. Individual rights – understood as the freedom to do whatever we choose – never was his agenda. But an assassin's bullet left the movement to those who welcomed that which he abhorred – the cult of the imperial self.

The cult of the imperial self is a philosophy of life that enthrones the individual. God, in any transcendent sense, ceases to exist. There is no eternally valid truth, only our various opinions. There is no universally applicable ethic, only personal preference. What matters, quite simply, is "choice" – and that choice is the "right" of each individual. Each of us defines our self, and each is obliged to acknowledge the other's self definition.

Some members of King's entourage – including social activist leaders of the Presbyterian Church (USA)[1] – shared his steps, but they did not know his heart. Ecclesiastical politicians, antinomian academics, loophole lawyers, media moguls and, of course, Hollywood forged an alliance that birthed an alien ideology.

Insisting on the right to define ourselves, this union of culture and the mainline church embraces tolerance and ignores the obvious: that had radical autonomy been our forebears' faith on Bloody Sunday, they would have had no moral warrant for judging Southern segregationists who were simply being themselves, according to their chosen definition.

Martin Luther King, Jr. did not sacrifice his life for individual autonomy. He knew it is not by accident that when America's pledge of allegiance speaks of "one nation," it adds the words, "under God." Only then does the word "indivisible" appear.

A Double-edged Sword

King's entourage brought obvious benefits to America's body politic. "Whites Only" signs no longer label bathrooms and drinking fountains, lunch counters and movie houses. And in many Southern towns, a race that was barred from the ballot now claims majority rule.

But those who participated for different purposes also made their mark. Their heirs chafe at the idea that we are one nation under God, accountable to him and designed to live under his authority. As a result, we have become increasingly divisible.

Such sentiments and the policies that they have engendered have been vigorously criticized by syndicated economist Thomas Sowell. An African American who participated in and personally benefited from the early civil rights movement, Sowell lamented what in its later stages the movement became. He warned his readers of "the evolution of idealistic movements into corrupt or tyrannical institutions." He observed that movements motivated by high minded ideals, can, and often do lead their followers into schemes that produce the opposite of their meritorious intent. "The sad fact is that the civil rights movement, after its great achievements of the 1950s and '60s, has not only begun to fizzle, but has even evolved into an institu-

1 The institution that is now called the Presbyterian Church (USA) is the result of a merger in 1983 between the United Presbyterian Church in the U.S.A. (the northern stream) and the Presbyterian Church (US), (the southern stream). This merged body, whose component parts are the result of previous mergers, claims the heritage, policies and assets of its antecedent bodies. In this sense, it is appropriate to refer to denominational officials who participated in the Selma to Montgomery march as leaders of the Presbyterian Church (USA).

tion serving only its own interests, both financial and ideological."[2]

Personal Reflections

I have often reflected on my participation in these events that occurred on the cusp of my ordination to the Presbyterian ministry. My identification with Dr. King, misinterpreted by Presbyterians who were there for different purposes, catapulted me into the ranks of denominational leadership. Assuming that I shared their ideology, they welcomed me onto national church boards, executive committees and agencies, a denominational task force, the inner sanctum of a mushrooming Presbyterian power structure whose passion was politics and the creation of a new world socioeconomic order. Thus, for a season, I saw from the inside that which I would oppose during most of my ministry, a collection of causes that led my denomination to pursue other gods.

From the Record

In the pages that follow, I have attempted to trace that ideological trajectory through a seminal period in the life of the Presbyterian Church (USA). Presbyterian history between 1926 and 2006 reveals a pattern. In the courtroom, it is called "the preponderance of evidence." It is in that evidentiary sense that I submit my verdict on what the character of the Presbyterian Church (USA) has become.

I acknowledge with deep appreciation the Presbyterian Lay Committee, brothers and sisters in Christ who have fought the good fight over many years, refusing to flinch in the face of adversity or to capitulate to cultural accommodation. I thank them for unswerving support of my ministry in their midst and for their encouragement that I pursue this writing project. Of particular note are Peggy Hedden, Robert Howard, Pamela Metherell, and W. Robert Stover who read the manuscript and offered valuable advice.

I offer a special word of thanks to my colleagues and friends: John H. Adams, whose editorship of *The Presbyterian Layman* was marked with integrity, courage and theological insight; Robert Mills, whose brilliant analyses laid bare each encounter with denominational obfuscation and whose counsel in all seasons was as generous as it was wise; Paula R. Kincaid, whose typographical skills gave shape and form to my thinking; and Gerrit Scott Dawson, whose superb articulation of the vision we share and

2 Sowell, Thomas, "A Road to Hell Paved With Good Intentions," *Forbes Magazine*, January 17, 1994, pp. 60-65.

unceasing prayers have sustained me.

Finally, I thank my wife, Patricia Jordan Williamson, whose research and proofreading proved invaluable, and who traveled many of the roads described in this book, always by my side.

Parker T. Williamson
Lenoir, North Carolina
August 31, 2007

INTRODUCTION

There was a time when Presbyterians knew what they believed. Rooted in Scripture, denominational leaders guarded the truth that had been entrusted to them. Aspiring ministers were tested for an unequivocal commitment to the Church's historic faith.

Essential beliefs were specified, and candidates for ordination subscribed to them in writing. No scruples, no behind the back finger crossing, no "wink, wink" reservations, no private definitions of Biblically conceived and confessionally affirmed doctrine. The lines between belief and unbelief were clearly drawn and commonly understood. If you felt you were called to be ordained as a Presbyterian leader, the church required that you profess what Presbyterians believe.

Proclaiming its convictions to the world, the Presbyterian Church (USA) grew exponentially. It established congregations in every state and many foreign countries, built colleges, children's homes, hospitals and hospices. Business, professional and government leaders numbered prominently among its ranks. At the peak of its influence in America, more than four and a quarter million Americans, many of them in leadership positions, claimed the name Presbyterian.

Today, having lost more than half its membership, decimated its budget, consumed its endowments, and jettisoned most of its missionary force, Presbyterian Church (USA) managers cling to the vestiges of a vanishing institution.

What happened? What caused an unparalleled witness to the gospel in the United States of America to be so rapidly swept toward oblivion? These are questions, not of conjecture, but of history.

In the pages that follow we will trace a critical segment of that history from the Presbyterian Church's General Assembly in 1926 to its General Assembly in 2006. We will examine the record of a denomination that, having rendered its core convictions and ethical imperatives optional, broke its covenantal bond and shattered its communion.

Presbyterians in the pews were horrified when they discovered that denominational leaders channeled church offerings into the hands of

African warlords (including Zimbabwe's mass murderer Robert Mugabe), underwrote tribal genocide in the name of peace and justice, and so destabilized churches in Latin America that their leaders found it necessary to evict our mission workers. Presbyterians have long been perplexed by their infrastructure's unrelenting assault on the institution of marriage, and its endorsement of sexual aberrations that the Bible condemns. Presbyterians shuddered when they learned that their leaders lobbied Congress on behalf of those who kill little children at the moment of their birth.

How shall we interpret these documented events in Presbyterian Church (USA) history? By what metamorphosis did a once-revered branch of Christ's holy catholic Church fall into such disgrace that God-fearing communicants now flee its ranks for the sake of their souls?

Examining the record, one observes an evidentiary pattern. Leaders of a denomination that claims the name of Jesus exchanged salvation for liberation. Pursuant to this exchange, they eviscerated the sacred, accommodated to culture, and invited their theologians, now devoid of "theos," into the exigencies of movement politics.

Church leaders undoubtedly will contest this assessment, arguing that the denomination's covenant – the theology and ethics that are expressed in its official documents and that purportedly constitute its character – has not been changed. But the evidence cited in this book clearly shows that the "official theology" of the Presbyterian Church (USA) which these leaders cite differs dramatically from its "working theology," the ideological composite that engenders its policies, programs and pronouncements.

What follows is a description of how this radical disjunction between the denomination's covenant and its character came to be.

Covenant

Holy Scripture

"I am astonished that you are so quickly deserting him who called you in the grace of Christ and turning to a different gospel – not that there is another gospel, but there are some who trouble you and want to pervert the gospel of Christ."

Galatians 1:6-10

The Constitution

"Insofar as Christ's will for the Church is set forth in Scripture, it is to be obeyed. In the worship and service of God and the government of the church, matters are to be ordered according to the Word by reason and sound judgment, under the guidance of the Holy Spirit."

The Book of Order
Preliminary Principles

Broken Covenant

"The Bible must always be transposed into a contemporary key to be understood by contemporary men. ..."

Edward A. Dowey, Chairman
Committee to Write a Brief Statement of Faith
Presbyterian Life, February 15, 1965

"And all the time – such is the tragic comedy of our situation – we continue to clamour for those very qualities we are rendering impossible ... In a sort of ghastly simplicity we remove the organ and demand the function. We make men without chests and expect of them virtue and enterprise. We laugh at honour and are shocked to find traitors in our midst. We castrate, and bid the geldings be fruitful."

C. S. Lewis
The Abolition of Man

Chapter One

1926

On May 22, 1922, Rev. Harry Emerson Fosdick stepped into the pulpit of First Presbyterian Church in New York City and delivered a sermon titled, "Shall the Fundamentalists Win?" A Baptist, Fosdick subscribed to no creed. Thus, he was the ideal front for Presbyterian leaders who chafed when required to subscribe to the denomination's five "fundamental" beliefs.[1] Modernists wanted more flexible standards, preferably, no standards at all. Finding the historic doctrines of Christianity too confining, they insisted that the essence of Christian faith lies not in specified beliefs, but in one's "Christian experience."

"Shall the Fundamentalists Win?" did not go unchallenged. Rev. Clarence E. Macartney, minister of Philadelphia's Arch Street Presbyterian Church, replied in a publication called *The Presbyterian*,[2] titling his article, "Shall Unbelief Win?" Macartney argued that grounding one's faith in spiritual feelings, no matter how powerfully experienced or sincerely held, was a poor substitute for the faith "once and for all delivered to the saints," as attested in Scripture and affirmed in the great confessions of the Reformed tradition. In themselves, one's personal feelings can play tricks on the heart and mind, he said, unless they receive confirmation from the benchmark of God's Word.

Christianity and Liberalism

Meanwhile, Rev. J. Gresham Machen, a distinguished professor of New Testament at Princeton Theological Seminary, jumped into the fray with the

---

1 Presbyterians aspiring to ordination were required to affirm: (a) the inspiration of the Bible by the Holy Spirit and the inerrancy of Scripture as a result of this inspiration; (b) the virgin birth of Christ; (c) the belief that Christ's death was atonement for sin; (d) the bodily resurrection of Christ; (e) the historical reality of Christ's miracles.

2 *The Presbyterian*, January, 1924.

publication of *Christianity and Liberalism*.[3] Machen argued that the basic tenets of liberalism that were espoused by Fosdick and his cadre of Presbyterian intellectuals represented not simply a different perspective within the Christian faith, but a different faith altogether.

"It may appear," said Machen, "that what the liberal theologian has retained after abandoning to the enemy one Christian doctrine after another is not Christianity at all, but a religion that is so entirely different from Christianity as to belong in a distinct category."[4]

Machen argued that liberalism differs sharply from Christianity in that, being based in one's personal experience, it rejects the objective, factual basis of Christian faith, namely, God's self revelation in the person and work of Jesus Christ and in Holy Scripture.

"The liberal preacher really is rejecting the whole basis of Christianity, which is a religion founded not on aspirations, but on facts. Here is found the most fundamental difference between liberalism and Christianity – liberalism is altogether in the imperative mood, while Christianity begins with a triumphant indicative. Liberalism appeals to man's will, while Christianity announces, first, a gracious act of God."[5]

A Different God

Liberalism's view of God, a force of nature or a projection of human ideals that causes humans to "feel spiritual," was utterly rejected by Machen as unBiblical and untrue. "Modern liberalism, even when it is not consistently pantheistic, is at any rate panthetizing. It tends everywhere to break down the separateness between God and the world, and the sharp personal distinction between God and man ... Very different is the living and holy God of the Bible and of Christian faith."[6]

A Different Humanity

Machen argued that not only is liberalism's view of God inadequate, but its resulting anthropology is false. He warned Presbyterians that liberals host an exceedingly optimistic view of human nature, finding little room for a doctrine of human sin. "According to the Bible, man is a sinner under the

3 Machen, J. Gresham, *Christianity and Liberalism* (Grand Rapids, Michigan: Wm. B. Erdman, 1923).

4 *Ibid*., p.6.

5 *Ibid*., p. 47.

6 *Ibid*., p. 63.

just condemnation of God; according to modern liberalism, there is really no such thing as sin. At the very root of the modern liberal movement is the loss of the consciousness of sin."[7]

Machen spared no words in his condemnation of liberalism's anthropology, identifying it not merely as an aberrant form of Christian faith but as an ideology that is utterly inconsistent with Christian faith. "Paganism is that view of life which finds the highest goal of human existence in the healthy and harmonious and joyous development of existing human faculties. Very different is the Christian ideal. Paganism is optimistic with regard to unaided human nature, whereas Christianity is the religion of the broken heart."[8]

A Different Jesus

In failing properly to assess the human condition, it is no wonder that liberalism had no use for a savior. Machen observed that the liberal preacher had much to say about Jesus as moral teacher, therapeutic friend and loving example. But Jesus as savior makes no sense to those who do not know that they need to be saved. Machen accused liberalism of adopting a "policy of palliation" in which Jesus displayed a consciousness of sonship with God that all humans may also experience. Palliation is the liberals' substitute for salvation.

What is missing in the liberals' Jesus is the fact that he is the Messiah. "Liberalism regards Him as an Example and Guide; Christianity as a Saviour: liberalism makes Him an example for faith; Christianity, the object of faith."[9]

A Different Scripture

Machen argued that the liberals' attitude toward Scripture was thoroughly anti-Christian. A scholar who knew not only the text but was thoroughly familiar with what post-Enlightenment interpreters were doing with that text, Machen could see the inevitable result of one's moving from the Word itself to one's "experience" of the Word. He knew that in elevating "Christian experience," undiscerning Christians might substitute their interpretations of the Word for the Word that speaks for itself. Thus he warned his fellow Presbyterians that their penchant for celebrating Christian experi-

7 *Ibid.*, p. 64.

8 *Ibid.*, p. 65.

9 *Ibid.*, p. 96.

ence would result in shifting from the Bible to "the Bible to me." Soon, preachers would replace "Listen to the Word of God," with an anemic substitute: "Listen for the Word of God." He saw that the Word was about to be equated with what we say it says.

A Different Church

Finally, Machen attacked the liberals' view of the church as an essentially open society whose permeable boundaries allow the inclusion of numerous beliefs and lifestyles. Liberalism builds its case on a doctrine of the brotherhood of humankind, he observed.

While conceding the fact that all humans experience a filial relationship by virtue of the fatherhood of God, Machen insisted that "the true brotherhood, according to Christian teaching, is the brotherhood of the redeemed."[10]

Machen found useful the Reformed tradition's distinction between the visible and invisible church. He lamented the "obvious weakness" of the visible church and inquired into its cause: "One cause is perfectly plain – the church of today has been unfaithful to her Lord by admitting great companies of non-Christian persons, not only into her membership, but into her teaching agencies … The greatest menace to the church today comes not from the enemies outside, but from the enemies within; it comes from the presence within the church of a type of faith and practice that is anti-Christian to the core ... It is highly undesirable that liberalism and Christianity should continue to be propagated within the bounds of the same organization. A separation between the two parties in the church is the crying need of the hour."[11]

A Different Religion

In the years that followed the publication of *Christianity and Liberalism*, Machen entered more deeply into the denominational debate. With each contest, he drew the lines more sharply. "The plain fact is," he told *The New York Times*, "that two mutually exclusive religions are being proclaimed in the pulpits of the Presbyterian Church."[12]

In an editorial that appeared in *The Presbyterian*, Machen said "the Presbyterian Church in the United States has apparently come to the parting of

---

10 *Ibid.*, p. 158.

11 *Ibid.*, p. 160.

12 *The New York Times*, January 10, 1924.

the ways. It may stand for Christ, or it may stand against him, but it can hardly hold the two opinions."[13]

The Auburn Affirmation

Alarmed by the fact that Machen enjoyed support from the majority of Princeton's faculty and was growing in popularity across the denomination, the liberals feared that "fundamentalists" were taking over. A group of Presbyterian ministers gathered at Auburn Seminary, and on January 9, 1924, they issued a document known as the "Auburn Affirmation."[14] Central to the affirmation was an attack on the inerrancy of the Scriptures. Other doctrines, the virgin birth of Christ and his bodily resurrection, were described as "theories." In essence, the Auburn Affirmation argued against any attempt by the Presbyterian Church to codify any particular belief as "fundamental" or "essential."

The Liberals' Strategy

Proponents of the Auburn Affirmation comprised a distinct minority in the Presbyterian Church. They knew that they did not have the numbers to overturn the General Assembly's requirement that persons standing for ordination must subscribe to specified "essential beliefs." The only way they could gain control of the denomination would be to forge an alliance with institutional Presbyterians, church leaders who loved organizational unity and structural maintenance more than theology. Thus, they devised a plan to turn the debate away from doctrine, which they could not win, toward a strategy for preserving the peace of the Presbyterian Church, a plan that they believed would attract institutionalists.

They knew that Machen, whose writings had shown their position not only to be non-Presbyterian but also non-Christian, would never play ball with them. But might it be possible to recruit someone close to Machen's camp, someone whose tone was more irenic, a recognized evangelical whose passion for preserving the institutional church might trump his theological integrity?

That person would not have to agree with them theologically. In fact, they would be better served if he did not. All they needed was for that known evangelical to make room for their views and help them recast the

13 *The Presbyterian*, April, 1924.

14 "*An Affirmation* designed to safeguard the unity and liberty of the Presbyterian Church in the United States of America with all signatures and the Note Supplementary," (Auburn, New York: The Jacobs Press, May 5, 1924).

denomination's focus from doctrinal differences ("essential beliefs") to unity (there's room under this tent for everyone). Such a person could tip the balance by pulling middle of the road Presbyterians, albeit unknowingly, into an alliance with the liberals.

The Triumph of the 'Middle'

Charles Erdman, Machen's Princeton Seminary colleague who described himself as an "evangelical moderate," fit that mold perfectly. Erdman was named moderator of the General Assembly in 1925, running on a peace platform. He urged the Presbyterian Church to get on with its ministry and not be distracted by troublesome doctrinal controversy.

Machen did not question Erdman's faith, but he was distressed by Erdman's willingness, either from political naiveté or misplaced priorities, to be used by those who would undermine the faith. "Dr. Erdman does not indeed reject the doctrinal system of our church," he said, "but he is perfectly willing to make common cause with those who reject it, and he is perfectly willing on many occasions to keep it in the background."[15]

Once elected, Erdman proceeded to appoint a commission of fifteen people "to study the present spiritual condition of our church and the causes making for unrest, and to report to the next General Assembly, to the end that the purity, peace, unity and progress of the church may be assured."[16/17] The group was largely comprised of liberals and peace seeking moderates. Missing were persons known to fight for doctrinal truth.

Erdman opened the 1926 General Assembly with a sermon that called on commissioners to work for peace and avoid being influenced by those who would foment disunity. "A man who is factious and causes separation among Christians shows that he is out of fellowship with Christ and is not controlled by his Spirit," the moderator said.[18]

Then the commission made its report. It called for doctrinal toleration, and it castigated unnamed Presbyterians who make "hasty or harsh judgments of the motives of brethren whose hearts are fully known only to God." In a tide-turning vote, the 1926 General Assembly adopted the com-

15 *The Presbyterian*, February 5, 1925.

16 Presbyterian Church in the U.S.A., *Minutes of the General Assembly*, 1925, p. 88.

17 Note the similar language used to describe General Assembly task forces in 1926 and 2006.

18 Erdman, Charles R., "The Power of the Spirit" (Philadelphia: General Assembly of the Presbyterian Church, 1926), p. 6.

mission's report,[19] which, according to church historian Bradley Longfield, "made it clear that the five essentials had no binding authority and the arguments of the Auburn Affirmation had essentially been accepted *in toto*."[20]

The 1926 General Assembly was a watershed moment in the life of the Presbyterian Church. From this moment on, presbyteries ordained persons who said they affirmed "the essential tenets" of Christian faith, but would not specify what those essentials are. Soon, it became clear that what one presbytery deemed "essential" might be regarded as "discretionary" by another. Having steadfastly refused to be tied to any particulars since 1926, presbyteries have ordained and installed denominational leaders who exhibit a wide variety of beliefs and practices.

During the nine years that followed the 1926 assembly, J. Gresham Machen continued his fight for Biblical and confessional integrity in the Presbyterian Church, but he was politically out gunned by the coalition that the liberal Auburn group had forged with Erdman and his moderate evangelical allies. Excoriated as a radical, Machen was forced to resign his professorship at Princeton Seminary. He was not charged with heresy, a theological debate that he would have welcomed and in which he would have been a formidable adversary. Instead, he was criticized for his "tone," "incivility," "lack of decorum," and unspecified "character issues." In 1935, after Machen refused to abandon an independent mission board that required its missionaries to subscribe to essential Christian beliefs, New Brunswick Presbytery stripped him of his ordination.

A Denominational Déjà vu

Presbyterians who know their history cannot help but be struck by parallels between the denomination's 1926 and 2006 General Assemblies. Both assemblies received reports from politically appointed, high level "peace, unity and purity" groups. In both cases, the dominant constituency of these groups embraced theological liberalism. Minority members from the "evangelical" sector of the denomination represented the most moderate, institutionally compliant faction within that sector. In 1926 and 2006, institutional preservation trumped doctrinal integrity. Theology succumbed to politics.

19 Note: Although the 1926 General Assembly "adopted" the report in principle, it honored the Special Commission's request for an extension in order to bring its final report to the 1927 General Assembly. When the final report was made in 1927, it was essentially unchanged, and the assembly adopted it unanimously. See Presbyterian Church in the U.S.A., *Minutes of the General Assembly*, 1927, p. 61.

20 Longfield, Bradley J., *The Presbyterian Controversy: Fundamentalists, Modernists, and Moderates* (Oxford: Oxford University Press, 1991), p. 160.

Covenant

Holy Scripture:

"Do not love the world or the things in the world ... The world passes away, and the lust of it, but he who does the will of God abides forever."

I John:15, 17

The Constitution:

"All synods or councils since the apostles' times, whether general or particular, may err, and many have erred; therefore they are not to be made the rule of faith or practice, but to be used as a help in both."

The Westminster Confession of Faith
Chapter XXXI

"... the Holy Scriptures are the only rule of faith and manners ... no Church governing body ought to pretend to make laws to bind the conscience in virtue of their own authority ... all their decisions should be founded upon the revealed will of God."

The Book of Order
G-1.0307

Broken Covenant

"The world sets the church's agenda."

The World Council of Churches, Uppsala, 1968

CHAPTER TWO

TURNING TO THE WORLD'S AGENDA

The debate over essential tenets and whether to require subscription to them as a prerequisite to ordination directed the denomination's focus inward to theology and institutional concerns. As this debate subsided, Presbyterian Church (USA) leaders in the mid-30s, 40s and 50s turned their attention beyond the sanctuary to a world where seismic events were taking place. Increasingly, the denomination's agenda took up the subjects of war, economics, race, and institutional mergers. To some extent, the impetus that turned its attention from spiritual matters to worldwide developments was driven, at least initially, by the denomination's passion for "foreign missions."

Membership on the Board of Foreign Missions was an esteemed and coveted position. It was, in fact, J. Gresham Machen's challenge to this board's theological integrity that triggered the removal of his ordination. Machen insisted that the board require Presbyterian missionaries to subscribe to essential tenets of Christian faith, and two presbyteries backed him up by sending overtures to this effect to the 1933 General Assembly. The assembly refused to enact such a requirement. To the contrary, it lauded the board with "the wholehearted, unequivocal, enthusiastic and affectionate commendation of the church at large."[1]

Machen and his supporters responded by establishing an independent foreign mission board that did, in fact, require strict adherence to specified principles of Reformed faith. That act of defiance was too much for General Assembly officials. They had tolerated Machen's theological challenges over the years – largely by attempting to ignore or isolate them – but

1 Presbyterian Church in the U.S.A., *Minutes of the General Assembly*, 1933, p. 159.

his creation of a competitive mission board was more than they could bear. No cause inspired greater generosity from Presbyterian donors than foreign missions, even during the Great Depression when contributions to church budgets were severely curtailed. Thus, Machen's threat became a pocketbook issue that denominational officials could ill afford to overlook.

In 1934, the General Assembly issued an edict that no ordained leader could participate in the newly organized independent foreign mission board.[2] Machen and other board members refused to resign their membership. So in 1935, the Presbytery of New Brunswick tried Machen on charges that he had defied the General Assembly's order.

Machen sought to defend himself with doctrinal arguments, namely that the official Board of Foreign Missions had deviated from Biblical standards by declining to require subscription to them by its missionaries, but the presbytery court ruled that it had no standing to question decisions of the General Assembly. Besides, said the presbytery, the General Assembly was not on trial, Machen was.

Machen's ordination was revoked, not on the basis of a heresy charge, but on grounds that he was in "rebellion."[3] In current Presbyterian parlance, such defiance is called "renouncing the jurisdiction of the Presbyterian Church (USA)."

Machen and other members of the independent foreign mission board who were similarly disciplined appealed their convictions to the 1936 General Assembly, but the denomination's highest court upheld its presbyteries' judgments.[4] Six months later, on January 1, 1937, while traveling among speaking engagements in North Dakota, Machen became ill and died.

Having effectively silenced leaders of the independent foreign missions board, denominational leaders mounted major campaigns in support of the official agency. Throughout the 1930s and 1940s, foreign missions commanded headlines in the church press. Of particular note were the denomination's missionary thrust into Korea and China, and its concerns over threats to these missionaries from a fast growing movement called "Communism."

---

2 Presbyterian Church in the U.S.A., *Minutes of the General Assembly*, 1934, pp. 115-116.

3 Presbyterian Church in the U.S.A., Presbytery of New Brunswick, "Action of the Presbytery of New Brunswick, April, 1935," Record Group 7, Box 1, Folder 3, Department of History, Presbyterian Church (USA), pp. 4-6.

4 Presbyterian Church in the U.S.A., *Minutes of the General Assembly*, 1936, pp. 99-101.

Presbyterians and Pacifism

Having dispatched more than a thousand missionaries around the globe, many of them landing in hot spots where Hitler's rise to power and clashes between Communism and Fascism with democracy was inexorably moving the world into war, the denomination could not avoid public policy issues.

Understandably, world peace became a major focus as the nation suffered through two world wars and a Korean conflict that some believed would trigger World War III. In 1936, for example, *The Presbyterian* ran a page one article by the Rev. David DeForest Burrell titled, "Presbyterians and Pacifism."[5]

Burrell's concern was with the fact that the Presbytery of Cayuga, with the concurrence of 71 other presbyteries, had submitted an overture to the 1936 General Assembly, asking it to strike from the *Westminster Confession of Faith* words that justify war: "So for that end, they may lawfully now under the New Testament, wage war upon just and necessary occasions."[6] The "end" referred to in the Confession is "to maintain piety, justice and peace, according to the wholesome laws of each commonwealth."[7]

While stating that his aversion to war equaled that of the pacifists, Burrell found the Cayuga overture troubling. "For some years," he said, "overtures concerned with various phases of the pacifistic movement have appeared at the assembly, but none has gone so far as this, and none has had so much support."[8]

"Any proposal to alter the Confession should receive the most deliberate consideration. It is the chief doctrinal Standard of our church, the expression of the Church's historical and established conviction as to the precise teachings of Scripture. It is the principle on which also, the Catechisms, our other doctrinal Standards, are constructed. Nothing has a rightful place in these constitutional documents which is not the plain teaching of Scripture; and nothing of their contents should be altered or removed which is the plain teaching of Scripture."[9]

Burrell said that Cayuga's "unconditional" opposition to war was not supported by Scripture. He charged supporters of the overture with a

5 Burrell, David DeForest, "Presbyterians and Pacifism," *The Presbyterian*, January 9, 1936.

6 *The Constitution of the Presbyterian Church (USA), Part One: The Book of Confessions* (Louisville, Ky.: Office of the General Assembly, 1999), paragraph 6.128.

7 *Ibid.*

8 Burrell, *op.cit.*

9 *Ibid.*

"Modernism [that] discards the Old Testament" and cites highly selective New Testament passages, thus giving the New Testament "an elective treatment."[10] On these scriptural grounds, Burrell and others were successful in convincing the 1936 General Assembly to reject the Cayuga overture.

While the Presbyterian Church (USA) has never subscribed to a full-blown pacifism, the pacifist ("peacemaking" is the label of choice in current General Assembly parlance) influence that surfaced in the Cayuga overture of 1936 continued to find strong support among denominational leaders in the three decades leading toward 1967.

Meanwhile, the rise of international totalitarianism evoked considerable concern among Presbyterians in the pews. The Rev. Wilbur M. Franklin penned a widely distributed article titled, "Will Germany Acknowledge God or State?" Franklin noted that all eyes were focused on what the churches in Germany would do in response to a growing national socialism that was being promoted by Hitler's Third Reich.

"Will the Church oppose national socialism?" asked Franklin. "One cannot but believe that a country which for four centuries has honored Martin Luther, who said, 'Here I stand! I cannot do otherwise. God help me,' and in whose heart lives the Spirit of the Reformation, will not and cannot acknowledge any authority higher than the authority of God."[11]

Franklin would soon learn, both in Germany and in his own United States, how a church that had been rooted in the Reformation could accommodate its theology to the pressures of surrounding culture.

In 1948, General Assembly Moderator Wilbur La Roe Jr., issued a strong pronouncement against communism. La Roe told Presbyterians that "great ideological battle lines" were being formed in the world. "One is a pagan battle line of the cohorts of totalitarianism, whether in the form of communism or fascism. Arrayed against this is the battle line of Christianity," he said.[12]

A widely known Presbyterian leader during this period was John Foster Dulles, director of the Federal Council of Churches Commission on a Just and Durable Peace and a member of the US delegation to the United Nations. In an article titled "Peace is Possible," Dulles lamented mounting criticism of the UN for its failures to prevent international armed conflict. He called on Presbyterians to defend the international body. Many people, said Dulles "are disappointed about the UN's past record, and they are

10 *Ibid.*

11 *The Presbyterian*, April 9, 1936.

12 *Presbyterian Life*, Jan. 17, 1948.

frankly pessimistic about its future ..."[13]

"... Political machinery only works well when it carries out community judgments as to what is right and what is wrong," continued Dulles. "The United Nations and its various bodies, particularly the General Assembly, provide places where representative men and women from all over the world discuss national conduct and national ideals and try to agree on what is right and what is wrong. Out of that discussion gradually will come common moral standards. That is the foundation of world order."[14]

"The religious people of the world, and especially Christian, should work enthusiastically to help build that moral foundation," said Dulles. "People should not feel and should not say that the United Nations has failed. For one, I am wholly optimistic about the United Nations. It is doing the kind of job which now needs to be done. ... Even as it now stands the UN is far more potent than the League of Nations ever was. Those who are dissatisfied are in the main those who would like to see a steeple built before the foundation is laid ..."[15]

Opposition to the Draft

Presbyterian leaders during this period were united in condemning communism as an evil ideology that was incompatible with Christian faith. But they differed on the means that the United States government should employ to combat this evil. Increasingly, General Assembly spokespersons denounced any move by the government to strengthen the military or to confront totalitarian regimes with military force.

When communist incursions began to overtake parts of Germany, Hungary, Bulgaria, Rumania and Czechoslovakia, and Fascists won major positions in Italy and Spain, US President Harry S. Truman proposed a program of "universal military training." This would be the nation's first peacetime military draft, and Presbyterian officials went on the warpath against it.

A lead article in the denomination's official magazine quoted Nebraska Congressman Howard Buffett: "The 'war scare' which is blanketing this country is a crime against America and all humanity. These are strong words, and are not used carelessly."[16]

The article reported Mr. Buffett's implication that "there were forces in the USA who are trying to provoke war: (1) to cover up Administration

---

13 *Presbyterian Life*, Feb. 28, 1948.

14 *Ibid.*

15 *Ibid.*

16 *Presbyterian Life*, April 24, 1948.

mistakes in foreign policy and (2) to rationalize the militarization of the nation."[17] It continued: "The churches and their people are concerned primarily with the growing control of the military in the United States. Their control centers upon the issue of universal military training. For the past six months, most of the nation's churches have joined with labor, educational and youth groups in opposition to U.M.T. [Universal Military Training]."[18]

"One month ago, March 19, officials of the Presbyterian Church again voiced opposition to peacetime training in an open letter signed by Dr. Paul N. Poling, secretary of the church's division of Social Education and Action, and the leader of the church's defense of its time-honored position … On March 30, Dr. Paul Payne, Dr. Ganse Little and Dr. Paul Poling went to Washington with a carefully prepared statement … for presentation to the Senate Armed Services Committee. It stated the 'historic position of opposition to peacetime military conscription.'"[19]

Poling and Payne said that the proposed draft "could be seen as 'the initiation of war.' It is not true that the measures proposed by President Truman are 'preventive measures' … The fact is that the sheer proposal of these laws, and the measures used by military leaders to stampede the American nation into the draft have intensified fears rather than brought reassurance and have created the conviction that we are moving toward, rather than away from war. To many American people the draft means war. For America it has never meant anything else."[20]

Poling and Payne continued: "We warn against likening the present crisis in all respects to the crisis at Munich, and postulating our national policy on the assumption that the two situations are identical, whereas they are just enough alike to be misleading. Hitler was the head of a nation armed as no other nation in history had ever been before. Russia, on the other hand, is critically weak both as to military establishments and industrial potential …"[21]

These church leaders' assessment of Russia's military potential and expansionist intentions was shared by John Foster Dulles: "Though some may agree with me in my optimism about the United Nations, they would point out that the most important problem today is the alleged 'impending war' between the United States and the Soviet Union. I do not believe in

17 *Ibid.*

18 *Ibid.*

19 *Ibid.*

20 *Ibid.*

21 *Ibid.*

such a war. The United States does not want it. The Soviet Union does not want it. The immediate ambitions of Soviet leaders are not of a kind which will be satisfied by military effort."[22]

When the 160th General Assembly of the Presbyterian Church U.S.A. met in the spring of 1948, it declared its opposition to peacetime conscription and, according to *Presbyterian Life*, "it urged 'constructive statesmanship' on the part of the U.S. in its dealings with Russia."[23]

The denominational magazine devoted much of its General Assembly coverage to speeches in opposition to Truman's military buildup proposals. It quoted heavily from a speech to the General Assembly by the Rev. Robert Skinner: "As Christians our struggle is not against Russia. It is against a godless, pagan, materialistic philosophy of life which has crystallized itself in a powerful, evangelistic, missionary-minded group called 'Communists' … We have been propagandized into thinking that we can stop Communism with universal military training, the draft, the atomic bomb, and a large military establishment. We know, however, that an idea cannot be stopped with guns … the only defense against the advance of a false faith is the establishment of a militantly active, evangelistic true faith."[24]

Presbyterian Life reported the decision reached by the 1948 General Assembly: "We believe the most ominous present threat to freedom and the peace of the world lies in the militarization of the nations. The United States as the leading world power should take bold steps to reverse such a trend. To date, our national tendency has been to fall in with and to accentuate rather than to retard this trend … We believe that a system of voluntary recruitment will provide adequate defense if administered by leaders who believe in it. Because of our industrial and military potentialities revealed in the last war, because of our capacity for mobilization, and because of the resources inherent in the voluntary system, we go on record as opposing compulsory military training and the use of the draft in peacetime."[25]

Despite significant lobbying efforts from Presbyterian Church spokespersons, President Truman's proposal made its way through Congress. General Assembly leaders took some comfort in the fact that the president's proposal was modified. It applied only to males between the

22 *Presbyterian Life*, February 28, 1948.

23 *Presbyterian Life*, June 19, 1948.

24 *Ibid.*

25 *Ibid.*

ages of 19 and 25, was limited to a period of twenty one months, and included numerous exceptions, the most significant being a marital exemption. *Presbyterian Life* noted that following congressional approval of the military draft, there was a marked increase in marriage ceremonies among 19-25 year old adults.

Military vs. Diplomatic Peace

After the Congress approved military conscription, *Presbyterian Life* ran an editorial by Francis Pickens Miller in which he called on church officials to monitor the training that the US government would impose on its draftees. Miller worried that the "moral character of America's young men might be considerably tainted if not actually corrupted by their experience in such a training program."[26]

"The effect of a military training program upon the moral character of American youth will depend primarily upon the moral character of the officers in charge," said Miller. "If they are of the type who think of their boys as being nothing more than young fighting animals whose natural off-duty recreation will be prostitutes and liquor, then widespread corruption can be expected ... Many Christians are skeptical about the peacetime draft because they are not sure that the youth of the country can be safely entrusted to the Armed Forces."[27]

Miller called on the Federal Council of Churches to serve as a watchdog over military training. He asked that the President of the United States set up an independent commission with power over the military to correct any offenses that might be reported by church overseers.[28]

While generally agreeing with Dulles and other General Assembly leaders that communism is best fought with the tools of economic development rather than by military standoff, Presbyterians in the pews hosted a deep love for their missionaries and argued for the safety of those who were increasingly standing in harm's way. During the early 1950s, *Presbyterian Life* ran numerous articles on the work of denominational missionaries in Korea and China, raising troubling questions about their safety in areas where communist regimes were becoming increasingly virulent. Denominational reporters in Korea spoke of "the Red invasions that began in June of 1950," and they posted stories including pictures of Presbyterian missionaries who had chosen to stay in South Korea and conduct worship services in

26 *Presbyterian Life*, August 7, 1948.

27 *Ibid.*

28 *Ibid.*

the midst of bomb craters and broken-down buildings.[29]

Articles in the denominational magazine focused on growing threats to missionaries in China as communist leaders increased the pressure on them: "Ever since last fall, Protestant mission boards have been in doubt about whether foreign missionaries on the mainland of China would be able, under Communism, to do effective work. Last month they had their answer: for many missionaries, it seemed to be 'no.'"[30]

One article reported new regulations that the communists had imposed on "foreign-supported" colleges, schools, hospitals and charity organizations. It reported that the mainland regime had taken over all American assets and had frozen bank deposits. "Because of this 'increased tension,' some American Protestant mission boards have called home their missionaries from China ... The PCUSA Foreign Mission Board has not ordered any of its sixty-four missionaries still in China to come home, because the church has always allowed mission workers to make their own decisions about leaving troubled areas."[31]

In 1951, divisions among Americans over diplomatic versus military responses to communist aggression reached feverish levels. The focus of this debate sharpened over the confrontation between President Harry Truman and General Douglas MacArthur. After MacArthur made his now famous speech to Congress, *Presbyterian Life* tried to pour editorial oil on Presbyterian waters: "We are united in our opposition to the Kremlin and all its works," said the editorial. "We want no part of it. Let us not then join in the service of Moscow by allowing ourselves to be divided into opposing camps because of our differences – at the moment, over the methods by which Communist aggressions can be checked."[32]

"Above all," continued the editorial, "let us avoid as the plague the temptation to vituperation, for such practice precludes all possibility of any intelligent facing of vital issues. These issues far transcend personalities, and it is a positive disservice to stoop to attribute sordid motives to the President or to General MacArthur ..."[33]

Finally, the denominational magazine came down on the side of diplomacy: "The question as to whether indefinite stalemate in Korea is the only alternative to World War III is one which no one can answer. Nevertheless,

29 *Presbyterian Life*, February 3, 1951.

30 *Ibid.*

31 *Ibid.*

32 *Presbyterian Life*, May 12, 1951.

33 *Ibid.*

if we label as appeasement all efforts to effect any kind of a compromise settlement, we are dangerously near the assumption that, unless all settlements with the communists can go our way, we are prepared to embark on a third world war."[34]

Struggles among Americans – and certainly among Presbyterians in their midst – were not limited to the subject of dealing with communists abroad. Church leaders expressed growing concern over "anti-Communist hysteria" that they observed among the American people, Congress and the FBI. Of particular concern were statements by members of Congress suggesting that denominational officials might be investigated for possible sympathies toward communism.

The 1951 General Assembly voiced such concerns. *Presbyterian Life* reported "Some forms of loyalty oaths … 'which stifle freedom of thought and inquiry' were condemned by the assembly … People are afraid to speak their convictions for fear of reprisal. Thus we lay the groundwork for a police society which destroys the freedom we seek to save. The assembly pronouncement warned against self-righteousness, fear and hysteria, militarism, unholy alliances, and moral flabbiness … from high government positions down to college athletics."[35]

In a follow-up editorial, the denominational periodical noted "Our worst danger at present is that we shall become so fearful of our enemies without and within that we shall try to save ourselves by armament against outside enemies, and the denial of freedom against inside enemies. In these two areas, the greatest sanity must be exercised, lest our vigilance result in our conquest by other enemies."[36]

The editorial continued, "Congressional investigations, loyalty oaths, the McCarran Act, and state laws today are employed to detect and eradicate the Communist virus in our body social. Some abuses have resulted from these methods: Men are accused of guilt before a legislative committee when they should be tried by a court of law before a judge; men are branded as guilty through widespread publicity and their careers are ruined even if they are innocent; men are regarded as guilty because of association with organizations which are suspect; and men are regarded with suspicion as enemies of their country if they earnestly criticize some of the policies of the United States."[37]

34 *Ibid.*

35 *Presbyterian Life*, June 23, 1951.

36 *Presbyterian Life*, November 24, 1951.

37 *Ibid.*

In 1954, Presbyterian officials' concerns became more personal when it was alleged that former General Assembly Moderator John Mackay had been the subject of investigation. Denominational leaders rallied at the 166th General Assembly. "The General Assembly voted to endorse a 'letter to Presbyterians' written by the General Council condemning attacks by congressional committees on human freedom of expression regarding communism and expressing confidence in Dr. John Mackay, 'the personal attack that has been made upon our beloved past Moderator, an attack so venomous and vindictive that the average person here would find it difficult even to imagine.'"[38]

Although it never went as far as the pacifism advocated by the Cayuga overture, the General Assembly repeatedly voiced a propensity for diplomatic rather than military responses to Communist expansionism. One General Assembly resolution suggested that the United States surrender its sovereignty to the United Nations. As reported by *Presbyterian Life*, it said that the denomination should "lend its backing to suggestions already made to seek the reduction of armaments on a collective basis, and subject all weapons of war including atomic weapons, to international jurisdiction under the proper safeguards … [and that it] should seek by every possible means to clothe the United Nations with the authority and the prestige which will give it the effect of world government …"[39]

An op-ed article by Casper Blackburn expressed a similar one-world government theme: "Ninety-one members of the United States House of Representatives recently joined to introduce a resolution asking that American foreign policy be aimed toward transforming the United Nations into a world federal government," said Blackburn. "Although many Christians consider the present time inappropriate to seek world federation, all can unite in supporting the action of these congressmen. The submitted resolution asks no immediate change in the United Nations. Its sponsors only wish to place the United States on record as refusing to adopt permanently the balance of power policy on which the prospects of peace rest uneasily today."[40]

Blackburn appreciatively quoted Charles Eaton, one of the congressmen who signed the resolution: "The passage of the resolution of which I am one of the sponsors will, I believe, help convince a doubting world that the United States wants to set up a world-wide communion table of peace

38 *Presbyterian Life*, June 12, 1954.

39 *Presbyterian Life*, June 23, 1951.

40 *Presbyterian Life*, September 17, 1949.

around which all the people of the world may sit with the Master. I do not expect to see this table set tomorrow. I may never see it. But I want to help in its construction."[41]

Addressing Economic Issues

Not only was world peace a preoccupation of Presbyterian Church leaders but the subject of economics, both at home and abroad, found its way onto the denominational agenda. This was partially due to the peace issue, for leaders like John Foster Dulles were convinced that the most effective front for engaging communism was economic aid rather than military defense. Dulles believed, and he convinced denominational officials to this effect, that communism could only take root in the soil of human deprivation and misery. Thus, although he affirmed it in altruistic and "Good Samaritan" terms, Dulles urged the Presbyterian Church to give strong public support to the Marshall Plan, an economic recovery program for war-ravaged countries in Europe.

Dulles challenged the Presbyterian Church in the U.S.A. to push economics to the forefront of the nation's struggle against communism: "The [Soviet leaders] are seeking first to overthrow free institutions by undermining them economically and taking advantage of their weaknesses. If they succeed and get control over much of the world, then the United States will be isolated and in a dangerous position. The defense against this control is not military, but economic and social. We must help to maintain free institutions by invigorating them with fresh ideas and with the economic aid needed to get these ideas to take root and to grow strong."[42]

"If the Marshall Plan becomes a reality," said Dulles in an address to Presbyterians, "peace will become a reality … It is here that the churches of America come in. It is important, not only that the plan be put through, but that it be put through in a spirit of brotherly love without suspicion, hatred and hysteria. Only the church people of America can assure that … Our program is clear. We must keep emotionally steady. We must support the Marshall Plan. We must support the United Nations. We must put forth this great creative effort animated by good will and not by hate."[43]

The denominational magazine promoted the Marshall Plan editorially. It said, "As we look at Europe the outlook is far from bright. There is no peace. Indeed, many are speaking of the imminence of another war …

41 *Ibid.*

42 *Presbyterian Life*, February 28, 1948.

43 *Ibid.*

Another war looms, this time between Russia and the USA, and Europe will be the battleground ... America needs and is in a position to lead Europe out of chaos. But we must change our hitherto negative attack on Communism to a positive demonstration that our democratic and Christian way of life is the better for the largest number of people. Somehow we must prove that our ERP [Economic Recovery Plan] is not primarily a means to combat Communism but an expression of good will and mercy and charity; moreover, that we are not out primarily to save ourselves by trying to save Europe but are giving expression to sincere altruism. To preach a gospel of anti-Communism and simultaneously to promote a dollar diplomacy just doesn't "click" with a suspicious and desperate Europe. Economic imperialism is worse under present economic conditions of the world than the political imperialism of our colonial epoch ...[44]

The Presbyterian Church in the U.S.A. did, in fact, endorse and promote economic recovery in Europe through adoption of the Marshall Plan. Reporting on this development, which mushroomed into a nationwide ecumenical campaign, *Presbyterian Life* said, "In the past few months, every major Protestant denomination in the United States has come out unequivocally for the Marshall Plan. The Federal Council of Churches, representing twenty-six Protestant faiths and some 26,000,000 church people, has issued a sweeping endorsement of the plan, calling it 'one of history's most momentous affirmations of faith' ... This week, on March 11, the Protestant Christian fight for the European Recovery Program will be climaxed by a special meeting in Washington, D.C. 'to demonstrate the concern of church people for the constructive principles essential to the success of the European Recovery effort.' Government and church officials, including Secretary of State George Marshall, Moderator Wilbur La Roe Jr., of the Presbyterian Church in the U.S.A., Bishop Angus Dun of the Protestant Episcopal Diocese of Washington, D.C. and Bishop John S. Stamm, vice-president of the Federal Council will attend. Speakers include John Foster Dulles and Willard Thorp, Assistant Secretary of State for Economic Affairs."[45]

European recovery was not the only economic concern that was addressed by Presbyterian Church in the U.S.A. leaders. Having suffered through the Great Depression, they were deeply motivated toward advocating governmental policies that might stimulate recovery at home. Not all proposals for economic recovery, however, met universal approbation from

44 *Presbyterian Life*, August 7, 1948.

45 *Presbyterian Life*, March 13, 1948.

denominational leaders. One such proposal, the Townsend Plan, received a sharp editorial rebuke from the Rev. Harry Rimmer on page one of *The Presbyterian*.[46]

The Townsend Plan, said Rimmer, proposes "(a) that the Federal government will pay to every person in the United States over 60 years of age the sum of $200 per month; (b) that recipients must spend the money within the calendar month in which they received it; and (c) that the cost of the project will be paid by a transaction tax of two percent on every business transaction."[47]

Rimmer argued that the Townsend Plan was based on faulty assumptions that (a) all persons over 60 years of age needed the stipend; (b) everyone who received this stipend would be capable of spending it wisely; and (c) the spending that the plan envisioned would bring about economic recovery. If this assumption can be trusted, said Rimmer, why stop at $200 per month? Why not make the stipend much larger?[48]

The Rimmer editorial was one of many pieces that appeared during the turbulent 1930s, when the nation was winding its way through a labyrinth of post-depression, economic recovery initiatives. Increasingly, denominational leaders lent their influence toward support for the imposition of government programs to alleviate the problem of poverty. A trend can be seen during this period in which church leaders migrated from an emphasis on charity (administered primarily by the churches and church institutions) to church support for governmentally funded and administered welfare programs.

Campaign for Racial Justice

In addition to peace and economics, another issue that increasingly captured headlines in the church press during the 1940s, 50s and 60s was racial equality. Presbyterian leaders began to press the issue in the late 1940s with mounting attention to conditions in the South.

In 1949, the General Assembly of the Presbyterian Church in the U.S.A. "condemn[ed] all organizations that seek to limit the opportunities and rights of any group on account of color or creed, and confess[ed] with shame that we have not fulfilled the spirit of our Lord with respect to race relations ..."[49]

46 *The Presbyterian*, February 13, 1936.

47 *Ibid.*

48 *Ibid.*

49 *Presbyterian Life*, June 25, 1949.

In October, 1949, *Presbyterian Life* ran a feature article and commentary on a civil rights case in Texas. Herman Marion Sweatt, "a Texas Negro" had sought admission to the University of Texas and was denied on grounds that he had opportunities for an education in other Texas schools that catered to black people. The Federal Council of Churches filed an amicus brief in the case, reported by *Presbyterian Life* to be "the first of its kind ever to be filed by the Federal Council," calling for the U.S. Supreme Court to strike down the doctrine of "separate but equal." The denominational magazine editorially supported the Federal Council's position and defended its ground breaking amicus brief.[50] In its unanimous decision, the court ruled that the Texas "separate but equal" policy was unconstitutional.

In July, 1950, the General Assembly of the Presbyterian Church US ruled for the first time in history that there would be no segregation in living quarters or in the assembly dining room for African American commissioners. The assembly also applied the desegregation rule to accommodations for adults and young people's council meetings at the assembly conference grounds in Montreat, North Carolina.

In 1954, the US Supreme Court issued its landmark *Brown v. Board of Education* ruling that struck down segregation in the nation's public school system. The General Assembly of the Presbyterian Church in the USA was ecstatic: "We receive with humility and thanksgiving the recent decision of our Supreme Court, ruling that segregation in the public schools is unconstitutional – with humility because action by our highest court was necessary to make effective that for which our church has stood in principle; with thanksgiving because the decision has been rendered with wisdom and unanimity."[51]

The General Assembly statement continued: "We urge all Christians to assist in preparing their communities psychologically and spiritually for carrying out the full implications of the Supreme Court's decision. We call upon the members of our churches to cooperate with civic organizations, neighborhood clubs, and community councils as effective means for the accomplishment of racial integration in the public school system, and to remember that integration must be indivisible in character, insisting that teachers as well as pupils be accorded full opportunity within the school system on the basis of interest, ability, and merit, without reference to race. We commend our church for its continued efforts to make the law of Christ relative to all areas of the church's life. We particularly commend the

50 *Presbyterian Life*, October 29, 1949.

51 *Presbyterian Life*, June 26, 1954.

increasing number of local churches which have become racially and/or culturally integrated and have learned the joy of full Christian fellowship."[52]

"It has been too frequently the practice of churches caught in the population movements which change the racial or cultural characteristics of the area to seek more 'desirable' locations in order to escape their Christian responsibility toward their community. It becomes ever more clear that sessions, ministers, and church members should make it their Christian concern to communicate the claim of Christ to every person within reach of their church."[53]

The General Assembly statement continued: "Local churches should do more than merely announce to the community a policy of open membership regardless of racial or cultural background. A mere statement by the session of a church may all too easily lead only to complacency and self-satisfaction. Our churches will be fulfilling their duty to evangelize all people only when they sincerely and personally offer church membership to all persons living within the communities served by them. We call upon all Christians to work for, not wait for a church and a society which rise above racial restrictions.

"Sessions and ministers particularly should take the initiative in preparing the hearts and minds of people for full fellowship in Christ through preaching, pastoral work, and through all educational channels in the church and community …"[54]

In June of 1954, the General Assembly of the Presbyterian Church (US) issued a resolution that paralleled that of its northern counterpart. It called on its congregations to open membership rolls to everyone, regardless of race. Further, it urged trustees of the denomination's colleges, seminaries and other institutions to adopt race neutral admission policies, and it urged its synods to adopt similar measures.

Between 1961 and 1965, the Presbyterian Church press carried articles on racial justice movements, primarily in the South. Stories of "freedom riders," voter registration drives, lunch counter sit-ins and other confrontations were frequently published. In its July, 1963 issue, *Presbyterian Life* carried a two-page center spread article on the Rev. Martin Luther King, Jr. that included his "Letter from a Birmingham Jail."[55]

In 1964, the 176th General Assembly of the United Presbyterian Church

52 *Ibid.*

53 *Ibid.*

54 *Ibid.*

55 *Presbyterian Life*, July 1, 1963.

in the U.S.A. made an unprecedented move by voting Elder Hawkins, "a Negro," to its highest elected office. Concurrent with Hawkins' election as Moderator, the General Assembly issued resolutions affirming "civil disobedience," approved new and controversial stands in support of antipoverty and unemployment legislation and encouraged the passage of legislation that would mandate residential desegregation.

The Urge to Merge

America's industrial production ran at a fast pace during and immediately after the war years. Increasingly, industry employed a hierarchical and highly centralized industrial model of organization. Power was vested at the corporate office, and it was transmitted to the workers through layers of bureaucratic supervision. Mergers were commonplace, for the prevailing view of America's industrial culture was that the larger the corporation, the greater its power.

Parallel to this centralization in the industrial sphere was the growth of federal government programs and the development of multiple administrative layers. Offices that had been initiated to alleviate the ravages of the Great Depression became permanent fixtures in the federal bureaucracy. Increasingly, political and economic power gravitated toward Washington, D.C.

America's mainline churches adapted themselves to this pattern of centralization. Originally conceived as servants to local congregations, the more inclusive governing bodies of presbytery, synod and General Assembly took on lives of their own.

Presbyterians at the local level began to look toward denominational headquarters as the locus of church leadership, and "loyalty" was measured by the degree to which local congregations carried out denominationally conceived programs and funded the denominational infrastructure. During this period, it would have been unthinkable for a local church to purchase curriculum materials that did not display the denomination's imprimatur. Ministers of local churches that did not meet contribution quotas established by higher governing bodies had some explaining to do, and presbytery offices were established to keep them in line.

Not only was this movement toward centralization a reflection of corporate and governmental trends, it also manifested a shift in denominational mission strategy. As secular world problems like peace, economics and racial conflict increasingly commanded the church's attention, its leaders sought political means of addressing them. Politics means power, and there is power in numbers. Thus, denominational leaders saw church mergers as the route toward greater influence in addressing societal issues. Although a theological rationale was often expressed to justify ecumenical alliances, the bottom line was politics.

Cross-Denominational Alliances

The centralization of ecclesiastical power within denominations was only the beginning, for this was also a period of vigorous cross-denominational activity. The Federal Council of Churches (later to become the National Council of Churches), the World Council of Churches, and the World Alliance of Reformed Churches grew exponentially in the 1930s through the 1950s. As was the case with industrial and governmental models, larger, more inclusive church structures were assumed to be better than the proliferation of smaller, congregationally oriented denominations.

John Foster Dulles' passion for cooperative ventures was not limited to his advocacy for the United Nations. He was also vitally interested in developing parallel structures among churches. Named to lead the Presbyterian Church in the U.S.A. delegation to the first assembly of the World Council of Churches, Dulles carried the banner for ecumenism. *Presbyterian Life* exuberantly anticipated the birth of the new world body: "Although the first assembly of the World Council of Churches is still five months away (August 22 to September 4, 1948), the assembly planners are taking no chances. They want this meeting to be the biggest event in the history of modern Christianity. Even at this early date, it looks as though they will succeed. Careful planning has already produced a clean-cut picture of the people and the issues involved at the Amsterdam assembly. The lineup for the meeting is amazing. Practically every Christian church in the world will be represented ..."[56]

Euphoric with the possibilities of world order that a united church might bring forth, denominational representatives forged increasingly inclusive relationships. In August of 1948, the World Council Assembly convened 350 representatives from 147 churches in 40 countries. Shortly thereafter, the Worldwide Anglican Communion convened its Lambeth Conference, the first since before the war. And during the week of August 10-17, the World Alliance of Presbyterian and Reformed Churches gathered in Geneva, its first meeting since 1937. *Presbyterian Life* called the Alliance "getting the Presbyterian family together again after the disruptions caused by World War II."[57]

56 *Presbyterian Life*, March 13, 1948.

57 *Presbyterian Life*, August 7, 1948.

In January, 1949, a merger was proposed among the Federal Council of Churches and seven other interdenominational agencies. The result of that merger would be called the National Council of Churches of Christ. The Federal Council called on all member churches to carry the consolidation proposal back to their governing bodies for ratification. Presbyterian Church in the U.S.A. representatives performed a leadership role in the merger.

The proposal was approved by many of the nation's mainline denominations, and on November 28, 1950, the National Council of Churches held its convening assembly in Cleveland. Applauding the event, *Presbyterian Life* said, "Through this merger Christian forces will have a new and powerful channel through which to register their conviction on moral and spiritual issues in the nation. The work of every individual church will be strengthened, but most important of all, this great organization will bring into its active and affiliate membership 90 percent of the nation's Protestant church membership. It means that now at last, these churches have united in facing their total task. It is the most important step that has thus far been taken toward Christian unity, for churches that are united in their work cannot indefinitely remain divided in their worship."[58]

For Presbyterians, the urge to merge did not stop with the World and National Councils of Churches. There was work to be done among several denominations that claimed the name "Presbyterian." In June, 1954, the General Assembly of the Presbyterian Church in the U.S.A. decided by unanimous vote to "seek union with its two sister denominations." The sisters that it had in mind were the United Presbyterian Church and the southern branch of Presbyterianism known as the Presbyterian Church in the United States. Notably absent from its sisters list was the Orthodox Presbyterian Church.[59]

One year later, at the 1955 General Assembly, the Moderator of the Presbyterian Church in the U.S.A. played the role of a spurned suitor. With sorrow, he announced that although the United Presbyterian Church was ready

58 *Presbyterian Life*, August 28, 1950.

59 In 1936, J. Gresham Machen and other members of the Independent Board of Presbyterian Foreign Missions founded a denomination that they called "the Presbyterian Church in America" when it was clear that the Presbyterian Church in the U.S.A. General Assembly would not overturn presbytery removals of their ordination credentials. In 1939, the Presbyterian Church U.S.A. filed and won a lawsuit against them, forcing them to drop the name, "Presbyterian Church in America." After losing the lawsuit, they chose to call themselves the Orthodox Presbyterian Church.

for marriage (the tally was two to one for union), the Presbyterian Church in the United States said "no." Since the proposal envisioned a three-way merger, the southerners' decision scotched the deal for everyone. Moderator Lloyd speculated that the rejection reflected the southerners' reaction to the 1954 US Supreme Court decision barring racial segregation in public schools.[60]

Moderator Lloyd's comments were seconded by the Rev. Wade Boggs, who appeared at the Presbyterian Church in the U.S.A. General Assembly to bring greetings from the southern church. Boggs' remarks were penitent, including a plea that northern Presbyterians be patient while their southern brothers and sisters worked through internal difficulties: "Many of you are aware of the fact that union was opposed in our church by a well-financed and closely organized group," he said.[61] Boggs did not identify the "organized group."

In 1956, the Presbyterian Church in the U.S.A. decided to consummate a two-way merger with the United Presbyterian Church. The plan was adopted by both denominations in 1958.

During this period, merger fever continued at a high pitch. Stated Clerk Eugene Carson Blake was elected president of the National Council of Churches in 1954, and he used this "bully pulpit" to promote ecumenical mergers at every turn.

In 1955, *Presbyterian Life* ran a prominently placed article by Episcopal Bishop James Pike titled "The Living Reformation." Pike said, "A church is not truly Protestant because it had a Reformation; it is Protestant when it realizes it always needs reformation."[62] Variations of that theme, often expressed in the form of the mantra "Reformed and Always Reforming," were commonplace.

In 1958, during a reorganization that followed the merger of the Presbyterian Church in the U.S.A. and the United Presbyterian Church, the new denomination, now called the United Presbyterian Church (USA), combined three major boards: the Board of Foreign Missions, the Permanent Commission on Inter-Church Relations and the Committee on Ecumenical Affairs.

On the one hand, the merger made sense, for on the foreign field where Presbyterian missionaries were proclaiming the gospel amidst pagan cultures, they experienced a bond of common faith with missionaries from

60 *Presbyterian Life*, May 28, 1955.

61 *Presbyterian Life*, June 11, 1955.

62 *Presbyterian Life*, October 29, 1955.

other denominations. On the other hand, it opened the door for a diversion of mission funds into unknown levels of ecumenical agencies.

In 1961, Eugene Carson Blake pulled out all the stops in his drive to achieve a major Protestant merger in the United States. In a sermon preached from the pulpit of Grace Cathedral in San Francisco, Blake "proposed to the Protestant Episcopal Church that it, together with the United Presbyterian Church invite the Methodist Church and the United Church of Christ to form with us a plan of church union, both catholic and reformed."[63]

The 1961 General Assembly adopted a resolution along the lines that had been specified by Blake, and an invitation was issued that paved the way for an organization that would later be known as the Consultation on Church Union.

A World Focused Church Needs a World Friendly Confession

During the 30s, 40s and 50s, Presbyterian Church leaders found the *Westminster Confession of Faith* too confining as they sought theological grounding for dealing with "this world" issues. Although *Westminster* was revered as an historical document, it was seen as increasingly irrelevant to the church's preoccupation with peace, economics and race. Thus, it was only a matter of time until denominational leaders began to call for a new statement of faith, a document that would be more in tune with the issues of the day.

In 1948, an editorial by Francis Pickens Miller expressed the view that the church must find more adequate theological benchmarks for underwriting its social policy.

Pickens wrote, "The doctrine that a man's soul belongs to God but his body to the state has cursed the world in which we live. Because of it the church fails to give its witness through men engaged in political activity; because of it the church fails to call down God's judgment upon unjust and immoral political programs, and because of it Christian laymen make no serious attempt to shape civil society according to God's purposes."

"Through its failure to proclaim the whole gospel to the whole man (body and soul) the church contributed directly to the creation of a moral vacuum in society into which rushed all the devils from hell. Hitler and creatures like him became inevitable wherever this vacuum existed."

"During the last third of a century these devils have shown what they

63 *Presbyterian Life*, May 1, 1961.

could do in the way of destroying a great civilization. Nor is their work finished. Society continues to live in mortal danger because Christian man has not yet begun to apply his mind and his will effectively to the affairs of the state …"

"As Christians, we intervene occasionally to prevent the government from doing something we don't want done. It gives us a feeling of great moral accomplishment to block, to thwart or to prohibit. But it seldom occurs to us that it is our duty as Christians to apply our minds positively and constructively to state policies in order that Christian thought may influence and guide developing government action …"[64]

In 1958, after the Presbyterian Church in the U.S.A. and the United Presbyterian Church merged their denominations and combined their boards of foreign missions, inter-Church relations and ecumenical affairs, they turned their attention toward creating a fresh statement of faith that they believed would enable them more adequately to address contemporary secular issues.

To that end, the 1958 General Assembly declared "that the church must reaffirm and apply the principles of our Reformed faith to the crucial issues of our time … To fail to know what we believe, why we believe it, and what it requires in meeting the problems of our day, is to forsake our heritage. The blazing contemporary issues such as the threat to freedom, war and peace, racism, economic imperialism, the deteriorating standards of home and family life, conflicting goals in education, youth delinquency, violation of property, and defiance of law and order devolve, in part, for their solutions upon citizens who hold membership in our church. The church itself cannot escape responsibility for seeking Christian answers to these problems …"[65]

In the early 1960s, denominational leaders engaged in lively theological debate as they struggled to forge a theological statement that they believed might be more relevant to their time than was the *Westminster Confession of Faith*. A special committee, headed by Dr. Edward Dowey, Jr., professor of theology at Princeton Theological Seminary, was commissioned to prepare "A Brief Contemporary Statement of Faith" for consideration by the 1964 General Assembly. In an interim report on the work of his group, Dowey said that his committee had in mind "current theological thinking, Biblical understandings, and the relation between a statement of faith and the church's social action."[66]

64 *Presbyterian Life*, March 27, 1948.

65 *Presbyterian Life*, July 15, 1958.

66 *Presbyterian Life*, July 1, 1963.

The chairman proceeded to say that his committee envisioned writing more than the "brief statement of faith," to which the General Assembly had assigned it. Speaking for his committee, he suggested that the *Westminster Confession of Faith* should be regarded not as the denomination's singular standard, but as one of several dated documents.

"In this way," said Dowey, "the present-day church can acknowledge its inheritance from the Reformed tradition of many lands, rather than harking back only to the work of the Westminster divines."[67]

By this time, after three decades of concentration on political, economic and sociological issues, the denomination that would become the Presbyterian Church (USA) was now fully wedded to an idea, later articulated by the World Council of Churches meeting in Uppsala, namely that "the world sets the church's agenda." In 1965, the General Assembly formalized that doctrine by adopting the work of Dowey's special committee, a *Book of Confessions* that contained a new "modern times" document, *The Confession of 1967*.

We turn to that confession and the theological shift that it represents in Chapter Three.

67 *Ibid.*

COVENANT

Holy Scripture

"All Scripture is inspired by God and profitable for teaching, for reproof, for correction, and for training in righteousness, that the man of God may be complete, equipped for every good work."

II Timothy 3:16, 17

The Constitution

"The authority of Holy Scripture, for which it ought to be believed and obeyed, dependeth not upon the testimony of any man or church, but wholly upon God (who is truth itself), the author thereof; and therefore it is to be received, because it is the Word of God."

The Westminster Confession of Faith
Chapter I

BROKEN COVENANT

"Scripture is nevertheless the words of men, conditioned by the language, thought forms, and literary fashions of the places and times at which they were written."

The Confession of 1967

The new confession "carefully avoids saying either that Scripture 'is' God's Word or that Scripture 'is' unique and authoritative as such or in its own right."

Edward A. Dowey, Jr.
A Commentary on the Confession of 1967

Chapter Three

1967

During the four decades that followed the 1926 General Assembly, generations of Presbyterian leaders were ordained without reference to any doctrine that the denomination deemed essential. During examination, candidates for ordination were asked to receive and adopt "the essential tenets of Reformed faith," but nowhere were these essential tenets specified. The result was precisely what J. Gresham Machen predicted, a broadly inclusive leadership that defied theological definition.

As it entered the 1960s, the Presbyterian Church faced a growing disparity between what the denomination officially claimed to be and what, since 1926, it had actually become. The denomination continued to identify itself as a constitutional church, standing under the authority of the *Westminster Confession of Faith*, a theologically precise and logically coherent statement of Reformed belief. But in reality, since 1926, many presbyteries had not been holding ordained leaders accountable to any particular doctrine, including centerpiece doctrines in the *Westminster Confession of Faith*.

Given the drift that had occurred since 1926, honesty required that the *Westminster Confession* be superseded, for, in practice, it could no longer be called the denomination's constitutional standard. Publicly acknowledging this reality via a constitutional amendment, however, was politically untenable. Thus, denominational leaders developed a plan to honor *Westminster* without obeying it. They would leave the confession in place, but envelop it within a compilation of other historical documents.

A key component in the plan was to add into this mix a new confession deemed more relevant to modern times. Thus, a clear and precise theological benchmark, a single standard by which the denomination's faith could be measured, was replaced with a library of multiple resources called *The Book of Confessions*.

Speaking for his special committee that had been assigned the task of bringing before the assembly a contemporary confessional base, Dr. Edward Dowey wrote an article for *Presbyterian Life* in which he outlined the denomination's problem with *Westminster* and its proposed *Book of Confessions* solution:

"While *Westminster* is a post-Reformation statement, it is by no means a modern one. It derives from an age of scholastic theology, of preoccupation with authority and law, of churchly and political absolutism ... But we can sense, behind the order, the precision, and the grandeur, a premonition that the world of classical and Christian culture in which the writers are at home is coming to an end. ... Church theology should not reflect every ripple of history and every wind of doctrine, but it must respond when it crosses over a major watershed such as the eighteenth century. It must be ready to respond again in the future to yet unknown but certainly profound changes that lie ahead ... The *Westminster Confession*, standing alone, is not modern enough to guide the present, nor is it ancient enough to represent the past. ... The committee will present a Brief Contemporary Statement of Faith, and at the same time will propose that the church alter its acknowledgement of traditional writings. The church will be asked, not to reduce the force of existing statements by amendment or removal, but to retain the *Westminster Confession and Shorter Catechism* and add to them creeds from other periods ... In addition, appropriate changes will be suggested in ordination vows."[1]

Turning From Scripture

Not only was the denomination's theological standard now diffused, but the inclusion of an additional document introduced self-contradiction into the picture. The special committee that had been appointed "to update Westminster" with more contemporary language went well beyond its assignment by proposing the insertion of a brand new confession, *The Confession of 1967*.

On the subject of Scripture, "C-67," as the new document was popularly labeled, differed radically from all other documents in the book. In every other confession, the divine authorship of Scripture and its consequent authority over the faith and life of the church was the central affirmation.

The Scots Confession states: "As we believe and confess the Scriptures of God sufficient to instruct and make perfect the man of God, so do we

1 *Presbyterian Life*, February 15, 1965.

affirm and avow their authority to be from God, and not to depend on men or angels."[2]

The Second Helvetic Confession says: "We believe and confess that canonical Scriptures of the holy prophets and apostles of both Testaments to be the true Word of God, and to have sufficient authority of themselves, not of men. For God himself spoke to the fathers, prophets, apostles, and still speaks to us through the Holy Scriptures. And in this Holy Scripture, the universal Church of Christ has the most complete exposition of all that pertains to a saving faith, and also to the framing of a life acceptable to God; and in this respect it is expressly commanded by God that nothing be either added to or taken from the same."[3]

The Westminster Confession of Faith says: "The authority of Holy Scripture, for which it ought to be believed and obeyed, dependeth not upon the testimony of any man or church, but wholly upon God (who is truth itself), the author thereof; and therefore it is to be received, because it is the Word of God."[4] A second section in this confession's extensive chapter on Scripture is also worthy of note: "The Supreme Judge, by which all controversies of religion are to be determined, and all decrees of councils, opinions of ancient writers, doctrines of men, and private spirits, are to be examined, and in whose sentence we are to rest, can be no other but the Holy Spirit speaking in Scripture."[5]

The Theological Declaration of Barmen, although stylistically different from other Reformed confessions, is consistent in its insistence upon the authority of Scripture as the Word of God: "If you find that we are speaking contrary to Scripture, then do not listen to us! But if you find that we are taking our stand upon Scripture, then let no fear or temptation keep you from treading with us the path of faith and obedience to the Word of God, in order that God's people be of one mind upon earth …"[6]

Again, Barmen is unequivocal with respect to Scripture: "Jesus Christ, as he is attested for us in Holy Scripture, is the one Word of God which we have to hear and which we have to trust and obey in life and in death. We reject the false doctrine, as though the church could and would have to acknowledge as a source of its proclamation, apart from and besides this

2 *The Constitution of the Presbyterian Church (USA), Part One: The Book of Confessions* (Louisville, Ky.: Office of the General Assembly, 1999) paragraph 3.19.

3 *Ibid.*, paragraph 5.001.

4 *Ibid.*, paragraph 6.004.

5 *Ibid.*, paragraph 6.010.

6 *Ibid.*, paragraph 8.04.

one Word of God, still other events and powers, figures and truths, as God's revelation."[7]

'The Words of Men'

C-67 also says that Scripture is the Word of God, but it adds an important modification. "Scripture," said the new confession, "is nevertheless the words of men, conditioned by the language, thought forms, and literary fashions of the places and times at which they were written."[8]

On its face, this qualifier can be accepted by Biblical scholars. No credible student of Scripture would deny that inspired human beings were the instruments by which God's Word was inscribed. But C-67 was headed in a different direction, one that would seriously weaken Scriptural authority. By employing subjective phrases, this confession suggested that the Scriptures are God's Word to the degree that the reader experiences them as God's Word. According to C-67, Scriptural authority is determined not by Scripture but the self who reads and interprets Scripture.

Following its adoption of C-67, the General Assembly approved substantial changes in the vows required of persons seeking ordination. The earlier vows asked, "Do you believe the Scriptures of the Old and New Testaments to be the Word of God, the only infallible rule of faith and practice?" The new vow asked, "Do you accept the Scriptures of the Old and New Testaments to be the unique and authoritative witness of Jesus Christ in the Church catholic, and by the Holy Spirit, God's Word to you?"

Commenting on this change in 1968, the Presbyterian Lay Committee wrote, "The new statement expresses the view that God was active in His Son, who is the living Word, and that the Bible is the 'unique and authoritative' testimony of men to what God did in His Son. But the high quality of the Scripture resides only in the fact that it was written by men who happened to be Jesus' earliest disciples and in some cases eyewitnesses of that about which they wrote. According to this view, the Bible is not the Word of God, but only a witness (and a potentially fallible one) to the Word of God."[9]

"Is a closed Bible God's Word?" continued the Lay Committee, "or does the Bible become God's Word only when He speaks to me through it? This is more than an academic matter. It is a question of authority … The new

7 *Ibid.*, paragraph 8.11.

8 *Ibid.*, paragraph 9.29.

9 *The Presbyterian Layman*, Vol. 1, No. 1, January, 1968.

view gives authority to our subjective experience of God speaking; the earlier view subjects the church officer and the church to the objective, written Word of God. The crucial point of dispute in the church as a whole today is that of final authority, and our denomination has just changed its position."[10]

Although the Lay Committee's arguments were dismissed by General Assembly commissioners who voted approval of C-67, they were confirmed after the vote by Dr. Edward A. Dowey, Jr., chairman of the General Assembly committee that drafted the new confession. Dowey celebrated what the Lay Committee lamented, namely, that in adopting a new book of confessions, the Presbyterian Church was completing what was begun by the General Assembly in 1926, the removal of any particular doctrine as essential or binding. Dowey wrote that the new confession "is a far cry also from the strait-jacket oath that once required Presbyterian seminary professors not to 'inculcate, teach, or insinuate' anything that 'directly or impliedly' appeared to them to 'contradict or contravene' the Westminster Standards. Both life and dogma are to be reformed, as new occasions, in God's providence, may demand."[11]

Dowey also agreed that C-67 represented a change in the denomination's understanding of Scriptural authority, although he welcomed the change while the Lay Committee opposed it. Dowey said that C-67 "carefully avoids saying either that Scripture 'is' God's Word or that Scripture 'is' unique and authoritative as such or in its own right. It is in the function of living witness to Christ, the Word, that it has its unique place ..."[12]

A Revisionist History

Commenting on denominational developments during this period, The Rev. Clifton Kirkpatrick, Stated Clerk of the General Assembly, said: "This broad, rather than narrow way of understanding our confessions is not new to Presbyterians. In the Adopting Act of 1927, our General Assembly made it clear that officers were not held to a 'fundamentalist' understanding of the confession (then only one, the Westminster Confession and catechisms), but to an upholding of its 'essential and necessary articles.' Adopting a Book of Confessions, as our church did in the late 1960s, is itself an invitation to theological diversity and dialogue in the

10 *Ibid.*

11 Dowey, Edward A., Jr., *A Commentary on the Confession of 1967 and an Introduction to the Book of Confessions* (Philadelphia: Westminster Press, 1968), p. 30.

12 *Ibid.*, p. 101.

best sprit of the Presbyterian tradition."[13]

Kirkpatrick's view that the Adopting Act provides an historical precedent for welcoming "theological diversity" and the practice of "scrupling" (declaring an exception to a doctrine or ethical tenet in the Confessions) has been cited in recent times as justification for setting aside selected theological/ethical standards in the denomination's Constitution. The most recent example is the "Peace, Unity and Purity" task force recommendation to the General Assembly of 2006 to allow candidates for ordination to "scruple" the Constitution's fidelity and chastity standard. This represents a faulty reading of history, for the Adopting Act of 1929 permitted no such license.

A review of the Adopting Act itself clearly shows that scruples called for by its authors were limited to one issue, the implied authority of the civil government over the church. American Presbyterians agreed wholeheartedly with the theological and ethical tenets of the *Westminster Confession of Faith*, and the purpose of the Adopting Act was to say so in precise and subscriptionist terms that allowed no exceptions. Their only problem with the Confession was in its Chapters 20 and 23 that express a church/state relationship view held by England's Parliament that Presbyterian leaders in America did not share. It was to this issue, the British interpretation of relative church/state authorities, that the scruples permitted by the Adopting Act referred. On all confessional standards relating to theology and ethics, strict subscription was required.

'Bird Bath' Theology

The Rev. Jack Rogers, Moderator of the 2001 General Assembly, expressed a similar interpretation during his opening speech to the assembly. Castigating Presbyterians who insist on doctrinal definition, Rogers said there are two ways of viewing the church's faith, "as a birdcage or a birdbath." He took issue with those who use the birdcage approach, saying that they see essential beliefs as iron bars, spending their time deciding "who is in and who is out."

Rogers said he prefers the birdbath approach, wherein the church views its faith like water. People who hold this view, he said, don't worry about walls. Rather, they spend their time splashing about in the water and inviting others to play in the spray.

Rogers' image invites reflection. Having spurned all boundaries, how

13 Kirkpatrick, Clifton, Column written for *The Presbyterian Layman*, Vol. 34. No. 1. Note: The Adopting Act was approved in 1929, not 1927. 1927 was the year in which a petition was sent to the Synod of Philadelphia, requesting the Adopting Act, but it was not approved until two years later.

shall we pool this living water for our enjoyment? Except in times of calamity, oceans are defined by shores, and streams flow within their banks. But when one eschews the very limits that produce shape and form, the precious water that is sought disappears and the bath becomes a dry and dusty place.

The Imperial Self

The adoption of C-67 completed what was begun by the General Assembly of 1926. Now, the great confessions of the Reformed tradition, and even Scripture itself, could be neatly arranged on the shelf, enshrined as historical documents, and revered as expressions of the culture from which they arose. Sufficiently sidelined, they would no longer inhibit those who were now rapidly developing what Machen had identified as a distinctly different religion.

It is instructive to note that in this same decade in which Presbyterian leaders undermined their confessional and Scriptural authorities, four books became best sellers among the denomination's clergy: Dietrich Bonhoeffer's *Letters and Papers from Prison,*[14] Bishop Robinson's *Honest to God,*[15] Harvey Cox's *The Secular City,*[16] and Thomas J.J. Altizer's *The Gospel of Christian Atheism.*[17] The themes were similar: the idea of a transcendent God who rules over human history has run its course. The world has "come of age," and we are entering a period of "religionless Christianity." Rather than looking beyond ourselves toward some "transcendent Other," we should look within ourselves, concentrate on self development, and aspire to the highest human potentiality.[18]

---

14 Bonhoeffer, Dietrich, *Letters and Papers From Prison* (New York: Macmillan, 1968).

15 Robinson, John A.T., *Honest To God* (Atlanta: Westminster John Knox Press, 1963).

16 Cox, Harvey, *The Secular City* (New York: Macmillan Company, 1965).

17 Altizer, Thomas J.J., *The Gospel of Christian Atheism* (Philadelphia: Westminster Press, 1966).

18 One should note that Bonhoeffer died a martyr at an early age, before he had developed a systematic theology. His imprisonment and death at the hands of Hitler elevated his status to that of hero among clergy admirers, and his scattered and often inconsistent writings were highly regarded, more because of who he was than because of any coherent theology that they reflect. Thus, while one may find themes in Bonhoeffer's writings – like the oft quoted "world come of age" and "religionless Christianity" phrases – that support the secularist thesis, it would be unfair to conclude from such fragments that they reflect a fully developed theological position.

Bishop Robinson's theme, "God is dead," gained widespread notoriety. Hardly an original idea – Friedrich Wilhelm Nietzsche had developed it decades earlier – Robinson's death-of-God notion was popularized by Presbyterian clergy/intellectuals who embraced the self-realization movement.

Harvey Cox, a Harvard professor with a flair for the dramatic, became a popular speaker on Presbyterian seminary campuses. Celebrating the secular, he encouraged institutional church leaders to focus on peace, justice and community development issues. The church was to be seen as an agent of societal transformation, a nexus of political power that could realize the kingdom of God through politics and community development.

Thousands of Presbyterian seminary students cut their theological teeth on these themes as they prepared to enter denominational pulpits across the country. These themes were, in fact, tenets of the alien faith that Machen identified decades earlier in *Christianity and Liberalism*: an immanent, pantheistic god rather than the transcendent God who reveals himself in his Word, an essentially good human being who needs only an opportunity for self-development, a vast array of culturally developed "authorities," available for selective utilization by humans as they maximize their inherent potentialities, and a church, now redefined as a political association, vectored toward community development goals.

Since the adoption of C-67, examples abound, illustrating the denomination's abandonment of Scriptural authority. In the Human Sexuality Report of 1991, rejected by that year's General Assembly but promoted as a recommended resource by denominational agencies, Scripture is placed under the authority of a new Justice/Love ethical principle: "Whatever in Scripture, tradition, reason or experience embodies genuine love and caring justice, that bears authority for us ... Whatever in Biblical tradition, church practice and teaching, human experience, and human reason violates God's commandment to do love and justice, that must be rejected as ethical authority."[19 /20]

Another example of the minimization of Scripture by denominational agencies can be seen in the 1991-1992 *Horizons* Bible Study, published by Presbyterian Women. The title, *We Decide Together: A Guide to Making Ethical Decisions*, offers a clue to its content, namely, that ethical judgments are to be made by autonomous human beings.

19 Presbyterian Church (USA), *Minutes of the General Assembly*, 1991, pp. 55, 263, Special Committee on Human Sexuality, section on Gays and Lesbians pp. 305-312.

20 A fuller discussion of the Justice/Love document appears in Chapter Six (page 175).

The Rev. Cynthia Campbell, author of *We Decide Together* asks, "How can we make the Bible speak clearly to us who must make all these difficult decisions?"[21] Implicit in the question is Campbell's assumption that "we" control Scripture and "make" it conform to our criteria for clarity. This assumption surfaces in the book's approach to the Ten Commandments: "We propose that, first of all, it is necessary to weigh and evaluate the many biblical imperatives against one another and that, finally, it is the image of God implied in the imperative that determines the persuasiveness of the command."[22]

Contrary to the Reformed principle of Biblical interpretation in which Scripture interprets Scripture, here the author pits various passages of Scripture against one another – in this case, the Ten Commandments – with the final arbiter in this pseudo disputation being the human who sets up the argument. Having established her contention that one passage of Scripture cancels out another, thereby leaving it to the human decision maker to "decide," Campbell's conclusion should come as no surprise: "In obedience to the Bible, we sometimes must disobey a given biblical imperative."[23]

21 Campbell, Cynthia McCall, *We Decide Together: A Guide to Making Ethical Decisions* (Louisville: Presbyterian Women – Presbyterian Church (USA), 1991), p. 4.

22 *Ibid.*, p. 10.

23 *Ibid.*, p. 16.

Covenant

Holy Scripture

"So Jesus said to the Jews who had believed in him, 'If you continue in my word, you are truly my disciples, and you will know the truth, and the truth will make you free.'"

John 8:31-32

The Constitution

And because the powers which God hath ordained, and the liberty which Christ hath purchased, are not intended by God to destroy, but mutually to uphold and preserve one another; they who, upon pretense of Christian liberty, shall oppose any lawful power, or the lawful exercise of it, whether it be civil or ecclesiastical, resist the ordinance of God.

The Westminster Confession of Faith
Chapter XX

Broken Covenant

"We need to continue to build ties of solidarity between all those who are working for human liberation both here and in other countries ... In order to understand the nature of the socio/political/economic reality of the American people as a basis for doing liberation theology, the tools of Marxist social analysis are crucial – especially its attention to class structures and the economic determinants of behaviors and institutions ... The present economic system is irreconcilable with the Christian faith ..."

Presbyterian Church (USA) Representatives
Joint Strategy and Action Committee, 1975

CHAPTER FOUR

SALVATION AS LIBERATION

If one believes that human beings are essentially good, then, as Machen argued in *Christianity and Liberalism*, there is no need for a savior. Jesus Christ serves as an example of the kind of person all humans can become. He is a moral leader who encourages us to do good deeds, building communities of peace and justice where all humans may flourish and share the earth's resources.

But how does such an optimistic anthropology explain the obvious fact that many persons live vastly below their potential? How does it account for a yawning gap between the rich and the poor? How does it explain poverty of mind, spirit and resources? Liberalism's answer is that the remedy for these inequities lies not in the transformation of persons, but in the overthrow of systems, socio-economic, political structures of oppression that enslave individuals, keeping them from becoming all that they can be. Secularized liberalism's answer to this problem is not salvation, but liberation.

As Presbyterian Church leaders substituted liberation for salvation, a radically different concept of missions began to surface among denominational boards and agencies. The church's call now was to engage in revolution, to participate in class struggles both at home and abroad, to declare that "God is on the side of the poor," and to support political and, if necessary, armed liberation movements ostensibly aimed at redressing inequities. Increasingly, the language of Presbyterian Church leaders included race, gender, and economic equality. They referred to "the tools of Marxist analysis," as essential for understanding and addressing the world's inequities.

An example of this growing ideological slant can be seen in "consensus documents" that emerged from a 1975 gathering of mainline denominational staff persons, sponsored by the National Council of Churches and held in Detroit. A newsletter published by the Joint Strategy and Action

Committee (JSAC), a coalition of the "national mission" agencies of the major Protestant denominations offered a detailed report of "points of agreement" that had been forged by conference participants, including representatives from the national staffs of the United Presbyterian Church (northern stream) and the Presbyterian Church US (southern stream). Listed among the group's "tasks that must be continued" was this: "There is a need to demystify Marxian thought and to legitimize the use of class analysis within the U.S. so that it can be heard rather than prematurely dismissed in our ecclesiastical and national life. We need to continue to build ties of solidarity between all those who are working for human liberation both here and in other countries."[1]

The Politics of Race

C-67 had identified racial reconciliation as a major challenge for the church of the 1960s. Thus, the civil rights movement became a fertile field for the application of liberationist ideologies. At the United Presbyterian General Assembly meeting in June, 1968, commissioners heard a report from Rev. Kenneth G. Neigh, General Secretary of the Board of National Missions, announcing a sweeping new policy designed to channel his agency's finances and personnel primarily to serving victims of racism and poverty. Included in the policy was a commitment to "make all Board-controlled properties available for use by community groups" and "establish a policy of participation in coalitions at every possible point in doing this work, concentrating first on linking United Presbyterians with black denominations and black church groups."[2]

This policy change opened the door for channeling church funds into secular organizations that denominational leaders believed shared their socio/political/economic goals. Since the mission of the church was being redefined in largely political terms (overturning unjust and oppressive systems and structures), the choice of secular and essentially political instrumentalities seemed appropriate.

The 1968 General Assembly approved a grant of $100,000 to the Martin Luther King, Jr. Poor People's Development Fund; gave $50,000 to help finance the Poor People's Campaign in Washington; announced that its National Missions Agency was paying the annual salary and benefits of Rev. Hosea Williams, Field Director of the Southern Christian Leadership Conference (SCLC), who had been named leader of Direct Action Demon-

1 Joint Strategy and Action Committee, *Grapevine*, Vol. 6, 1975.

2 *The Presbyterian Layman*, Vol. 1, No. 6, June, 1968; see also *Presbyterian Life*, June 15, 1968.

strations in Washington; and that it had "loaned" national missions staff member, Rev. Oscar McCloud to the SCLC for full-time work for a three-month period. Finally, the assembly adopted a report from its Standing Committee on Church and Society, calling on the abolition of "the present welfare system and for the establishment of an adequate income for all with restorative services as a basic human right."[3]

Left undefined in the General Assembly's statement was any specification as to what constitutes an "adequate income for all." It was also unclear as to what "restorative services" meant. What was clear was the fact that denominational leaders were replacing an ethic of charity with an ideology of income redistribution. Equality, not merely of opportunity, but of assets, was to be seen as a "basic human right."

The Black Manifesto

Supported by these General Assembly policy statements, leaders of denominational agencies, particularly the Board of National Missions, believed they had been given sufficient authority to fund secular community organizations that were actively engaged in income redistribution campaigns.

On May 15, 1969, the San Antonio General Assembly of the United Presbyterian Church invited "Black Manifesto" activist, Rev. James Forman to share the podium with General Assembly Moderator John Coventry Smith and Stated Clerk William P. Thompson. Hailed as "a modern prophet," Forman received a standing ovation. Then he proceeded to castigate the church as a "racist, capitalist, financial institution." Meanwhile, members of his organization, the Black Economic Development Corporation, stormed the offices of the United Presbyterian Church in New York and occupied them for the seven days of the General Assembly meeting.[4]

At the General Assembly meeting in San Antonio, denominational leaders reprinted copies of Forman's "Black Manifesto" and distributed them to commissioners. The document called for $500 million in "reparations" ($80 million of which was to come from the United Presbyterian Church) to be paid by the churches to the black people of America "for their share in the injustices suffered during and since the period of slavery in this country." Included in the Manifesto was a warning that its signatories would "use whatever means necessary, including the use of force and the power of the gun, to bring down the colonizer."[5]

---

3 *Ibid.*

4 *Presbyterian Life*, June 15, 1969.

5 *The Presbyterian Layman*, Vol. 2, No. 7, July/August, 1969; See also: *TIME* Magazine, May 16, 1969.

The General Assembly took no action on Forman's reparation demands, but it did invite Forman's Black Economic Development Conference (BEDC) and leaders of other militant groups to attend official meetings of the denomination's General Council, where "concessions" would be considered. By September, 1969, the BEDC raised its reparation demand from $500 million to $3 billion. According to a survey conducted by *The New York Times*,[6] congregations across the country responded with no more than $18,000. The survey disclosed that the leaders of many congregations were incensed over Forman's tactics, and they rejected outright the demands of his organization.

Responding to Reparations

But at the headquarters of the National Council of Churches in New York, the United Presbyterian Church in Philadelphia, and the Presbyterian Church (US) in Atlanta, Forman's group was taken seriously. The Inter-religious Foundation for Community Organization (IFCO) was established as a channel for denominational funds, and the United Presbyterian Church gave it an initial grant of $100,000. Recognizing that Forman's rhetoric had made him a political lightening rod, denominational leaders distanced themselves from him, some even criticizing him publicly, but their agencies continued to channel funds into community organizing projects that coincided with Forman's purposes.

The Council on Church and Society of the Presbyterian Church US issued a statement saying that it could not "uncritically endorse the Manifesto," but, it continued, "to reject the Manifesto outright would be equally irresponsible. To do this would be to close our ears to an impassioned cry of the neighbor, to ignore the urgency of this present moment in history, and – quite possibly – to miss an opportunity to hear the Word of God."[7]

On June 23, 1969, the Board of National Missions of the United Presbyterian Church distributed a paper on the Black Manifesto, written by Rev. Gayraud S. Wilmore, Chairman of the board's Division of Church and Race. In his introduction to the document, David Ramage, Jr., Executive Secretary of the General Department of Mission and Strategy and Evangelism of the Board of National Missions, stated that although the paper was "not a statement of policy or program," his board had chosen to distribute it for the edification of the church and as a statement "out of which policy and program will grow."[8]

6 *The New York Times*, July 27, 1969.

7 *The Presbyterian Layman*, Vol. 2, No. 8, September/October, 1969.

8 United Presbyterian Church in the U.S.A., Board of National Missions, Division of Church and Race, unpublished paper, dated June 23, 1969.

The Wilmore paper urged Presbyterians to accept the view that the Black Manifesto "with the legal concept of reparations ... may be seen, through the eyes of faith, to be redemptive." It suggested that the Manifesto is an expression of "God's judgment on the church" for its complicity in racial injustice. "By the witness of men like James Forman ... the church as an institution is called to be renewed, to become the revolutionary vanguard of God's in-breaking Kingdom." The paper called for "a radical theology of revolution which can impel churchmen, beyond Black Power and White Power, to grasp the reality of the new being of humanity which Christ came to bring and which he made possible by the dethronement of all the principalities and powers of this world."

The paper defended the Manifesto, commending it for revealing "this crisis of theological clarity and ethical commitment within the churches and synagogues of America." It noted the fact that "the rhetoric of the introductory material and of the Manifesto itself is Marxist and revolutionary." Identifying black people in the United States with oppressed people in Asia, Africa and Latin America, the paper commended the Manifesto for its condemnation of capitalism as "basically an exploitative economic system, because in the final analysis it 'puts profits before people.'"[9] It affirmed the Manifesto's charge "that the ownership of the means of production by the state is preferable to the concentration of massive power in the hands of private interest," and "that militant blacks in the United States represent what is potentially the most skilled and technologically advanced revolutionary vanguard among the oppressed peoples of the world."[10]

The paper called on Presbyterians to receive the Manifesto "in the tenor of prophetic Christianity ... that says that the judgment of God begins in his own household, often by the witness of those who do not claim to know Him, and that such judgment also points to the perennial revolution of the coming Kingdom of God by which the whole of mankind is saved." In conclusion, the paper urged agencies of the Presbyterian Church to "join in the black revolution, wherever collaboration is possible and desirable, by supporting enthusiastically the demands of the Black Manifesto."[11]

Back Channel Funding

Presbyterians in the pews largely rejected these and other pleas by denominational leaders who sought to garner support for the Black Mani-

9 *Ibid.*

10 *Ibid.*

11 *Ibid.*

festo. Sparked by a resolution from Shadyside Presbyterian Church, Pittsburgh Presbytery adopted a statement at its October 9, 1969 meeting that said, "We will not use any funds under our control to give aid or comfort to those who foment violence or racism, black or white." Other presbyteries followed suit, distancing themselves from agencies that operated out of national church headquarters. These statements by local congregations and their presbyteries reflected widespread opinion across the United States. A Gallup Poll survey conducted between May 23 and May 27 showed that 90 percent of the population opposed and only 4 percent favored the nation's religious institutions giving $500 million to blacks because of "past injustices."

Clearly, church members in general and Presbyterians in particular opposed any move by their denominational agencies to send money to Forman's Black Manifesto organization (BEDC). Under these circumstances, a direct grant from denominational headquarters would have been political suicide. Thus Presbyterian Church leaders sought an indirect method for accomplishing their purpose.

In April, 1970, the Associated Press released a story by its religion writer, George Cornell, in which he revealed that $50,000 in United Presbyterian Church funds had been transferred to BEDC through the Inter-religious Foundation for Community Organization (IFCO). William P. Thompson, stated clerk of the General Assembly, told Cornell that the money was part of a $100,000 grant that the denomination had previously awarded to IFCO. Thompson insisted that no United Presbyterian funds had been given directly to BEDC, but that it was perfectly proper for IFCO to send money to BEDC if, in its sole discretion, it chose to do so. "IFCO serves in the role of a broker for a number of major denominations and secular groups which support its program," said Thompson, "and it is up to IFCO to determine which agencies merit funding."[12]

12 Note: This use of a third-party agency to launder funds that might not have been approved by a denominational governing body has become commonplace in recent years. Denominational officials often fund activities as members of the National Council of Churches (NCC) or the World Council of Churches (WCC) that their own governing bodies would probably not approve. IFCO, the Inter-faith Center for Corporate Responsibility (the ecumenical group that coordinates shareholder resolutions and divestment activities), the NCC and the WCC are essentially consortiums of denominational bureaucrats operating under cover of a different name, one step removed from the organizations to which they are accountable. Presbyterian Church staff members exercise virtual control over the governing boards of these ecumenical associations because the denomination which they purport to represent is their primary funding source.

Presbyterians and Panthers

As their commitment to secular liberation movements deepened, Presbyterian Church leaders became particularly enamored with "self-development" organizations, preferring to channel denominational funds to non-church organizations whose philosophy and leadership were controlled by "the poor, oppressed, and disenfranchised." It was argued that making bloc grants to these groups affirmed the right of the oppressed to control their own destiny, whereas funding church ministries designed to alleviate poverty was an act of "paternalism."

But making bloc grants was not only an expression of ideology; it had accountability repercussions. In the event that the funds were misused or applied to programs that angered Presbyterians in the pews, denominational agencies could offer the disclaimer that they were not directly responsible for the programs in question.

Among the groups that won approbation from denominational leaders was the Black Panther Party, founded by Huey Newton and Bobby Seale in 1966. Unhappy with the more moderate leadership of Martin Luther King, Jr., the Panthers developed a full-blown Marxist philosophy, viewing the plight of black people as an element of a world-wide class struggle between the haves and the have-nots. Point number seven in their ten-point program stated: "We want an end to the robbery by the capitalists of our black and oppressed communities."[13] The Panthers believed that change could only come through revolution, both at home and abroad, and that violence was a necessary tool. Police were viewed as agents of oppression whose primary function was to brutalize and murder black people.

Considering its philosophy, it should have come as no surprise to discover that the Panthers were involved in shoot-outs, both with the police and among themselves. By 1970 numerous Panthers and police had been killed in flare-ups that occurred in Los Angeles, Chicago and New York.

Motivated by the undocumented assumption that 28 recent Panther deaths were the result of "a nationwide strategy to harass, repress and eliminate the Black Panthers ..." the four highest officers of the United Presbyterian Church sent a telegram to the President of the United States, calling for a presidential commission "to investigate police and judicial actions against Black Panthers and similar groups in the past two years; to report its findings concerning particular incidents and possible connections between incidents; and its recommendations for necessary action in light of

13 Newton, Fredrika and Hilliard, David, *The Huey P. Newton Reader* (New York: Seven Stories Press, 2002), p. 49ff.

its findings." The telegram was signed by Rev. George E. Sweazey, Moderator of the General Assembly, William P. Thompson, Stated Clerk of the General Assembly, Rev. Elder Hawkins, Chairman of the Council on Church and Race, and J. Henry Neale, Co-chairman of the Council on Church and Race.

In a published objection to the telegram, the Presbyterian Lay Committee noted that the church officials' suggestion of "a nationwide strategy to harass, repress and eliminate the Black Panthers" was strikingly similar to a statement released by the Panther organization itself and that no evidence substantiating these serious charges had been cited.

The Lay Committee referenced a *New York Times* investigation into the alleged 28 Panther deaths. That investigation revealed that when questioned by *The New York Times*, San Francisco lawyer Charles R. Garry, who represented the Black Panthers and had made the initial allegation, reduced his total to 19 Panther deaths. Of this number, it turned out that four were killed by a rival black organization, two died "for unexplained reasons," one was shot by a storekeeper during a robbery of his store, one allegedly was shot by other Panther members who were subsequently indicted for the crime, one was shot after he threatened a policeman, seven were shot while exchanging gunfire during a shoot-out with Oakland, California police, and two died in a Chicago shoot out with police.

The Lay Committee questioned why General Assembly officials had so quickly endorsed unsubstantiated allegations by spokespersons for the Panthers, smearing the credibility of Los Angeles and Chicago police departments, while ignoring official F.B.I. reports and the published findings of *The New York Times* investigation. "Why should our church leaders take only one side of this complex issue, implying evil intent to our law enforcement agencies, purely on the basis of news reports and apparently without checking the facts with the police or the F.B.I. for the other side of the story?" asked the Lay Committee.[14]

The Angela Davis Grant

In 1971, another Panther made the news. It was announced that self-avowed Marxist and Black Panther member Angela Davis received a $10,000 grant from the United Presbyterian Church Fund to Combat Racism. Davis had been arrested following an attempt by Panther Jonathan Jackson to free his brother, George Jackson, from a courtroom in Marin County, California, August 7, 1970. During George Jackson's trial, Jonathan Jackson and two accomplices burst into the courtroom with guns and took

14 *The Presbyterian Layman*, Vol. 3, No. 2, February, 1970.

Judge Harold Haley and Prosecutor Gary Thomas hostage. Jackson and accomplice William Christmas were shot and killed while driving away from the courthouse, but not before they killed Judge Haley. The .38 caliber revolver that was used by Jackson was registered in Angela Davis' name.

Later, on August 21, 1971, George Jackson was killed while a prisoner in San Quentin Prison. Guards said he was trying to escape. A 9mm automatic pistol had been smuggled into the prison, and Jackson had it in his possession when he was shot. The gun was traced to Angela Davis.

Davis went underground, but two months later she was arrested in New York and held for trial where she was ultimately acquitted of all charges. It was during her incarceration that United Presbyterian Church officials contributed to her legal defense fund.

Presbyterians in the pews were furious when they learned of the grant, and thousands sent letters to General Assembly officials, protesting the allocation. Damage control strategists tried to contain the Angela Davis incident as a one-of-a-kind misjudgment, an isolated failure of discernment. But a review of denominational policies and programs that preceded and followed the grant, suggests that the gift was not at all isolated, but part of a continuous stream of events wherein denominational officials supported proponents of liberationist ideologies.

During the ensuing denominational controversy, Robert E. Hunt, a circuit court judge from Peoria, Illinois with 30 years' experience on the bench, published an analysis that laid bare the ideological purpose of denominational officials in making the grant. Hunt's commentary, published by *The Presbyterian Layman*,[15] pointed out that there is a public defender system throughout the United States, "designed to assist in the representation of persons accused of crime who are indigent." He said that these public defenders represent all persons, "regardless of race." He said that if the accused does not want a member of the public defender staff, "the court appoints another qualified attorney to defend him … these services are free to the accused."

"The indigent is entitled to a free attorney, not only at the trial level, but also on appeal to the highest courts," Hunt continued. "A complete record is made of every statement, argument, motion, and shred of evidence at every stage of the proceedings. This is typed up and furnished to him without charge. These same services are available to Miss Davis in California, free."

Hunt said that he queried attendees at a conference of trial and appellate court judges in Chicago. He asked them "If Angela Davis is tried, and if she defends herself on the issues framed by the indictment and uses the offices

15 *The Presbyterian Layman*, Vol. 4, No. 8, September, 1971.

of the public defender, do you believe that she will receive a fair trial without the aid of private counsel?" Hunt said he received a unanimous "Yes."

Hunt said that all of the attorneys whom he queried agreed that "political defenses" claiming "that the accused's political motives at the time of the event justify his actions" would not pass muster. He cited arguments increasingly employed by ideological activists, namely, that the end justifies the means. Labeling the tactics employed in this type of defense as public relations rather than law, Hunt said the Angela Davis strategy was "an open attempt to make a public carnival out of orderly judicial process. To do this, the accused must hire private counsel at tremendous fees. For this, one must raise a defense fund of $100,000 or more."

Judge Hunt then specified the tactics used in Davis' defense. "She has already disqualified all the judges in the area where the murder took place. She tried to get the case transferred to the federal courts and to disqualify the federal judge. That judge sent the case back to the state courts, since the federal courts do not try state murder cases, noting that she was obviously trying to delay trial and frustrate justice. Her attorney announced he would appeal this decision to a higher court to further delay the matter. She also tried to get out a warrant for Governor Reagan on charges of conspiracy – which was refused. She has a battery of lawyers representing her, and the sources of funds for them are many."

Hunt then drew his conclusion: "In essence, then, the church has garnered a substantial fund for 'Legal Aid' and has misappropriated it to a legal defense fund to be used to destroy our courts and system of justice ... Those diverting church funds for such purposes should do so openly and acknowledge the true purpose of such a gift, and not misrepresent it to be legal aid for the poor."

Following her release from prison, Davis spent a period of time in Cuba where she endorsed the Castro regime. She returned to the United States and has continued her advocacy for egalitarian politics, teaching and lecturing at several California colleges and universities. She was the Communist Party's vice-presidential candidate in 1980 and 1984. She is currently a professor with the History of Consciousness Department at the University of California, Santa Cruz and director of the Feminist Studies Department. She publicly declared herself a lesbian in 1997 and has expanded her initial African American liberationist interests to include gay, lesbian, bisexual and transgendered liberation causes as well.

Going Global

Although the Presbyterian Church's embrace of liberationist ideologies was initially limited to the civil rights movement in the United States and, in particular, to the politics of race, it soon gravitated toward global applications. At the core of this expansion lay the Marxist vision of a transnational classless society. According to Marxist theory, oppression in any part of the world inhibits revolutionary progress everywhere else. Thus, it was not sufficient for the church to address inequities between the races at home. It had to understand, as James Forman and Angela Davis so vigorously articulated in their speeches and writings, that racial conflict in the United States is simply one symptom of a worldwide war between the haves and the have-nots.

The vehicle that denominational officials chose to transport them into global liberation movements was hunger. During the 1970s, mainline denominations turned their focus on the problem of hunger, at home and abroad. Both northern and southern Presbyterian denominations created high level hunger task forces, and their congregations proved exceedingly generous in supporting their hunger projects. Millions of dollars were contributed to direct feeding and development efforts by the denominations, whose task forces often coordinated their work through parallel agencies in the World Council of Churches, World Alliance of Reformed Churches, and National Council of Churches.

The Politics of Hunger

Eager to mine this mother lode of compassion, liberationists at the national staff level developed a plan to channel funds for the hungry into international politics. Their approach appeared innocuous on its face. They simply said that in addition to direct feeding programs and development projects like well digging, irrigation, flood control, and exporting agricultural technology, hunger funds would also be used to "address the root causes of hunger." The language was so vague that few parishioners saw the potential expansion that such words made possible. In time they would learn that in agreeing to address "the root causes of hunger," they had written a blank check to international liberationist causes. Money that was given to feed hungry people would soon be spent on ideology, bullets and bombs.

In 1973, International Documentation of North America (IDOC), an intellectual think tank that operated under the umbrella of the National Council of Churches and distributed its findings to a limited audience, primarily the seminary communities and national staffs of mainline denominations, circulated a paper among its constituencies.

"The purpose of this paper," said authors Eugene Toland, Thomas Fenton, and Lawrence McCulloch, "is to say that many of the injustices we see all around us cannot be understood and dealt with effectively if we treat them in isolation. It is something like the weather. If we want to explain why it is cloudy one day and sunny the next, or why it snows in one place and rains in another, we have to know as much as we can about the weather system … In the same way, a child dying of malnutrition in one of the slums of Rio, or a black steelworker out of work in Gary, or an important banker riding comfortably in his limousine down Park Avenue in New York – these are not merely isolated events. They are related to and dependent upon one another. They are part of a system."[16]

Then IDOC made its point: "To be more specific, this paper contends that the system which creates and sustains much of the hunger, underdevelopment, unemployment, and other social ills in the world today is capitalism ... As such, it is an unjust system which should be replaced."[17]

In the IDOC paper, the meaning of "root causes of hunger" that denominational executives had left vague and undefined now became crystal clear: "We can better see the roots of many of the injustices which we face today. Bloated stomachs, refugees, chronic unemployment, crowded urban ghettos … and the continuance of imperialistic wars are all products of a system which reaps excess for the few and scatters crumbs to the many. As men and women thirsting for justice, we are naïve if we fail to take a hard, critical look at this system … A characteristic common among white workers, most women, Chicanos, blacks, farmers, Indians, office workers – be they in the U.S. or in other countries – is that they are exploited by the super rich in a system designed to be unfair."[18]

Two years later, in 1975, the Joint Strategy and Action Committee (JSAC) of the National Council of Churches convened its Detroit conference for staff members of the mainline denominations. National staff from the United Presbyterian Church and the Presbyterian Church US attended. They concluded their conference with a "consensus statement" that included "points of agreement, questions left unresolved, and a list of tasks to be completed."

Among the "points of agreement" were these: "God acts in history for human liberation from every kind of oppressive condition – including the oppressions of poverty, racism, sexism, and colonialism. Liberation theology is thus a theology of salvation for the whole person … In order to understand the nature of the socio/political/economic reality of the American people as a basis for doing liberation theology, the tools of Marxist

16 *International Documentation of North America*, Number 54/Summer, 1973, p.1.

17 *Ibid.*

18 *Ibid.*, p. 7.

social analysis are crucial – especially its attention to class structure and the economic determinants of behaviors and institutions ... The dynamic impulse of transnational corporations results in the exploitation of people both here and abroad. The present economic system is irreconcilable with the Christian faith ... Anti-communist socialization and hysteria ... have prevented the development of class consciousness among oppressed and exploited people in the U.S."[19]

The consensus statement listed questions that participants left unresolved: "Given that Marxist social analysis is an essential tool in the praxis of Liberation Theology, what form of Marxism is most adequate to these tasks? What is the significance between Marxism and Christianity? What can Marxism add to the practice of Christianity; what can Christianity add to Marxism? Recognizing that equality among all peoples and the elimination of oppression cannot be achieved without radical social transformation, what kind of transformation, as Christians, should we work for?"[20]

Finally, the consensus statement listed tasks to be continued. Among them were, "The task of developing a more holistic structural analysis of the U.S. – one which makes clear the inter-structuring of racism, sexism, class exploitation, American and economic imperialism, and one which deals with the ecological crisis – must be continued ... We need to continue to build ties of solidarity between all those who are working for human liberation both here and in other countries."[21]

In 1973, denominational leaders attended The World Conference on Salvation Today, in Bangkok, Thailand. Here, Presbyterian Church representatives, freed by their own C-67 to promote liberation as salvation, played a leading role.

The Bangkok event offered the ecumenical community an expanded definition of salvation. No longer confined to the work of Jesus Christ in the heart of the believer, salvation became a World Council of Churches code word for socio-economic change. At the Bangkok event, WCC leaders called for a "moratorium" on Christian churches sending missionaries to non-Christian countries. Instead, Christians were encouraged to work together with non-Christian religions to achieve liberation from oppressive socio-political, economic regimes.

According to Marlin VanElderen, Executive Editor, WCC Publications, the Bangkok event "called churches to overcome the idea of mission as a

19 *Grapevine* (Joint Strategy and Action Committee), Vol. 6, 1975.

20 *Ibid.*

21 *Ibid.*

one-way movement from 'Christians' to 'non-Christian' countries, to take up the challenges of living in community with people of other faiths, to link their verbal proclamation of the gospel with engagement in the struggles of communities against oppression, poverty and hunger ..."[22]

Bishop Desmond Tutu, General Secretary of the South Africa Council of Churches described the shift most graphically: "Jesus is a revolutionary. I am a revolutionary. Every Christian must be a revolutionary."[23] Again, speaking to a reporter for the London *Daily Telegraph*, Tutu said, "One young man with a stone in his hand can achieve far more than I can with a dozen sermons."[24] Writing to a WCC publication, Tutu said, "When justice prevails over injustice as in Zimbabwe, it shows that the kingdom of God is here already."[25]

Later, in 1985, Tutu told a reporter for London's *Sunday Times*, "I am a socialist. I hate capitalism."[26] Writing for the publication *Inside South Africa* in 1988, he said, "I think I would use Marxist insights, 'From each according to his ability, to each according to his need.' That, I think, is in line with what our Lord, himself, would have taught."[27]

'Internationalization of Mission' Conference, 1975

In February, 1975, a conference of mainline denominational staff members was held in New York. National mission and world mission executives from the United Presbyterian Church and the Presbyterian Church US participated. The event was initiated by JSAC and sponsored by two units of the National Council of Churches and the Inter-religious Foundation for Community Organization (IFCO), the organization through which United Presbyterian Church officials had channeled funds to James Forman's Black Manifesto reparations campaign and related organizations, like the Black Panthers.

As reported in *Grapevine*, participants concluded that "American churches which seek to be in mission must take into account both their past complicity in the structures of U.S. power and imperialism and their present dialectical relationship with the centers of multinational corporate power.

22 World Council of Churches 8th Assembly, Feature No. 1, "Happy Birthday WCC," January, 1998.

23 *Rapport*, April 20, 1986.

24 *Daily Telegraph*, London, November, 1984.

25 *Ecunews*, November 19, 1980.

26 *Sunday Times*, London, December 29, 1985.

27 *Inside South Africa*, April, 1988.

Third World peoples are increasingly demanding of us that we look critically at our links to capitalist power and seek to disengage ourselves from it. The church is still divided over the question of whether it is possible to reform the multinationals or whether it should in some way be working for their dissolution."[28]

Participants agreed that if one measured the effectiveness of world missions in socio/political/economic development terms, missionaries from their churches had done a poor job: "Everywhere, the claim that Western Christianity has made for truth is being challenged by socialist movements, such as those in Tanzania, North Vietnam, China and Mozambique which in many instances have proven more effective in bringing about social and economic justice for large groups of the oppressed than have all the efforts of Western Christian missionaries abroad."[29]

In a conclusion voiced by United Presbyterian representatives, they announced that radical changes must be made in their 'foreign missions' efforts, including declaring a moratorium on sending out additional missionaries and, instead, sending bloc grants to "foreign churches or projects" in the developing world.[30]

Acknowledging the influence of Presbyterian participants, conference leaders said, "Whatever else the Christian faith means," states a United Presbyterian document on internationalization, "it implies that Christian existence in the world cannot be understood apart from a political conception of the world."[31]

DETROIT CONFERENCE ON LIBERATION THEOLOGY, 1975

In August, 1975, the Religion News Service reported on a week-long conference on Liberation Theology, held in Detroit for 126 "theologians, social scientists and activists." The conference was sponsored by the Latin American Division of the U.S. Catholic Conference and the Latin American Working Group of the National Council of Churches. Prominent among the leaders and platform speakers at the conference were Presbyterians Robert McAfee Brown, a United Presbyterian theologian who was teaching at the Graduate Theological Union, Berkeley, California, and James E. Goff, a Presbyterian missionary who had long been a leader of revolutionary movements in Latin America.

---

28 *Grapevine*, Vol. 5, No. 7, pp. 1, 2.

29 *Ibid.*, p. 2.

30 *Ibid.*, p. 3.

31 *Ibid.*

Brown told conferees that he found liberation theology in Latin America "exciting" and a contemporary version of the Exodus. He called on U.S. participants to back liberation movements in Latin America. "Somehow, we're on the side of people engaging in oppression. American business is ripping off Latin America all over the place," he said.[32]

James Goff told the Religion News Service, "the various groups taking part [in the Detroit event] had 'quite a consensus on the usefulness of Marxist tools of social analysis. They felt we have to have a more sophisticated analysis and they hammered steadily at the role of U.S. imperialism.'"[33]

Shortly thereafter, Robert C. Lamar, Moderator of the United Presbyterian Church, convened five regional conferences on "The Theology of the Church in Mission." Lamar invited Letty M. Russell, Assistant Professor of Theology and Women's Studies at Yale Divinity School and author of "Human Liberation in a Feminist Perspective" to be a keynote speaker. Russell argued that the mission of the church is "human liberation" and "revolution of freedom."

On July 9, 1975, Alexander Solzhenitsyn delivered a speech to the AFL-CO in New York in which he castigated the liberationist leadership of Angela Davis and the aftermath of her ideology: "There's a certain woman here named Angela Davis. I don't know if you are familiar with her in this country, but in our country, literally for one whole year, we heard of nothing at all except Angela Davis. There was only Angela Davis in the whole world, and she was suffering. We had our ears stuffed with Angela Davis. Little children in school were told to sign petitions in defense of Angela Davis. Little boys and girls, eight and nine years old in schools, were asked to do this. Well, they set her free. Although she didn't have a rough time in this country, she came to recuperate in Soviet resorts. Some Soviet dissidents – but more important, a group of Czech dissidents – addressed an appeal to her: 'Comrade Davis, you were in prison. You know how unpleasant it is to sit in prison, especially when you consider yourself innocent. You now have such authority. Could you help our Czech prisoners? Could you stand up for those persons in Czechoslovakia who are being persecuted by the state?' Angela Davis answered, 'They deserve what they get. Let them remain in prison.' That is the face of Communism. That is the heart of Communism for you."[34]

32 Religion News Service, August 26, 1975.

33 *Ibid.*

34 Solzhenitsyn, Aleksandr, *Warning to the West* (New York: Farrar, Straus and Giroux, 1976), pp. 60-61.

In a 1975 editorial, *Christianity Today* laid bare the NCC liberationist thesis that had so readily been adopted by Presbyterian Church leaders in both the northern and southern streams. "'A basic contradiction exists between the capitalist system and biblical justice, mercy, stewardship, service, community and self-giving love,' decided the delegates to 'An Ecumenical Consultation on Domestic Hunger' convened last month by the National Council of Churches. 'We were blinded to these basic contradictions between the values inherent in our faith heritage and the operative social reality … Now, however, the contradictions are too apparent, and we are forced to confess our complicity – whether through ignorance, apathy, fear or deliberate venality – with a system that is basically unjust.'

"The delegates went on to say that Christians are called upon to make a difficult decision: 'We must choose either to serve God and our neighbor or to perpetuate the prevailing values and systemic arrangement. There is no other choice. To end hunger, then, means to work for radical change in the economic, political and religious values and institutions in this society.'

"If they were saying that the capitalistic system operating in the United States today has evils that need to be corrected, we would certainly agree. But they are going much further. They are saying that capitalism is inherently evil and must be abolished. This we must certainly reject.

"The question we must ask this NCC panel is, what other system do you advocate? Where is there evidence of a better system, one more consonant with 'justice, mercy … and self-giving love?' Certainly not in the state capitalism of Russia and China, one that makes possible the worst examples of the dehumanization of man. Certainly not in a system that denies to its citizens such basic human freedoms as freedom of speech, religion, and movement. Certainly not in a theory that makes fairy-tale promises of the disappearance of the state and of a future communal society in which all people will work for the common good without coercion from anyone."

"The alternative to capitalism is socialism. But the socialism of China and Russia has shown itself incapable of producing enough food to feed the people. For the foreseeable future, both of those nations will have to depend on the achievements of what the hunger consultation called a 'basically unjust' system to keep them going (while they work to kill the goose that lays this golden egg).

"The time has come for Christians who believe in capitalism, which they admit can be abused and is indeed in need of correction, to make themselves heard. The best way for them to get their message through to the NCC is to cut off their churches' financial support of that body. Money talks; so does its absence. If the NCC wants to promote the destruction of capitalism, it should do so with money contributed by persons who favor that goal. Much of its constituency does not."[35]

Liberationists Target Latin America

As objections to Liberation Theology began to increase among their churches, denominational leaders turned to JSAC for assistance in interpreting the import of this theology for the life of the church. JSAC responded to the challenge by publishing an article in February, 1977 whose theme was that all theology is the product of culture and that as such, the theology of European and North American churches is inadequate for churches in Latin America. "The theologies from Europe and North America," said JSAC, "are dominant today in our churches, and represent one form of cultural domination. They must be understood to have arisen out of situations related to those countries and therefore must not be uncritically adopted without our raising the question of their reliance in the context of our [Latin American] countries."[36]

"Theology," continued JSAC, "is not neutral. In a sense all theology is committed, conditioned notably by the socio-cultural context in which it is developed." JSAC commended the Soviet Union and Eastern Europe for supporting the indigenous theologies of Latin Americans in contrast to and as "a counter-balance against the imperialist domination by the North American powers."[37]

Presbyterians Follow Suit

The Presbyterian Church in the U.S.A. General Assembly of 1977 approved a resolution calling on the United States government to remove any obstacle of policy or practice imposed by the United States preventing normal relations with the Cuban government. It voted "no action" on an overture from the Presbytery of Box Butte calling for "discontinuance of support by IFCO of organizations whose militant means include violence," approved a resolution affirming continuing financial support for IFCO, and defeated a motion which stated, "The General Assembly affirms that the United Presbyterian Church does not and will not support any organization that uses violence to bring about social change."[38]

The 1977 General Assembly also approved recommendations from a

35 *Christianity Today*, November, 1975.

36 *Grapevine*, February, 1977.

37 *Ibid.*

38 Presbyterian Church in the U.S.A., *Minutes of the General Assembly*, 1977, p. 119.

Special Committee on the Theology of Liberation and Renewal calling on the General Assembly Mission Council to coordinate churchwide theological reflection "based upon the Scriptures, *The Book of Confessions*, and *The Book of Order* of the United Presbyterian Church, USA, seeking to maintain both freedom and openness of theological inquiry, and commitment to Jesus Christ in the quest for understanding." The approved recommendations affirmed "the need to continue listening to the renewing insights of Liberation Theologies being developed in such groups as Asian Americans, Hispanic Americans, Native Americans, Blacks and Women."[39]

Reflecting the United Presbyterian Church's deepening commitment to incorporating Liberation Theology into its world mission policies, the 1977 Mission Yearbook for Prayer and Study included a promotion of the "Conscientization" work of liberationist Paulo Freire. It commended the work of the Europe-Third World Center and the Institute of Cultural Action, identifying the latter group's function in helping people engage in "the process through which we learn to identify the contradictions in our reality and take action against oppressive forces in our lives."[40]

Missionary Cites Theological 'Betrayal'

This documented support of Marxist writers and associated groups that prepare study documents, leadership for seminars and workshops throughout the denomination triggered an angry rebuke by Rev. Richard Baird. Born of Presbyterian missionary parents in Korea, Baird himself became a missionary, giving a lifetime of service in Korea, agricultural missions in Colombia, and ending his career as Missionary Field Secretary for the Caribbean area of Latin America, working in Mexico, Guatemala, Colombia and Venezuela. Having seen firsthand the work of liberation theologians in Latin America and their devastating impact on mission work among the Latin American churches, Baird declared the denomination's endorsement of this theology "a betrayal."

"This drift toward Humanism has been greatly aided by our connection with the World and National Councils of Churches (WCC and NCC), which have wandered from their original legitimate goals, and by the ambiguities of the Confession of '67, plus confusion attendant upon Restructuring," he said. "It has led us into a breach of faith with our sister-daughter churches, especially, but not exclusively, those of Colombia and Korea. In dishonoring

39 *Ibid.*

40 Presbyterian Church in the U.S.A., *Mission Yearbook for Prayer and Study*, 1977, p. 78.

its commitments to these sister churches the United Presbyterian Church has betrayed its own missionaries who, like myself, drew up the Covenants of Mutual Agreement and Cooperation which our church has (unilaterally) dishonored."[41]

'Theology of the Americas'

200 Roman Catholic and Protestant educators, social and political scientists, social activists and theologians from North and South America gathered in New York, June 21, 1978 to address the issue of capitalism. Leaders of the "Theology of the Americas" event and members of the drafting committee that produced its consensus statement were two United Presbyterian Church theologians from Union Theological Seminary in New York, Robert McAfee Brown and Beverly Harrison. The ecumenical group called on Christians to "explore a more radical alternative – including "humanistic socialism" – to the prevailing western capitalistic system."[42]

"All of us sense that capitalism is the fundamental problem," said the statement drafted by the United Presbyterian theologians and approved by conference participants. The statement called capitalism "an idol" and as such "a violation of the first Commandment, for it demands human sacrifice to preserve the system."[43]

Christian/Marxist Dialogues

Denominational leaders' infatuation with Marxism, seen in their councils' statements during the 1970s, would grow in intensity during the next decade, until the collapse of the Soviet Union. In 1987, the World Council of Churches initiated a program for "Christian/Marxist Dialogue." The Rev. Wesley Ariarajah, a WCC official, justified the program because of "a softening in attitudes toward Christian churches in the German Democratic Republic (East Germany) and Hungary, as well as in Cuba." He also referred to developments in Zimbabwe and Nicaragua "where leaders of Marxist-oriented governments have Christian roots while often being at odds with some church authorities." The view that Marxism is anti-religious in some Eastern European countries is "gradually falling apart," he said. Regarding peace movement issues, Ariarajah said, "there is common ground between Christians and Marxists."[44]

41 *The Presbyterian Layman*, Vol. 10, No. 7, September/October, 1977.

42 Religion News Service, June 21, 1978.

43 *Ibid.*

44 Religion News Service, November 10, 1986.

Protests From Colombian Presbyterians

United Presbyterian Church (USA) leaders did more than talk about implementing principles of Marxist analysis in developing countries, they practiced it. Denominational grants in the early 1970s to ROSCA, a Marxist organization in Colombia, South America prove illustrative.

In 1972, The Presbytery of the South, with the concurrence of two additional presbyteries in the Presbyterian Church of Colombia, issued a sharply worded "Declaration," protesting a $75,000 grant to ROSCA from the United Presbyterian Church's National Committee for the Self Development of People.

The stated purpose of the grant was "to work with peasant organizations in rural areas, Indian civil rights, labor unions in the city, basic community organization all over the country, and to do a great deal of adult education work in the country."[45]

The three Colombian presbyteries complained in their "Declaration" that leaders of ROSCA "are men with known Marxist views who are totally unrelated to our Colombian church." "These men," continued the Declaration, "reject the order now established in Colombia and propose the establishment of a socialist regime with the logical implication of the destruction of economic and political structures which at present operate in our country."[46]

A member of the United Presbyterian Church's National Committee for the Self Development of People who was named in the Colombian church's declaration, was Dr. Orlando Fals-Borda, a sociologist who led the committee when it addressed Latin American issues. Fals-Borda's liberationist views were well known. He was the author of several books, including *Subversion and Social Change in Colombia*[47] and *The Significance of Guerrilla Movements in Latin America*.[48]

Delivering the Eleventh Annual Foyer John Knox Lecture in Geneva, Switzerland, Fals-Borda said, "As we are witnessing today the birth pangs of a new society in Latin America, it is necessary to become acquainted with its prophets, builders, and martyrs – the human heart and arms of sub-

45 United Presbyterian Church in the U.S.A., Report of the National Committee on the Self Development of People, 1972.

46 Presbytery of the South, Ibague, Colombia, "Declaration," enacted and delivered to the United Presbyterian Church in the U.S.A., January, 1972.

47 Fals Borda, Orlando, Skiles, Jacqueline D., trans., *Subversion and Social Change in Colombia* (New York & London: Columbia University Press, 1969).

48 Fals Borda, Orlando, *The Significance of Guerrilla Movements in Latin America* (New York: Association for Religion and Intellectual Life, 1968).

version seen as a truly significant social development."[49]

Among the "prophets" whom Fals-Borda listed was Cuban revolutionary leader, Che Guevara. "In this field, which is eminently moral, the writings of Che Guevara are paramount. In his 'Notes for the Study of the Ideology of the Cuban Revolution,' Guevara starts by pointing out the 'moral system' that distinguishes the guerrilla from the regular army soldier. Essentially, they differ in commitment: the former is willing to offer his life to the cause and to forego all comforts, while the second is a simple mercenary. Moreover, the use of violence is conditioned to the resistance shown by the reactionaries who impede the birth of the new society: thus, the guerrilla is not a violent man *per se*, and should not be confused with a bandit."[50]

Fals-Borda extolled the work of Fidel Castro: "The case of Cuba is outstanding because it is a demonstration of the great potential of the Latin American peoples in both the social and the technical fields, once the oppressive rules of the present economic and political game have been discarded."[51] He concluded his lecture by expressing his hope that Latin America's movement toward creating a Marxist "New Society" might influence similar developments in Africa, Asia and Europe. This was apparently the rationale that he employed in his efforts to channel $75,000 from United Presbyterian Self Development funds into Colombian revolutionary activity.

Strained Relations with Colombian Presbyterians

The protest from Colombian Presbyterians created quite a stir at the 1972 General Assembly. When the matter came before one of the assembly's standing committees, the majority sought to bury it. But a minority report was filed, along with a motion calling for a special General Assembly committee to investigate ROSCA. In the ensuing debate, denominational staff persons, led by Rev. John H. Sinclair, secretary for Latin America on the Commission on Ecumenical Mission and Relations (COEMAR) staff, imported an impressive line up of consultants, advisors and "experts" to testify before the committee. Among those whom he invited was Fals-Borda, who, according to news reports, told commissioners that he was a member of the Colombian Presbyterian Church and that, in his opinion, the

49 Third World Center, "Foyer John Knox Lecture," Geneva, Switzerland, June 19, 1970, p. 11.

50 *Ibid.*, p. 13.

51 *Ibid.*, p. 16.

Colombian church did not know or care much about self-development. A commissioner asked Fals-Borda if he denied that "ROSCA has a Communist stand." The sociologist replied sharply, "I thought the McCarthy era was over in this country," and he left the microphone.[52]

Commissioner Francis Scott asked, "Is Dr. Fals-Borda saying that we should cut off relations with the Colombian Presbyterian Church and establish relations directly with ROSCA? Why does he not work with his own church there?"[53]

Although he may not have realized it at the time, Scott was pointing to a trend that included but went far beyond the ROSCA issue. Increasingly, Presbyterian officials were making connections with secular liberationist groups in other countries, often over the objections of Christian churches in those countries with whom the denomination had fraternal agreements and missionary partnerships. The attitude expressed by denominational bureaucrats toward their fellow Presbyterians in other countries bordered on arrogance.

The 1972 General Assembly did commission a study of the ROSCA grant, but it took care to indicate that its action should not imply that there was any wrongdoing on the part of denominational agencies. "The committee believes that the request for a study is not questioning at all the integrity of our national staff nor the National Committee for the Self-Development of People. But, rather, the study is to affirm our Presbyterian process. It is to give confidence in our connectional design."[54]

Several months later, the special committee issued a written report affirming the propriety of the ROSCA grant and commending the denomination's national staff for having acted within General Assembly guidelines. The committee rejected "the accusation that ROSCA's leaders are Marxist or Communist motivated." It said that it was "impressed with the sincerity and dedication of ROSCA's leaders," and that "they operate neither as a political party nor as a political influence within one party, but as sociologists committed to helping people help themselves."

The committee concluded that problems with the Colombian Presbyterian Church arose primarily because "the grant to ROSCA was not fully understood by the Colombian church." Thus, the committee suggested that an appropriate remedy would be "open discussions" between Colombian church leaders and United Presbyterian Church leaders in the Committee

52 *The Presbyterian Layman*, Vol. 5, No. 6, June/July 1972.

53 *Ibid.*

54 *Ibid.* See also *Presbyterian Life*, July, 1972, pp. 51, 52.

on Ecumenical Mission and Relations.[55/56]

On January 27, 1973, the National Committee on the Self-Development of People voted to validate and fund a second grant to ROSCA in the amount of $75,000. In 1975, after *The Presbyterian Layman* published articles revealing the contents of ROSCA magazines, books and other publications that were being distributed in Colombia for the purpose of inciting revolutionary activity, the General Assembly overturned an additional $90,000 grant to ROSCA that had been approved by the National Committee on Self-Development of People.

In 1979, Fals-Borda was arrested in Colombia along with members of a left-wing guerrilla organization which, on January 2, 1979, allegedly tunneled from a nearby house into an army arsenal near the capital of Bogota and stole some 5,000 weapons. It was further reported that some of these weapons were found in Fals-Borda's home. Fals-Borda disclaimed any responsibility for the storage of weapons, saying that the home belonged to his wife.[57]

Redefining Missions as 'Mission'

The United Presbyterian Church was not alone in pushing liberationist themes into its mission policies. Leaders of its sister denomination to the south, the Presbyterian Church US, engaged in similar efforts. In 1978, leaders of the Presbyterian Church US world missions program initiated a major effort to incorporate liberationist initiatives by organizing a "Consultation on Overseas and Domestic Mission," that was held at the denomination's conference center in Montreat, North Carolina.

The use of the word "mission" rather than "missions" was intentional and significant. Previously, mainline denominations used the plural term when referring to their response to the Great Commission. They understood that their task was to take the gospel to those who have not heard it and to make disciples of Jesus Christ. "Missions" meant evangelism, pure and simple, and when Presbyterians gave money to missions, this is precisely what they intended to fund.

55 United Presbyterian Church in the (USA), *General Assembly Minutes*, 1973, pp. 422-435.

56 This type of response is often used by denominational leaders when they face criticism from Presbyterians in the pews. The problem is the people's ignorance, and "dialogue" is the proffered remedy. Implicit in this "solution" is the assumption that if the people really studied a matter or engaged in extended conversation about it, they would come around to the establishment's more enlightened point of view.

57 *The New York Times*, March 11, 1979.

Using the singular term to differentiate it from its traditional meaning, denominational leaders broadened mission to include not just evangelism but everything the church does. Richard Hutcheson, an observer of organizational development in the Presbyterian Church (US) described this evolution of "mission." He pointed out that in the traditional sense, missions had been related to sending missionaries overseas to preach the gospel and plant churches, but that contemporary usage was not so clearly focused. Mission came to include the entire range of functions and activities of the church. In this sense, meals for the poor, advocacy for the oppressed, education for children, health care for the infirmed, day care for children of the congregation, recreation programs for youth, housing for seniors, painting the church parsonage, padding the pews and paying the pastor was defined as mission.[58]

One major signal that highlighted the changing definition of mission came in 1969 when the *International Review of Missions*, an established journal of missiology, changed its name to the *International Review of Mission*. The editorial discussing the name change explained that the term "mission" was more acceptable to church leaders outside of the west.[59]

On its face, the change from missions to mission seems innocent. Who would argue against the social implications of the gospel? It is the church's duty to heal the sick, strengthen the brokenhearted, and rescue the helpless. The model of Christ himself is one of servant leadership. The world cries out for help with health, educational, economic and social needs of all kinds. But when missions becomes mission, and mission becomes everything that the church is doing, then something precious is lost, namely, the highest goal of the church and the first priority of mission – the Great Commission to make disciples.

Presbyterians who were aware of their history should not have been surprised by the subtleties inherent in changing missions to mission. J. Gresham Machen predicted it in the 1930s, when he took issue with a document called *Rethinking Missions*,[60] that had been funded by the Rockefeller Foundation and was in vogue among liberal church leaders. Machen argued that when liberal theology substituted personal and class liberation for the doctrine of original sin, it opened the door to an entirely different under-

58 Hutcheson, Richard G. Jr., *Mainline Churches and the Evangelicals: A Challenging Crisis?* (Atlanta: John Knox Press, 1981), p. 82.

59 *Ibid.*

60 Hocking, William E., *Rethinking Missions: A Layman's Inquiry after One Hundred Years* (New York: Harper & Brothers, 1932), p.70.

standing of missions, one whose purpose is to change the structures of society rather than bring individuals into a personal relationship with Jesus Christ.

Karla Koll summarizes the report as suggesting that "the greatest division in the world was not between Christians and non-Christians, but between enlightened people of different religions seeking the moral and social betterment of humankind and those trapped by superstition in oppressive social structures. Therefore, the report also urged missions to cooperate with non-Christian groups in efforts aimed at social improvement."[61]

Although Presbyterian Church mission boards did not adopt *Rethinking Missions* as a matter of official policy, Machen could see evidence that they were incorporating its themes into that policy. In this observation, Machen was prophetic. Historians John R. Fitzmier and Randall Balmer have argued that the report proved to be a blueprint for mission board policies in future decades.[62]

Machen called on the General Assembly of the Presbyterian Church in the U.S.A. to require its missionaries to sign a statement of faith in Jesus Christ as their personal savior and a commitment that they would teach this Biblical theology on the mission field, not the social restructuring doctrines of liberalism. Consistent with the General Assembly decision in 1926 eschewing any requirement that ordained leaders subscribe to essential tenets of belief, denominational leaders refused to require such subscription from their missionaries. Machen responded to this refusal by helping to organize an independent mission board.

In 1978, when Presbyterian Church (US) leaders announced their Consultation on Overseas and Domestic Mission, they said they would invite representatives from partner churches in developing countries to come to Montreat. These Third World Christians would help those who manage the Presbyterian Church US world mission enterprise come to a new understanding of "mission."

But were the putative representatives of Third World Christian communities truly representative? It turns out that they were handpicked, in many cases not by leaders of the churches that they purported to represent, but by

61 Koll, Karla Ann, *Journal of Presbyterian History*, Vol. 78, No. 1, p. 90.

62 Fitzmier, John R., and Balmer, Randall, "A Poultice of the Bite of the Cobra: The Hocking Report and Presbyterian Missions in the Middle Decades of the Twentieth Century," in *The Diversity of Discipleship: Presbyterians and Twentieth Century Christian Witness*, ed. Milton J. Coalter, John M. Mulder and Louis B. Weeks (Louisville: Westminster/John Knox, 1991), pp. 105-25.

staff persons of the Presbyterian Church US. Several of these "voices of the Third World" proved to be vigorous promoters of liberationist ideologies who castigated the United States for alleged economic imperialism. In general, the theme was that rich nations achieved their wealth by exploiting developing countries.

Exposing a Fraud

In a move that proved offensive to the Presbyterian Church of Brazil, Presbyterian Church US officials bypassed that church's evangelical and popular president, Rev. Dr. Boanerges Ribeiro, and, instead, invited a relatively unknown Marxist to attend the PCUSA mission consultation, pretending that he represented the Presbyterian Church of Brazil.

A veteran Presbyterian Church US missionary knew that denominational officials had chosen an imposter. Together with friends who offered to provide funding for travel, he encouraged Ribeiro to attend the meeting. Ribeiro understood that he might not be welcomed by Presbyterian Church US officials, but he agreed to attend the conference. When he presented his credentials, officials had no choice but to recognize him as the elected leader of his denomination.

Given the program format and the choice of "voices from the Third World," the consensus statement that emerged from this event was predictable. The consultation's document, "One Mission Under God," was loaded with liberationist rhetoric. Sin was no longer seen primarily as a flaw in the human soul, but as a socioeconomic structure. In particular, sin was equated with capitalism, and repentance required "solidarity with the poor in their entitlement to justice and liberation ... and help in creating the political will for a new international economic order."[63] Jesus, the Savior, was reinterpreted as Jesus, the Liberator.

Ribeiro vigorously opposed the consultation's sociopolitical product. When the document was approved over his objection, he insisted that his written dissent be recorded in the minutes. Arguing that the new Presbyterian Church US mission policy presented a watered-down Jesus, Ribeiro said: "I disagree with the theology underlying the paper, *God's Claims*, [a working draft of the consultation's final report] since in my opinion, it does not clearly state that only through belief in Jesus Christ can anybody be saved."[64]

63 Presbyterian Church in the United States, *Minutes of the General Assembly*, 1978, pp. 142-151.

64 *Ibid.*, p. 151.

Included in the mission consultation's report to the 1978 General Assembly were these statements:

"Surely the great disparity and imbalance between the rich and poor nations of the world ... call for urgent and radical solutions."[65]

"They [invited spokespersons purportedly representing Presbyterian Churches in developing countries] have said to us that the capitalistic system ... is for the majority of their people, in effect, exploitative and oppressive; and that acquiescence in such a system is a sin ..."[66]

The report called on the Presbyterian Church US to "face up to the truth of these statements from our fellow Christians so that we may be able to engage more effectively in programs and activities designed to combat the root causes of injustice ... Christ calls us to help create the political will for a new international economic order."[67]

The 1978 General Assembly adopted the report of its mission consultation, thereby making it the denomination's official policy statement on its overseas and domestic mission program. This action provided an important denominational imprimatur for funding and otherwise supporting revolutionary activity in Third World countries.[68]

Presbyterian Church of Brazil Issues Protest

The Presbyterian Church of Brazil broke relations with the United Presbyterian Church in 1973, after a year in which it declared two USA missionaries *persona non grata* and demanded that four other couples leave the country. The complaint: United Presbyterian Church missionaries were losing their passion for evangelism and turning their attention toward liberation theology and the politics of revolution.[69]

"Our churches were growing rapidly. We needed help in developing leadership and growing new churches," remembers the Rev. Ludgero Bonilha Morais, executive secretary of the Presbyterian Church of Brazil's Supremo Concilio (General Assembly), "but we did not need what the United Pres-

65 *Ibid.*, p. 145.

66 *Ibid.*

67 *Ibid.*

68 For a sympathetic interpretation of Presbyterian Church (US) mission policy changes, see Brown, G. Thompson, "Overseas Mission Program and Policies of the Presbyterian Church in the U.S., 1861-1983," *American Presbyterians: Journal of Presbyterian History*, (Summer 1997).

69 Joao Dias de Araujo, *Inquisition without Burnings*, trans. James N. Wright (Rio de Janiero: Instituto Superior de Estudos da Religiao, 1982), p.1012.

byterian Church was sending to us, so we had to ask it to leave."[70]

After 1973, Presbyterian missionaries from the Presbyterian Church US continued to receive a warm Brazilian welcome because at that time they remained committed to evangelism, leadership development and ministries of compassion in the name of Jesus. But as leaders of the southern denomination began plans to merge with the northern branch of Presbyterianism, they developed parallel policies that would pave the way toward reunion. Concerned Brazilian church leaders responded by tightening the reins on Presbyterian Church US mission agencies, demanding that the Brazilian church exercise control over their missionary assignments.

Severing All Relations

That Presbyterian Church US leaders were crafting liberationist policies similar to those of the United Presbyterian Church deeply troubled Brazilian church leaders. "We warned them that we could not accept this," said Morais, "but they would not listen to us."

In fact, Brazilians had been warning the Presbyterian Church US for several years. In 1974, sensing that a merger between the northern and southern branches might soon occur, representatives from the Presbyterian Church of Brazil sent a letter to the southern church's Division of International Mission, advising it that such a merger would adversely affect its missionary work in Brazil. Reflecting on this document, Frank L. Arnold, a 32-year veteran PCUS missionary to Brazil, wrote, "The document came across as a warning, and it was not well received by mission leaders in the United States, who saw it as unwanted pressure against reunion."[71]

In 1983, when the northern and southern branches merged to become the Presbyterian Church (USA), Ribeiro, who led the Brazilian delegation to that assembly, announced that the Presbyterian Church of Brazil would sever its ties with the reunited denomination, just as it had done earlier with the United Presbyterians. All former southern church missionaries were allowed to complete their terms of service. The Brazilian church agreed to take full responsibility for planned Bible Institutes and all former Presbyterian Church (US) properties in its country.

Seeking to put a happy face on this sad occasion, the Rev. Clifton Kirkpatrick expressed pleasure "that our churches have been able to part still

70 *The Presbyterian Layman* interview with the Rev. Ludgero Bonilha Morais, executive secretary of Supremo Concilio, Iglesia Presbyteriana, October 22, 2004.

71 Arnold, Frank L., "From Sending Church to Partner Church: The Brazil Experience," *Journal of Presbyterian History*, Fall, 2003.

friends in Christ, to wind the work down gradually, and in an orderly manner. We are glad that the Presbyterian Church of Brazil, in 122 years of working with us, has now reached a time that they are strong enough to stand alone and proceed with their emphasis of continued evangelism."[72]

Kirkpatrick's "strong enough to stand alone" comment may have been lost when translated into Portuguese, but for those who watched the soaring growth of the Brazilian church and the simultaneous, precipitous decline of the US Presbyterians, such words must have sounded as strange as they were paternalistic. US Presbyterians did not leave Brazil because they believed their Brazilian Presbyterian progeny had matured and no longer needed our mission workers. They left because the Presbyterian Church of Brazil kicked them out for having brought an alien ideology into its land.

Warning Their People

Brazilian church leaders point to massive declines in the Presbyterian Church (USA) as a warning to their own people. "The liberalism in your denomination is not just a different perspective," says the Rev. Dr. Augustus Nicodemus Lopes, Chancellor of the 50,000 student Mackenzie University, professor at Sao Paulo's Andrew Jumper Institute and assistant pastor to a Presbyterian congregation in the city. "It is, as your own J. Gresham Machen so clearly pointed out many years ago, a different faith."[73]

Presbyterian Church of Mexico Evicts US Mission Workers

Brazil and Colombia were not the only Latin American countries in which indigenous Presbyterian Church leaders objected to the liberationist political activities of US missionaries. In 1972, the Presbyterian Church of Mexico declared a five-year moratorium on accepting missionaries and money from both northern and southern Presbyterian denominations in the United States.

Having been evicted by the Mexican Presbyterians, US denominations redeployed their missionaries to Central American countries, notably Nicaragua, where two of them, J. Gary and Margaret Chase Campbell began to channel US Presbyterian support to the revolutionary junta of Marxist Sandinista Daniel Ortega.

72 Presbyterian Church News, November 17, 1983.

73 *The Presbyterian Layman* interview with the Rev. Dr. Augustus Nicodemus Lopes, Chancellor, Mackenzie University, October 30, 2004.

Supporting the Sandinista Revolution

In 1983, the reuniting General Assembly of the Presbyterian Church (USA) received and adopted a report on Central America that had been prepared by agencies of the two former Presbyterian denominations, the General Assembly Mission Board of the Presbyterian Church (US) and the Advisory Council on Church and Society of the United Presbyterian Church.

The report was replete with lavish praise for revolutionary regimes in some countries and guerrilla insurgencies in others. Throughout the volume, United States policy in Central America was heavily denounced as imperialistic and detrimental to people's movements in the region. Its chapter on Nicaragua was particularly colorful.

In glowing terms the report described the Sandinista Front of National Liberation (FSLN) as a flourishing expression of Christ at work among his people. Romanticizing the revolution, it said, "Priests and nuns organized 'Christian Base Communities' which raised the social consciousness of Nicaraguans and, indirectly, helped FSLN recruitment, and peasants disrupted military movements by felling huge trees or cutting trenches across major highways. The degree to which citizens of all types were mobilized in the Nicaraguan 'War of Liberation' was unprecedented in Latin American history."[74]

The report's description of US President Ronald Reagan's administration was particularly graphic: "The behavior of the Reagan administration simply confirmed the Sandinistas' worst fears ... Almost immediately upon Reagan's inauguration and with flimsy evidence at best, Nicaragua was accused of being a major conduit for arms flowing to the Salvadoran rebels."[75]

The Sandinistas were lauded for having made "great progress" in governance. In spite of the "external threat" and "obstructionist behavior" by the US, "the Sandinists, in their first three and a half years in power, were remarkably effective in establishing a new governmental system, in reactivating the war-ravaged economy, and in implementing a wide variety of social programs. In the area of politics and government, the Sandinists behaved with considerable constraint and moderation."[76]

It is not at all clear what the writers of this report had in mind when

74 *Adventure and Hope: Christians and the Crisis in Central America* (Interim Stated Clerks of the Presbyterian Church (USA), 1983), p. 72.

75 *Ibid.*, p. 73.

76 *Ibid.*, p. 74.

speaking of the Sandinists' reactivating their economy. In reality, the economy was in ruins, a fact that is admitted later in the report: "And in spite of the government's moderate and pragmatic approach to the economy, a number of factors largely beyond its control were causing serious economic, and therefore political difficulties."[77]

Of particular interest was the report's attempt to explain away the regime's persecution of the free press. Referring to *La Prensa*, the country's only independent newspaper, the report offered a justification for the Sandinistas' attempts to muzzle opposition voices: "For almost three years, it [*La Prensa*] was subject to no precensorship. During most of this period it published bitterly hostile, usually distorted, and frequently false information about the new revolutionary system. During these years the government shut it down as a punitive measure for two to three-day intervals on only six occasions. Only in 1982, as the counterrevolution mounted and part of the CIA's strategy for Nicaragua was disclosed in the U.S. press, was *La Prensa* finally placed under precensorship as part of a general state of prewar emergency declared by the government that spring."[78]

There is abundant evidence of the fact that Daniel Ortega's regime operated as a police state and that the people lived under oppressive controls. Unable to ignore these policies completely, the authors of the Presbyterian Church (USA) report suggested that the policies were justified in light of US government policies: "This is not to say that in 1982 all was well in Nicaragua. Intense counterrevolutionary pressures from abroad and from within were forcing the government to adopt emergency measures which tended to restrict civil liberties."[79]

During this period, there was mounting international pressure on Nicaragua to hold free, internationally supervised elections. Finally, the Sandinistas agreed to do so, confident – as were Presbyterian Church (USA) supporters of their revolution – that the people would confirm their leadership. That confidence made its way into the Presbyterian report: "There is little likelihood that the Sandinist Revolution will, as U.S. officials apparently naively believe, 'fall like a house of cards in the wind,' in the face of U.S.-sponsored efforts at destabilization and counterrevolution … The CIA's program of harassment and infiltration can undoubtedly cause considerable hardship and misery and might drive the government to become more authoritarian, but it holds very little likelihood of turning

77 *Ibid.*, p. 76.

78 *Ibid.*, p. 75.

79 *Ibid.*, p. 76.

back the pages of history."[80]

During the pre-election political campaign, Presbyterian Church (USA) mission workers invested heavily in Daniel Ortega's bid for a continuation of the Sandinista regime. Among those who worked for the Sandinista campaign while on the payroll of the Presbyterian Church (USA) were J. Gary Campbell, Margaret Chase Campbell, Charles R. Hughes, Anne Hughes, Derek Coursen, Donald Reasoner, and Karla Ann Koll. In a Nov. 23, 1989 statement released by "Presbyterian Church workers in Nicaragua" they said: "We are giving thanks this day for the Nicaraguans who have opened their lives up to us and allowed us to work beside them in this historical experiment known as the Popular Sandinista Revolution."

One of the key tools which Presbyterian Church (USA) mission workers used to influence the national election was called the "Accurate Information Project." Throughout the campaign, this project produced "Fact Sheets." These documents displayed data which appeared to support Ortega and discredited data which might be used against him.

A major target of the "Fact Sheets" was *La Prensa*, the independent newspaper that criticized the Sandinista regime. During the campaign *La Prensa* conducted a poll that indicated that Ortega was losing ground against his opponent Violetta Chamorro. An "Accurate Information Fact Sheet" voiced an immediate reaction, denouncing the *La Prensa* data as "a lie." It stated the *La Prensa's* poll included "questionable bias and faulty methodology [which] make the poll as a whole unreliable ... misleading and deceptive." The "Fact Sheet" then displayed contrasting claims indicating that Daniel Ortega was "the preferred candidate for president."

Presbyterian staffers in Nicaragua made no secret of their feelings regarding *La Prensa*. In "Fact Sheet 3" they stated "*La Prensa* has historically and systematically been used for disseminating reactionary, anti-Sandinista viewpoints. Its style of attack is sensationalist and often full of non-truths. *La Prensa* often needs to publish corrections of such printed lies after one of the other dailies investigates the outrageous accusations."

But the "Fact Sheets" did not limit themselves to *La Prensa* during the campaign. As Violetta Chamorro's popularity climbed, their attacks became more personal. Concerned that she might attract votes from Nicaragua's women, they tried to portray her as the anti-feminist candidate: "Dona Violetta has recently asked the women of Nicaragua to put aside their new feminist consciousness and don their aprons in order to return to their historical role as housewives," they declared.

---

80 *Ibid.*, p. 76.

In addition to its contribution of salaried personnel who were sent to Nicaragua to perform Christian missionary work, the Presbyterian Church (USA) poured thousands of dollars into Sandinista support projects. Much of this money was laundered through a labyrinth of interconnecting, quasi-independent ecumenical organizations. CEPAD, CEPRES, the Antonio Valdiviso Ecumenical Center, the InterChurch Center for Theological and Social Studies, and Witness for Peace constitute a partial list of pro-Sandinista groups that were working in Nicaragua to whom mission workers were assigned by denominational headquarters in Louisville. These organizations also received grants from various Mission Units of the Presbyterian Church (USA). Money was also provided from the Presbyterian Church (USA) treasury through "bloc grants" to the National and World Councils of Churches where accountability for the use of the funds was virtually non-existent. Thus, the total amount of money that the denomination channeled into Ortega's operation would have been impossible to calculate.

In 1990, *Reader's Digest* ran an article by John S. Tompkins, former staff correspondent for the *Wall Street Journal, New York Times* and *TIME Magazine* that detailed activities of Presbyterian Church (USA) mission workers in support of the Ortega political campaign. Tompkins, who was at the time a freelance writer, was a member of Madison Avenue Presbyterian Church in New York. Tompkins wrote that leaders of the Presbyterian Church (USA) "have substituted social, economic and political action for the real business of religion – worship, the study of Scripture, a spiritual vision of life and death, and a code of moral conduct." He quoted the results of church polls that "confirm the widening political gulf between church bureaucrats and the people in the pews."[81]

Members of the General Assembly Council were quick to respond to Tompkins' article with an eight-page attempt at damage control. Published and distributed by denominational headquarters in Louisville, the paper claimed that the Presbyterian Church (USA) is governed by a representative system, that national staff members are chosen by elected leaders, and that public positions taken by the national staff are based on policies adopted by elected leaders.

Responding to Tompkins' well documented charge that Presbyterian mission workers in Nicaragua campaigned for Daniel Ortega, the paper quoted Global Mission Unit director Clifton Kirkpatrick: "None of the mission personnel of the Presbyterian Church (USA) in Nicaragua – or anywhere

81 Tompkins, John S., "Look What They Have Done to My Songs," *Readers' Digest*, December, 1990.

else – have been campaign workers for any candidate."[82]

One of the organizations that received grants from the Presbyterian Church (USA) was the Council of Protestant Churches of Nicaragua (CEPAD). One of the organization's textbooks for the Nicaraguan people declared "We must therefore see socialism as the system which comes closest to the gospel ideal, whereas capitalism is incompatible with Christianity because it is based on egoism, implacable competition and the exploitation of man by man. As to Marxism, one can be a Christian and a Marxist, and in fact there are very many Christian Marxists in Latin America today."[83]

CEPAD's Nicaraguan textbook continued, "Instead of leaving the factories and other means of production in the hands of capitalists, Marx says that these must be in the hands of the people. Thus, instead of enriching the few, the profits go to benefit the people and are used for free education for all children, free medicines and medical care, and to build more schools, hospitals, clinics and highways."[84]

Finally, the CEPAD publication brought Sandinista party politics into the picture: "Daniel S. Ortega said: 'I feel proud to share with revolutionary Christians … In our country, there came about a coincidence in time of a renewed church, a Christian church with a Christian, Sandinista people …'"[85]

Ignoring the Facts

The Sandinistas' Soviet and Cuban connections and their commitment to a one-party totalitarian state were well known during the period that Presbyterian Church (USA) leaders were applauding Ortega's regime. Humberto Belli, former editorial page editor of *La Prensa*, who had collaborated with the Sandinista revolution before becoming a Christian in 1977, fled the country in 1982 and made public the policies and practices of this Marxist enterprise. Citing evidence from Sandinista memoranda and documented activities, he demonstrated how Sandinista policies were following a trajectory toward the development of a full police state.

82 Presbyterian Church (USA), General Assembly Council and Office of the General Assembly: Statement by Rev. S. David Stoner, Executive Director, General Assembly Council, and the Rev. Clifton Kirkpatrick, Stated Clerk of the General Assembly, December, 1990.

83 Council of Protestant Churches of Nicaragua, "Capitalism and Socialism for Beginners," Introduction, 1980.

84 *Ibid.*, p. 15.

85 *Ibid.*, p. 32.

Belli documented the gradual suppression of freedom of expression (*La Prensa*); a gradual suppression of political pluralism (non-Sandinista political parties were denied access to the media and barred by law from political campaigning); a progressive increase in the use of local and regional controls on the population (Sandinista Defense Committees on nearly every block in urban areas); a gradual suppression of independent labor organizations (the Sandinistas created their own trade union with the official slogan, "Only one workers' class, only one trade union."); a systematic use of government-organized mobs to intimidate opponents; the merger of State and Party, effectively wiping out checks and balances; redefining free elections (Commander Humberto Ortega, Daniel Ortega's brother, declared in 1980 that unlike elections in "bourgeois countries," Nicaraguan elections would be used to "select the best among the revolutionary vanguard, for power has been conquered forever by the people and it shall never be gambled again."); and the alignment of Sandinista foreign policy with that of the Soviet Union (the Sandinistas imported more than 8,000 Cuban "advisors" and other personnel from the Communist bloc, primarily East Germans, Bulgarians and Soviets.)[86]

Belli's revelations were widely publicized by the Puebla Institute and were picked up by the Associated Press, *The New York Times* and numerous newspapers across the United States, including *The Presbyterian Layman.*[87] Given the widespread dissemination of Belli's revelations in both the secular and church-related press, in addition to massive documentation by the United States State Department, it is beyond the realm of credulity to assume that officials of the Presbyterian Church (USA) were unaware of the facts. What is more likely is that in their ideological passion for what they believed was "the people's revolution" and the cardinal tenet of liberation theology that "God is on the side of the poor," they simply chose to ignore the facts.

Bolstering their romanticized version of what was happening in Nicaragua, Presbyterian Church (USA) agencies pumped tens of thousands of mission dollars into "travel/study" excursions into the country, where participants saw exactly what their Sandinista hosts wanted them to see. Former General Assembly Moderator Dorothy Bernard, an alumnus of one such tour, testified before a commissioners' committee at the 1987 General Assembly that she had seen Nicaragua for herself, "and I did not see a single Soviet tank while I was there!"

86 Belli, Humberto, *Christians Under Fire* (Garden City: The Puebla Institute, 1984), p. 45.

87 *The Presbyterian Layman*, Vol. 17, No. 4, July/August, 1984.

Mission Funds Underwrite Propaganda Tours

From November 17 to 24, 1990, 27 persons were dispatched by the denomination's Global Mission Unit to a meeting in Managua, Nicaragua. Of these, 20 persons went from the US and six came from Europe, Africa, and Nicaragua. Operating under a sub-unit called "Bi-National Servants," the group assessed conditions in Nicaragua and developed recommendations to the Global Mission Unit on plans to coordinate Presbyterian Church (USA) tours in the country that would result in a favorable impression of the Sandinista regime and generate resistance to US policies in the region.

The denomination's Nicaraguan tour project was part of a coordinated effort that included other denominational offices, the National Council of Churches, liberationist organizations like CEPAD and Witness for Peace. PCUSA mission workers J. Gary and Margaret Chase Campbell, who had been evicted from a former mission assignment by the Presbyterian Church of Mexico, led many of the tours, some of which were financed by the Ecumenical Exchange office of the Global Mission Unit, the campus ministry of Virginia Tech University in Blacksburg, Virginia, and the Soviet Peace Fund of Moscow.[88]

Not everyone in the denomination's program agency favored the "study" trips that it funded. In 1986, the Rev. Cecilio Arrastia, a program agency official, expressed skepticism in an open letter to participants: "Many Presbyterian groups, agencies, and governing bodies are planning 'study' trips to Nicaragua. (Sometimes we wonder if the church is becoming a travel agency.) In view of this fact, it is wise to ask some favors from those taking these 'study' trips.

"Please do remember that you are taking this 'study' trip to a country in which freedom is non-existent. Recently, all the civil liberties were eliminated officially. No freedom of the press. No freedom of association. No freedom to keep the privacy of correspondence. Any study under these circumstances will be limited and incomplete.

"Please do remember that in any totalitarian state (Marxism is always totalitarian, as well as Facism) these 'study' visits are controlled by the government. You will see only that which the government wants you to see. You will talk (listen) to those trained by the government to talk with and lecture to guests …

"Please … if you do not know Spanish, be aware of the fact that you will

88 Presbyterian Church (USA), Mutual Mission Office Report, Paper 25, January 1991, p. 185.

depend on translations. This is always risky and will limit your understanding of the situation. Both your 'optic' and your 'audio' will be determined by interpreters ...

"Please do not come back to us as an 'expert' on the Sandinista revolution and the Central American situation. One week in Nicaragua, on a 'study' trip so limited and contaminated, does not make you an expert in this complex process ..."[89]

Rev. Arrastia's pleas to the contrary notwithstanding, Presbyterian Church (USA) agencies stepped up their propaganda campaign in favor of the Sandinista regime. Parallel "travel/study seminars," also funded by the denomination, were coordinated by the "Gift of New Eyes" program, and International Designs for Economic Awareness (I.D.E.A.), which described itself as "an economically focused travel/study seminar." I.D.E.A. included Jamaica, Cuba and Brazil on its itinerary. The organization's director during 1990 was John Sinclair, whose salary was funded by the denomination's Global Mission Unit.[90]

The "Gift of New Eyes" program was administered by Gaspar Langella, a denominational "Peace and Justice Specialist," whose focus was on developing support for revolutionary movements in Latin America.[91]

Also included in the Global Mission Unit's budget (purportedly a budget dedicated to sending missionaries) was the annual salary of Sara Campbell-Evans, to serve as Coordinator of Central America Issues at the denomination's Stony Point Conference Center in New York. Stony Point served as a training center for church personnel who were actively supporting revolutionary activities, primarily in Latin America.[92]

Missions money was also allocated to Stony Point for William Jordan, Program Assistant for Latin American issues, who divided his time between leading liberation theology seminars at Stony Point and studying for an M. Div. degree at Maryknoll, a Roman Catholic Order whose area of concentration was Third World revolution, primarily in Latin America.[93]

Another missionary salary went to Karla Koll, a "theology teacher" in Nicaragua, working under the supervision of the Inter-Church Center for Theological and Social Studies (CIEETS).[94] The Global Mission Unit also

89 *Monday Morning*, March, 1986.

90 *Ibid.*

91 *Ibid.*, p. 307.

92 *Ibid.*, p. 275.

93 *Ibid.*, p. 274.

94 *Ibid.*

provided a stipend for Jean M. Peacock to serve as a "community organizer" in Tucson, Az., while attending graduate school for a Masters Degree in social work from Arizona State University.[95]

Journalist Shunned on Nicaragua Trip

Francis Meeker, Religion Editor of the *Nashville Banner,* had a long-running personal interest in Central America. Fluent in the Spanish language, she had made five trips to the region, interviewing people representing every caste. When national religious groups began to focus on Nicaragua, El Salvador and Guatemala, Meeker's personal and professional interests merged. Aware that denominational agencies were sponsoring "study" tours to Nicaragua, the Nashville journalist decided to participate.

Meeker learned that an organization called Witness for Peace, funded in part by the Presbyterian Church (USA) and her own United Methodist Church, was sending teams to observe the final days of the Nicaraguan political campaigns and the elections. The advertised purpose of the visit was to provide onsite reports for U.S. newspapers, members of Congress, and church communications offices. Meeker sensed a perfect fit between her church and journalism backgrounds, and she said so in her application to Witness for Peace.

Meeker's application was accepted, and she immediately sent in the required money for her transportation, lodging and specified expenses. But somewhere between her welcome letter acknowledging receipt of payment and her arrival at the group's staging area in Miami, Witness for Peace entertained second thoughts about her participation. When she arrived, she was told that she was not the kind of person that the group needed. Since a contract had been signed and money had changed hands, Witness for Peace said it felt obliged to include Meeker if she would not voluntarily resign. Despite the chilly welcome, Meeker decided to continue.

The group leader told Meeker that she would be allowed to travel with the group as an observer, but because she was a professional journalist she could not participate in "group reflections on our daily experiences."

"Much of the time I had to be by myself," she said in an interview with *The Presbyterian Layman*.[96] "One night I walked into a garden area near our hotel and sat down in the corner of a small structure. The Presbyterian group came down [Witness for Peace teams were clustered in denominational groups] and began sharing their excitement over indications that

95 *Ibid.*

96 *The Presbyterian Layman*, Vol. 23, No. 4, July/August 1990.

Oretga would win the election. Then one of the men saw me and came over to the place where I was sitting. 'We don't want you in on this,' he said."

Meeker told the Presbyterians that she had been sitting in the garden for some time and that it was they who had joined her. "This is our meeting place," he replied. "You need to go somewhere else."

The pro-Sandinista bias of Meeker's group (Methodist) and others with whom they traveled was clear by the second day of their visit. On that day, group leaders announced that they would travel together from Managua to Leon. "We were not told the purpose of this excursion," she said.

"On the way out of town we drove through a huge campaign rally for Violetta Chamorro. People were dancing in the streets. There were bright colors everywhere. People rushed up to our vehicles and offered leaflets."

Meeker reported that the occupants of her vehicle became "rigid and silent." They faced forward and appeared not to acknowledge the existence of the rally that surrounded them. "I reached out of the window and accepted a leaflet from a smiling demonstrator," said Meeker. "I smiled back."

Meeker said that she felt scorn from her fellow travelers and had second thoughts about having accepted the leaflet since the group of which she was a part was purportedly a neutral observer group. But on the outskirts of Leon, the situation changed dramatically, and so did her entourage. A Sandinista rally was underway in that city. At the moment it came into view, Meeker's traveling companions exploded with enthusiasm. They cheered, left their vehicle and hugged people in the streets.

"It was then that I realized the purpose of this day trip," she said. "It became obvious to me that we went to Leon not simply to report, but to participate in the Sandinista rally."

Meeker said that in Leon her group was hosted by people who worked with CEPAD (Evangelical Committee for Aid and Development), an organization that received funding from the Presbyterian Church (USA). "They told our group that Ortega was 'a charismatic leader' and that Chamorro was 'so low profile' that she could not possibly be a strong leader in Nicaragua."

Four or five days before the election, Meeker's group met with Witness for Peace representatives who told them that they had prepared news releases on the election in advance. The stories announced that Daniel Ortega had won, and they included background on the candidate, identifying him as the voice of the people. The press releases were personalized in the names of various members of the group. Meeker noted that one of the sheets said, "According to Francis Meeker ..."

"The fact that these releases were written ahead of time was not unusual," said the journalist. "When a reporter works on a tight deadline, stories which report each of the probable outcomes are often written in advance, with space left for last minute details." But what she found unusual about the Witness for Peace releases was the fact that none were prepared which declared a win for Violetta Chamorro. "They simply did not anticipate that possibility," said Meeker.

Results of the internationally supervised election, monitored by former US President Jimmy Carter and a delegation of world leaders, were announced on February 27, 1990. Chamorro had won the election by a landslide vote.

Witness for Peace was caught with nothing to say. The prepared press releases were obviously worthless. Meeker observed that members of her group were so stunned that they couldn't find words to describe what had happened. "The election occurred on Sunday," said Meeker, "and when we left Nicaragua on the following Thursday we still didn't have any statement from Witness for Peace."

Meeker filed her own story with the *Nashville Banner* from a hotel in Managua.

Interpreting the Election

Reeling from news of the election results, Sandinista supporters in the Presbyterian Church (USA) mission program blamed the US government for Ortega's defeat. In a statement to Larry Rohter of *The New York Times*, another organization funded in part by the Presbyterian Church (USA), the Ben Linder Council said, "US policy has brought death, destruction and economic strangulation to this fledgling democracy." Ortega's defeat, the council explained, happened because "Nicaraguan voters feared that an FSLN victory would bring a continuation of US policy."[97]

The council, whose leaders included J. Gary Campbell, Charles Hughes and other Presbyterian Church (USA) workers said that the US government had sabotaged "the democratic achievements of the first ten years of the Sandinista government."

Campbell told *The New York Times* reporter that he had every intention of staying in Nicaragua and continuing the revolution that was started by Daniel Ortega. "There is no way to be politically neutral," he said. "We will try to use common sense and respect the difficult situation here. But if the mass organizations with which we have worked are critical of repression

97 *The New York Times*, March 1, 1960.

and unjust policies [policies of the new government] we will stand with them as long as we are permitted to be here."[98/99]

Lobbying for the Sandinistas

The Washington Office of the Presbyterian Church (USA) played a leading role in lobbying against the Reagan administration's requests to Congress for appropriations that would aid the Contras in Nicaragua. On Feb. 14, 1986, the Rev. George Chauncey, director of the Washington Office and leader of Presbyterian Advocates on Central America, dispatched an "Act Now!" message to his network of supporters, urging them to pressure Congress to reject aid to the Nicaraguan resistance forces. Chauncey set a goal of "generating 12,000 letters to Congress in the next few days and 12,000 phone calls."

On August 4, 1986, Chauncey was arrested for his participation in a demonstration in the rotunda of the Capitol.[100] In 1987, Chauncey helped orchestrate a demonstration in the streets of Washington, calling for the impeachment of President Reagan. He promoted the event in a Feb. 5 memo to "Former Moderators of the General Assembly Mission Board and Program Agency members and staff; Advisory Council on Church and Society; Presbyterian Seminary Presidents; Presbyterian College Presidents; Synod Executives; National Capital Presbytery leaders; members of the Advisory Council on Social Witness Policy's Taskforce on Central America; members of the Presbyterian Witness for Peace Delegation; and other interested parties." Those who wished to participate were instructed to meet at Washington, D.C.'s New York Avenue Presbyterian Church on the morning of April 25. When they arrived, several were dispatched by Chauncey to CIA headquarters, where, according to *The New York Times,* they lay down in the agency's parking lot, blocking its entrance, while shouting "Si Si, Sandinistas. No, No, CIA!"

Although he organized the affair, Chauncey did not take part, probably owing to the fact that he was already on probation for having engaged in

---

98 *Ibid.*

99 Interestingly, after a period of political exile, Ortega won a return to power in Nicaragua's 2006 election. This time around he disclaimed any connection with Marxism and affirmed a desire for open and free economic relations with the United States. Whether this disavowal of his former ideological connections is honest remains to be seen, but it is at least clear that he perceived some political advantage in severing his ties with a Soviet-inspired past.

100 Presbyterian Church News, August 4, 1986.

civil disobedience in the Capitol rotunda.

Chauncey's office received more than $400,000 in support from the 1987 General Assembly mission budget.

In 1988, Chauncey officiated at a rally, held at New York Avenue Presbyterian Church, at which Daniel Ortega was the principal speaker. Chauncey led the crowd in a raised-hand "blessing" of Ortega, applauding him for his "contributions to peace and justice."

That same year, Chauncey found himself in the midst of a political crossfire. Defying the General Assembly policy that he promoted, a policy that opposed any U.S. aid to the Contras, Chauncey urged lawmakers to vote for an aid package that had been proposed by the Democratic Party. His rationale, as reported by *The Los Angeles Times*, was that Congress was "almost certain" to pass some aid to the Contras, and the Democrats' package was less than that of the Republicans.'

"Chauncey apparently decided to defy the General Assembly's position after hearing from Mike Lowry, Chairman of the Democratic Study Group in the U.S. House of Representatives. Lowry urged peace group leaders to 'actively support the Democratic alternative and let their members know why the Democratic plan should be supported.' Lowry continued: 'Allowing the Republican substitute to prevail would be unconscionable …'"[101]

Chauncey's war on U.S. Central America policy received notice by *The Washington Post*: "In this country church efforts on Central American issues are significant. Since 1983, George Chauncey, a member of a four-member Washington lobbying staff for the Presbyterian Church (USA), has worked on nothing else."[102]

The grants, stipends and salaries reported above demonstrate the results of the denomination's altered policy, defining "missions" as "mission." With this new definition in place, church officials believed they had denominational approval to transfer missionary support funds into any program that fit their expanded understanding of "mission."

Initially, Presbyterians in the pews, who have historically been most generous in their support for world missions, were unaware of the nuanced definition that was being employed by those who managed their gifts. Several years of liberationist funding passed before Presbyterians caught on as to how their mission money was being diverted into political adventures that they found objectionable. As that realization took hold, those who understood missions as having to do with the Great Commission created founda-

101 *The Presbyterian Layman*, Vol. 21, No. 3, May/June, 1988.

102 *The Washington Post*, April 14, 1988.

tions that were independent of denominational agencies in order to channel their mission gifts into programs whose managers they could trust.[103]

Adventures in Africa

During the 1970s, both northern and southern streams of the Presbyterian Church made significant investments in liberation movements, largely guerrilla activities, operating in Southern Africa. Many of these grants were channeled through the World Council of Churches Fund to Combat Racism, to which the Presbyterians constituted the largest denominational contributors. In 1974, the WCC grants to terrorist groups in Southern Africa (called "liberation groups" and "freedom fighters" by denominational officials) totaled $322,000.

The largest single grant, $100,000, went to the African Independence Party of Guinea and Cape Verde Islands (PAIGC), a movement that declared the independence of Guinea-Bissau from Portugal on September 24, 1973.

Other sizeable grants to South African liberations movements included $30,000 to the Southwest Africa People's Organization (SWAPO) in Namibia, and $60,000 to the Mozambique Institute of FRELIMO, which had amassed a guerrilla army of some 7,000 fighters by the early 1970s.

One of FRELIMO's operations occurred at the Nhacambo Hamlet where 120 of the town's 186 huts were burned. Seventeen villagers were killed, of whom three were small boys, three were youths, two were baby girls, seven were women and two were men. Reports of the massacre and FRELIMO's responsibility for it were authenticated by the International Red Cross.

Although the WCC frequently issued statements criticizing Portuguese colonialists in Mozambique, not one word was said by WCC spokespersons following the Nhacambo atrocity. United Presbyterian Church officials defended the WCC grant to FRELIMO, assuring critics that none of the money given to the guerrilla forces was used for weapons. FRELIMO finally gained control of Mozambique's government and established a one-party state based on Marxist principles. The new government received substantial funding from the Soviet Union and Cuba.

Funds were also given to the People's Movement for the Liberation of Angola, the Revolutionary Government of Angola in Exile, the Zimbabwe African People's Union and the Pan African Congress.

---

103 This erosion of trust in denominational mission agencies led to the creation of the Outreach Foundation, the Medical Benevolence Foundation, and Presbyterian Frontier Fellowship.

Massacre in Rhodesia

On September 3, 1978 guerrilla forces under the command of Robert Mugabe and Joshua Nkomo opened fire on an Air Rhodesia civilian airliner that was transporting Christian missionaries. A handful of survivors, including women and children crawled out of the wreckage, where ten of them were shot and mutilated by the guerrilla fighters. Eyewitnesses who managed to escape the massacre described it in detail.[104]

Subsequent investigations revealed that Mugabe and Nkomo's Patriotic Front of Zimbabwe had received an $85,000 grant, including United Presbyterian Church funds that had been filtered through the World Council of Churches Programme to Combat Racism.

Denominational officials argued that they had given the money to the guerrilla organization with the understanding that it would be used for "food, health, and social and educational programs," not guns and rockets. But Rev. Eugene Carson Blake, former head of the World Council of Churches and Stated Clerk of the United Presbyterian Church admitted that there could be no guarantee "that funds destined for liberation movements might not be used to buy weapons."[105] As the top national staff person for the United Presbyterian Church, Blake had been instrumental in setting up the controversial fund.

In 1975, Blake's successor at the World Council of Churches, Dr. Philip Potter said that his organization "would not send inspectors to see whether the money had been spent in the way that it was given" because "there could be no real sense of solidarity with people if you did not trust them."[106]

Shooting the Messenger

General Assembly Moderator William T. Lytle defended the grant and lashed out at *The Presbyterian Layman* for its reporting of the massacre. "My own feeling on this is that if the church is going to be involved in the world, in helping people, it's always going to be vulnerable. There is no way that we can be in the world and be involved in assisting where there is a need without taking risks. Those risks are of several kinds: One is of making a mistake. It is always a possibility. I'm not suggesting that this was a mistake. I really do not think that it was … I'm frankly concerned about the approach that I saw in *The Layman* on this particular issue, with the pictures of the coffins of missionaries who had been slain … It almost seems

104 *TIME* Magazine, September 18, 1978.

105 *The Presbyterian Layman*, Vol. 11 No. 6, September/October, 1978.

106 *Ibid.*

journalistically to be trying to get across 'those terrible people who did this – why are we helping them? – you know, these murderers,' and so on."[107]

Moderator Lytle's criticism was amplified by Frank H. Heinze, Editor of *Monday Morning*, a publication of the United Presbyterian Church. "We were as appalled as was Bill Lytle by the 'Hearstilian' technique used by *The Presbyterian Layman* (sic) in its reporting on the World Council of Churches' grant to the Patriotic Front of Zimbabwe. To so blatantly exploit the deaths of eight missionaries and their four children seems to us to go far beyond the bounds of good taste. And of good journalism. As we viewed the front page picture spread in the September issue of the Layman (sic), the words of Attorney Joseph Welsh to Senator Joseph McCarthy during the infamous Army-McCarthy hearings came to our mind: 'Have you no shame, sir? Have you no shame?'"[108]

With support from the Presbyterian Church and other members of the World Council of Churches, Mugabe consolidated his control of the country that he now called Zimbabwe. In a cleanup operation designed to cut off potential challenges to his power, he unleashed his Fifth Brigade against his former ally Nkomo's Ndebele tribe, committing wholesale genocide and insuring the fact that he would rule a one-party state.

Thanking the WCC

In 1980, Robert Mugabe greeted a delegation from the World Council of Churches and thanked it for the WCC's support of the liberation struggle in his country. He said, "It is an honor to express gratitude for the role you have played and to send through you to other people struggling for justice the message of our firm commitment to the principles for which you and we have struggled together, including the principles of non-racism."

Commenting on the visit, Ninan Koshy, executive secretary of the Commission of the Churches on International Affairs, said, "The elections have produced the best possible solution in terms of peace and stability. It is a unique situation where a revolutionary armed struggle has been given the stamp of overwhelming popular approval."

According to the WCC official, "the leaders of the new government are committed to the building up of a non-racial society and in the words of the prime minister, 'to beat its swords into ploughshares and build a new country which would be the pride of all Africa.'"[109]

107 *Monday Morning*, November 6, 1978.

108 *Ibid.*

109 Religion News Service, May, 1980.

In 1998, when the World Council held an assembly in Harare, Zimbabwe, Mugabe paid a courtesy call to the assembly in order to thank denominational leaders – including an entourage of Presbyterian Church officials led by Stated Clerk Clifton Kirkpatrick – for supporting his revolution.

"Today I present to you the country towards whose liberation you struggled, a free Zimbabwe" said Mugabe to vigorous applause. "Zimbabwe thanks you, the World Council of Churches."[110]

While acknowledging that Christian missionaries built schools in the bush, providing the only education available to his generation, and hospitals and clinics that still provide almost all the country's rural health care, Mugabe hammered hard on the evil that he said was committed by them. He said that most missionaries came as agents of "the empire builder" who paid them off with land and money "not for sound spiritual reasons, but to use 'religion as opium' to take the indigenous population." Laced with fragments of the phrase first employed by Karl Marx, Mugabe's diatribe against Christian missionaries brought loud and sustained applause from the audience in which "indigenous" has been equated with holiness.

Mugabe said that all Christians were not collaborators with evil. Some, he said, took the role of liberators who were willing to fight against colonial injustices. The WCC, he said, is representative of that kind of Christianity.

Mugabe paid his guerrilla fighters with land that he confiscated from white families who had farmed the land for more than three generations. The new owners ruined it, hurling what had once been a food exporting country into a massive hunger crisis. Inflation in Zimbabwe is soaring to record highs, having hit 7,634.8 percent in August, 2007, according to the British Broadcasting System, and most Zimbabweans are starving. Meanwhile, Mugabe continues to torture and kill those who oppose his one-party rule.

Supporting 'Liberation' in the Philippines

In 1989, *The Presbyterian Layman* received correspondence from a Presbyterian Women circle mission study leader, objecting to program material published by the denomination. She said that when the study material was announced, "to understand faith in struggle through a study of the Philippines," she "anticipated a stimulating and exciting time" with her women's circle. But when she read the recommended study book, *Rice in the Storm*,[111] she was deeply troubled.

110 *The Presbyterian Layman*, Vol. 32, No. 1, January/February, 1999.

111 Asedillo, Rebecca and Williams, B. David, *Rice in the Storm* (Cincinnati, Ohio: Friendship Press, 1989).

"The entire 'study,' she said, "is one-sided and apparently delights in bashing the U.S. It overwhelmingly espouses the so-called 'liberation theology,' very succinctly described in the July 1986 *National Geographic* as being 'a doctrine of social revolution influenced by Marxist-Leninist theory and practice.' This ill-conceived doctrine perceives the many problems of the Filipino people – poverty, hunger, economic chaos, etc. – as solely the fault of the U.S. presence in the Philippines."[112]

Mrs. Stewart's letter is typical of thousands that have been sent to *The Layman* over the years from Presbyterian women regarding publications either published by their denominational organization or, as in this case, by the publishing arm of the National Council of Churches (Friendship Press) and included as a "recommended resource" by Presbyterian Women. The message in these letters has been corroborated on numerous occasions by Voices of Orthodox Women, a denominationally independent organization of Presbyterian women that promotes the doctrines and practices of historic Christian faith as expressed in the ecumenical creeds of the Church.[113]

In his analysis of *Rice in the Storm*, a researcher for the Institute for Religion and Democracy, said, "*Rice in the Storm* attempts, in short, an amazing feat of political stealth. It seeks to lead church study groups right to the brink of rejecting a democratic government [the government of Corazon Aquino] and endorsing a communist movement [The National Democratic Front (NDF) that describes its goal as "overthrowing U.S. imperialism"], while barely whispering the names of the government's head and the communist movement ... One thing is sure: because the NCC chose to tailor its materials to fit a narrow and questionable political agenda, U.S. Christian laypeople have been deprived of the broad view of Christian life in the Philippines to which they were entitled."[114]

Peacemaking: "Are We Now Called to Resistance?"

In a move that was largely motivated by the liberals' objection to US military resistance to the spread of Soviet-styled communist regimes, the denomination's Advisory Council on Church and Society sent a "peacemaking" paper to the 1987 General Assembly. Titled, "Presbyterians and Peacemaking: Are We Now Called to Resistance?" the document declared the United States guilty of "Militarism" and suggested that the appropriate

112 Correspondence from Mrs. E.L. Stewart, Jr., December 19, 1989.

113 Voices of Orthodox Women, 2409 Estrella Avenue, Loveland, CO. 80538.

114 *Religion & Democracy*, December, 1989.

Christian response was "a stance of non-cooperation."[115] Among proposals listed in the paper were the refusal to support corporations that do business with the military;[116] calling on citizens to refuse to register for the draft or submit to the draft if one were reinstituted;[117] encouraging "acts of symbolic witness, legal or civilly disobedient forms of confrontation, marches, sit-ins, and public rallies;"[118] calling on military personnel to go absent without leave (AWOL),[119] the refusal to pay the percent on one's income tax that supports military expenditures,[120] calling on churches to offer "sanctuary" to "tax resisters, AWOL service-persons, those who climb fences into nuclear weapons installations."[121]

Ironically, at the same time that the "Peacemaking/Resistance" paper was being released by some agencies at denominational headquarters, other agencies were aggressively channeling funds to guerrilla and terrorist groups in Africa and Latin America, leading one to conclude that Presbyterian leaders' opposition to "militarism" was highly selective.

In the months leading up to the 1987 General Assembly, scores of local church sessions and presbyteries issued statements condemning the peacemaking document. By the time of the assembly meeting, opposition to the paper was overwhelming. Drafters withdrew their motion that the controversial paper be adopted and urged simply that it be sent to every congregation "for study." This the General Assembly agreed to do, but later in the meeting, when informed that the cost of printing and mailing the document would exceed $130,000, the assembly reversed itself and sent the paper back to its Advisory Council on Church and Society.

In a related action that was sure to appease those who supported the document, the assembly condemned the United States for its Central America policy, called for "a negotiated end to the conflict" in Nicaragua, and urged congregations "to engage in other creative means of registering moral opposition to current U.S. policy … and to consider seriously whether public non-violent civil disobedience as a symbolic act of resistance is called

115 Wilbanks, Dana W. and Stone, Ronald H., *Presbyterians and Peacemaking: Are We Now Called To Resistance?* (New York: Advisory Council on Church and Society, Presbyterian Church (USA), 1986), p. 45.

116 *Ibid.*, p. 51.

117 *Ibid.*, pp. 52, 53.

118 *Ibid.*, p. 55.

119 *Ibid.*, p. 53.

120 *Ibid.*, p. 50.

121 *Ibid.*, p. 55.

for in today's situation." The assembly also called on the U.S. government to "stop all direct or indirect assistance to the contras," to "end the economic embargo against Nicaragua," and to "cease all efforts, direct or indirect, to destabilize or overthrow the present government of Nicaragua."[122]

The Peacemaking and Resistance paper returned at the 1988 General Assembly in a different, milder form and with the title *Christian Obedience in a Nuclear Age*. Although its rhetoric was greatly subdued, the paper reflected identical presuppositions.

This time, denominational staffers did their homework. They waited until the eleventh hour to release the paper, making it difficult for opposition forces to prepare their case. At the assembly they inundated commissioners with resource persons and individuals who had been dubbed "experts" on foreign policy. The paper was adopted by a whopping 509-35 vote.

The Middle East

In recent years, the world has turned its focus to the Middle East and, in particular, to the war that has been raging between Israel and its Arab neighbors. Presbyterian Church (USA) spokespersons have found in this conflict a fertile field for applying the theology of liberation. The facts in this exceedingly complex international conflagration to the contrary notwithstanding, denominational bureaucrats have identified the oppressor and the oppressed. Having decided that God is on the side of the Palestinian Liberation Organization, official Presbyterian task forces, study groups, tour guides, media specialists and funding sources have climbed onboard a one-issue railroad.

It matters not that Syria, Iran, and Lebanon have, as a matter of policy, declared that Israel has no right to exist. What matters is that when Israel defends itself against attacks by those whose stated purpose is its annihilation, Israel is deemed "the aggressor." When Israel claims land that it won in a war that it did not initiate as a buffer zone against future attacks, it is deemed "imperialist." When Israel builds a wall, not to keep its own people in, but to keep terrorists and suicide bombers out of civilian shopping centers, school districts and synagogues, it is condemned for having isolated its neighbors.

While there is no question but that in retaliation for terrorist attacks, Israel has collaterally injured and killed non-combatant women and children who reside in terrorist staging areas, it is also true that Israel is fighting for its life against those who have declared publicly their intention to obliterate it from the face of the earth.

Several US government administrations – both Democrat and Republican – have addressed this issue, bringing representatives of Israel and the Palestinian Liberation Organization to the table. At Camp David, President Clinton came within a hairsbreadth of an historic peace agreement that was scuttled at the last minute by Yasser Arafat's refusal to sign. Israel, on the other hand, has agreed to many demands by US administrations in the hope that such agreement might facilitate a peaceful solution to a crisis that it alone cannot solve. Israel's compromises have not been met by reciprocity from the Palestinian side of the table.

None of this has been helped by official Presbyterian Church delegations visiting terrorist organizations like Hezbollah, and issuing one-sided statements.[123] Nor has the situation been improved by calls from the National Council of Churches Interfaith Center for Corporate Responsibility, its Presbyterian partner, the General Assembly on Mission Responsibility Through Investment, and the General Assembly itself to divest stock holdings in companies that do business with Israel.[124]

The fact of the matter is that Israel will not agree to its self-annihilation. Thus, the situation is exacerbated by media orchestrated pronouncements from purported representatives of the Presbyterian Church (USA), who attempt to bestow legitimacy on those who will not affirm Israel's right to exist.

Presbyterians in the pews may not be cognizant of every action by their denominational officials, but when they have been informed, for example, of visits by their Advisory Committee on Social Witness Policy with Hezbollah and press conferences with the terrorists in which Israel was condemned and the liberationists were affirmed, they have reacted with anger and disgust. The interventionist activities of denominational leaders into complex and highly nuanced issues of Middle East relationships have alienated Presbyterians who intrinsically sense that there is more to the story.

Support for Sabeel

Presbyterian Church (USA) Middle East policymakers lean heavily on a liberationist group that has extolled the late Yasser Arafat, terrorist leader of the Palestinian Liberation Organization, and rationalized the deeds of suicide bombers who have murdered hundreds of Israelis.

123 Press release during Oct., 2004 visit with Hezbollah by Presbyterian Church (USA) Advisory Committee on Social Witness Policy.

124 *General Assembly News*, Presbyterian Church (USA) News Service # GA04121, 2006.

The organization is the Sabeel Ecumenical Liberation Theology Center, which is based in Jerusalem. The Presbyterian Church (USA) lists Sabeel as one of its ecumenical partners and gives it a substantial voice on the PCUSA Web site. Among other things, it has made available a Sabeel-produced church bulletin insert and sent delegations, including young people, to Sabeel seminars.

The material produced by Sabeel on its Web site includes many of the themes that have become woven into PCUSA policy statements that overwhelmingly favor the Palestinians over the Israelis in complicated political, theological and security issues. The Sabeel statements condemn the construction of the separation barrier, investment in Israel, the U.S. relationship with Israel, the occupation of Palestinian areas and Israel's military response to the suicide bombers.

Consistent with liberation theology, Sabeel advocates for the Palestinians because they are the oppressed group and Israel holds the greater power. Justice, liberation theologians argue, requires the church to side with the "oppressed," regardless of what they believe or how they act. Sabeel calls Israel "the enemy."

"For forty years Arafat struggled for the liberation of his beloved country, Palestine," Sabeel said in its eulogy of Yasser Arafat. "He was the father figure of the Palestinians. In his life, Arafat traveled the world tirelessly presenting the just case of his people. He met with kings and queens, presidents and prime ministers. He represented the Palestinians before many international forums, not least the United Nations. He was able to wrest international recognition of the right of the Palestinian people to a sovereign and independent state. For his faithful endeavors in seeking peace, he was awarded the Nobel Peace Prize. He came to embody and personify the struggle of his people. The Arabs in general and the Palestinians in particular saw Arafat symbolizing and epitomizing the spirit of Palestine. Through his hard work and persistence, the Palestinian people regained their Palestinian identity."[125]

There was no mention in the eulogy of the way Arafat gained power and wielded it – raising billions of dollars and using much of it for his own benefit. Much of that which he did not appropriate to himself, he used to pay militants, including suicide bombers, to encourage their attacks against Israel. According to the Bloomberg financial reporting service, Arafat did not use any of the money for improving the bleak economic condition of the Palestinians.[126]

125 http://www.sabeel.org/documents/Arafatweb.html.

126 vtsilver@bloomberg.net, December 21, 2004.

In a media release called "A Word of Respect and Esteem for a Great Leader," Sabeel came close to declaring Arafat a messianic figure: "Mr. Arafat died lifting his voice for the liberation of Palestine. While awaiting his funeral, a little Palestinian boy was interviewed on TV. He was wearing the kufiah, the Palestinian head dress, as President Arafat always wore it. With great confidence and pride the boy said, 'we are all Yasser Arafat.' In essence this is the message of the Palestinians. They will continue the struggle and carry on the legacy of their late president until the illegal Israeli occupation ends and Palestine is free."[127]

Sabeel's justification of suicide bombers is expressed in a long essay by Naim Ateek, the organization's executive director. Ateek expresses regret for suicide bombings and other acts of terrorism, but he also rationalizes them, drawing a parallel with the Old Testament story of Samson.

"Read in the light of today's suicide bombers how do we evaluate the story of Samson?" Ateek wrote in the summer 2002 issue of Sabeel's journal, *Cornerstone*. "Was not Samson a suicide bomber? Was he acting on behalf of the God of justice who wills the liberation of the oppressed? Was God pleased with the death of thousands of men and women of the Philistines? Are we confronted with many similar stories today in the experience of suicide bombers?"[128]

Ateek argues that "many countries in the world are against suicide bombings" because "Israel was successful in its media campaign internationally."[129]

'Christian' Economics and Politics

Liberationists who manage the Presbyterian Church (USA) infrastructure often introduce their policy proposals through a General Assembly-level group called the Advisory Committee on Social Witness Policy (ACSWP). Envisioned as a quasi-independent denominational think tank, this group is one of three that are accorded special privileges. It is allowed to present its papers directly to the General Assembly, bypassing the vetting process required of other committees, and it is given the privilege of providing written commentary and oral testimony on any presbytery overture, commissioner resolution or other business that comes before the General Assembly. Thus the committee's position papers come to General Assembly policy-

127 Sabeel Ecumenical Liberation Theology Center, (Jerusalem: Nov. 15, 2004).

128 Ateek, Naim, "What is theologically and morally wrong with suicide bombings? A Palestinian Christian Perspective." *Cornerstone*, Issue #25, 2002.

129 *Ibid.*

makers wearing the mantle of intellectual expertise.

From the outset, ACSWP membership has almost unanimously reflected liberationist ideologies. Occasionally, as in the case in the mid-1990s of Frank Lankford, a Birmingham, Ala. businessman, a conservative has been placed on the committee, purportedly to achieve "a balance of perspectives," but there is no evidence that such tokenism has made any difference in policy proposals that are promoted by majority members.

An example of ACSWP's approach to formulating denominational policy can be seen in the development of its document on international economics. The committee's procedure calls for having a small subgroup, often "resourced" by an outside consultant of its own choosing, produce a "prospectus" for the project. The prospectus lays out the approach the committee will make to the subject, including any theological or ethical guidelines. Then the committee chooses a writer whose task is to produce a draft document whose content reflects the prospectus.

In August, 1991, ACSWP commissioned a Task Force on Sustainable Development, Reformed Faith and U.S. International Economic Policy. Starting with a preliminary budget of $118,500, the 12-member task force was asked to produce a major policy paper for submission to the 1996 General Assembly. One had only to read the approved prospectus to anticipate the ultimate outcome of the task force's labors.

The approved prospectus for this project called on the task force to examine the ways in which developed countries consume the world's resources at an "unsustainable rate," and the ways in which they impoverish community life in the poorest nations. The prospectus identified two systems: "basic biological systems" and "basic social systems." It argued that these systems are threatened by "the onslaught of individualistic economic structures and the imposition of artificial political boundaries."

The prospectus anticipated resistance to the not-yet-written policy paper because "acceptance will imply fundamental shifts in the social, economic, and moral character of our society." Nevertheless, the task force was commissioned to "develop a comprehensive and integrated statement of social witness policy on sustainable development, especially as it relates to the impact of American international economic policies on the economies and societies of the poorest countries, and to derive from it programmatic recommendations for study and action at all levels of the church."

ACSWP planners took great pains to insure that the task force document would include a liberationist perspective. The prospectus called for "a carefully focused point of view" which required that the task force "include in its membership and its sources of information people who already know from experience the feelings of personal and societal impotence which accompany poverty." In liberationist language, that meant that ACSWP wanted the task force to view development issues "from the perspective of the poor," much in the same way that the Montreat Consultation on Mission Policy had handpicked "representatives" from developing countries so they could "hear the voice of the Third World," and a later Task Force on Human Sexuality was directed to treat its subject "from the perspective of the marginalized" (homosexuals and radical feminists).

The ACSWP prospectus also instructed the task force to include "feminist theology, liberation theology, and process theology" in its interpretation of environmental and economic data. Further, it called on the study's writers to "be thoroughly contextual" in their work.

This process is illustrative of the manner in which denominational insiders have channeled General Assembly-level projects toward predetermined outcomes. The original proposal that was approved by the General Assembly was to commission "a study." Filled with vague euphemisms that expressed the denomination's concern for the poor, what compassionate Christian could have opposed it? But the devil proved to be in the details. The prospectus that presaged the study's conclusion was written by ACSWP insiders, after the General Assembly had given its broad-brush authorization. In essence, ACSWP's prospectus was the paper. Given the constraints that it placed upon the writers, the outcome of their work was eminently predictable.

When the paper was presented to the 1996 General Assembly, much was said about how thoroughly ACSWP had gone about its work, the high degree of professionalism that was represented on the task force, the three years of hard labor that had been invested in the project, and the affirmation that it had been "mandated" by a previous General Assembly. Attempts by commissioners at the 1996 General Assembly to amend offensive sections of the document were generally unsuccessful, for it was a whole-cloth work product whose underlying premises as outlined in ACSWP's prospectus ran through the entire piece. For all practical purposes, the document was impervious to amendment. Commissioners would have to either approve or reject ACSWP's work product, something that polite, "loyal" and generous delegates to a church meeting are loath to do.[130]

Thus, subject to a bit of tinkering here and there in order to make the doc-

130 A minority report from a commissioners' committee at the 208th General Assembly (1996) was handily defeated during the assembly's plenary session, and the sustainable development paper was approved. See: Presbyterian Church (USA), *Minutes of the General Assembly*, 1996, p. 107.

ument their own, General Assembly commissioners, with rare exceptions, routinely adopt ACSWP's policy papers. This having been accomplished, ACSWP sends its staff to every relevant agency of the General Assembly infrastructure, insisting that the policy be implemented in that agency's programs. Having played the role of author, ACSWP assumes the role of internal police within the bureaucracy, ensuring compliance with its policy.

Economics via the World Council of Churches

One of the methods employed by Presbyterian Church (USA) liberationists to move their economic theories onto the international stage is to utilize the voice of the World Council of Churches, an organization that is heavily dependent on Presbyterian Church (USA) funding. This influence was evident during the 8th Assembly of the World Council of Churches, meeting in Harare, Zimbabwe, Dec. 3, 1998.

Here, capitalism took a major hit when delegates enacted a resolution on international economics. Condemning "globalization," its term for free-market economies that invest capital in developing nations, the WCC said it would work for the establishment of "global governance" that will rein in the activities of transnational corporations, making them accountable to an international body. All eleven delegates of the Presbyterian Church (USA) voted for the resolution.

During discussion – there was little debate – of the resolution, United Church of Canada Moderator William Phipps, who had earlier denied central doctrines of the Christian faith, including the virgin birth, the bodily resurrection of Christ, the existence of heaven and hell, and, most directly, the deity of Christ, told the WCC, "We need to be serious about redistributing income."[131]

Referring to transnational corporations, Phipps said, "These global predators need to be held accountable ... Our people need a conversion experience ... and conversion has to do with economic relationships. Economic relationships are central to our understanding of the faith."[132]

After Phipps concluded his speech, the WCC adopted a statement that said, in part, "In view of the unaccountable power of transnational corporations and organizations who often operate around the world with impunity, we commit ourselves to working with others on creating effective institutions of global governance. The search for alternative options to the present economic system and the realization of effective political limitations and

131 *The Presbyterian Layman*, Vol. 32. No. 1, January/February, 1999.

132 *Ibid.*

corrections to the process of globalization and its implications are urgently needed."[133]

Similar themes were voiced by the 9th Assembly of the World Council of Churches, meeting in Porto Alegre, Brazil on Feb 23, 2006. Here, the international body issued a statement on Latin America that reaffirmed its commitment to "Liberation Theology," decried US sanctions against Fidel Castro's regime, called for statist solutions to "economic injustice," and criticized development policies by the World Bank and the International Monetary Fund.[134]

Having chosen Latin America as the site of its assembly, the WCC declared that it had seen "signs of transformation" in several countries, e.g., "the first indigenous person to be elected as President of Bolivia and the first woman to be elected as president of Chile." These political improvements are to be celebrated, said the WCC, but there is also much to lament in the "Latin American context," it added.[135]

A principal concern for the WCC is poverty in the developing countries, which the WCC believes is caused by "unjust distribution of wealth, natural resources and opportunities." Continuing its endorsement of liberation theology, the WCC statement gave special recognition to persons who encouraged revolution in Latin American countries. "The blood of these martyrs has helped to fertilize the seeds of God's kingdom, which have borne the fruits of solidarity, life and democracy," said the WCC.[136]

But the fact of the matter is that wherever the liberationist approach has been tried in Latin America, it has met with failure and the exacerbation of poverty. Thus, several countries are moving toward development models that, with the assistance of the World Bank and the International Monetary Fund, have encouraged free market economies and international trade, precisely the direction that the WCC opposes. Even in Brazil, the country chosen by the WCC for its assembly meeting, President Lula, who came into power with the backing of his workers' party and the Communists, has made significant concessions to capitalism and international trade, with corresponding economic success.

These movements away from statist economies and toward the privatiza-

133 *Ibid.*

134 World Council of Churches, 9th Assembly, "Statement on Latin America, Document # PIC-01," February 23, 2006.

135 *Ibid.*

136 World Council of Churches, 9th Assembly, "AGAPE Call For Love and Action," February 16, 2006.

tion of state companies have produced improvements that the WCC cannot ignore. Thus a WCC statement, somewhat begrudgingly, recognized those improved conditions, but it suggested, without explanation, that they won't last. "The privatization of state companies brought in short-term relief and economic welfare in a few cases. Even in those countries where poverty is relatively less, the gap between the rich and the poor is enormous and the distribution of wealth continues to be unjust."[137]

Delegates Confess 'Sins' of the United States

As the first week of the World Council of Churches 9th Assembly drew to a close, with its incessant bashing of capitalists, environmental imperialists, militarists, fundamentalists and heterosexists, a handful of U.S. delegates declared their shame at being Americans.

In an open letter to the WCC that was read to the assembly on February 18, 2006, the Americans, who identified themselves as "The US Committee of the World Council of Churches," confessed to being "complicit in a culture of consumption that diminishes the earth." Specifically, they lamented violating rivers, oceans, lakes, rainforests, wetlands and "the air we breathe," along with leaving global warming unchecked.[138]

According to the letter, the US is also guilty of being rich while people of other nations are poor. The letter suggested that American wealth has actually caused other nations' poverty. Thus, the delegates repented of US responsibility for "crushing poverty" wherever it is found, HIV/AIDS, racism and "the grim features of global economic injustice." "In the face of the earth's poverty, our wealth condemns us," they confessed.[139]

The US delegates launched the final paragraph of their confession with a thank-you note: "Sisters and brothers in the ecumenical community, we come to you in this assembly grateful for hospitality we don't deserve, for companionship we haven't earned, for an embrace we don't merit."[140]

But gratitude soon returned to lamentation: "From a place seduced by the lure of empire we come to you in penitence, eager for grace, grace sufficient to transform spirits grown weary from the violence, degradation, and poverty our nation has sown, grace sufficient to transform spirits grown

137 World Council of Churches, 9th Assembly, Letter from the US Committee of the World Council of Churches, February 18, 2006.

138 *Ibid.*

139 *Ibid.*

140 *Ibid.*

heavy with guilt, grace sufficient to transform the world. Lord, have mercy. Christ, have mercy. Lord, have mercy. Amen."[141]

There were no signatures on the letter, the only identification being "The US Committee of the World Council of Churches," of which Rev. Clifton Kirkpatrick and leaders of most mainline denominations in the US are members. But its supporters were far from anonymous. In a press conference following the letter's presentation, Rev. John Thomas, leader of the United Church of Christ delegation, spoke for the group, sharing the podium with Michael Livingston, President of the National Council of Churches in the United States, an ordained minister in the Presbyterian Church (USA) and former member of the faculty at Princeton Theological Seminary.

Kirkpatrick did not participate in the press conference. Asked why he had not signed the letter, he told George Conger, reporter for the Church of England newspaper, that no signatures were necessary since it came from a committee. In answer to Conger's follow-up question, Kirkpatrick said that although he did not sign the letter, he agreed with it.

Kirkpatrick's comment was consistent with positions he has taken in other contexts. In August, 2004, meeting in Accra, Ghana, the World Alliance of Reformed Churches elected Kirkpatrick as its president and declared that capitalism is an "immoral economic system defended by empire ... In biblical terms such a system of wealth accumulation at the expense of the poor is seen as unfaithful to God and responsible for preventable human suffering." Kirkpatrick lauded the alliance as "a community that truly covenants for justice in the economy and the earth."[142]

Statist vs. Free-market Economies

The WCC and WARC statements provide a classic example of the difference between statist and economic development approaches to poverty. The statist emphasizes wealth redistribution, whereas development emphasizes wealth creation. Development economists argue that unless one's policies result in growing the pie, those who merely wish to slice it will find a smaller pie to slice. This observation leads economist Amy L. Sherman to say that statist solutions "fail to recognize that the poor's standard of living is inevitably related to economic growth."[143]

141 *Ibid.*

142 Ecumenical News International, August 13, 2004.

143 Sherman, Amy L., *Preferential Option: A Christian and Neoliberal Strategy for Latin America's Poor* (Grand Rapids: Wm. B. Erdmans Publishing Co., 1992), p. 31.

Sherman cited a statement by the World Bank in 1990: "No country has achieved substantial reductions in poverty without economic growth."[144] Sherman continues, "Macroeconomic growth is a prerequisite of poverty alleviation. It is not sufficient: the pattern of growth must be such that broad segments of the population benefit from increased opportunities. But wealth creation is essential if low-income families are to have the opportunity to lift themselves out of poverty. Certain types of income transfers or government interventions in the market system may be appropriate in assisting the poor during the transition period. But in general, an overemphasis on distribution through state controls at the expense of growth via the free market will neither help the poor nor produce a healthy economic environment for sustainable development, increased opportunities, and social mobility."[145]

Development economists do not discount the WCC's concerns about the "gap between the rich and the poor," but they view such concerns as "relative rather than absolute." A program that makes the rich richer is acceptable as long as it makes the poor richer too," says Sherman. In fact, when countries move from the statist model to the development model, it often occurs that there is a short-term increase in the income gap, but this gap must be assessed in light of the fact that the whole economic pie is being enlarged.

Economist Peter L. Berger refers to this phenomenon as "the Kuznet's effect." Berger describes the theory as follows: "as modern economic growth continues over time, there occurs first a sharp rise in inequality, and then later, a leveling effect."[146] Economists like Sherman and Berger criticize the WCC for its narrow focus on the income gap alone, a focus that they say is typical of statist ideologies.

'Freedom is Not a Luxury'

A review of the regimes that Presbyterian Church (USA) officials and spokespersons have either supported or defended demonstrates a marked propensity to endorse highly centralized governments, often one-party rulers from the totalitarian left, and controlled economies. As we have seen, Fidel Castro, Daniel Ortega, Robert Mugabe have been lifted up as revolutionary heroes.

The endorsements given by Presbyterian Church (USA) leaders to Fidel

144 *Ibid.*

145 *Ibid.*

146 Berger, Peter L., *The Capitalist Revolution: Fifty Propositions about Prosperity, Equality and Liberty* (New York: Basic Books, 1986), p. 44.

Castro have been particularly painful to Christians who have suffered in that country. U.S. Ambassador to the United Nations Commission on Human Rights Armando Valladares addressed a gathering of Presbyterians in Washington, D.C. on Oct. 14, 1989. Reflecting on his 22-year imprisonment under the Castro regime, Valladares spoke of the sense of betrayal that he felt when during his imprisonment, he learned of visits by Presbyterian delegations that praised his captors. "Even when my Christian friends and I were in solitary confinement," Valladares told the group, "we were given newspaper accounts of visits by these church delegations. It was another form of torture used by the regime upon us. We Christians who opposed Communism waited, year after year, to be embraced by our Christian brothers and sisters. But in the end, those who were embraced were our jailers, our torturers."[147]

A frequent and prominent participant in such delegations has been the Rev. Clifton Kirkpatrick, who has brought greetings to Castro on behalf of his denomination, posed with the Cuban dictator for photo opportunities, publicly expressed his confidence that Christians in Cuba are free to worship God, unencumbered by interference by the state, and declared his opposition to US sanctions against the Castro regime.

Even North Korea's Kim Il Sung and his successor Kim Jong Il – universally condemned for their ruthless treatment of their own people – have been beneficiaries of Presbyterian Church (USA) largesse. Proposals that human rights guarantees be added to the denomination's call for the reunification of North and South Korea in 1992 and 1993 were vigorously opposed by national staff members Syngman Rhee and Insik Kim.

During General Assembly meetings in both years, the two staff members testified that they had made several trips to North Korea in support of reunification efforts that were orchestrated by the National Council of Churches. They returned from those trips with glowing reports of having worshiped freely with North Korean Christians in their churches.

During the 1992 General Assembly, Rhee visited the commissioners' committee on Peacemaking and International Relations in order to counter a letter by the Rev. Alan Wisdom, director of Presbyterians for Democracy and Religious Freedom. Wisdom's letter reminded commissioners of the denominational leadership's penchant for condemning human rights abuses of right-wing governments but excusing or ignoring similar abuses committed by Marxist-Socialist regimes. He urged the commissioners to

147 Valladares, Armando, Speech at The Mayflower Hotel, Washington, D.C., October 14, 1989.

include a human rights clause in a proposed resolution on the reunification of North and South Korea. Rhee opposed the insertion, urging committee members not to take "anti-communist positions" that could impede the church's reunification efforts.

Rhee said that he had made ten trips to North Korea and could say that while that country does not experience freedom "in the same sense that our country does," it has a type of religious freedom. "Constitutionally," said Rhee, "there is a guarantee of religious freedom in the law."[148]

Rhee's testimony was challenged by the Rev. Dean Turbeville, a member of Amnesty International, who said that his organization had received a plethora of reports documenting human rights abuses under the Kim Il Sung government, which Amnesty International viewed as one of the repressive regimes in the modern world.[149]

Following a spirited debate, commissioners inserted a human rights clause in the Korean reunification statement.

One year later, during the 1993 General Assembly, a new proposal for Korean reunification was introduced, this time without the human rights clause. Again, Rev. Rhee argued vigorously against any attempt to insist that North Korea respect human rights.

John Boone, an elder from Nashville, TN, and a member of a team from Presbyterians for Democracy and Religious Freedom, cited a US State Department report that referred to government-organized religion in North Korea: "The regime has summarily executed political prisoners, political opponents of Kim Il Sung and Kim Jong Il, repatriated defectors and others ... Based on defector testimony and other sources, the Republic of Korea estimates that North Korea detains about 150,000 political prisoners and family members in maximum security camps in remote, isolated areas. North Korean officials deny the existence of such gulags or prisons, but admit the existence of 'education centers' for people who 'commit crimes by mistake.' One credible report lists 12 such prison camps believed to exist in the DPRK."[150]

The State Department document continued, "The regime is making a major effort to use government-sponsored religious organizations to advance its foreign policy goals ... A few Buddhist temples are in operation, and the country's first two Christian churches – one Protestant and one

148 *The Presbyterian Layman*, Vol. 25, No. 4, July/August, 1992.

149 *Ibid.*

150 US Department of State, "Country Reports on Human Rights Practices for 1992," February, 1993.

Catholic – were built in 1988. The churches are included in the fixed itinerary for many foreign visitors to Pyongyang."[151]

During his testimony before the General Assembly committee, Syngman Rhee insisted that the services were authentic, but other witnesses who testified said they appeared to be staged public relations events.

This favoritism by denominational officials toward political and economic systems that restrict the freedom of their own people makes little sense when one looks beyond ideology to measured outcomes. "Freedom is not a luxury. It is a very powerful instrument, without which no person and no country in the world can have sustained prosperity, security, development or respect," says Andrei Illaronov, president of the Institute of Economic Analysis in Moscow and former chief economic advisor to the president of the Russian Federation.[152]

FREEDOM ENGENDERS ECONOMIC GROWTH

Illaronov cites the Heritage Foundation's *Index of Economic Freedom*, the Fraser Institute's *Economic Freedom of the World*, and Freedom House's *Freedom in the World* for evidence that economically and politically free countries are much richer than non-free countries, "with a GDP per capita, on average, between $28,000 and $30,000, compared to approximately $4,000 per person in non-free or repressed countries."[153]

Further, Illaronov shows that "the economies of free countries grow faster. During the past 30 years, completely free countries doubled per capita income and partially free countries increased per capita income 40 percent on average. By contrast, non-free countries reduced per capita income roughly 34 percent."[154]

Illaronov concludes that the lack of freedom "creates an insurmountable barrier to prosperity and economic growth." He says that there are no examples in world history of non-free countries overcoming a GDP per capita barrier of $15,000. He named Spain, Portugal, Greece, Taiwan, South Korea and Chile as countries that crossed the barrier when they became free. Conversely, countries that were rich and then became non-free, also became poor, "even oil-exporting countries in years of high energy prices." The GDP per capita in Iran, Venezuela, and Saudi Arabia

151 *Ibid.*

152 *Imprimis*, Vol. 36, No. 1, January, 2007.

153 *Ibid.*

154 *Ibid.*

has plummeted in recent years. “The lack of freedom always destroys wealth,” says Illaronov.[155]

NARROWING THE GAP

Writing for *The Wall Street Journal*, which co-sponsored the 2007 Index of Economic Freedom with the Heritage Foundation, Mary Anastasia O’Grady emphasizes the measurable effects of “a gradual global shift that reflects the basic human longing for individual liberty.”[156] O’Grady said the index shows not only a worldwide trend toward greater economic liberty, “but the incomes of poor individuals across the globe are rising as a result. The world isn’t only growing richer. The gap between the per-capita income of have-not populations and that of the developed world is narrowing.”[157]

The ideals of economic freedom and private property, regularly dismissed by Presbyterian Church (USA) leaders in their “justice” offensives, are not new. In 1945, Frederick Von Hayek wrote, “What our generation has forgotten is that the system of private property is the most important guaranty of freedom, not only for those who own property, but [also] for those who do not. It is only because the control of the means of production is divided among many people acting independently that nobody has complete power over us, that we as individuals can decide what to do with ourselves. If all the means of production were vested in a single hand, whether it be nominally that of “society” as a whole or that of a dictator, whoever exercises this control has complete power over us.

“Who can seriously doubt that a member of a small racial or religious minority will be freer with no property so long as fellow-members of his community have property and are therefore able to employ him, than he would be if private property were abolished and he became owner of a nominal share in the communal property. Or that the power which a multiple millionaire, who may be my neighbor and perhaps my employer, has over me is very much less than that which the smallest *functionary* [i.e. bureaucrat] possesses who wields the coercive power of the state and on whose discretion it depends whether and how I am to be allowed to live or to work?”[158]

---

155 *Ibid.*

156 *The Wall Street Journal*, January 16, 2007.

157 *Ibid.*

158 F. V. Hayek, *The Road to Serfdom* (Chicago: University of Chicago Press, 1945), pp. 103-104.

Character and Capitalism

In 1982, theologian Michael Novak laid an invaluable theological framework for economic theory. In it, he argues that democracy does not flourish without capitalism and that capitalism cannot thrive without morality. Concepts such as freedom and responsibility, equal opportunity for individuals to succeed, and the threat to the market by human sinfulness provide the components necessary for a vibrant culture and economic stability.

"No traditional society, no socialist society – indeed, no society in history – has ever produced strict equality among individuals or classes, observed Novak. Real differences in talent, aspiration, and application inexorably individuate humans. Given the diversity and liberty of human life, no fair and free system can possibly guarantee equal outcomes. A democratic system depends for its legitimacy, therefore, not upon equal results but upon a sense of equal opportunity. Such legitimacy flows from the belief of all individuals that they can better their condition. This belief can be realized only under conditions of economic growth. Liberty requires expanse and openness.

"Not only do the logic of democracy and the logic of the market economy strengthen one another. Both also require a special moral-cultural base. Without certain moral and cultural presuppositions about the nature of individuals and their communities, about liberty and sin, about the changeability of history, about work and savings, about self-restraint and mutual cooperation, neither democracy nor capitalism can be made to work. Under some moral-cultural conditions, they are simply unachievable."[159]

Clergy Ignorance

Although widely published, Novak's economic insights have apparently made little headway with Presbyterian Church (USA) officials. In 1985, for example, the General Assembly adopted a 40-page paper on economics that was submitted by the assembly Committee on Justice and Social Issues. Titled "Toward a Just, Caring, and Dynamic Political Economy," the paper declared, "For the first half of the 1980s, our tax system is making the rich richer and the poor poorer. When you add in the effects of the higher Social Security taxes, the Sheriff of Nottingham effect is even more onerous."[160]

Novak's book, *The Spirit of Democratic Capitalism*, speaks to the dearth of competence in economics among the ranks of the clergy: "It is, there-

159 Novak, Michael, *The Spirit of Democratic Capitalism* (New York: Simon and Schuster, 1982), pp. 15-16.

160 Presbyterian Church News, June 10, 1985.

fore, a sad commentary on the sociology of knowledge in the Christian churches that so few theologians or religious leaders understand economics, industry, manufacturing, trade and finance. Many seem trapped in precapitalist modes of thought. Few understand the laws of development, growth and production. They demand jobs without comprehending how jobs are created. They demand the distribution of the world's goods without insight into how the store of the world's goods may be expanded. They desire ends without critical knowledge about the means. They claim to be leaders without having mastered the techniques of human progress. Their ignorance deprives them of authority. Their good intentions would be more easily honored if supported by evidence of diligent intelligence in economics."[161]

Novak argues that capitalism succeeds because it is an economic theory designed for sinners of whom there are many, just as socialism fails because it is a theory designed for saints of whom there are few. Capitalism is able to convert individuals' private ambitions into the creation and distribution of wealth so that everyone has a solid material base. Unintended consequences make moral systems out of a variety of motives (e.g., when individual self-interest leads to a system that produces economic abundance, political liberty, and a free pluralistic culture) and makes immoral systems out of moral motives (e.g., tyrannies that have emerged from modern experiments in collectivism). Capitalism demands freedom in order to function and thus liberates those who live under it; socialism ostensibly supports such liberation but, in fact, requires sharp restrictions of freedom in order to function.[162]

PROMOTING 'ECONOMIC TRANSFORMATION'

Despite voluminous evidence demonstrating that the poor fare better in free market economies than in managed economies, Presbyterian Church (USA) leaders have consistently favored various socialist schemes. At the Third Economic Justice Conference, in El Paso, Tex., Feb 27, 1992, sponsored by the General Assembly Justice for Women Committee, plenary speakers touted capitalism as the root cause of poverty. Their solution was "economic transformation," a concept borrowed from liberation theology.[163]

The theme of the conference was "SISTER," "Sisters in Solidarity Transforming Economic Reality." The 250 participants, mostly women, spent

161 Novak, Michael, *The Spirit of Democratic Capitalism* (New York: Simon & Schuster, 1982), p. 238.

162 *Ibid.*, p. 242.

163 Cyre, Susan, *The Presbyterian Layman*, Vol. 25, No. 3, May/June, 1992.

part of one day in "solidarity groups" visiting various agencies in the border cities of El Paso and Juarez. After the solidarity groups saw examples of extreme poverty, they attended plenary sessions at their conference site where capitalism was identified as the root cause of the economic problems that they had observed. Liberation theology's twin dicta, that class struggle defines the human condition and that salvation means the redistribution of material assets, were presented as the undergirding human and spiritual truth which moves Christians to "transform economic realities."

A keynote speaker at the conference was the Rev. John Fife, a member of the General Assembly Mission Responsibility Through Investment Committee who later was elected moderator of the Presbyterian Church (USA). Fife's presentations, called "theological reflections," redefined the doctrine of original sin as capitalism. He espoused the Marxist view that humanity is caught up in a class struggle and gave it a theological twist by adding that God has taken sides in the struggle. "God has always been present in preferential treatment for the poor," said Fife. "God is not everywhere with all people. If you believe that he is with everyone, you have not read the Bible but Greco-Roman idolatry. God is only with the poor. He is not with the patriarchs who cling to greed. God is not with the managers who pay workers $1 per hour and poison the earth. He is not with the Pharaoh ... The Bible was written by the poor for the poor."[164]

Also on Sept. 24, 1992, the Stony Point, N.Y. conference center, an official conference center of the Presbyterian Church (USA), hosted a Central America "education program," called "Y Ahora Que?" ("And What Now?"). The theme of the conference was "A Brave New World Order," and it featured presentations by Fr. Miguel D'Escoto, spiritual leader of the Sandinista revolution in Nicaragua. On display in the reception area was a huge poster portraying two armed guerrilla fighters who were embracing doves and olive branches. The conference theme equated support for armed revolution in Central American countries with "the peacemaking mission of the church."[165]

In 1984, the General Assembly adopted "Christian Faith and Economic Justice," which was commended to the churches by the 1985 General Assembly, along with a 40-page paper called "Toward a Just, Caring, and Dynamic Political Economy." Both papers were heavily slanted toward managed economies and confiscatory tax policies aimed at redistribution.

Economist Walter Williams called this Presbyterian venture into the

---

164 *Ibid.*

165 *The Presbyterian Layman*, Vol. 25, No.5, September/October, 1992.

world of economics "an exercise in fantasy." "Much of what is said is either untrue or can have merit only if we view the attainment of a Utopia or heaven-on-earth a real possibility," said Williams.[166]

Williams criticized the Presbyterian document, together with a similar paper that was released concurrently by the US Catholic Bishops, as an "attack on private property rights; confusion and demagoguery over the sources of income; and a recipe for collusion" whose chief victims are the poor whose interests the papers claim to champion.[167]

A review of economic history shows that human beings have tried various means to allocate the world's limited resources, said Williams. Violence by government or individuals, government fiat, intimidation or threat have all been employed. "Then there is the market mechanism of capitalism where allocation of resources take place on a voluntary basis. It is a matter of moral judgment to decide whether coercion ... or voluntary relations are most in keeping with Christian principles," he said.

"Capitalism is not a Utopia," continued Williams. "However, of all the ways of organizing economic activity capitalism has done the best job at solving traditional human problems such as famine, disease, and gross poverty. The fact that capitalism wins hands down in comparison to any other system does not mean that we do not have problems in America. But as suggested throughout this discussion, capitalism has been the most successful system in the history of mankind in bringing the material means for our spiritual development."[168]

Economist Thomas Sowell shared Williams' assessment of the bishops' and Presbyterian prelates' misadventures into the realm of economic theory. He found in the clerics' views an ample supply of wishful thinking that had little relevance to real world interactions of wealth and labor. Sowell saw grave danger in church leaders' admixtures of idealism and politics, due to the fact that such combinations often lead to endorsements of the totalitarian state.[169]

Sowell and Williams' assessments suggest that clergy leaders in the mainline denominations are not just wrong in matters of economics, they are ignorant. Samuel Gregg, director of research at the Acton Institute, author of

166 Williams, Walter, *Notre Dame Journal of Law, Ethics and Public Policy*, Fall, 1985.

167 *Ibid.*

168 *Ibid.*

169 Sowell, Thomas, "The Economics of the Bishops' Letter," *St. Louis University Public Law Review*, 1986, Vol. V, pp. 297-308.

Morality, Law, and Public Policy and *The Art of Corporate Governance*, places much of the blame for clergy ignorance on the seminaries. "Despite the attention given in seminaries and schools of theology to public policy issues, it is curious that few seminarians are currently exposed to one subject that is especially relevant to matters such as poverty: economics. As an intellectual discipline, economics has a potentially important role to play in the development of Christian social thought. Christian clergy, theologians, and philosophers engaged in the study of what is often described as 'the social question' risk failing to grasp much of the complexity of social issues if they lack a basic understanding of the insights offered by economics ... Unfortunately, many theological schools and seminaries do not offer courses that provide their students with such knowledge."[170]

'BAD SOCIAL SCIENCE AND BAD THEOLOGY'

Those who review the Presbyterian Church (USA)'s complicity with liberationist adventures, ranging from courtroom shoot-outs in Los Angeles to the slaughter of missionaries in Zimbabwe, may wonder how events so alien to the Christian ethic could have won the support and sometimes active involvement of this denomination. The answer is found, not in the events themselves – all but the most virulent denominational apologists condemn such acts – but with an idea that was birthed by the General Assembly of 1926 and further explicated in the denomination's Confession of 1967, namely, that there are no "essential tenets" of Christian faith. Having declared as optional foundational truths that are rooted in Scripture, church leaders opened the door for a pluralism that knows no boundaries. Devoid of theological benchmarks by which to discern truth from falsehood, they fall prey to utopian movements promising "justice," which, although undefined, is usually understood to be some form of redistribution.

Evangelical theologian Carl F. H. Henry observes that poverty and human discontent have long spawned ideologies that promise utopian solutions. Liberation theology – which is a misnomer because there is no "theos" in this essentially secular world view – offers one such utopia. Henry says, "Confusing material with spiritual poverty, Liberation Theology misses the central biblical truth that Jesus Christ is the hermeneutical key to the Bible. Political involvement is not the test of Christian authenticity, but confession of and obedience to Christ is the test. He stands supreme over every manmade system of ethics and every proposal for cultural and

170 Gregg, Samuel, *Economic Thinking for the Theologically Minded* (Lanham, Maryland: University Press of America, 2001), p. ix.

sociopolitical change."[171]

Henry continues, "Christianity is not a utopian religion; it takes seriously original sin and human selfishness. But it is a religion of ideal justice and continuing compassion nurtured by the transcendental gift and grace of God. It is tragic that in its call to social justice Liberation Theology should so sadly have missed the biblical way."[172]

Theologian Clark Pinnock says that the alignment of some Christians with Marxism can be explained by invoking the category of the utopian myth. "Socialism," says Pinnock, "is one of the most powerful myths of the modern era, and the fact that it is nowhere realized only adds to its appeal."[173]

"It is vital to understand that a fugitive vision of this sort forever tantalizes those who long for it," continues Pinnock. "Capitalism may produce better results in terms of productivity. It may produce a better car at a cheaper price. Capitalism, however, cannot compete with socialism in the area of romantic appeal. This quality of romance has enabled Marxists to disregard the empirical data and persist in policies long after they have been seen to be ruinous."[174]

Pinnock's observation parallels that of sociologist Peter Berger: "Socialism is one of the most powerful myths of the modern era. To the extent that socialism retains this mythic quality, it cannot be disconfirmed by empirical evidence in the minds of its adherents."[175]

Pinnock suggests that Christians who are not careful thinkers can be highly vulnerable to seduction from the utopian left. He says that because Christians are sensitive to their own sins and failings, they can be easily alienated from their own admittedly imperfect society. "Indeed some of us feel so keenly the shortcomings of Western culture that we are prone to accept even false charges hurled against it and idealize societies just out of view, especially if they make a claim to social justice as Marxist regimes always do."[176]

171 Henry, Carl F. H., *Evangelical Response to Liberation Theology* (Costa Mesa, CA: National Citizens Action Network, 1989), p. 25.

172 *Ibid.*

173 Pinnock, Clark H., *Freedom, Justice, and Hope: Toward a Strategy for the Poor and the Oppressed*, ed. Marvin Olasky (Westchester, Ill: Crossway Books, 1988).

174 *Ibid.*

175 Berger, Peter, *The Capitalist Revolution: Fifty Propositions about Prosperity, Equality and Liberty* (New York: Basic Books, 1986).

176 Pinnock, p. 29.

"Paradoxically, it is easy for us to become estranged from our own society at the very moment millions are desperate to emigrate to it. Somehow that socialist utopia just over the horizon must be a better place, we think . . ."[177]

But Pinnock believes that the deepest cause of our "willing seduction" comes from the "millennial dimension of the gospel message itself." Christians do pray for God's kingdom to come on earth, just as it is in heaven. We do long to see a time when there will be no more suffering, no pain or death any more. Inequities – whatever their cause – spark our sympathies and move us to compassion toward those who have fewer possessions. Thus, we are predisposed to welcome "hucksters peddling the miracle ideology guaranteed to deliver the millennium for us" without asking the hard question of economics and the social sciences, namely, can these utopian visions deliver the goods?

Pinnock says that any intelligent assessment of statist solutions to human inequities tells us that they cannot deliver. As a matter of historical fact, there has never been a Marxist state that could feed its own people. Every attempt has ended in the loss of productivity, the loss of basic human freedoms, and a benefit only to those who manage the system, albeit by coercion.

"How easy it is to be indifferent about practicalities in the realm of hope and religion; how easy to want to treat all people as if they were saints – not sinners; how easy to relish a foolish course of action in the name of a greater faith! Whatever moral grandeur can be found in the rhetoric of Marx is more than destroyed in the deadly havoc which has resulted from the implementation of his theories."[178]

During the peak years of Presbyterian Church (USA) support for regimes of the totalitarian left, Regnery Gateway published *The Coercive Utopians*, by Rael Jean and Erich Isaac. In this publication, the Isaacs laid bare the ideological assumptions that were prevalent in US mainline denominational bureaucracies: "They are called utopians because they assume that man is perfectible and the evils that exist are the product of a corrupt social system. They are coercive because in their zeal for attaining an ideal social order, they seek to impose their blueprints in ways that go beyond legitimate persuasion."[179]

In 1983, the year prior to Regnery Gateway's publishing *The Coercive Utopians*, *Readers' Digest* published an article by Rael Jean Isaac in which

177 *Ibid.*

178 *Ibid.*

179 Isaac, Rael Jean and Erich, *The Coercive Utopians* (New York: Regnery Gateway, 1984), p. 33.

she focused on the leadership of mainline Protestant denominations and described "the extent to which mainline Protestant denominations had become supporters of revolutionary activism both in the United States and abroad." The climate in some church agencies has grown so fevered that "they have literally become breeding grounds for terrorists," she said.[180]

Reflecting on the propensity of Presbyterian ministers to endorse various socialist schemes, one is tempted to insist that every Presbyterian seminary include a course of basic economics in its curriculum. Such training might have prevented the Presbyterian Church (USA)'s gargantuan losses in an adventure called PEDCO (The Presbyterian Economic Development Corporation). PEDCO's vision, spawned by social activists who believed that the banking industry was insensitive to the offense of poverty, was to make low interest loans to the poor. Led primarily by clergy with no demonstrable business skills, PEDCO lost $6,985,359 before it was shut down, and many of the business ventures that it funded failed. Commenting on PEDCO's losses, the Rev. Donald Wilson, director of the program said, "You win some and lose some, and in the course of it a lot of good things happen."[181]

UTOPIA MEANS 'NO PLACE'

Presbyterian ministers who chase after utopian ideals often do so at the cost of abandoning the Great Commission, said the Rev. James F. Miller to Charlotte, NC's Covenant Presbyterian Church in 1992. Miller reminded his congregation of utopia's definition. "It is a combination of two Greek words. The first, 'topos,' means a 'place.' When you put the Greek letter 'u' in front of any Greek noun, it means 'no,' or 'not.' It is a negation and a denial. U-topia means no place, nowhere."

Miller urged his congregation to learn the danger of chasing after utopias by examining the failure of Marxism, one of the modern world's most virulent utopian movements. The alternative to such movements' dream-like vapidity, said Miller, is Jesus Christ. "He was no utopian, but a flesh and blood person. He died on Calvary, no utopia, but a real place, the place where all silly manmade dreams come to perish and from which there is unleashed the unstoppable power that will one day bring to us, not of our own making nor by our own efforts, not a 'brave new world,' but a 'new

180 Isaac, Rael Jean, "Do You Know Where Your Church Offerings Go?" *Reader's Digest*, January, 1983, p. 122.

181 *The Presbyterian Layman*, Vol. 23, No. 4, July/August, 1990.

heaven and a new earth.' And in the meantime, he charges us to go and make disciples!"[182]

Theology vs. Ideology

The Christian faith originated, not in human ideas – no matter how inventive – but in revelation. When Simon Peter affirmed that Jesus is the Christ, Son of the living God, Jesus responded, "You have been blessed, for flesh and blood did not reveal this to you, but my Father, who is in heaven." Simon's affirmation was not his idea. He was a conduit for the truth that had been revealed to him.

The core of Presbyterian belief is revealed truth. God spoke in his Word made flesh and in his Word written. Authentic Presbyterian communion gathers around a faith that arises from a Word that is not its own. When the General Assembly of the Presbyterian Church decided that truth originates with culture, it replaced the Truth with truths, ideas of human invention.

A 'Wandering Church'

Speaking of that loss and the consequent forfeiture of the Presbyterian ethos, Dr. James I. McCord, former President of Princeton Theological Seminary, said, "We in the Presbyterian Church, in suffering from a corporate theological amnesia, have lost our sense of identity. We are leaders in the ecumenical movement and, in my view, we should be. But the ecumenical movement is far broader and deeper than mere ecclesiastical joinery ... Until we discover what it is to be Presbyterian in faith, polity, and life, I think we shall be a wandering church."[183]

Ideas have consequences, as anyone who examines the effects of liberationist ideology must attest. Liberationism is a bad idea. It is, as political scientist René Williamson correctly concluded, "bad social science and bad theology."[184] Its optimistic assessment of human nature, identified by Machen during the debates of the 1920s as alien to the gospel, has led it to proffer statist solutions for problems whose only answer is the gospel.

In liberationism's blanket indictment of capitalism, says Williamson, it ascribes to one social system "what is part of the universal human condi-

182 *The Presbyterian Layman*, Vol. 25, No. 3, May/June, 1992.

183 McCord, James I., "Address to the Geneva Forum," Philadelphia, November 18, 1976.

184 Williamson, René de Visme, *The Integrity of The Gospel* (Atlanta: John Knox Press, 1979), p. 3.

tion, and fails to recognize that every social system is afflicted with the same vices."[185]

McCord also saw the theological flaw implicit in denominational policies arising from an incessant contrition over putative corporate sins: "One problem, I think, with the mainline churches is that we have developed a guilt complex – what I have spoken of as a 'death wish.' We know there are many things that are wrong and that there has been complicity. And we who are 'Wasps' feel our complicity, and respond with guilt. But there are two kinds of guilt. One is positive – you confess it before God, and God forgives you. He cancels your past and He opens for you a new future. The other kind of guilt is negative and unhealthy – it is the guilt that says, 'Beat me more and more, heap up the abuse.' When we opt for this kind of guilt, we shirk our responsibility to get on with the mission of the church."[186]

And what is the mission of the church? Is it found in efforts to replace one human system with another? Human sin cannot be eradicated by the liberationists' schemes of socio-economic restructuring. Sinners need a Savior. His name is Jesus, and He is the Christ.

185 *Ibid.*, p.11.

186 McCord, *op. cit.*

Covenant

Holy Scripture

"Jesus said to him, 'I am the way, and the truth, and the life; no one comes to the Father, but by me.'"

John 14:6

The Constitution

We believe in one Lord, Jesus Christ, the only Son of God, eternally begotten of the Father, God from God, Light from Light, true God from true God, begotten, not made, of one Being with the Father; through him all things were made."

The Nicene Creed

All power in heaven and earth is given to Jesus Christ by Almighty God, who raised Christ from the dead and set him above all rule and authority, all power and dominion, and every name that is named, not only in this age but also in that which is to come. God has put all things under the Lordship of Jesus Christ and has made Christ Head of the Church, which is his body.

The Book of Order
G-1.0100

Broken Covenant

"What's the big deal about Jesus?"

Dirk Ficca, July 29, 2000

Jesus is "unique."

General Assembly of the Presbyterian Church (USA),
June, 2001

Chapter Five

The PCUSA's Problem with Jesus

On July 29, 2000, Presbyterians across the country were shocked when they received reports of a speech delivered by Rev. Dirk Ficca, keynote speaker at a Presbyterian Peacemaking Conference. The theme of the event focused on how to maintain complementary relationships with persons of other faiths in an increasingly pluralistic world. Ficca's thesis was that much of the discord that has fractured human communities is fomented by groups that host exclusive religious convictions. His solution was to recognize that God works in the world through people of many faiths.

After all, asked Ficca, "If God is at work in our lives, whether we're Christian or not, what's the big deal about Jesus?"[1]

Thousands of Presbyterians wrote to the denomination's General Assembly Council telling this agency to which the Peacemaking Program is accountable that Jesus is a very big deal, and, according to Scripture, the only deal that can secure our salvation.

Denominational staff members defended Ficca' presentation. Rev. Victor Makari, coordinator for the Middle East and the Office of Interfaith Relations in the Worldwide Ministries Division, called Ficca's question about Jesus "rhetorical, not dismissive." Sara Lisherness, coordinator of the Presbyterian Peacemaking Program, said that Ficca's approach to interfaith relations was "cutting edge, not radical."[2]

On August 23, Council chairman Peter Pizer and executive John Detterick released a statement, emphasizing Ficca's right freely to express his views and their belief that discussions of interfaith relations such as had

---

1 Presbyterian Church (USA) News Note #6154, August 16, 2000.

2 *Ibid.*

occurred during the peacemaking conference should be welcomed. "Rev. Ficca speaks for himself," they said, "and not for the Presbyterian Church (U.S.A.). Given the open dialogue encouraged at the Peacemaking Conference and given the urging of previous General Assemblies to engage in interfaith relationships, we support discussion that responsibly explores how we are to live faithfully as Presbyterians in a religiously plural world."

On October 25, General Assembly Council's executive committee issued a letter, stating its own faith in Jesus Christ but defending the peacemaking event: "We reaffirm Dr. Ficca's right to his own views and we reaffirm the propriety of the Peacemaking Conference Planning Team's decision to invite Dr. Ficca to be one of the speakers at this particular conference."

The letter continued, citing statements in the Presbyterian Church (USA) *Book of Order* that executive committee members believed cleared the way for church leaders to hold different views, including – as in Ficca's case – different views about Jesus. "Our church's Historic Principles of Church Order (G-1.0300) declare that 'God alone is Lord of the conscience, and hath left it free from the doctrines and commandments of men which are in anything contrary to his Word, or beside it, in matters of faith or worship.' These Historic Principles also declare that 'there are truths and forms of truth with respect to which men of good characters and principles may differ. And in all these we think it the duty both of private Christians and societies to exercise mutual forbearance toward each other.'"

Neither Detterick's statement nor that of the council's executive committee quelled dissent across the denomination. Presbyterians who can read between the lines understood not only what was being said but, more importantly, what was being left unsaid. The unsaid message was, "we may believe what the Scriptures say about Jesus, but we respect the right of other Presbyterians, denominational personnel, and speakers at official church events, to express contrary beliefs."

Detterick and the executive committee might have claimed some warrant for that position, particularly in light of the General Assembly's 1926 decision not to require ordained persons to subscribe to any particular doctrine. If Chicago Presbytery, where Ficca was a member, had no problem with Ficca's faith – apparently it did not, for there was no move by the presbytery to correct or discipline him after his speech was made public – then, following the 1926 ruling, no one else in the denomination should be troubled by what he believed or did not believe.

But some Presbyterians were troubled, namely, the sessions of Highland Park Presbyterian Church and Montreat Presbyterian Church, both of whom sent notices of their intention to file judicial complaints against the General

Assembly Council for failing to uphold the church's faith. These and other warnings inspired Detterick to reassess his position.

On October 31, 2000, Detterick addressed a gathering of evangelicals in Indianapolis that was sponsored by the Presbyterian Coalition. In that speech, he said that he now believed Ficca's "What's the big deal about Jesus?" message "conflicts with a basic tenet of the church's faith" and was "out of bounds."

Detterick admitted that official responses issued by himself and council leaders were inadequate. "Some of you have found [the executive committee's letter] inadequate because while it affirms our core beliefs, it does not hold the speaker accountable for his out-of-bounds statements," he said.

Detterick said that upon reflection, he had concluded that if the conference had invited a non-Christian speaker to address the subject from the perspective of that tradition, it could have been helpful. But the fact that the speaker who expressed this non-Christian perspective was "a Presbyterian minister of the Word and sacrament … exacerbates our problem," he said.

Although evangelicals who attended the event applauded Detterick and expressed appreciation for his candor, many saw the need for a theological control mechanism, a General Assembly requirement that might ensure the leadership's conformity to Biblical truth. Overtures were dispatched to the General Assembly, calling on the assembly to declare that Jesus Christ is "the singular saving Lord as understood through Scripture, our confessions, and the *Book of Order*."

Jesus Christ is 'Unique'

When the General Assembly met on June 14, 2001, a vigorous debate ensued. Some commissioners insisted that declaring Jesus Christ "the singular saving Lord" must be a requirement for church leaders. Others wanted the denomination to continue being "inclusive, generous, welcoming and diverse."

Some commissioners quoted John 14:6: "I am the way, the truth and the life. No one comes to the Father but by me." The Rev. Catherine Purves said, "There comes a time when a clear and strong singular affirmation of the Lordship of Jesus must come, and this is the time."

Seminary student Jeff McDonald said, "If salvation isn't singular through Jesus Christ, does that mean that it is plural? If it is plural, who are the others?"

But former General Assembly moderator Freda Gardner opposed the affirmation of Christ alone: "Words can become stumbling blocks," she said.

The Rev. Robert Rea, Jr., a presbytery executive, said, "I do not have the right to say other people cannot find God in other ways. If God is all powerful, God can find ways to save Hindus, Jews, and other people."

Timothy Sakelos suggested that different religions are like a basket of fruit. "The taste, smell and look are different, but they are all fruit. If you look more deeply, you can see the sunshine, rain and minerals. Only their manifestations are different. All religions have similarities and differences, but the real difference only exists in their emphasis."

As polarities sharpened, moderates raced to the microphones, expressing their fear that the denomination might split if either position were affirmed. Former General Assembly Moderator Syngman Rhee suggested a compromise, "why not approve both?" he asked. "Couldn't we put these two positions together?"

And that is exactly what the commissioners did. By a vote of 369-163, the General Assembly declared that Jesus is "unique." Calling the decision "namby-pamby at best," *Christianity Today* paraphrased it: "Jesus may not be the only way to salvation, the denomination essentially said, but he's the only way we are sure of."[3]

Commenting on what he heard during the assembly debate, The Rev. Joe Rightmyer, executive director of Presbyterians for Renewal, made a statement that could have been taken from J. Gresham Machen's *Christianity and Liberalism*. Rightmyer said, "What has crept into the life of the Presbyterian Church is not just differences of opinion, it is unbelief."[4]

The denomination-wide reaction to the assembly's compromise launched a surge of public declarations from local church sessions. In these declarations, they aligned themselves with a rapidly growing "Confessing Church Movement" that attracted 1,214 congregations, representing more than 434,000 Presbyterians. "The General Assembly may not be able to say who Jesus is, but we can!" said the Rev. Paul Roberts, pastor of Summit Presbyterian Church in Western Pennsylvania, the first church session publicly to declare its faith in contradistinction to the assembly's ambivalence.

That reaction moved the succeeding assembly to issue another compromise, albeit somewhat less ambiguous, called "Hope in Jesus Christ."

The Kaseman Case

The "What's the big deal about Jesus?" controversy was not the first occasion in which the issue of Christology had been debated among Presbyterians. In 1981, the case of the Rev. Mansfield Kaseman came before

---

3 *Christianity Today*, July, 2001.

4 *Ibid.*

the General Assembly Permanent Judicial Commission, the highest court in the denomination. At issue was the fact that during his ordination examination, Kaseman denied the divinity of Jesus Christ. In answer to the question, "Was Jesus God?" Kaseman replied, "No, God is God."[5]

Later, in an attempt to explain his position, Kaseman tried to improve his answer. "Saying Jesus is one with God is a better way of saying it." But, he continued, "I, too, am one with God."[6]

Kaseman's denial of Biblical faith to the contrary notwithstanding, the high court upheld National Capital Union Presbytery's decision to ordain him. The issue, the court reasoned, was not a matter of theology, but one of polity. Instead of asking if it was right for the presbytery to ordain Kaseman, the court asked if the presbytery had the right to ordain Kaseman. To that question, the court answered in the affirmative. The heart of the issue in this case, the court said, was the "inherent powers of the presbytery."

The Permanent Judicial Commission's decision upheld a ruling of the Synod of the Piedmont that Kaseman's answers to theological questions "were within the acceptable range of interpretation" of doctrine in *The Book of Confessions* and that in accepting his answers, the presbytery correctly and properly reflected the spirit of theological pluralism. "The arguments presented by both parties in this case force us to recognize that there are several valid ways of interpreting the creedal symbols and the confessions of our faith," said the synod court in its ruling that was subsequently upheld by the denomination's high court.[7]

The Kaseman decision emphasized doctrinal freedom, the linchpin of the 1926 General Assembly's decision that the denomination would no longer require its ministers to subscribe to specific beliefs. It affirmed that Kaseman "recognized and accepted the fact that the creeds of the church are extremely important ... the church does not require that its ministers be possessed of a photographic mind ... indeed it appears to this commission that by his refusal to use theological language in answering the questions asked at his examination, Mr. Kaseman was being true to the spirit of the Confession of 1967."[8] This was precisely the kind of aberration against which Machen warned the church in the 1920s debates.

5 *The Presbyterian Layman*, Vol. 13, No. 5, September/October, 1980. See also: *Rankin v. National Capital Union Presbytery* (Remedial Case 193-10, UPCUSA).

6 *Ibid.*

7 *The Presbyterian Layman*, Vol. 14, No 2, March/April, 1981.

8 United Presbyterian Church in the USA, *Minutes of the General Assembly*, 1981, p. 117.

Evangelism: The Case of the Missing $15 Million

The 1988 General Assembly delivered major victories and great encouragement to evangelicals in the Presbyterian Church (USA) who were determined to see the name of Jesus affirmed "above every name in heaven and on earth." During that assembly, renewal organizations orchestrated an all-out effort to have the denomination's highest governing body declare that evangelism was its top priority. Social activist forces resisted but were unable to turn the tide. The assembly voted to direct its General Assembly Council, the body that implements General Assembly decisions and acts on behalf of the General Assembly between its annual meetings, to add to the budget of its Evangelism and Church Development Ministry Unit each year from 1990 to 1995 an amount equal to one percent of the total General Assembly mission budget. The money was to be earmarked for spending on evangelism within the United States. Estimates at the time of the General Assembly action suggested that it would provide approximately $15 million for evangelism.

By March, 1989, Evangelism and Church Development director Pat Roach had assembled a crack team of 13 professionals, including the Rev. Gary Demarest, a nationally known evangelical pastor from California, to lead the evangelism program. "It's fun to be a part of this evangelism unit at a time when interest is expanding far beyond anything I have ever experienced in my ministry. I take all of this to be a sign of renewal," said Demarest.

Segmented into three divisions, Presbyterian Evangelism, Rural and Urban Church Development, and Mission Financial Resources, the team crafted a host of evangelism initiatives designed to rejuvenate static congregations and jump-start new ones. Training events were developed to help Presbyterians understand the gospel message and articulate it in business, professional and social contexts.

But the jubilation expressed by Demarest and others in the evangelism unit was not universally shared at denominational headquarters. The General Assembly's windfall allocation for evangelism had come in the midst of a severely declining income stream from congregations to the national church. In effect, the action guaranteed that the evangelism program would be the only "cut proof" ministry at General Assembly headquarters for five years, while other programs and their staffs would face major retrenchments.

Denominational executives met in a frantic attempt to mitigate the damage done to their agenda by the 1988 General Assembly. In a matter of months, they launched two strategies that resulted in scuttling any effective implementation of the evangelism program.

Strategy One: Re-define Evangelism

One strategy was to re-define "evangelism." On its face, the General Assembly Council's definition declared: "Evangelism is joyfully sharing the good news of the sovereign love of God and calling people to repentance, to personal faith in Jesus Christ as Savior and Lord, to active membership in the church, and to obedient service in the world." Council officials let that public definition stand unchallenged, but they broadened their in-house operational definition of evangelism to such a degree that it could encompass any existing program. Soon everything the church does – from lobbying Congress to fomenting revolution in Third World countries – would be considered a form of evangelism.[9]

These sentiments were expressed by the Rev. Constance Baugh, pastor of the Church of Gethsemane in New York, and featured speaker at a 1990 General Assembly breakfast sponsored by the Presbyterian Health, Education and Welfare Association. "The church has a new emphasis on evangelism, and evangelism is a justice issue," said Baugh. "Evangelism is a relational issue. We can respond to the cry of the poor in new and transforming ways." Baugh suggested that tapping the $15 million fund was simply a matter of how one describes what one is doing.[10]

Additional formulas for re-defining evangelism were attempted by the denomination's Global Mission Ministry Unit at an August 18, 1990, retreat in Nazareth, Ky. In a paper that was approved by the unit, the concepts of "Partnership, Mutuality and Incarnational Solidarity" were propounded as important elements in the unit's understanding of mission. The "solidarity" section of the paper voiced the Global Ministry Unit's justification for supporting Third World revolutionary movements and political campaigns. The paper suggested that acts of solidarity should be given priority over evangelism, as evangelism is normally understood by people in the pews. "It [solidarity] hears a kind of divine impatience with us when we put piety and worship – and having the right theology and making the right verbal confessions – even, in a sense, believing the right things – before doing the right things."[11]

9 Note similar tactics that were employed by Presbyterian Church (USA) missions leaders when they re-defined missions as "mission," (Chapter Four, page 55) and efforts by Christ Church in Burlington, Vt. to defy the Constitution's sexual behavior standards by re-defining "fidelity" and "chastity." (Chapter Six, page 175).

10 *The Presbyterian Layman*, Vol. 23, No. 4, July/August, 1990.

11 Presbyterian Church (USA), Global Mission Ministry Unit, Bi-National Servants Advisory Group, "Partnership, Mutuality, and Incarnational Solidarity," August 18, 1990.

Although the paper was approved without objection by the Global Ministry Unit, the concerns of some members over how it might be interpreted to the Presbyterian public were discussed. The Rev. Gerrit Van Brandwijk said, "I don't think the people have caught on to our move from paternalism to partnership yet, and now we're talking about mutuality and solidarity." The Rev. Brent Coffin asked, "How do we move this from the table to the church?" Presbytery executive Virginia Robertson said, "This is mostly for our own people. I am sorry that most people out there in the church don't understand what we do on the mission field in the same way that we who do it understand it."[12]

This conflict of "understandings" came to the surface later in the meeting when Ministry Unit members reviewed an early draft of a mission policy document titled "Turn to the Living God: A Call to Evangelism in Jesus Christ's Way." The draft contained strong evangelical language: "The Proclamation of the gospel includes an invitation to recognize and accept in personal decision the saving lordship of Christ … Christians owe the message of God's salvation in Jesus Christ to every person and every people … We cannot point to any other way of salvation than Jesus Christ."[13]

Reflecting on the anti-conversionist views expressed in the "Solidarity" paper that the Ministry Unit had just adopted and the call to conversion in Jesus Christ alone found in the draft mission policy statement that was before them, the Rev. Brent Coffin, a member of the unit's mutual mission subcommittee, asked, "How do we put together all these pieces? They contain very different concepts?"[14]

The apparent solution to this dilemma was to adopt policy papers expressing evangelical language that Presbyterians in the pews will support (*Turn to the Living God*), while also adopting internal working documents that include radically different operational definitions of those terms (*Partnership, Mutuality and Incarnational Solidarity*).

Another example of in-house attempts to undermine the General Assembly's evangelism emphasis can be seen in a paper that was circulated through denominational headquarters by the Office of Ecumenical and Interfaith Relations shortly after the General Assembly action. The paper said, "We condemn proselytizing efforts which de-legitimize the faith tradition of the person whose conversion is being sought. Deceptive proselytiz-

12 *The Presbyterian Layman*, Vol. 23, No. 5, September/October, 1990.

13 *Turn to the Living God: A Call to Evangelism in Jesus Christ's Way* (Louisville: Office of the General Assembly, 1991).

14 *The Presbyterian Layman*, Vol. 23, No. 5, September/October, 1990.

ing efforts are practiced on the most vulnerable of populations – residents of hospitals and old age homes, confused youth, college students away from home. These proselytizing techniques are tantamount to coerced conversions and should be condemned."[15]

Jesus told his disciples to make disciples of all nations. Commissioners to the 1988 General Assembly instructed the General Assembly Council to do precisely that. So how did Louisville headquarters end up circulating documents full of proscriptions against "proselytizing?" and what, pray tell, was wrong with introducing away-from-home college students to Jesus Christ? Knowing that the General Assembly was in session for only a few days, members of its national staff simply bided their time. Then they proceeded to undermine its directives.

Strategy Two: Reinterpret the General Assembly Action

The second strategy involved a reinterpretation of the 1988 General Assembly's action. General Assembly Council budget managers said that what the General Assembly really meant to say was that congregations would be challenged to produce $15 million new dollars for evangelism, not that dollars they had already given would be reallocated.[16]

Politically astute executives knew better than to announce these two strategies, for they would most certainly have evoked protests from the pews. Instead, they simply implemented them operationally. Ministry Unit managers re-crafted the language that described many of their existing programs, inserting evangelistic phrases that might justify the use of evangelism funds. Evangelism proposals that would have required new funds were approved, but General Assembly managers never got around to implementing them.

It was as if the system had acquired wads of bubble gum on the soles of its shoes, making any forward step very difficult. As it became clear that little would be done, evangelism experts whose skills were lying fallow left the program. Demarest redirected his ministerial efforts to growing congregations in California. Strategic planner Stan Wood accepted a professorship

15 Presbyterian Church (USA), Office of Ecumenical and Interfaith Relations, "Ecu-Dialogue Newsletter," 1989.

16 Arguably, the most egregious example of defiance by reinterpretation occurred in 2006, when liberals who had been unable to remove the denomination's ordination standards by constitutional amendment effectively did so by enacting an "authoritative interpretation" that allows governing bodies to permit practices that the Constitution expressly forbids.

at Columbia Seminary. Over time, others jumped ship until the evangelism program, lost in a shuffle of papers, died quietly from neglect.[17]

Blowing Smoke: Assembly Adds Pagan Rituals and Removes Christian Essentials

Meanwhile, denominational leaders continued in their affirmation of "alternative pathways to God." In a planning meeting for the 1992 General Assembly, denominational staff member the Rev. Daniel Hamby told the General Assembly Council that "on the whole" plans for worship services at the General Assembly were progressing very well. Hamby's keen-eared listeners, however, caught the qualifying phrase and pressed him for specifics.

"Well," said Hamby, "the moderator has some very definite ideas about the opening communion service." Hamby explained that Moderator Herbert Valentine had a strong interest in Native American spirituality, and he planned to burn sage and pass the smoke over the people. The practice is called "smudging." Hamby continued, "Since the moderator insists that we do this, we are all trying very hard to make it fit into the liturgy."

When the 1992 General Assembly was convened in Milwaukee, Valentine's opening ritual went up in smoke. Chief Paul Firecloud, the moderator's choice to lead the ritual, suffered a heart attack, so the Rev. Ron Moccasin was quickly dispatched to the scene. But Moccasin forgot to bring his sage. After a quick skirmish in the back room, Moccasin appeared with smoke of unidentified origin. He "purified" General Assembly commissioners, purporting to expel unwanted spirits and attract favorable spirits by wafting an eagle feather through the smoke and toward the four corners of the assembly.

Dr. John H. Leith, Pemberton Professor of Theology at Union Theological Seminary in Virginia, walked out of the communion service, saying that

17 The denominational infrastructure's defiance of General Assembly mandates, sometimes by the process of re-definition, sometimes by reinterpretation, and often simply by an outright refusal to implement General Assembly actions, occurred often in the period between 1965 and 2006. Other instances are noted in Chapter Six, which documents the fact that General Assembly policies on sexual ethics have been routinely violated by its offices and agencies. This has distressed independent renewal organizations that have attempted to reform the denomination by working within the constitutionally defined structures of its polity. Hard fought victories at the General Assembly level have often been for naught, leading growing numbers of renewal leaders to conclude that barring some miraculous intervention by the Lord of all creation, the Presbyterian Church (USA) infrastructure has proven itself virtually impervious to reform.

the inclusion of a pagan ceremony violated the integrity of Christian worship. But Moderator Valentine dismissed his critics, saying that they "need to worry about the essentials, like people starving to death in the Sudan." Valentine did not clarify how his practice of "smudging" the General Assembly would solve Sudan's hunger problem, nor did he elaborate on the meaning of "essentials."

What needed no clarification was the fact that the highest elected official of the Presbyterian Church (USA) had chosen to incorporate a non-Christian ritual into the General Assembly's opening communion service. In doing so, Valentine was not unique, for representatives of the Presbyterian Church (USA) were already deeply involved in syncretism through their participation – and leadership – in gatherings sponsored by the World Council of Churches.

Denying the Atonement of Jesus Christ

In 1993, a new religion was promoted at a Minneapolis, Minnesota event, sponsored by the World Council of Churches and funded with a $60,000 grant from the Presbyterian Church (USA). The purpose of the event was to "re-imagine god," and, in the process, to reconfigure Jesus Christ. In order to accomplish these goals, leaders of the event proposed a god who is "within" rather than transcendent, and a "Christ" who does not resemble Scripture's witness to Jesus of Nazareth and the cross on which he died.

Planned and funded by a group that included Mary Ann Lundy, Director of the General Assembly Council's Women's Ministries Division, and other high level executives of the Presbyterian Church (USA), the new religion was referred to as a "bottom up" religion. Speakers began with their own experiences as women from a variety of cultures and religions. They announced that God is teaching them, as women, new teachings that are superior to Scripture's revelations.

Jesus' incarnation, his divinity and his atonement on the cross were soundly rejected. Conference leader Rita Nakashima Brock quoted an author who declared, "not transcendence – that orgy of self-alienation beloved of the fathers – but immanence, god working out god's self in everything." Brock argued that there was nothing particularly unique about Jesus. In fact, she said, in Jesus' encounter with the Canaanite woman (Matthew 15) "she is the incarnation of god to Jesus."[18]

18 Quotations derived from audio tapes purchased by *The Layman* from *Resource Express*, a Minneapolis, MN vendor that was under contract with conference management to record plenary presentations.

Virginia Mollenkott expressed her view of Jesus as "our elder brother, the trailblazer and constant companion for us ... ultimately one among many brothers and sisters in an eternally, equally worthy siblinghood. First born only in the sense that he was the first to show us that it is possible to live in oneness with the divine source while we are here on this planet."[19]

Delores Williams, professor at Union Theological Seminary in New York, told the group, "I don't think we need a theory of atonement at all. I think Jesus came for life and to show us something about life ... I don't think we need folks hanging on crosses and blood dripping and weird stuff."[20]

Mollenkott claimed that Jesus' death was the ultimate in child abuse and a model for human child abuse. "As an incest survivor, I can no longer worship in a theological context that depicts God as an abusive parent and Jesus as the obedient, trusting child," she declared.[21]

Aruna Gnanadason, director of the sub-unit on Women in the Church and Society of the World Council of Churches, condemned the church as a patriarchal institution that "centered its faith around the cruel and violent death of Christ on the cross, sanctioning violence against the powerless in society."[22]

Chinese feminist Kwok Pui-lan – a World Council of Churches leader who was the featured speaker at a meeting of the Presbyterian Church (USA) Theology and Worship Ministry Unit in 1992 and whom Mary Ann Lundy invited to "resource" members of her Women's Ministry Unit – told conference participants that the Chinese reject the Christian belief in the depravity of all human beings who can only be reconciled with God through the death and sacrifice of Jesus the Christ. Instead, she pointed to Confucius, who "emphasized the propensities in human nature for good rather than evil ... We Chinese believe there is a genuine possibility of human beings to achieve moral perfection and sainthood," she said.[23]

"We cannot have one savior," she argued. "Just like the Big Mac ... prepackaged and shipped all over the world. It won't do. It's imperialistic." When asked a question about the Trinity, Pui-lan said she favored her culture's religion, which has 722 gods and goddesses, but that if the church wouldn't accept 722, at least three gods are better than one because

19 *Ibid.*

20 *Ibid.*

21 *Ibid.*

22 *Ibid.*

23 *Ibid.*

"monotheism used in the wrong way can be extremely dangerous ... If you have one and only one we are even more oppressive," she said.[24]

Pui-lan offered a radical feminist view of salvation, quoting the ancient Gnostic gospels. "If you bring out what is within you, what is within you will save you. But if you cannot bring out what is within you, what is within you will destroy you." She justified her use of the Gnostic gospels, which were rejected as heresy by the Christian church in the second century, by telling the participants that the canon (the contents of the Bible) was decided by men and therefore, women are not obliged to accept a book or 'Constitution' they had no part in framing.[25]

Conference Themes Promoted

Presbyterian Church (USA) staff members who promoted the "ReImagining God" conference lost little time introducing its themes into the denomination's regional infrastructure. On March 24, 1994, Kwok Pui-lan appeared at the denomination's Stony Point conference center to teach Hudson River Presbytery leaders about "Pluralism and the Mission of the Church."

Pui-lan's theme was reminiscent of ReImagining, calling on participants to eschew Scripture and the teachings of the church in order to discover the god that already dwells within them. Quoting from one of her books, she said that a new, more inclusive theology "requires us to shift our attention from the Bible and tradition to people's stories." She continued: "With full confidence, we claim that our own culture and our people's aspirations are vehicles for knowing and appreciating the ultimate."[26]

Pui-lan told Hudson Presbytery leaders that our gods are the products of our own experiences. It follows, therefore, that many experiences will generate many gods. This is no problem, said Kwok Pui-lan, so long as one avoids "superior attitudes." She warned her Stony Point audience not to get hung up on "the myth of Christian uniqueness," which leads to an unhealthy attitude in a pluralistic world.[27]

Pui-lan said that the key problem for pluralism arises when people tend to view life in terms of polarities. We see ourselves (and our beliefs about God) as "A" and everything else as "not A" she said. That way of looking at the world, she insisted, is "imperialistic." She described it as the kind of

24 *Ibid.*

25 *Ibid.*

26 Pui-lan, Kwok, *Inheriting Our Mothers' Gardens* (Louisville: Westminster John Knox Press, 1988).

27 *The Presbyterian Layman*, Vol. 27. No. 3, May/June, 1994.

attitude that was exhibited by Christian missionaries who went into other lands and destroyed traditional faiths and customs. "When missionaries arrived in Asia, Africa and Latin America, trying to convert the people, they condemned our ancestors, trashed our gods and goddesses, and severed us from our indigenous culture," she wrote in a printed handout that was distributed to conference participants.[28]

If two affirmations are mutually contradictory, said Pui-lan, this is a problem only for Westerners who insist on logic. For Asians who were brought up in a yin-yang background, opposites may be seen as "correlated, interdependent, and inter-penetrating." One can accept anything; one is required to deny nothing.

Meanwhile, news reports of the ReImagining God conference created quite a stir across the denomination. General Assembly officials hired a public relations firm to handle damage control, but Presbyterians in the pews were not to be mollified by attacks on "male," "sexist," "fundamentalist" critics, or statements that *The Presbyterian Layman* that reported the event was lying (*The Layman* report was verified by tape recordings), nor were they moved by affirmations that those who planned the conference meant well. When the 1994 General Assembly met in Wichita, Kansas, it rejected many of the themes expressed in the ReImagining God conference, declaring that they "not only extended beyond the boundaries of the Reformed theological tradition but also beyond that tradition's understanding of what makes faith Christian."[29]

But after the General Assembly made its affirmations, printed versions of the conference presentations were archived by staff members of the Presbyterian Church (USA) Women's Ministry Unit, where they became "recommended resources" for various denominational programs, including studies conducted for the National Network of Presbyterian College Women and seminars led by Sally Hill, a steering committee member for the ReImagining Conference at the denomination's Ghost Ranch conference center.

Lundy's Revolving Door

Mary Ann Lundy, executive of the Women's Ministry Unit and a principal in planning and funding the ReImagining God conference, became a political liability for the denominational establishment. So General Assembly Council executive James Brown fired her. The following day approximately 200 members of the denominational staff in Louisville showed up

28 *Ibid.*

29 Presbyterian Church (USA), *Minutes of the General Assembly*, 1994, p. 87.

for work wearing bells around their necks, a symbol of protest and a declaration that they would not remain silent over this "injustice."[30]

But their lamentations were brief, for soon thereafter, an announcement was made in Geneva, Switzerland, that Lundy had been hired by the World Council of Churches. The Rev. Clifton Kirkpatrick, head of the Presbyterian Church (USA) Worldwide Ministries Division, was a member of the World Council's Central Committee, the group that hired Lundy. The Presbyterian Church (USA) gives more money to the World Council than any other US denomination. As his denomination's primary advocate for such funding, Kirkpatrick wields a powerful influence over World Council activities. So the right hand, James Brown, fired Lundy, and the left hand, Kirkpatrick, hired her.

Lundy's quip after the firing/hiring scenario was, "I've been fired up!" In 1998, during a gathering of Presbyterian Church (USA) leaders attending the World Council of Churches meeting in Harare, Zimbabwe, Kirkpatrick publicly recognized Lundy, thanking her for her "extraordinary leadership and the gifts you have brought to the church." His words evoked a standing ovation.

The Decline and Drift of Union Theological Seminary

By a hairsplitting vote of 68-64, the Presbytery of Coastal Carolina decided, on Feb. 24, 1996, not to adopt a session resolution that questioned the commitment of Union Theological Seminary in Virginia to Reformed theology and its adequacy as a training center for ministers of the Presbyterian Church (USA).

The resolution was submitted by the Pineland Presbyterian Church session after it learned that Union's theology professor, Douglas Ottati, refused to affirm the bodily resurrection of Jesus Christ and denied that Christ lived a sinless life.

Ottati states in his book, *Jesus Christ and Christian Vision*,[31] that he affirms "the resurrection," but not the bodily resurrection to which Scripture attests. Ottati's version of the resurrection suggests a "continuing presence" of Christ in the lives of his disciples. He believes that they "experienced" Christ's presence after his death, although it is not clear how he differentiates this experience from a residual memory.

---

30 *Presbyterian Outlook*, Vol. 176, No. 23.

31 Ottati, Douglas F., *Jesus Christ and Christian Vision* (Louisville, Ky.: Westminster John Knox Press edition, 1996), pp. 93-94.

Recognizing that his denial of the bodily resurrection could be a problem, Ottati wrote, "I am not insensitive to the fact that this interpretation yields few hard and fast rules for the preacher at Easter."[32] He was also clear that his views might prove challenging to those who affirm the authority of Scripture: "When I say that it is not necessary or appropriate to insist on Jesus' sinless perfection I do in fact depart from Hebrews."[33]

The Pineland church session said it was troubled that an institution of the church whose purpose is to prepare Presbyterians for ordained ministry would employ faculty members who deny "essential doctrines" of the faith.

Union's president Louis Weeks, who had earlier predicted in an interview that Ottati would one day be recognized as "a premier theologian," spent three days visiting Coastal Carolina Presbytery leaders during the week before the vote. He dismissed the theological controversy surrounding Ottati as a minor "fundamentalist" disturbance and said that the matter had been "put to rest."

During the Coastal Carolina Presbytery debate, supporters of the seminary lauded its years of service to the denomination. But the Rev. Brown Caldwell, a minister member of the presbytery and alumnus of the seminary, said, "This is not a peripheral dispute. It is about a central tenet of the Christian faith. We are talking here about Union's commitment to the historical resurrection of Jesus Christ. Without the resurrection, we have nothing to say."

A year later, Union Seminary again made the news when it invited Rosemary Radford Ruether to deliver the prestigious Sprunt Lectures. Ruether calls the resurrection of Jesus Christ "a myth created by males to assuage their own fear of death."[34] Her theology makes room for multiple deities that are encompassed into "the great womb within which all things, Gods and humans, sky and earth, humans and non-humans, are generated."[35]

Responding to public criticism for his having issued an invitation to Ruether, President Weeks told the *Richmond Times Dispatch* that he "enthusiastically endorsed her" and that "she is one of the pioneers in feminist theology."[36] Weeks added that he was surprised by the criticism that had

32 *Ibid.* p. 93.

33 Ottati, Douglas F., "My Christology," A paper distributed to Union Theological Seminary in Virginia trustees on May 6, 1995.

34 Ruether, Rosemary Radford, *Sexism and God-Talk* (Boston: Beacon Press, 1993), pp. 257-58.

35 *Ibid.*, p. 48.

36 *Richmond Times-Dispatch*, January 31, 1998.

been leveled in light of the fact that conservative scholar John Leith "used her books here in the 1970s."[37]

Leith responded in a letter to the newspaper: "This statement by Louis Weeks is misinformation and leaves the wrong conclusion. If I used her books in the seventies, it was as a reference or an illustration."[38] Leith said he was "dismayed" that Ruether had been invited to Union. She is "a person whose recent writings have denied every basic Christian doctrine from creation to redemption," he said.[39]

Building Community Among Strangers

A controversial study paper that called for building community by denying the lordship of Jesus Christ was derailed by the 1998 General Assembly, meeting in Charlotte, North Carolina. By a vote of 418-86, the Assembly rejected *Building Community Among Strangers*, a product of the Advisory Committee on Social Witness Policy (ACSWP). "I don't think tightening a few screws here and touching up a paint job there will be enough to fix this paper," said Rev. Thomas Theriault, one of two commissioners whose objections brought the issue to the floor. "This paper needs a dramatic redirection."[40]

A central thesis of the committee's paper was that religious differences divide people and that Christians can affirm Jesus Christ's lordship for themselves while affirming the validity of other people's gods. The paper equated believers in the truth of God's revelation with followers of "a jealous tribal God." It urged Presbyterians to become "Christian humanists," religious pluralists who believe that all beliefs about God are equally valid. To illustrate its point, the paper included an image of a banquet in which the food is blessed not only in the name of Jesus, "but also in the name of Allah, the Lord Krishna, Siddhartha Buddha, and the Goddess Gaia."[41]

When confronted by widespread criticism, committee members dropped the banquet illustration, but the theologically inclusive theme that the ban-

37 *Ibid.*

38 *Ibid.*, February 2, 1998.

39 *Ibid.*

40 *The Presbyterian Layman*, Vol. 31, No. 4, July/August, 1998.

41 Quotation from *Building Community Among Strangers*, a paper submitted to the 210th General Assembly (1998) of the Presbyterian Church (USA) and rejected by a vote of 418-86. A revised version that omitted this phrase was approved by the 211th General Assembly (1999) and published as a resource of the Office of the General Assembly, Item #OGA99028.

quet was meant to convey continued to run through the fabric of the document. That is what led Theriault, minister commissioner from San Diego, and Louise Holert, minister commissioner from Seattle, to challenge the committee's work before the entire General Assembly.

Theriault made a motion, which he called "a friendly amendment," that the committee produce a paper that "(1) is clearly centered around the confessional and biblical teaching about Christ as Lord of all the world and its only hope of reconciliation, and (2) embodies a tone of mutual respect for differing opinions within our church." Holert stated that the study paper needed this change because it "blurs the lines between 'cultural' and 'religious' pluralism."[42]

Allen Dean of Tres Rios Presbytery responded: "This amendment has been described as 'friendly.' With friends like this you don't need any enemies." Byron Schaffer, from the Presbytery of New York City agreed: "The very nature of this enterprise is to incorporate the broadest possible theological diversity." [43]

But Glenn Weaver of Lake Michigan Presbytery declared the paper not only outside the Presbyterian Church (USA)'s confessions, but "an act of hostility against them." Paul Pierson of San Gabriel Presbytery said, "I am a former missionary, and I find this material offensive. It is hostile to the world mission of the church."[44]

Rev. Donald Shriver, former President of Union Theological Seminary in New York and a member of the committee that produced the study, told commissioners that he thought rewriting the paper was unnecessary and that it would cost the church a great deal of money. He said that his committee had heard from the church and would make revisions in its final policy document. "Just trust us," he pleaded.[45]

But Theriault responded "Trust involves a track record, and the track record of this committee has been deeply troubling. We must give the world the best of what we have to offer. And our best is Jesus Christ. He is the only basis of bringing together our fractured world."[46]

At the conclusion of its debate, the 1998 General Assembly approved Theriault's motion, sending *Building Community Among Strangers* back to the committee, and asking that it produce a paper "more clearly centered

42 *The Presbyterian Layman*, Vol. 31. No. 4, July/August, 1998.

43 *Ibid.*

44 *Ibid.*

45 *Ibid.*

46 *Ibid.*

around Christ as Lord of all the world and its only hope of reconciliation ...."[47]

The following year, the 1999 General Assembly approved a revised version of *Building Community Among Strangers* that had removed much of the offensive language.[48] Members of the Presbyterian Renewal Network cheered the assembly's action, only to learn during a meeting in Louisville, Ky. two years later that the original, unabridged document was being offered for sale at the denomination's book store in the Presbyterian Church (USA) headquarters building. "Get a load of this," said Rev. Ilona Buzick, executive director of Presbyterian Elders in Prayer, as she displayed her newly purchased copy. "Why did we bother with the debate? It is as if the General Assembly never acted."

What Buzick discovered is illustrative of a frustration often experienced by Presbyterians who have fought for Biblical integrity within the Presbyterian Church (USA). While they have won significant victories at General Assembly meetings or at the presbytery level where General Assembly amendments to the Constitution must be ratified, they have found themselves unable to counter a denominational infrastructure that refuses to implement policies with which it does not agree.

Christ's Atonement Declared an Outdated Doctrine

Two Presbyterian theology professors, echoing one of the central themes of the ReImagining God conference, told a national conference of the Covenant Network of Presbyterians on Nov. 11, 2002 that the atoning death of Jesus Christ is an outdated doctrine.[49]

Not the cross, but "the incarnation itself may be redemptive," said a paper that was prepared for the conference by Anna Case-Winters, associate professor of theology at McCormick Theological Seminary. "He became as we are that we may become as he is – the incarnation that accomplishes our salvation."[50]

Parenthetically, the irony of Anna Case-Winters' affirmation should not go unnoticed. A radical feminist, she has painted herself into a corner by

47 Presbyterian Church (USA), *Minutes of the General Assembly*, 1998, p. 744.

48 Presbyterian Church (USA), *Minutes of the General Assembly*, 1999, pp. 30, 31.

49 Although the Covenant Network was organized for the purpose of overturning the denomination's ethical ordination standards, it subsequently broadened its scope to oppose the imposition of theological standards as well.

50 Case-Winters, Anna, "Who Do You Say That I Am? Believing in Jesus Christ in the 21st Century," Covenant Network Conference Address, November 9, 2002.

propounding a view that mirrors male-dominated Mormon doctrine. According to the Church of Latter Day Saints' belief, Mormon men (women are excluded) will become gods, co-equals with Christ.

In an affirming response to Case-Winters' paper, Paul Capetz, a theology professor at United Theological Seminary of the Twin Cities and formerly a member of the faculty at Union Theological Seminary in Virginia, agreed. "What about atonement? We don't need any more crucifixions." Nonetheless, Capetz said the cross is important to Christianity as a "symbol of the faith" – not as the redemptive work, but as a reminder that suffering is a part of the Christian life.[51]

Both Case-Winters and Capetz have been prominent in the left flank of the Presbyterian Church (USA). Case-Winters was appointed by controversial moderator Jack B. Rogers to be chair of the 214th General Assembly's Committee on Confessions and Theology. She has also served as a PCUSA delegate to the World Alliance of Reformed Churches.

She is the author of *God's Power: Traditional Understandings and Contemporary Challenges*, in which she says the Biblical view of an all-powerful God as well as the use of such terms as King and Father for God promote male superiority.

Capetz is known among Presbyterians for the fact that he forfeited his ordination to protest the prohibition against ordaining practicing homosexuals.

Case-Winters repeated the argument that some radical feminists have against the atonement: That it is child abuse for a father to sacrifice his son and serves to foster abuse in today's world.

She also quarreled with the righteous wrath of God. "It's not a matter of God's anger causing God to turn from us, but we turn from God," she said.

The theological views of Case-Winters and Capetz – which are far off the center of Reformed doctrine and classical Christian understanding – reflected the Covenant Network's growing kinship with "progressive theology" – the notion that Scripture is the product of a particular culture and that as cultures change, Scriptural interpretation must adapt in order to remain relevant to the context within which it is being read.

Capetz emphasized that point when he addressed the issue of atonement. He said Jesus was crucified and died in a time when many religions practiced animal sacrifice because they were influenced by the culture of their times.

51 Capetz, Paul, "Response to Anna Case-Winters' 'Who Do You Say that I Am? Believing In Jesus Christ in the 21st Century,'" Covenant Network Conference Address, November 9, 2002.

"Read the Scripture in context," Capetz said. "Insisting on an atonement for the remission of sin provided for an end to the sacrificial system. Paul uses the word sacrifice metaphorically."

'Witch' Addresses San Francisco Seminary

McCormick and Union in Richmond are not the only seminaries that have exposed aspiring Presbyterian ministers to syncretism and undermined the integrity of the gospel. On March 3, 1989, Starhawk, a west coast woman who describes herself as a witch, addressed students and faculty members from the pulpit of Stewart Chapel at San Francisco Theological Seminary. Her presentation included prayers offered to "powers under the earth."

When reports of Starhawk's visit appeared in the media, San Francisco's president, J. Randolph Taylor, issued a damage control statement. He described Starhawk's "lecture" (as opposed to a worship presentation) in Stewart Chapel as "a wide-ranging presentation which was focused primarily on creation spirituality and the interrelationship of all of life." Taylor insisted that there was "no service of worship, no sermon preached, and no corporate prayers."

Starhawk's religious views were well known prior to her visit to the seminary campus. Founder of two covens in San Francisco and a licensed minister of the Covenant of the Goddess, a legally recognized "church," she called herself "a priestess of the Old Religion," and claimed that her faith pre-dates Christianity by centuries.

The witch's visit was sponsored by the Feminist Perspectives Committee, a campus group composed of both students and faculty advisors. Committee members were drawn to Starhawk because of her belief that religion has special relevance to the women's movement. "Since the decline of the Goddess religions," she wrote in *The Spiral Dance*, "women have lacked religious models and spiritual systems that speak to female needs and experience … Through Goddess we can discover our strength, enlighten our minds, own our bodies, and celebrate our emotions."[52]

Starhawk's appearance at San Francisco Theological Seminary was both a reflection of ideologies being promoted by seminary leaders and a portent of things to come. In the year preceding her presentation, the Rev. Cynthia Campbell, a professor at Austin Theological Seminary who would later become president of McCormick Theological Seminary, authored a paper

52 Starhawk, *The Spiral Dance: A Rebirth of the Ancient Religion of the Great Goddess* (San Francisco: Harper, 1989).

titled "Theologies Written from Feminist Perspectives" that was distributed by the Presbyterian Church (USA) General Assembly to all pastors in February, 1988. In her paper, Campbell explained why, from the feminist perspective, many of traditional Christianity's standards were being abandoned. "No aspect of traditional Christian theology can remain immune to reconsideration and reconstruction," she said.

In 1993 similar ideologies would blossom to full flower in the Presbyterian Church (USA) – funded ReImagining God conference.

Problems with the Incarnation and Resurrection

It is not only in seminaries and national conferences that the denomination's Jesus problem has come to light. Several presbyteries have struggled with it.

In 1983, a theological controversy that had broken out in 1977 with the publication of *The Myth of God Incarnate*,[53] resurfaced among California Presbyterians. On Sept, 13, Professor John Hick, who had formerly taught theology at Birmingham University in England, Princeton Theological Seminary in New Jersey and had come to the faculty at Claremont Graduate School in Los Angeles, applied for membership in San Gabriel Presbytery. The presbytery admitted him on a 98-92 vote after a lengthy debate.

At issue was Hick's belief concerning Jesus Christ, which had surfaced in *The Myth of God Incarnate* and a more recent book, *God Has Many Names*.[54] According to Religion News Service, Hick had written that the idea of the incarnation has no literal meaning.[55]

Hick wrote: "Incarnation, in its full and proper sense, is not something directly presented in scripture. It is a construction built on the variegated evidence to be found there. Increased historical knowledge has enabled our generation to see this truth about the way in which incarnational doctrine emerged more clearly than some earlier generations."[56]

In a passage that Presbyterians who did away with "essential tenets" of Christian faith at the 1926 General Assembly could applaud, Hick wrote, "Many people, including both conservative believers and perhaps a still larger group of conservative unbelievers, will take exception to the thinking that is going on in this book. They will hold that Christianity consists and

53 Hick, John, *The Myth of God Incarnate* (Louisville: Westminster John Knox, 1977).

54 Hick, John, *God Has Many Names* (Louisville: Westminster Press, 1982).

55 Religion News Service, November 15, 1983.

56 Hick, John, *The Myth of God Incarnate*, p. 3.

always has consisted in a certain definite set of beliefs, and that theologians who seek to modify or 'reinterpret' those beliefs are being disingenuous: it would be more honest of them frankly to abandon the faith as no longer tenable. To this it must be replied that modem scholarship has shown that the supposed unchanging set of beliefs is a mirage."[57]

For Hick, the doctrine of the Trinity was an add-on by the early church, reflecting the language of ancient culture. "The proper conclusion seems to me to be that the notion of a special human being as a 'son of God' is a metaphorical idea which belongs to the imaginative language of a number of ancient cultures. The Christian tradition, however, has turned this poetry into prose, so that a metaphorical son of God became a metaphysical God the Son, second Person of a divine Trinity; and the resulting doctrine of a unique divine incarnation has long poisoned relationships both between Christians and Jews and between Christians and Muslims, as well as affecting the history of Christian imperialism in the Far East, India, Africa, and elsewhere."[58]

In 1987, after being ordered by the General Assembly Permanent Judicial Commission to review its decision, San Gabriel Presbytery voted to withdraw Hick's clergy status. In a statement following the decision, Hick said that the central issue was "my view of the other great world religions as spheres of salvation and my consequent diminution of the traditional absolute and exclusive claims of Christianity."[59]

Although he lost his bid to maintain clergy status, Professor Hick's prediction that his "type of Christology is developing within Presbyterianism" appears to have been on the mark. His argument against the Trinity surfaced full bloom in the 2006 General Assembly's reception of a paper on the subject, submitted by the denomination's Office of Theology and Worship. His suggestion that believing in the Incarnate Son would damage interfaith relations showed up, as we have discussed earlier, in Dirk Ficca's "What's the big deal about Jesus?" And the reader will recall that his view that Jesus is a stumbling block to peace was a dominant theme in *Building Community Among Strangers.*

That these themes have found their way onto the floor of other presbyteries can be seen in three presbytery incidents that are illustrative, one in Missouri, one in New Jersey and another in North Carolina.

---

57 *Ibid.*

58 *Ibid.*

59 Religion News Service, February 10, 1987.

Heartland Presbytery Debates "The Only Way?"

During a Nov. 15, 1995, Heartland Presbytery meeting, the Rev. Stu Austin, who was being examined for presbytery membership, said, "I believe that Jesus Christ is the Son of God and that He is the only way to salvation." According to those present, the Rev. Hal LeMert challenged the assertion, saying, "If that's your position, then I cannot vote for you." Later, in a telephone interview, LeMert was asked if "an essential tenet of the Reformed faith [is] that Jesus Christ is our only access to God?" "No. I don't think it is," he responded.[60]

Prompted by this discussion, the Roanoke Presbyterian Church of Kansas City submitted an overture that would have required ordained members of the presbytery to declare that "Jesus Christ is the only mediator between God and humankind and the only access to God is through Jesus Christ." Either sign it or resign your ordination in good conscience, the overture said.

Roanoke's overture triggered two days of "colloquy" by the presbytery on the question, "Who is Jesus?" Professors from McCormick Seminary, Union Seminary (Va.) and the General Assembly Office of Theology and Worship were invited to make presentations. McCormick's John Burkhart told the presbytery that attempts to define essential tenets of faith are "spawned and nurtured in mistrust." Opposing Roanoke's overture, he urged presbytery members to "look to the confessions, honor diversity of conscience, and trust the presbytery."

During the ensuing discussion, Rev. Merrill Proudfoot stated his belief that there are many truths. Rev. Doug Shulse said that persons of other faiths have approaches to God that are valid for them. Asked whether a Hamas terrorist who blew himself up with a schoolroom of children, believing that to be his sure path to God, was having a valid faith experience, Shulse snapped, "We are not here to cast aspersions on the Islamic faith."

Several elders shared their faith, giving testimonies of their belief that "Jesus Christ is the only mediator between God and humankind and the only access to God."

Finally, the presbytery adopted a revised version of Roanoke's overture, one that affirmed Jesus Christ as "the sole reconciler between humankind and God," but did not include any requirement that ministers subscribe to it as a condition of their continuing ordination.

---

60 *The Presbyterian Layman*, Vol. 29, No. 2, March/April, 1996.

THE 'IDEA' OF THE ATONEMENT REJECTED

On Nov. 20, 2002, the Presbytery of West Jersey opened its evening session with the sacrament of the Lord's Supper, voicing the familiar words, "This is my body broken for you. Do this in remembrance of me." Then it received into ministry a person who denies the divinity of Jesus Christ and rejects the "idea" that he died to save us from our sins.

The candidate, Helen Dekker, had little to say about the relationship between Jesus of Nazareth and God. She said she was thankful that Jesus "brought me under the wings of God's love," but beyond that it was not clear that she saw much more in him.

That led to questions. "Is Jesus God?" asked a member of the presbytery. "No," she replied. "He was filled with the spirit of God."

A woman who had served on the committee that recruited Dekker said "She teaches us to find the Spirit in ourselves, and she has helped us rewrite our mission statement. It is a little different from what we are used to, but we feel the Spirit with Helen leading us."

Another church member said, "I'll never forget the first sermon I heard her preach. It was on racism and tolerance."

When the vote was taken, Dekker was approved by a 3-1 majority.

BODILY RESURRECTION DENIED

Citing a lack of agreement among witnesses, a Presbytery of Western North Carolina investigating committee decided in November, 2003, not to call for a trial of a minister accused of heresy for allegedly denying that Christ rose bodily from the grave.

The committee said that Robert W. Martin III's "statements on the resurrection of Jesus Christ could and should have reflected the full witness of Scripture and the Confessions. They do not, however, place him outside of the Reformed tradition and he cannot properly be called a heretic."

At issue was the fact that, when asked "Do you believe in the literal, physical, bodily resurrection and ascension of Jesus Christ?" Martin said "No." Persons who were present during Martin's examination had mixed recollections of how Martin subsequently explained and possibly qualified his response.[61]

REIMAGINING'S GOD REVISITED

The 1993 General Assembly's rejection of ReImagining God themes did not put them to rest. In fact, denominational leaders who influence the

61 Presbytery of Western North Carolina, "Report of Investigating Committee," November, 2003.

selection of speakers for conferences, seminars and other events have kept ReImagining ideologues on a preferred speakers list. Following the 1993 General Assembly, Kwok-Pui-Lan was invited to address the Presbyterian Church (USA) Theology and Worship Ministry Unit. There she told her listeners that people who do not profess a belief in Jesus Christ are "anonymous Christians." She said that while Christ is central, "others are not excluded." "While Christ is unique for me, I understand that Buddha is unique for others ... The important thing for me is not to convince others that Christ is unique," she said.

Another invited speaker was Virginia Ramey Mollenkott. She became a hot item on the lecture circuit after publishing her views that God is not a divine personal "other" who judges us. Instead, God is a divine force that binds all of creation and is present in all of creation. For Mollenkott, human beings are a manifestation of the divine. She writes, "I am a manifestation of God. God Herself! God Himself! God Itself! Above all. Through all. And in us all."[62]

Later in the year, the Women's Ministry Unit of the General Assembly Council met on retreat in Daytona Beach. Using a liturgy from *Birthings and Blessings*,[63] a booklet funded in part by the Justice for Women subcommittee, the women confessed liturgically, "We have discovered the truth of the Divine within us, around us, and among us." Then they called on God to "challenge us to reach the stage of autonomy where we are authorities of our own experience."

Commenting on this trend toward self divinization, Philip Turner, Dean of the Berkeley Divinity School at Yale University, suggested that Jesus' summary of the law had been inverted to read: "Thou shalt love thy neighbor with all thy heart, soul, mind and strength. This is the first and great commandment. And the second is like unto it, namely, thou shalt love God as thyself."[64]

In 1994, Kwok Pui-lan was chosen to write for Presbyterian Women's official publication, *Horizons*.[65]

In December, 1994, the Presbyterian Church (USA) co-sponsored an ecumenical student conference in St. Louis called "Celebrate! Gathering at

62 Mollenkott, Virginia R., *Sensuous Spirituality: Out from Fundamentalism* (New York: Crossroad Publishing Company, 1992).

63 Mitchell, Rosemary Catalano and Ricciuti, Gail Anderson, *Birthings and Blessings: Liberating Worship Services for the Inclusive Church* (New York: Crossroad Publishing Company, 1991).

64 Turner, Philip, *First Things*, October, 1992.

65 *Horizons*, September/October, 1994.

the Crossroads." The program, which attracted more than 1,800 students, campus ministers and denominational staff spread a thin veneer of traditional teaching over neopagan and radical feminist ideologies.

Keynote speaker Edwina Gately told the group, "I believe God lives about three inches from my belly button ... if we're in touch with the God-given seed in each of us then we know what we have to do."[66] Gately was associated with the dissident Catholic group Call to Action. In her book, *A Warm Moist Salty God*, which quickly sold out in the conference bookstore, Gately wrote, "We have within us everything that is necessary for transformation, everything that is required for fullness of life."[67]

Also participating in the program was Rita Nakashima Brock. In her "Bible Study" presentation, she compared Jesus' wilderness temptations to Lakota Indian vision quests, his baptism to sweat lodge purification rites, and John the Baptist to a spirit guide. Jesus thus became a human model of one seeking self-understanding through altered states of consciousness.[68]

Those who bought the Bible study leader's book *Journeys by Heart: A Christology of Erotic Power* in the conference bookstore read, "Christ is a major problem in feminist theology. That problem has been born of an unholy trinity, father-son-holy ghost, that has cradled Christ in its patriarchal arms." Brock continued, "I will be developing a Christology not centered in Jesus, but in relationship and community and the whole-making, healing center of Christianity. In that sense, Christ is what I am calling Christa/Community."[69]

In March, 1995, Presbyterian Survey, an official denominational publication, ran a series of articles promoting feminist theology, including one by ReImagining speaker Delores Williams, which rejected "the theory of Christ's atonement." Williams was also featured in June in a weeklong seminar at Ghost Ranch, a Presbyterian Church (USA) conference center.

In 1996, ReImagining speaker Ada Maria Isasi-Diaz was the keynote speaker at the Presbyterian Peacemaking Conference. There, she described the church as "a human construct ... oppressive to women." She called on her listeners to "prophetic actions of complaint and recriminations, of denunciation, and calling to conversion."

66 *The Presbyterian Layman*, Vol. 28, No. 1, January/February, 1995.

67 Gately, Edwina, *A Warm Moist Salty God: Women Journeying Toward Wisdom* (Naperville, Il.: Source Books, 1993).

68 *The Presbyterian Layman*, Vol. 28, No. 1, January/February, 1995.

69 Brock, Rita Nakashima, *Journeys By Heart: A Christology of Erotic Power* (New York: Crossroad Publishing, 1988).

In June of 1996, the Women's Ministries Program Area, National Ministries Division and Congregational Ministries Division published *Sisters Struggling in the Spirit: A Women of Color Theological Anthology*.[70] Contributors included Delores Williams, Kwok Pui-lan, Ada Maria Isasi-Diaz and Jacquelyn Grant.

Also celebrated by Women's Ministries as a "recommended resource," was Miriam Theresa Winter, keynote speaker at the follow-up 1995 ReImagining conference, where she told her audience that relying on Scripture alone is "like peering at the universe through a straw." In her book *WomanWord*, she included "A Psalm in Search of a Goddess," that made supplication to pagan goddesses Sophia, Ishtar, Inanna, Hathor, Cybele, Nut, Hera, Athene, Aphrodite, Artemis, Demeter, Isis and Gaia.

Winter's poems were quoted in Presbyterian Youth Curriculum and the Presbyterian College Women's Network Issues packet in 1996. At the "HerStory 1996" conference at the Presbyterian Church (USA) Massanetta Springs conference center, Winter's songs were sung and prayers were offered to Sophia.

The 1996 lineup of speakers and seminar leaders at Ghost Ranch included Beverly Wildung Harrison, "Discerning the Signs of the Times: A Forum in the Christianity and Crisis Tradition." Lesbian Episcopal priest Carter Heyward joined Harrison in leading the seminar. In Heyward's book, *Touching Our Strength: The Erotic as Power and the Love of God*,[71] she announces, "sexual pleasure [is] a delightful relational happening that needs no higher justification ... God is our relational power ... we are the womb in which God is being born."

At the fourth ReImagining conference in 1997, lesbian activist and former Presbyterian Church (USA) minister Letty Russell led a seminar in which she said, "In my local presbytery last year, I went to the ministerial relations committee and told them I was retiring from the presbytery because of the church's position on the ordination of homosexuals." She continued, "As a lesbian, I decided to use my energy on subversion and not on church committees. I've decided to be in, but not of, the church."[72]

70 Lewis, Nantawn, Hernandez, Lydia, Locklear, Helen, Winbush, Robina, *Sisters Struggling in the Spirit: A Women of Color Theological Anthology* (Louisville: Presbyterian Church (USA), Women's Ministry Unit, 1994).

71 Heyward, Carter, *Touching Our Strength: The Erotic as Power and the Love of God* (New York: Harper and Row, 1989).

72 *The Presbyterian Layman*, Vol. 30, No. 1, January/February, 1997.

Sexuality and Pagan Spirituality

Appearing in the 1997 General Assembly edition of *More Light Update*, a bimonthly publication of Presbyterians for Lesbian and Gay Concerns, was a request for contributions to a book on "dykes and spirituality." The announcement suggested that homosexuality involves not simply a choice of sexual partners, but a religion that differs in significant respects from Christian faith.

"We're putting together a big, fat, eclectic book about dykes and our spirituality – our connection to The Source, the sacred, the realm of the spirit, the depths, our essential selves, and all the other ways of describing IT," said the announcement.[73]

The advertisement continued, "Dykes! Send us writing or art about what inspires you, particularly: profound mystical experiences, connection to The Source ... the connection between being a dyke and your spiritual expression ... the connection between sex and spirit ... How do you connect to The Source? Prayer? Art? Ritual? Magic? Sex? Meditation? Music? Dreams? Trance? Dance? Mind-altering substances?"[74]

An additional advertisement in the paper called for contributions to an anthology of "writings by bisexual people of faith (Jews, Christians, Pagans, Quakers, UUs [Unitarian Universalists], those following other spiritual paths)." The advertisement identified the focus as "connections/intersections/links between your sexuality and your spirituality?" It called for contributors with "a range of handling bisexuality,"including "swingers, singles, couples, celibate folks, etc."[75]

Presbyterians for Lesbian and Gay Concerns, which changed its name to More Light Presbyterians in order to reflect its inclusion of bisexual and transgendered persons, is no peripheral lobbying group in the denomination, for several of its leaders also hold memberships in the denominationally funded Presbyterian Health, Education and Welfare Association, and attorney Tony De La Rosa, a member of Presbyterians for Lesbian and Gay Concerns' board, has served as chairman of the General Assembly Advisory Committee on Litigation, the committee that guides Stated Clerk Clifton Kirkpatrick on the filing of Presbyterian Church (USA) amicus briefs.

This organization's attempts to forge connections between religious and sexual activities do not represent a new phenomenon in church history. The prophets of Israel often did battle with fertility cults and temple prostitution

73 More Light Presbyterians, *More Light Update*, July/August, 1997.

74 *Ibid.*

75 *Ibid.*

that infiltrated Israel's religion from Canaanite culture. And New Testament passages, particularly Paul's epistles, warned the early church to beware of those who would introduce both homosexual and heterosexual aberrations into the community of faith. The Old and New Testaments describe these practices as unethical, but they also describe them as pagan.

More Light Presbyterians similarly recognize a connection between their avowed sexual behavior and non-Christian religions. Presbyterian Jane Spahr, who describes her role as that of a "lesbian evangelist," contrasts her movement's ideology with that of historic Christian faith, saying, "Maybe we're talking about a different God."[76]

Appearing with the sex and spirituality advertisements on the inside cover of *More Light Update* were advertisements for gay/lesbian/bisexual conferences at Stony Point and Ghost Ranch, two official conference centers of the Presbyterian Church (USA) that are supported by its mission budget.

'ReImagining Revival'

In 1998, almost 900 women, including 180 Presbyterians, many of whom were employed by denominational offices at national and regional levels, seminaries and colleges, and Christian educator positions, gathered in St. Paul, Minn. in an attempt to "revive" the movement that had begun with their 1993 ReImagining God conference. Presbyterian minister Sally Hill, an organizer of the event who has taught seminars at the Ghost Ranch conference center, led the group in a "Milk and Honey" ritual: "This is the body of God for healing the bitterness of the human heart ... We have seen the power, rising from the earth ... Together, we have given birth to a ReImagining Community which extends to every corner of the world!"[77]

The event attracted a collection of speakers who have been featured at Presbyterian Church (USA) conferences and seminary gatherings around the country. Beverly Harrison, a Presbyterian professor of ethics at Union Theological Seminary in New York confessed her embarrassment at being a Presbyterian at a time when the denomination was beginning to reaffirm biblical sexual standards for its ordained leaders. "Don't get me started on the heartbreak of being a Presbyterian," she said.[78]

76 Macksound, Anne, and Ankele, John, "Maybe We're Talking About A Different God: Homosexuality and the Church" (Lanham, MD: National Film Network, 1994).

77 *The Presbyterian Layman*, Vol. 31, No. 3, May/June, 1998.

78 *Ibid.*

Mary Ann Lundy was given a standing ovation when she appeared at the conference. Lundy, an official of the World Council of Churches, encouraged members of the audience to develop alliances, "to be ecumenical in the broadest sense of the word." Specifically, she encouraged connections not only across lines of gender and geography but those of religion as well. "We are learning that to be ecumenical is to move beyond the boundaries of Christianity," she said. "You see," concluded Lundy, "yesterday's heresies are becoming tomorrow's *Book of Order*."[79]

Delores Williams, a Presbyterian professor at Union Theological Seminary in New York, who attracted national attention at the first ReImagining conference by suggesting, "I don't think we need folks hanging on crosses and blood dripping and weird stuff," called for a "church without walls ... a community where people can be free ... where no sexuality is unclean. In the heart and soul of the deities, we are all loved, and it doesn't matter who we're sleeping with."[80]

Carter Heyward, a professor at Episcopal Divinity School in Cambridge, Mass. who was recommended by the Women's Ministry Unit of the Presbyterian Church (USA) as a "theological resource," expressed her view that all of life is simply an extrusion of divine reality, meaning that all persons and things are essentially divine and that no person can claim to be unique, not even Jesus: "While nobody, even Jesus, is divine in and of him or herself, everybody, like Jesus, is able to god, and I use this [god] as a verb ... That is what we are to do ... to god, and that is what the Jesus story is all about."[81]

Resurrection Re-imagined in Texas

The Rev. Jim Rigby, minister of St. Andrews Presbyterian Church in Austin, Tex., has made the news on several fronts in recent years. In 2005, he participated in a marriage service for 50 same-sex couples, violating a ruling of the General Assembly Permanent Judicial Commission that prohibits such services. A formal accusation was brought against Rigby, but an investigating committee of his presbytery declined to charge him with an offense, so the matter was dropped.

In 2006, Rigby again drew attention when his congregation admitted Robert Jensen to its membership. Writing for an online magazine, Jensen

79 *Ibid.*

80 *Ibid.*

81 *Ibid.*

explained, "Why I am a Christian (Sort of ...)." Jensen said, "I don't believe in God. I don't believe Jesus Christ was the son of a God that I don't believe in, nor do I believe Jesus rose from the dead to ascend to a heaven that I don't believe exists."[82] Jensen said he joined the church because he approved of its social service projects and political stands.

Rigby defended the decision to admit to the membership of a Christian church a person who does not believe what the church believes. He said that it was important to "build bridges" with non-believers and that policies of inclusiveness and diversity would widen Christian fellowship.

In 2007, Rigby's sermon on the Resurrection drew public attention. Writing for *Texas Monthly's* Faith Based Series, William Martin reported on his visit to St. Andrews Presbyterian Church and a sermon by Rigby. In the article, Martin quotes Rigby: "The Resurrection took place when the community was born. What rose was the body of Christ. Maybe a body got up; I don't care. That's not the point ... It's a symbol of something deeper ... What the great saints and sages have discovered ... is that they are not just one little life; they are the Big Life and so are you. And they set up ways of understanding, through rituals, through Communion, through baptism, to teach you that you also are the One Life ... What these symbols are talking about are not things that happened; they are things that are always true. The Resurrection is happening now ... Heaven is not another world someplace else. It's a profound understanding of this world, of that which is not born and that which does not die."[83]

The January, 2007 Saint Andrews church newsletter referred church members to the *Texas Monthly* piece, calling it "quite an interesting article," and announcing that copies of the article were available in the church foyer. The newsletter announcement offered no disclaimers or suggestions that Rigby's sermon was misquoted.[84]

'Christ' in Other Places

On the ecumenical scene, The World Council of Churches is taking giant strides toward stretching its boundaries to include non-Christians. On February 15, 2006, his Holiness Aram I, moderator of the WCC's Central Committee and leader of the Armenian Apostolic Church in Lebanon, addressed the 9th assembly of the WCC, calling on ecumenical Christians to "come out of our frozen, ossified, petrified churches" and recognize the Christ in

82 *Counterpunch*, March 7, 2006.

83 *Texas Monthly*, January, 2007, p. 38.

84 The AGAPE News, Vol. 2, No. 1.

other places. "We cannot confine the economy, practice, activity, and saving action of Jesus Christ within the church," he said.[85]

In his message to the assembly, Aram I recognized that institutional ecumenism is "facing tremendous difficulty." Underscoring his point, he referenced leading member denominations, including the Presbyterian Church (USA), that are losing members at an increasingly rapid rate. "The world context today challenges institutional ecumenism, which must go through the process of transformation, no longer being confined within institutional structures," he said.[86]

The Christian church today lives in a pluralist world, a fact that is amplified by "globalization," Aram I said. "The new environment in which we live questions exclusivist, monological, and self-centered self-understanding, and calls for a dialogical self-definition," he said.[87]

This means that we must redefine the concept of "otherness," which has heretofore meant separateness. Encouraging inter-religious dialogue, Aram I said, "to discover the 'other,' is to rediscover oneself. The churches' missionary outreach must not be perceived as a reaction 'against' the stranger, but as a proactive engagement 'with' our neighbor."[88]

The "engagement" to which Aram I referred is to be experienced in "dialogue," not in attempts to persuade others to the truth of the gospel. He said that he believes the gospel is true, but that Christians should not insist on it. "The specificity and integrity of each religion should be respected in dialogue," he said.[89]

Aram I argued that his approach toward non-Christian religions is based on faith in the Triune God. He suggested that if one revisits "the Logos Christology" of the early church, he will see that "the Christ embraces the whole cosmos," not just the church. "The Holy Spirit's work is cosmic; it reaches in mysterious ways to people of all faiths. Therefore, the church is called to discern the signs of the 'hidden' Christ and the presence of the Holy Spirit in other religions and in the world, and bear witness to God's salvation in Christ."[90]

During a press conference, Aram I was asked if his pluralist view con-

85 World Council of Churches, 9th Assembly, "Report of Moderator Aram I," Document No. A01. See also *Transforma Mundo* #3, February 16, 2006.

86 *Ibid.*

87 *Ibid.*

88 *Ibid.*

89 *Ibid.*

90 *Ibid.*

stituted a theological equivalency between Christianity and non-Christian religions.

"I do not choose to answer in these terms," he replied. "Jesus does not belong to the churches. He belongs to all humanity. He is savior of the world. There are people who accept him and those who do not. But he belongs to us all."[91]

What do Presbyterians Believe?

A perusal of presbytery debates across the denomination reveals that the question, "What's the big deal about Jesus?" refuses to go away. It is asked in numerous forms, often in the context of presbytery ordination examinations. In recent years, the trend among presbyteries has been to refer such discussions to small groups, typically their examinations committee or committee on ministry, thereby keeping potentially inflammatory disputes under wraps. On those occasions when committee decisions are challenged before the whole presbytery, they are often settled, not as theological issues, but on questions of polity, e.g., did the committee have the right to make such a decision? rather than the more substantive question, did the committee make the right decision? After all, without standards, who is to determine if a decision is right?

Occasionally, in the midst of such disputes, the suggestion is made that the underlying theological issue be referred to higher governing bodies – ultimately to the General Assembly – for a definitive ruling that would apply to all churches. Inevitably, such suggestions are scuttled by reference to the 1926 General Assembly, where it was determined that each presbytery may determine for itself what constitutes "essential tenets of Christian faith." Apparently, one presbytery's tenet is as good as another.

Over the years that have passed since 1926, ministers who entertain radically different beliefs regarding the person and work of Jesus Christ have been ordained. In the course of their careers, they have moved from one presbytery to another, thus stirring the pot of variant beliefs. It is not surprising, therefore, that attempts to establish a denomination-wide standard have failed. The pluralism that has been so thoroughly woven into the fabric of denominational life, and the manner in which postmodernism allows words to mean whatever their speakers (or listeners) want them to mean, makes it impossible to assess what the Presbyterian Church (USA) believes about Jesus.

91 World Council of Churches Press Conference, Porto Alegre, Brazil, February 14, 2006.

Presbyterians and Pluralism

Pluralism argues that all religions and philosophies contain elements of truth, and that no religion can claim final and definitive truth. Underlying that view is the assumption that religions are philosophies of life that are of human origin. They are human attempts to conceive a divine reality that cannot be fully known.

Pluralism insists that all religious ideas are equally valid and equally defective. Its adherents promote their view as a generous, gracious, respectful and humble way to embrace theological differences. Conversely, they regard those who profess exclusivist convictions as narrow-minded, intolerant, bigoted, and inhospitable toward persons of other faiths, or, as some prefer to describe it, "other faith perspectives."

The Parliament of the World's Religions

A colorful celebration of pluralism occurred at the 1993 Parliament of World's Religions in Chicago. According to the Presbyterian News Service, the involvement of evangelical Christians was "noticeably lacking."[92]

That did not stop some 20 Presbyterian leaders from attending, including a key Parliament organizer, the Rev. David Ramage, who had recently retired from the presidency of McCormick Presbyterian Theological Seminary. Ramage, who served as chair of the Parliament's board of trustees, said he hoped the Chicago event would serve as "a documentation of a new era." He told reporters, "We live in the midst of genuine religious and multicultural reality. There is a mammoth transformation going on in religious and cultural life. Yet most people in the suburbs have blinders on."[93]

Ramage was not the only prominent Presbyterian Church (USA) leader to attend the Chicago event. Joining him were former General Assembly moderator Thelma Adair, the Rev. Syngman Rhee, who was serving as transitional manager of the denomination's Worldwide Ministries Division, the Rev. Jay Rock, director of interfaith relations for the National Council of Churches and a Presbyterian leader, and Margaret O. Thomas, associate for interfaith relations in the Worldwide Ministries division.

Referring to the event as "an exotic extravaganza of the first order," John R. Coyne, Jr. described what he saw: "Hindus, Sikhs, Muslims, Jains, Bahais, Zoroastrians, neo-Pagans, Indians of both the Calcutta and Rosebud variety, witches, warlocks, goddesses, and at least one old Beat poet –

92 Presbyterian News Service, Nov. 1993. See also Gill, Theo Jr., "The Parliament of World Religions," *Presbyterian Outlook*, Vol. 175, No. 36.

93 *Ibid.*

garbed in a great variety of robes, dresses, gowns, cylindrical Egyptian headdresses, turbans, cowls, hoods, Chicago Cubs baseball caps, at least one tam-o'-shanter, and in the case of Andras Arthen, a member of the Covenant of the Goddess, a wolf's head headdress, which he would wear to great effect on September 1, capering in the light of the full moon with his fellow wiccans and wiccanettes in the wold, a/k/a Grant Park."[94]

The centerpiece of the Parliament's agenda was a "Declaration of a Global Ethic" that the event's planners hoped all participants would sign. Given the diversity of the group, there were problems from the start over using the word, "God." Swiss theologian Hans Kung, author of the declaration's initial draft, explained that including God would have "excluded all Buddhists and many faith groups with different views of God and the divine."[95]

Kung said that when Parliament participants finally came to agreement, his draft had been drastically reduced. "We have here a minimum ethic," he said of a document that, according to Coyne, "condemned environmental crimes, anti-woman violence, and hate crimes in general."[96]

"The high point of the meeting," reported Coyne, "came with the blessings administered by Lady Olivia Robertson of the neo-Pagan (no paleos were in attendance) Fellowship of Isis, much to the delight of the Rev. Baroness Cara-Marguerite Drusilla of the Pagan (also neo-) Lyceum of Benus of Healing, who nodded her Egyptian headdress and waved her hands. Lady Olivia shook a rattle and chanted in a loud voice: 'Holy Goddess Isis, Mother of all beings, come to thy children.'"[97]

Parenthetically, the Rev. Dirk Ficca, keynote speaker for the Presbyterian Peacemaking Conference whose "What's the big deal about Jesus?" caused a denominational stir in 2000, is employed by the Parliament of the World's Religions. His ministry with that organization has been deemed valid by Chicago Presbytery.

The Impossibility of Pluralism

Gavin D'Costa, a Trinitarian Catholic and world-renowned philosophical theologian at Bristol University, once held the pluralist view. But in 1994, D'Costa astounded an audience at Kings College, London when, in the

94 Coyne, John R. Jr., "Ultimate Reality in Chicago," *The National Review*, November, 1993.

95 *Ibid.*

96 *Ibid.*

97 *Ibid.*

course of a lecture, he renounced his pluralist position. He told his audience that after careful analysis of numerous religions, he was obliged to recognize that every religion's truth claim necessarily excludes contrary positions.[98]

Lesslie Newbigin, who served for nearly 40 years as a missionary in India and was long active in international ecumenical organizations, clearly understood the exclusivist nature of every religion and ideology: "It is understandable that anyone faced with the clashing diversity of religious commitments should seek some basis for unity among them, or at least some agreed common framework. The difficulty is that we are dealing here with ultimate commitments, and the basis that I accept can only be my commitment. There have been many attempts to find a basis that all could accept, but none of them escapes this necessity."[99]

Disciples of Jesus Christ attest to the fact that he is God Incarnate. Islam says that he is not. Both positions cannot be true. To affirm, as the pluralists do, a position that encompasses these contradictory religious claims is to embrace a self-contradiction. As the prophet Elijah saw centuries ago, pluralism's attempt to encompass mutually exclusive faiths represents a self-inflicted injury. "How long will you go limping between two opinions?" he asked. "If the Lord is God, follow him; but if Baal, follow him!"[100]

Based on a self-contradiction that defies the most elementary principle of rational thought,[101] the pluralist position self-destructs. This observation led Friedhelm Hardy, a comparative religions scholar at Kings College, London to declare, "Religious pluralism is demonstrable nonsense."[102]

Contrary to their claim of graciousness, hospitality and humility, pluralists host an arrogance of their own, for, like other religions whose exclusiveness they criticize, their scheme rejects every truth claim except their own. Pluralism simply creates another, separate religion that is as exclusive as those it seeks to combine. D'Costa observes, "All pluralists are committed to holding some form of truth criteria and by virtue of this, anything

98 D'Costa, Gavin, "The Impossibility of a Pluralist View of Religions" Religious Studies 32, Cambridge University Press, June, 1996, pp. 223-232.

99 Newbigin, Lesslie, *The Open Secret* (Grand Rapids: Wm. B. Erdmans, 1995), p. 162.

100 I Kings 18:21.

101 The first rule of logic is that a proposition and its opposite cannot both be true at the same time.

102 Hardy, Friedhelm, *The Religious Culture of India* (Cambridge: Cambridge University Press, 1994).

that falls foul of such criteria is excluded from counting as truth."[103]

To suggest that the ailing Presbyterian Church (USA) legitimize a system that encompasses theological opposites (Jesus is the way, the truth, and the life vs. Jesus is a way, a truth, and a life) is to endorse pluralism. It institutionalizes a competing religion that lacks both intellectual and theological integrity. It has been thoroughly discredited by scholars like Lesslie Newbigin,[104] Gavin D'Costa, Thomas F. Torrance,[105] Friedhelm Hardy, Alvin Plantinga,[106] Nicolas Wolterstorff,[107] and others who have devoted their lives to the engagement of the gospel with world religions.

That this pluralism, which has contributed so substantially to the Presbyterian Church (USA)'s theological crisis, could now be proffered as a solution to that crisis strikes rational observers as the height of absurdity. There is, of course, an acceptable diversity of ethnicity, culture, and expression in the life of a world-wide church. But, as the Book of Acts clearly demonstrates in its description of Pentecost, the glue that anchors that diversity is a common commitment to the Lord Jesus Christ as he is revealed in Scripture to people of every race and nationality.

Choosing diversity as an end in itself suggests that Presbyterians are best united by being divided on foundational issues of Christian faith and life. Such a notion is foreign to the gospel. Allowing a denomination to balkanize itself into mutually exclusive faith groups, e.g., the 2001 General Assembly's decision to encompass incompatible convictions concerning the singular saving Lordship of Jesus Christ, has resulted in a denomination that believes everything. But a denomination that believes everything, in effect, believes nothing, and a denomination that believes nothing has nothing to offer to an unredeemed world.

Early Warnings

It should have come as no surprise to denominational managers that their plunge into pluralism would result in massive membership losses. In 1993,

103 D'Costa, Gavin, "The Impossibility of a Pluralist View of Religions" *Religious Studies 32*, Cambridge University Press, June, 1996, pp. 223-232.

104 Newbigin, Lesslie, *Foolishness to the Greeks* (London: SPCK, 1986) (BR115, C8).

105 Torrance, Thomas F., *The Christian Doctrine of God, One Being Three Persons* (Edinburgh: T. & T. Clark, Ltd., 1996), p. 22 ff.

106 Plantinga, Alvin, "Advice to Christian Philosophers," *Faith and Philosophy: A Journal of the Society of Christian Philosophers*, Vol. 1, 1984.

107 Wolterstorff, Nicolas, *Reason Within the Bounds of Religion* (Grand Rapids: Erdmans, 1976).

sociologists Dean Hoge, Benton Johnson and Donald Luidens released a study of declining mainline denominations, paying particular attention to the Presbyterian Church (USA) as representative of the mainline groups. They attributed the decline in membership to a "lay liberalism" that they found among former members of the denomination and among current members whose membership was at risk.

"Lay liberalism" was defined by Hoge, Johnson, and Luidens as a general belief in a higher being, a desire to follow the golden rule, and belief in universal salvation which denies the unique work of Christ and instead holds that all the world's religions teach basically the same thing. The authors wrote, "Most lay liberals 'prefer' Christianity to other faiths, but they are unable to ground their preference in strong truth claims. A few simply told us that Christianity is 'true for me,' whereas Buddhism or Islam may be true for others and some explained that they preferred Christianity because they were raised in that faith."[108]

The authors concluded that the reason for mainline denominational decline and, in particular, the losses of the Presbyterian Church (USA) lies in the prevalence of this "lay liberalism." They noted that "the single best predictor of church participation turned out to be belief – orthodox Christian belief, and especially the teaching that a person can be saved only through Jesus Christ. Virtually all ... who believe this are active members of a church ... 95 percent of the dropouts ... do not believe it."[109]

Hoge, Johnson and Luidens' observations suggest that the Presbyterian Church (USA)'s losses are the result of two membership movements. "Lay liberals" drift into non-participation, wherein they are ultimately placed on the inactive roll, and persons who are committed to orthodox Christian belief are moving their membership to evangelical churches, often nondenominational, that they find more theologically compatible.

Mega-Church Lessons

In the same period in which Hoge, Johnson and Luidens were conducting their study of denominational decline, the Rev. A. Russell Stevenson, senior minister of First Presbyterian Church in Baton Rouge, La. conducted a study of Presbyterian congregations that were growing. Stevenson listed the 48 largest Presbyterian congregations, measured not by membership, but by average weekly attendance at worship. Citing church growth experts

108 Hoge, Dean, Johnson, Benton, and Luidens, Donald, "Mainline Churches: the Real Reason for Decline," *First Things*, March 1993.

109 *Ibid.*

Lyle Schaller and Carl George, Stevenson said that membership statistics in themselves are meaningless as indicators of a congregation's vitality.

When Stevenson applied average weekly attendance and annual giving per member statistics to the 48 largest Presbyterian congregations, nine congregations were deemed "not very healthy" and were dropped from the list. The remaining 39 congregations were reshuffled on the vitality scale according to the new criteria.

"I am at least passingly acquainted with 34 of these 39 churches," said Stevenson, "and the remarkable common factor which emerges is that *they are all evangelical churches!*

"I recognize that my statement reflects an opinion rather than the results of a scientific study, but I think that anyone who knows these churches would confirm their significant, theological similarity."[110]

Stevenson continued, "My own observation of these mega-churches leads me to the inescapable conclusion that the key factor which puts them in the vital, high-growth category is *theological*. In many other areas of inquiry (demographics, for example) these churches span a broad spectrum of differences. Theology is clearly a common bond."[111]

Stevenson expressed his hope that the denomination in which his 39 churches and "the hundreds of [vital] smaller churches which resemble them theologically" live would not "undermine and offend" the theology that spawns their growth by surrounding them with theological pluralism. "Such a future," he said, "would discourage the development of mega-churches."[112]

'Who do you say that I am?'

One must conclude that the Presbyterian Church (USA) has a problem with Jesus. It cuts to the core of his question to his disciples, "Who do you say that I am?"[113] When Peter responded in faith, "You are the Christ, son of

110 *The Presbyterian Layman*, Vol. 26, No. 5, September/October, 1993.

111 *Ibid.*

112 *Ibid.*

113 Those who remember Moses' encounter with the Lord will recognize the "I Am" in Jesus' question. A devout Jew would fall on his face before that word, for YHWEH is the Lord's revelation of himself. Composed solely of consonants, the word is indecipherable, bathed in the divine mystery. The Creator of heaven and earth alone chooses how much of himself he will reveal. Sinful humanity is ill equipped to look into the face of God. In Jesus' question, he makes the crucial connection between himself and the fullness of God, offering the listener an opportunity to respond in faith.

the living God," Jesus acknowledged that Peter had been blessed. "Flesh and blood did not reveal this to you, Peter, but my Father who is in heaven."

The Presbyterian Church (USA) has been toying with "flesh and blood" answers to Jesus' question, speculation derived from human imagination and culture. In so doing, it has chosen philosophy over theology, cutting itself off from the source of truth. "Who do you say that I am?" can be answered only by the One who poses the question. He is the one Word of God who reveals himself to us, full of grace and truth.

Covenant

Holy Scripture

"I appeal to you therefore, brethren, by the mercies of God, to present your bodies as a living sacrifice, holy and acceptable to God, which is your spiritual worship. Do not be conformed to this world, but be transformed by the renewal of your mind, that you may prove what is the will of God, what is good and acceptable and perfect."

Romans 12:1-2

The Constitution

Q. What does the seventh commandment teach us?
A. That all unchastity is condemned by God, and that we should therefore detest it from the heart, and live chaste and disciplined lives, whether in holy wedlock or in single life.

The Heidelberg Catechism

"They who, upon pretense of Christian liberty, do practice any sin, or cherish any lust, do thereby destroy the end of Christian liberty; which is, that, being delivered out of the hands of our enemies, we might serve the Lord without fear, in holiness and righteousness before him, all the days of our life."

The Westminster Confession of Faith
Chapter XX

Broken Covenant

"Do anything that appeals to both partners. You are in complete control over what you do sexually and with whom."

Brochure for teenage boys, distributed at
The Presbyterian Youth Triennium, 1989

Chapter Six

Human Sexuality

In 1966, denominational leaders began mentioning that which had heretofore been deemed publicly unmentionable. In November of that year, the United Presbyterian Church Council on Church and Society initiated "a study of the Christian concept of sexuality in the human community." The council said it would "explore the mystery of sexuality in a broad range of human experience; identify and analyze the forces that enhance or inhibit the realization of sexual values; and evaluate the church's role and responsibility in interpreting the meaning of sexuality and in bringing a Christian ethical view to bear upon its expression in human relationships."

The fact that the Council on Church and Society was initiating this study was itself instructive and could well have presaged the direction that it would take. Paramount on the council's scale of values was "justice."

Only one pastor made it into the study group. Other participants were drawn from academia, professional associations (with special emphasis on psychology), media and denominational bureaucracies.

The Report and Its 'Attachment'

In November, 1969, the Task Force's 200-page report, "Sexuality and the Human Community," was received and studied by the Council on Church and Society. In 1970, the Council concluded its study and directed that its report be transmitted to the 1970 General Assembly with the request that the assembly "receive the report, direct that it be published and recommend it to the churches for study and appropriate action."

The 1970 General Assembly voted 485-259 to approve the council's request, noting that "this action is not to be construed as an endorsement of this report." The assembly's action was itself a compromise after a long and arduous debate. Two factors made this vote possible. One was the disclaimer referenced above. The other was the passage of an amendment that received vigorous opposition from supporters of the Task Force. The amendment required that an "attachment" be printed and "included as part of the Task Force report."

The General Assembly's "attachment" constituted a 180 degree contradiction to the message of the report. It read: "We, the 182nd General Assembly (1970), reaffirm our adherence to the moral law of God as revealed in the Old and New Testaments, that adultery, prostitution, fornication, and/or the practice of homosexuality is sin. We further affirm our belief in the extension Jesus gave to the law, that the attitude of lust in a man's heart is likewise sin. Also, we affirm that any self-righteous attitude of others who would condemn persons who have so sinned is also sin. The widespread presence of the practice of these sins gives credence to the Biblical view that men have a fallen nature and are in need of the reconciling work of Jesus Christ which is adequate for all the sins of men."[1]

Members of the Council on Church and Society were furious, for the attachment undermined their message and they knew that joining opposite statements in one document would create confusion across the denomination.

Contrary to the message of the attachment, their treatise embraced the principles of "situation ethics," replacing fixed moral principles with a morality that chooses the behavior that is deemed "appropriate" in each situation. Condoned, under certain circumstances were premarital and extramarital sex, homosexual relationships and other practices long considered immoral on the basis of Biblical teaching.

During the General Assembly debate, the Rev. Richard Unsworth, a member of the task force, was asked, "Does the Bible have a definite set of sex ethics?" He replied, "It depends on who holds the Bible – Darryl Zanuck would answer differently than Billy Graham."[2]

Thus, Presbyterian congregations got a package deal, two statements for the price of one, each statement contradicting the other. Ironically, although the Council on Church and Society opposed the package, its approval worked to the council's advantage. Had its report simply been rejected by the assembly, agencies of the assembly would have had no warrant to implement it. But because it was adopted, albeit with the attachment, denominational agencies could now promote parts of it, the parts that represented their views.

Selective Implementation

In the ensuing years, this has been a popular tactic when church leaders

1 United Presbyterian Church in the U.S.A., *Minutes of the General Assembly*, 1970, p. 469.

2 *The Presbyterian Layman*, Vol. 3, No. 7, July, 1970.

face substantial opposition during General Assembly meetings. In the name of moderation, peace and mutual respect, they seek a fallback, compromise statement that affirms both points of view. Even if the resulting statement is self-negating by virtue of its inherent self-contradiction, it becomes policy. Staff members are then free to implement the portion that they prefer, pointing to the particular clause that warrants their activity, and ignoring the clause that they deem objectionable.

Even before the 1970 General Assembly adopted its both/and package on human sexuality, denominational agencies and their publications were promoting the Council on Church and Society's ethic. In April, just prior to the General Assembly meeting, *Church and Society* Magazine, an official denominational publication, ran an article titled "Female and Single – What Then?" The author was Margaret Kuhn, Coordinator of Administration for the Division of Church and Race. Included in the article was the following paragraph:

"The church should point the way with compassion and wisdom to a way of life that enables those who are single to express their sexuality and to establish deep sustaining relationships with men who may or may not be married; to begin to experiment with ways in which particular members of a congregation may become an extended family – or at least take on the characteristics and functions of an extended family. Such relationships between single women and married men might or might not involve coitus."[3]

Homosexuality Study

On November 11, 1975, New York City Presbytery sent an overture to the 1976 General Assembly, requesting guidance on the ordination of a homosexual candidate whom the presbytery deemed otherwise qualified for the ministry. At about the same time, the Advisory Council on Church and Society initiated a "Prospectus for Study" of homosexuality and an "Advice and Counsel Memorandum" on homosexuality as resource material for the assembly that would receive New York City Presbytery's overture.

During the 1976 General Assembly, there was no question but that a study of homosexuality would be authorized. The only question was, who would oversee the study? In that contest, the Advisory Council on Church and Society won a proposal that the study be supervised by the Office of the Stated Clerk. Likewise, Church and Society prevailed in having members of the study task force appointed by the Moderator (Thelma Adair) and Church

3 Presbyterian Church (USA), *Church and Society* Magazine, March/April, 1970.

and Society member Jeanne Marshall. The task force would be resourced by the Church and Society staff rather than by the staff from the Office of the Stated Clerk. These shape-of-the-table decisions proved to make a major impact on subsequent task force decisions and recommendations.

The task force report to the 1978 General Assembly was predictable, given the composition of the group. It stated that homosexuality "is a strong, enduring, not consciously chosen and usually irreversible affectional attraction to and preference for persons of the same sex." It declared that homosexuality is "a minor theme in Scripture ... not mentioned by any of the prophets or by Jesus himself." The primary ethical issue in relationships between Christians said the report "is not whether the relationship conforms to a concept of orders of creation, but whether the persons involved in the relationship encourage and support growth in faith and self-giving love."[4]

Moving to its major conclusion, the report asked: "May a self-affirming, practicing homosexual Christian be ordained? We believe so, if the person manifests such gifts as are required for ordination." It recommended that decisions on the fitness of candidates for ordination continue to be lodged with the presbyteries, recognizing that "this constitutional situation may lead to divergent actions by different congregations and presbyteries."[5]

Five members of the 19-member task force filed a minority report: "Our study has led us to conclude that homosexuality is not God's wish for his children ... it is neither a gift from God nor a state or a condition like race; it is a result of man's fallen condition."[6]

The minority report continued, "Though none of us will ever achieve perfect fulfillment of His will, all Christians are responsible to view their sins as He viewed them, and to strive against them. To evade this responsibility is to permit the church to model for the world forms of sexual behavior which may seriously injure individuals, families, and the whole fabric of human society."[7]

When the General Assembly met in June of 1978, it voted by an overwhelming majority (600-50) to replace both the majority and minority reports with a new statement forged by its own commissioners' committee. The assembly declared that homosexual behavior is a sin and accordingly

4 United Presbyterian Church in the U.S.A., *Minutes of the General Assembly*, 1978, pp. 261-266.

5 *Ibid.*

6 *Ibid.*

7 *Ibid.*

"our present understanding of God's will precludes the ordination of persons who do not repent of homosexual practice."[8]

Included in the action was a condemnation of "homophobia;" the acceptance into church membership of homosexuals who affirm "Jesus Christ is my Lord and Savior;" the possibility of ordination of repentant homosexuals who are committed to celibacy; the support of civil rights for homosexuals; the need for reconciling ministry with homosexual persons and the cautioning of committees examining candidates for ordained office not "to make a specific inquiry into the sexual orientation or practice of candidates."[9]

The assembly approved one amendment that has proved to be problematic in succeeding years, to "declare that these actions shall not be used to negatively affect the ordination rights of any … deacons, elders and ministers who have been ordained prior to this date."[10]

The General Assembly's use of the term "ordination rights" would figure prominently in future demands by homosexual activists. These words turned the terms of the ordination debate from the field of ethics (what is the right thing to do?) to the field of entitlement (do I have the right to do it?). We have seen this migration before, in the General Assembly Permanent Judicial Commission's handling of the Kaseman case. In that case, the Commission changed the terms of the discussion from theology (right belief about Jesus Christ) to entitlement (the presbytery's right to approve beliefs about Jesus Christ). We will see this migration again when we examine the denomination's approach to the abortion issue, placing its emphasis on a woman's right to choose rather than the more substantial question of which choice is right.

This tactic has proved a skillful political maneuver that makes radically liberal positions more palatable to persons who define themselves as moderates. One declares oneself for "choice" in lieu of publicly saying that one is for same-sex genital activity or killing children in the womb. But while it may make for effective politics, such a declaration is nonsensical as a principle of ethical judgment. What does it mean, as a moral principle, that one is "for choice?" Surely all but the most totalitarian among us would stipulate that humans are free to make choices. That freedom is inherent in our humanity. But the mere possession of the right to choose has no moral consequence. Morality enters the picture only when a choice is made, for it is not choice in general, but in the particular act of choosing that a person

8 *Ibid.*

9 *Ibid.*

10 *Ibid.*

makes a value declaration.

When the church replaces ethical judgments with politics, it acts beneath itself, forfeiting its role as a moral influence in society. Such forfeiture sentences the church to irrelevance, for in its refusal to make its own judgment on the basis of ethical principles, much less to persuade the world, it abandons its uniqueness, its warrant to say something that no other entity can say.

The irony of this irrelevance lies in the fact that it is the result of attempts by church leaders seeking, above all, to be more relevant to the world of politics. Apparently they assumed they could get a hearing on Capitol Hill if they removed the theological/ethical dimension of the church's message. But this has made the institutional church simply one of the many secular lobbyists that flood congressional hallways. Politicians read the polls, and they know that lobbyists from the denomination's Washington Office represent the views of a tiny constituency, the Presbyterian Church (USA) bureaucracy, which does not reflect the opinions of Presbyterians in the pews.

The voice of the church would be most relevant if it spoke not the language of politics but the Word of the Lord. That is a Word that only the church has been commissioned to proclaim. It is that "Thus says the Lord" declaration, the prophetic proclamation of the church, that will draw the world's attention. But a church that does not know what it believes is incapable of declaring the Word of the Lord to the world.

This, of course, takes us back to 1926, when in setting aside any required essential tenets of belief for its ordained leaders, the General Assembly created a denomination composed of Presbyterians without principles. Theology and ethics go hand in hand. Persons who do not know what they believe have no basis on which to act. Granted, they have a choice, but they do not know what to choose, so they simply assign a value to choice itself, which from the standpoint of ethics is meaningless.

Southerners Follow Suit

In 1979, the General Assembly of the Presbyterian Church (US), anticipating merger with the United Presbyterian Church, approved an interpretation of its ordination standards that paralleled the United Presbyterian Church's 1978 ruling, denying ordination to persons who practice homosexual behavior. Meanwhile, the 1979 United Presbyterian Church General Assembly defeated a proposal to reconsider its position on homosexuality. Special interest groups representing homosexual rights causes lobbied General Assemblies in both branches of the Presbyterian Church until their reunion in 1982.

Alarmed by the position taken by the General Assemblies of their two previous denominations, 70 executives from 14 of the 20 synods of the newly merged Presbyterian Church (USA) met at the Stony Point center for two days. Their purpose was to consider ways to counter the denomination's policy denying ordination to persons who engage in homosexual behavior. The consultation was coordinated by the Program Agency and was warranted by claims that it was part of an educational project on "homophobia" which the Program Agency was developing.[11]

Participants in the consultation included synod and presbytery staff, pastors and elders of key church committees. Invited participants also included members of the Presbyterians for Lesbian/Gay Concerns.

In a plenary address, Dr. Robert Hawkins, associate professor at the State University of New York, Stony Brook, said that homophobia "is a fear that has no basis in fact," while at the same time "it is fear that has social and legal support. If you believe homosexual people are unfit for coaching football, you are homophobic ... Until we believe that gay people can experience as happy a life as heterosexual people, homophobia will continue to be a disease – what you Presbyterians call a sin."[12]

'Justice/Love'

In 1991, the General Assembly of the now merged northern and southern denominations, the Presbyterian Church (USA), was confronted by a major offensive from homosexual activists and their allies in the denomination's national staff. Before the assembly was a "Human Sexuality Report" promoting the theme "Justice/Love."

Ironically, the impetus for the creation of this task force came from evangelicals. Troubled by a proliferation of un-Biblical themes on sexual morality that were being promoted in denomination publications, youth conferences, and various agency documents, the session of Highland Park Presbyterian Church, Dallas, Tex., had given one of its associate ministers, the Rev. Harry Hassall a leave of absence in order to promote a campaign

11 The Stony Point consultation provides a clear example of an oft recurring practice in which an official agency of the General Assembly, whose mandate is to uphold and implement General Assembly policies, subverts a policy by means of a loophole in its language. The 1978 General Assembly policy stated with crystal clarity that homosexual behavior is "sinful" and contrary to the teaching of Scripture, and persons who practice such behavior may not be ordained. The loophole was the General Assembly's additional statement condemning "homophobia," the fear of homosexuals that drives persons to treat them unjustly.

12 Presbyterian News Service, September 19, 1984.

called A Witness to Biblical Morality. For six months, Hassall traveled throughout the denomination, asking local church sessions to sign onto the "Witness," a document declaring that in the area of sexual ethics, this particular congregation stood on a Biblical foundation and would not accommodate to the views expressed by denominational leaders. Thousands of church leaders signed the statement.

The grass-roots campaign also generated petitions, calling on denominational leaders to bring their policies, programs and publications in line with Biblical morality standards. It was as a result of this evangelical momentum that the 1987 General Assembly commissioned a task force on human sexuality and asked it to bring a major policy paper to a future General Assembly.

The motion before the 1987 General Assembly that created the task force called for its study to include "understanding of the variety of expressions of human sexuality." This, of course, was hardly what the Witness to Biblical Morality signatories had in mind. An amendment was attempted that would have had the assembly declare that "sexual intercourse is a gift from God to be used only within the covenant of marriage" and that responsible Christian behavior means "faithfulness within the covenant of marriage" and "chastity of all unmarried men and women." The amendment was defeated.[13]

Appointed by General Assembly Moderator Isabel Rogers, a professor at the Presbyterian School of Christian Education and a vigorous advocate of homosexual, bisexual and transgendered causes, the task force membership was heavily lopsided. In fact, during the first year of its existence, two of the token evangelicals who had been appointed to the task force resigned, stating that the deck was so stacked against persons who represented Biblical morality that there was no point in their investing any more effort in the project.

When the 1988 General Assembly met, it called on its new moderator, the Rev. Kenneth Hall, to make new appointments to the task force "in order to give it balance." Hall's appointees ensured that the task force would have a vocal minority of two persons, but it made little impact on the group's predominant point of view.

The task force was staffed by "ethicist" James Nelson, whose published commitment to virtually unfettered sexual couplings was widely known.[14] Considering his published views, Nelson's guidance to the task force was

13 *Presbyterian Church News*, June 10, 1987. See also: *The Presbyterian Layman* Vol. 20, No. 4, July/August, 1987.

14 Nelson, James, *Sexuality and the Sacred* (Louisville, Ky.: Westminster John Knox Press, 2006).

predictable. In 1978, he wrote that "sexual theology is body theology." He argued that Christian theology had gotten off track when it began with God or, in Reformed thought, with the Word of God. Nelson argued that this "top-down approach" results in a theological dead end. He said that humans are "body-persons," that we think with our bodies, that we view everything, including God, from the perspective of our sexuality. "How we experience ourselves and others sexually will condition and affect the style and contents of our Christian beliefs," said Nelson.[15]

Nelson's views on marital fidelity were spelled out in *Embodiment*: "An increasing number of couples are rejecting sexual exclusiveness as essential to marriage and are seeing intimate 'satellite' relationships as positively supporting both marriage and personal growth," he said. He suggested that the church should re-think what it means by fidelity and maintained that marital fidelity and adultery can be compatible, depending on one's definition of terms.[16]

Following Nelson's lead, the task force promoted "Justice/Love," a theme whose controlling premise was that all sexual activity among adults – whether marital or extramarital, heterosexual or homosexual – is good if it occurs by mutual consent that is not coerced (that's the justice part) and is motivated by a sincere desire to please the other (that's the love part).

Obviously, Scripture says something quite different about sexual morality, so the committee had to address the issue of Scriptural authority. On this point, the Confession of 1967 was a significant help, since it had already concluded that Scripture ("the words of men") is derived from culture. The task force said, "Whatever in Scripture, tradition, reason or experience embodies genuine love and caring justice, that bears authority for us and commends an ethic to do likewise. Whatever in Biblical tradition, church practice and teaching, human experience, and human reason violates God's commandment to do love and justice, that must be rejected as ethical authority."[17] Thus, Scripture was made to conform to the task force's "justice/love" principle, not the other way around.

The 1991 General Assembly rejected the Human Sexuality Report by an overwhelming vote (534-31), but not before the liberals achieved their compromise: The assembly agreed that the report could be used as "a study resource" for the church. That's all that the denomination's infrastructure

15 Nelson, James, *Embodiment* (Minneapolis, MN: Augsburg Publishing House, 1978), p. 20.

16 *Ibid.*, p. 131.

17 Presbyterian Church (USA), *Minutes of the General Assembly* 1991, p. 275.

needed to turn their defeat into victory. Justice/love themes appeared subsequently in numerous denominational conferences, study guides, curricula, and promotional materials. Considering the proliferation of such materials, one would have thought that the Human Sexuality Report of 1991 had been approved.

The Spahr Case

On Nov. 26, 1991, the Presbytery of Genesee Valley voted 121 to 46 to approve the call of the Downtown Presbyterian Church in Rochester, NY to the Rev. Jane Adams Spahr, who was engaged in a lesbian relationship. Spahr said of her lifestyle, "as a lesbian Christian Presbyterian minister, my life reflects a claiming of all who I am."[18] Spahr received her Doctor of Ministry from San Francisco Theological Seminary. Her thesis was "Lesbian Spirituality: A New Model for Ministry." She had been ordained prior to the 1978 General Assembly that outlawed ordination for persons who openly practice homosexual relationships.

A longtime favorite of the same-sex community, Spahr was honored in the 1992 "More Light Prayer Book" with the dedication, "To the Goddess that preceded and includes the God we affirm, in thanksgiving for the life and ministry of Dr. Jane Adams Spahr."

On Nov. 3, 1992, the General Assembly Permanent Judicial Commission "set aside" Spahr's call to the Rochester, NY church. The commission ruled that while the 1978 General Assembly's grandfather clause protected homosexuals who were ordained prior to 1978, it did not accord them a permanent exemption from the denomination's sexual behavior standards. The fact that she continued openly to engage in homosexual activity made her ineligible to receive a call, said the court.

In the Spahr decision, the General Assembly commission was particularly direct in its communication to Genesee Valley Presbytery. It warned that "a presbytery (or any governing body) is not free to exercise its own judgment contrary to our constitutional standards or the lawful injunctions of higher governing bodies without jeopardizing the entire fabric of our Presbyterian system."[19]

This ruling and a similar ruling in the case of *Londonderry v. the Presbytery of Northern New England* represent an oasis in the "local option" proclivity that has characterized Presbyterian polity since 1926. The two rulings, holding presbyteries accountable to a General Assembly standard,

18 *The Presbyterian Layman*, Vol. 25, No. 1, January/February, 1992.

19 Presbyterian Church (USA), *Minutes of the General Assembly*, 1993, pp. 66-170.

were effectively undermined by the 2006 General Assembly's adoption of a new policy, allowing presbyteries to exempt themselves from national standards by declaring the standards "non-essential," and therefore optional.

The reaction from homosexual activists in the denomination was swift and vitriolic. Chris Glaser, moderator of Presbyterians for Lesbian and Gay Concerns, whose books advocating the homosexual lifestyle are published and marketed by the Presbyterian Church (USA) Publishing Corporation, was particularly hostile. "No words can convey the rage I experience today," he said on Presbynet, a denominationally funded computer network. "May God damn the Presbyterian Church (USA)'s pride and hypocrisy."[20]

In an apparent reference to strategies which homosexual activists would soon employ to influence future appointments to the denomination's highest court, Glaser said, "Thank God the 'Permanent Judicial Commission' is a misnomer when it comes to the word 'Permanent.'"[21]

The Church and its Leaders

Numerous polls have been conducted by the denomination's department of research services, each indicating that Presbyterians in the pews honor the sacred covenant of marriage between a man and a woman, and they do not favor the ordination of persons who openly engage in sexual activity outside of that covenant of marriage.[22]

One may wonder why homosexual pressure groups are able to command such attention in Presbyterian Church (USA) circles when they represent so small a minority of the Presbyterian population. The answer to that inquiry is twofold:

(1) Homosexual activist groups maintain a vigorous, persistent and well organized political lobby. Presbyterians for Lesbian and Gay Concerns and its later manifestations, More Light Presbyterians and That All May Freely Serve, maintain active alliances with The Witherspoon Society, Voices of Sophia, and The Covenant Network of Presbyterians. These alliances have been able to mount formidable campaigns on behalf of their causes during General Assembly meetings.

(2) The staff infrastructure of the Presbyterian Church (USA) is strongly

20 Presbyterian Church (USA), *Presbynet*, November 4, 1992.

21 *Ibid.*

22 In 1993, the PCUSA Office of Research Services reported that 74 percent of Presbyterians opposed the ordination of practicing homosexuals, and in 1991, more than 94 percent of commissioners to the General Assembly voted their opposition to the Human Sexuality Report that affirmed moral approbation for same-sex and extramarital sexual behavior.

committed to the agenda of homosexual activists. This commitment is manifested in rulings favorable to the same-sex lobby at every level of denominational governance above the local congregation.

The Office of Research Services at denominational headquarters conducts a professionally respected polling service that indicates by random selection of 5,000 participants where Presbyterians stand on various issues before the denomination. Results of that "Presbyterian Panel," are segmented into the following categories: Members, Elders, Pastors, Specialized Clergy.

Data from the 2005 report is revealing.[23] 19 percent of the members say they are "very liberal to liberal," while 45 percent of the specialized clergy identify with that category.

41 percent of the members and 43 percent of the elders identify themselves as "very conservative to conservative," while only 21 percent of the specialized clergy choose that designation.

Only 25 percent of members and 24 percent of elders say they would "like to see the PCUSA permit ordination of sexually active gays and lesbians as ministers," but 58 percent of the specialized clergy say "yes" to that issue.

On a query regarding "political preference," 27 percent of the members and 30 percent of the elders identified with the Democrats, while 64 percent of the specialized clergy chose that designation. 53 percent of the members and 51 percent of the elders chose "Republican," while 17 percent of the specialized clergy identified with that party.

National and regional staff members represent the "Specialized Ministry" category, ministers who serve in non-pastoral positions. Stated Clerk Clifton Kirkpatrick, for example, followed his seminary training with employment by ecumenical organizations. From there he was recruited by national church headquarters. He has never served in the pastorate of a local church. This is not unusual for national church bureaucrats, many of whom pursued a direct-line track through college, seminary, graduate school, and into denominational leadership positions.

The heavy influence of national and regional staff on deliberations at General Assembly meetings has long been a bone of contention for Presbyterians who advocate Biblical theology and ethics. At each General Assembly meeting, hundreds of staff persons are recruited to serve as "resource persons" for the elected commissioners. In some years, there have been

23 Source for the data cited on this page: Presbyterian Church (USA), Office of the General Assembly, Department of Research Services, "A Presbyterian Panel Snapshot: Characteristics of Presbyterians, 2005."

almost as many resource persons as voting commissioners attending a General Assembly.

The rules of the General Assembly provide for open hearings by its committees. Non-committee members are allowed a limited time to testify, rarely more than three minutes. But testimony from staff resource persons is not bound by the restriction. The number of staff persons and their virtually unlimited access to commissioners throws a huge weight toward the point of view they represent.

In each room where General Assembly committees convene, a small desk with telephone is stationed beside the door. From this location, a person designated as adjunct General Assembly staff monitors the proceedings. If it appears that the committee opinion is drifting toward a position that General Assembly officials do not favor, a call is made to the General Assembly "tracking office." Within minutes, official resource persons are dispatched to the committee room to testify before the committee. The documented bias of General Assembly staff, ratio of official resource persons to voting commissioners, and the elaborate communications system that has been developed among General Assembly officials help explain why General Assembly decisions often reflect a vastly different viewpoint than that which is held by Presbyterians in the pews.

Examples of Agency Bias

While there is abundant evidence of cooperative efforts between homosexual activists and denominational agencies, a few incidents are listed here as illustrative.

On December 4, 1990, Chris Glaser, a nationally known homosexual activist led worship for the Presbyterian Church (USA) staff in a chapel service at the Presbyterian Center in Louisville. Glaser, whose publisher is Westminster John Knox Press, the official publishing house of the Presbyterian Church (USA), spoke to an unusually large audience of national staff members.

When asked by *The Presbyterian Layman* why Glaser had been invited to speak to the staff, the Rev. Jerry Van Marter, director of the Presbyterian News Service, said "Whenever a dignitary comes to town – General Assembly moderators, overseas guests, etc. – we invite them to speak to us in our chapel service." Van Marter said that chapel services at the Presbyterian Center usually drew approximately 75 people, but that the Glaser service drew an estimated crowd of 175 staffers.[24]

24 *The Presbyterian Layman*, Vol. 24, No. 1, January/February, 1991.

While in town, Glaser also made an appearance at Louisville Presbyterian Theological Seminary, where he told his audience that he perceived "a different attitude" toward homosexuals in the church and that he hoped the denomination's human sexuality task force would "find ways for the church to be realistic ... and give guidelines for responsibility in sexual relationships, whether those relationships are within marriage or outside marriage."[25]

On July 17, 1992, the Justice for Women Committee of the Presbyterian Church (USA) conducted a meeting in St. Louis at General Assembly expense. Five homosexual activists were invited to spend six hours with the committee, developing implementation procedures for current policy and new policy proposals for future General Assembly meetings. Participants in the event included the Rev. Lisa Bove, co-moderator of Presbyterians for Lesbian and Gay Concerns, the Rev. Jane Spahr and the Rev. Coni Staff, a minister at Metropolitan Community Church in San Francisco.[26]

During the denominationally sponsored 1989 Presbyterian Youth Triennium, Presbyterians for Lesbian and Gay Concerns was invited to set up an exhibit from which sexually explicit brochures were distributed. A brochure for women offered advice on same-sex intimacy: "First I would ask myself if I felt ready. Then I would talk to my partner and see if she felt ready ... Only you can know when it is and isn't right for you to have sex ... You may feel very scared at the thought of having sex with another woman. That's OK. Lots of us do, especially if it is our first time."[27]

A brochure for boys was similarly explicit, urging them to trust their instincts. Assuring teenage boys that they would know when the time was "right," the brochure told them that when that time comes they should be able to "do anything that appeals to both partners. You are in complete control over what you do sexually and with whom."[28]

The brochures provoked a churchwide explosion in 1989, which produced several overtures to the subsequent General Assembly. In response to these overtures, the assembly chided the denomination's Louisville staff for allowing the brochure affair to occur.[29]

When the Presbyterian Youth Triennium met in West Lafayette, Ind. in 1992, Presbyterians for Lesbian and Gay Concerns was denied booth space

25 *The Louisville Courier-Journal*, December 1, 1991.

26 *The Presbyterian Layman*, Vol. 25, No. 5, September/October, 1992.

27 *Ibid.*

28 *Ibid.*

29 Presbyterian Church (USA), *Minutes of the General Assembly*, 1990, p. 757.

in the exhibit hall. But denominational staff members were not to be deterred by this omission. The Triennium design team decided to invite two members of a "More Light" church (a congregation that commits itself to the homosexual agenda) to assume leadership roles in the Triennium program. The two homosexual leaders, Kathleen Moran and Scott Miller, members of the Rochester, NY church that had called Jane Spahr to become its minister, were given carte blanche to present their position on the moral approbation of homosexual behavior at a seminar during the Triennium event. No one was invited to present alternative views, including the position of the Presbyterian Church (USA) that homosexual practice violates the teachings of Scripture.

National Capital Presbytery Council Challenged over Same-Sex Wedding

In 1990, Mr. Ralph Westfall, an elder in a Falls Church, Va. congregation learned that homosexual "weddings" were being conducted at Westminster Presbyterian Church in Washington, D.C. Believing that the sponsorship of same-sex ceremonies by a Presbyterian Church session and the conduct of such rituals by ordained Presbyterian ministers constituted a violation of Scripture, *The Book of Order*, and the stated position of the Presbyterian Church (USA) General Assembly, Westfall wrote a letter on Nov. 15, 1990 to National Capital Presbytery officials. He stated that the events at Westminster constituted "a delinquency within the bounds and under the jurisdiction of the presbytery," and he warned officials that if they did not initiate remedial action, he would file a judicial complaint.

On December 3, 1990, the moderator of National Capital Presbytery, the Rev. John W. Wimberly, responded to Westfall in writing. He stated the presbytery council's opinion that members of the Westminster Church session "were well within their rights according to *The Book of Order* to decide what is the appropriate use of their building." Referring to Westfall's charge that Westminster and its ministers had violated *The Book of Order* and the General Assembly's policy, the presbytery's stated clerk "found no specific violation of church polity."

In his letter of response, Westfall said that he had not challenged the right of a session to determine the "appropriate use of its building." Rather, he said, the essence of his complaint centered on "the inappropriate use of the building."

"It may be," continued Westfall, "that persons responsible for these actions seek to defend them on the technical, semantic grounds that no actual 'wedding' was performed, and that what occurred was a 'blessing' of a 'religious union,' or some like verbiage. If anyone should seek to follow this line of defense, they will merely insult the intelligence and offend the deeply felt beliefs of those many Presbyterians who find these actions reprehensible. Those who consider one of the most sacred elements of their faith to be mocked and degraded will not be convinced by theological 'spin doctors' seeking to pretend that an abomination is really a blessing. Any such obfuscation will not work: it is merely to further aggravate an already unhappy state of affairs."[30]

National Capital Presbytery's council met and prepared a statement for the presbytery's January 22 meeting.[31] The council's recommendation urged "that members of the denomination not participate in the exclusion and discriminatory treatment of our lesbian sisters and gay brothers; that National Capital Presbytery pledge itself to the development of full and open fellowship with all disciples ..." The recommendation recognized that *The Book of Order* "affirmed marriage to be a male-female relationship," but it urged churches of the presbytery to commit themselves to a study of the issue. The council suggested that the denomination's position was constitutionally unclear and it stated its hope that congregational study would develop "constitutional clarification and the commitment to the inclusive life in our churches."[32]

Bloody but unbowed, Ralph Westfall continued to stand in what had heretofore been a solo protest. Then the tide shifted. The session of the prestigious National Presbyterian Church entered the fray, warning the presbytery of dire consequences should it continue to allow gross violations of Scripture, *The Book of Order* and General Assembly policy. On September 24, 1991, nine months after Westfall publicly and single-handedly challenged National Capital to uphold the Constitution, the presbytery blinked. Setting aside the recommendation of its council, the presbytery called on its ministers to "prayerfully heed" General Assembly policies on the sanctity of marriage.[33]

---

30 Letter by Ralph Westfall to the Rev. John W. Wimberly, December 5, 1990.

31 Statement by National Capital Presbytery Council, January 2, 1991.

32 The opinion that Scripture, the Constitution and the will of the church are "unclear" on matters of sexual morality has been frequently expressed by General Assembly officials. Even after the people of the Presbyterian Church (USA) embedded a Biblical sex ethic in its constitutional ordination standards (G-6.0106(b)) and defeated attempts to remove it by overwhelming majorities, Stated Clerk Clifton Kirkpatrick has continually declared that the mind of the church has not been discerned on this matter.

33 National Capital Presbytery, *Minutes*, September 24, 1991.

Twin Cities 'Certifies' Lesbian for Ministry

Meanwhile, in that same year, in defiance of the General Assembly's determination that same-sex intimacy does not accord with the teachings of Scripture, the Presbytery of the Twin Cities area voted to certify as "ready to receive a call to the ministry" Lisa Larges, a petitioner who told the presbytery that she was engaged in homosexual behavior and did not believe that it was morally wrong. The presbytery's certification constituted a necessary endorsement that frees candidates to seek ordination.

On June 24, 1992, the permanent Judicial Commission of the Synod of Lakes and Prairies ordered Twin Cities to rescind its action. That order was sustained by the General Assembly Permanent Judicial Commission on an appeal by the presbytery.

Presbyterian Women 'Shape' Scripture

In Louisville, Presbyterian Women released its 1991-92 Bible Study, *We Decide Together: A Guide to Making Ethical Decisions*. As suggested by its title, the study book contended that Christian ethics is based on contextual authorities rather than on Scripture. The study suggested that the Bible, taken as a whole, lacks clarity. It presumed that "we" control Scripture and are in a position to "make" it respond according to our will.

An explicit example of the authors' elevation of human authority above Scripture is found in this quote, "In obedience to the Bible, we sometimes must disobey a given biblical imperative."[34] This theme would come in handy when later in the year, the denomination's Special Committee on Human Sexuality presented its report to the General Assembly declaring "Whatever in Scripture, tradition, reason or experience embodies genuine love and caring justice, that bears authority for us ... Whatever in Biblical tradition, church practice and teaching, human experience, and human reason violates God's commandment to do love and justice, that must be rejected as ethical authority."[35]

Annulment of 'Irregular' Ordinations Deemed 'Inappropriate'

In 1993, Central Presbyterian Church of Eugene, Ore. acknowledged that it had ordained "two persons who made known to the session and con-

34 Campbell, Cynthia M., and Donelson, Lewis R., *We Decide Together: A Guide to Making Ethical Decisions* (Louisville: *Horizons*, 1991), p. 16.

35 Presbyterian Church (USA), *Minutes of the General Assembly*, 1991, pp. 55, 263; Special Committee on Human Sexuality, section on Gays and Lesbians, pp. 305-312.

gregation their homosexual orientation and practice." But it denied that in doing so it had "disregarded the authority of Scripture and the position of the denomination." The Presbytery of the Cascades, acting on a complaint by Hope Presbyterian Church of Portland, Ore., ruled "There was an irregularity in the ordination of the two practicing, self-affirming homosexuals by the Session of Central in that current Presbyterian law prohibits these ordinations."[36] But the presbytery declined to annul the two ordinations, opining that doing so would be "inappropriate."[37]

When the matter ultimately arrived before the General Assembly Permanent Judicial Commission, the high court sided with the presbytery. "While this Commission recognizes that the ordinations were not in accordance with constitutional law in the Presbyterian Church (U.S.A.), they must stand in accordance with G-14.0203. The Commission stated that no precedent exists supporting the annulment of an irregular ordination.[38]

Mr. Richard Paul, attorney for the Hope Church, called the decision "confusing." "If it is unconstitutional to ordain persons who practice homosexual behavior," said Paul, "then these two 'irregular' ordinations should have been declared null and void." Paul warned that this kind of ruling would render the Constitution unenforceable and open the door to numerous violations.[39]

In January, 1993 the Synod of the Northeast met to deal with a major budget crisis due to dwindling contributions from congregations. In a stopgap measure, the synod excised four full-time staff positions. Then, having taken care of the emergency at hand, it turned to the subject of sex. By a vote of 68-52, the synod declared itself a "More Light Synod." "More Light" was a label coined by Presbyterians for Lesbian and Gay Concerns, a homosexual caucus, to identify churches and organizations that favor "sexual orientation inclusiveness." The synod's resolution declared its opposition to the General Assembly policy that prohibits the ordination of persons who openly engage in same-sex conjugal behavior. Although merely symbolic, since it had no force of law, the resolution did serve as an encouragement for defiance of General Assembly policy in the region.

During a meeting of Pittsburgh Presbytery on Feb 11, 1993, representa-

36 Note the use of the word "current," which implies that this mandate in the constitution is temporary, subject to change. This has been the hope/intention of the PCUSA infrastructure since the denomination's position was codified by the 1978 General Assembly.

37 Presbyterian Church (USA), *Minutes of the General Assembly*, 1993, p. 142.

38 *Ibid.*

39 *The Presbyterian Layman*, Vol. 26, No. 6, November/December, 1993.

tives of Pittsburgh area churches discovered that a private arrangement had been made between the presbytery's Race and Social Justice Unit and lesbian activist Jane Spahr to bring her into the presbytery for lobbying purposes. The unit had allocated $500, half of which was to be taken from the presbytery's Special Committee on AIDS budget, to underwrite some of Spahr's travel expenses.

A motion was made to block payment to Spahr, but Presbytery Moderator Mark Krauland ruled the motion out of order. He said that the Race and Social Justice Unit had already conveyed the invitation and Ms. Spahr had accepted it. This constitutes an agreement, he said, that Pittsburgh Presbytery is legally obliged to honor.[40]

Faced with a refusal by the courts and governing bodies to enforce denominational standards, the General Assembly standard on the sexual behavior of ordained members became increasingly difficult to uphold. This was particularly true when those who were elected to be spokespersons for General Assembly policies openly opposed them. During General Assembly Moderator John Fife's term he told a gathering of Princeton Theological Seminary faculty and students that he regarded the General Assembly's position on homosexuality "intolerable." He said that while 70 percent of the denomination's membership might support the policy, the remaining 30 percent saw it as "a devastating blow to our hope that our church, over the last two years, was moving to be more inclusive."[41]

Fife's speech at Princeton triggered a meeting of the Grace Presbyterian Church session in nearby Montclair, NJ. "We were dismayed by the public comments made by the Rev. John Fife, Moderator of the General Assembly, in a message given recently at Princeton Theological Seminary," said the session in a communication to the Rev. James E. Andrews, Stated Clerk of the General Assembly. The session objected to the fact that "Fife, while acting in his official capacity as moderator, made public statements contravening the official position of the General Assembly that elected him."

Divided Opinion

On Nov. 12, 1993, the Rev. James Brown, Executive Director of the General Assembly Council, and the Rev. James Andrews clashed during a meeting of the National Council of Churches Governing Board. At issue was a proposal to admit a homosexual organization, the Universal Fellowship of Metropolitan Community Churches, to "observer status" in the NCC.

40 *The Presbyterian Layman*, Vol. 26, No. 2, March/April, 1993.

41 *The Presbyterian Layman*, Vol. 26, No. 1, January/February, 1993. See also *The Presbyterian Outlook*, Jan. 1993.

Andrews voted against the proposal, arguing that as a member of the Presbyterian Church (USA) staff, he believed he had an obligation to reflect the policies of his denomination. Brown voted for the proposal, saying that he was also a representative of the Presbyterian Church (USA) and was aware of his denomination's policy regarding homosexuality, but that he didn't agree with it.

As executive director of the General Assembly Council, Brown functioned as the Chief Executive Officer, responsible for implementing General Assembly policies through the programs and agencies of the denomination. His defiance of Presbyterian Church (USA) policy sent a signal to the more than 600 national staff members who were accountable to him that they were free not to honor the denomination's sexual behavior standards.

Promoting Defiance

On Brown's watch, numerous General Assembly Council agencies and offices promoted the homosexual agenda. The National Network of Presbyterian College Women, a group that was organized and funded by the Women's Ministries Unit, included on its web page, whose server was the property of the Presbyterian Church (USA), located and maintained at denominational headquarters, a link to a lesbian dating service. The web page was removed in 1998 "for renovations" after *The Presbyterian Layman* published an article revealing its contents.

During the same period, the Congregational Ministries Division published a sex education curriculum whose message contradicted the denomination's policy on same-sex behavior. The 1999 General Assembly ordered the General Assembly Council to revise the curriculum to conform with Biblical standards, as did the 2000 and 2001 General Assemblies, but the national staff dragged its feet. In 2002, the General Assembly Council pleaded with the General Assembly to give it more time to conform to denominational standards. The assembly gave it a two-year reprieve. Finally, opponents of the curriculum lost hope, momentum and energy, and their effort to force the General Assembly Council to comply with Biblical standards died a quiet death.

Seeking Judicial Relief

On May 13, 1994, Dr. Alexander Metherell, a radiologist and an elder in the Saint Andrews Presbyterian Church of Newport Beach, CA, and representatives of 12 church sessions filed charges against the General Assembly Council with the General Assembly Permanent Judicial Commission, often called "the Supreme Court of the Presbyterian Church (USA)." The remedial complaint charged that various officers and agencies of the General

Assembly Council have taken actions and issued public statements that contradict the express policies of the General Assembly. The text of the complaint cited numerous instances in which the General Assembly policy on sexual behavior standards for ordained officers had been deliberately undermined by members of the assembly staff and their agencies.

The complaint requested four remedies from the court: that the General Assembly Council (1) publicly disavow the views expressed by the ReImagining God conference; (2) declare that it will not support or participate in the work of any organization whose leadership affirms any or all of the views expressed by leaders of the ReImagining God conference; (3) declare that any employees who affirm these views in the performance of their duties as employees be found in violation of the PCUSA Constitution and be disciplined appropriately; (4) declare that all employees who affirm the ordination of practicing, unrepentant homosexuals will be found in violation of the PCUSA Constitution and dealt with accordingly.

Representatives of the General Assembly Council asked the Permanent Judicial Commission to dismiss the case on grounds that presbyteries, not the General Assembly Council, have disciplinary jurisdiction over ministers on the council's staff and that sessions, not the General Assembly Council, have disciplinary jurisdiction over elders on the council staff.

Speaking for the complainants, Metherell argued that insofar as the General Assembly Council is an employer, it has a duty to supervise all persons who are acting as employees. Insisting that the case was "remedial, not disciplinary," Metherell argued that the case had been appropriately filed. Metherell said that the denomination's structure reveals a clear chain of responsibility. The council is responsible to the General Assembly for implementing the policies of the General Assembly, he said. It carries out this responsibility through the work of its employees and officers who perform their duties under its supervision.

The General Assembly Permanent Judicial Commission decided not to hear the case on grounds that the General Assembly Council is not a governing body of the denomination.

The ruling suggested that since the council is actually an extension of the General Assembly that operates between its meetings, the General Assembly itself might be the appropriate defendant in such a case.[42]

42 Note that Dr. Metherell had previously attempted to follow the approach suggested by this Permanent Judicial Commission. In 1992, he filed charges against the General Assembly itself on grounds that the denomination's highest governing body had violated Scripture and the Constitution of the Presbyterian Church (USA). The high court dismissed those charges in 1993, saying that Metherell did not have standing to bring an action against the General Assembly. See page 237 for a discussion of this case.

Reconciling the Broken Silence

In 1994, the Congregational Ministries Division of the General Assembly Council continued its defiance by publishing *Reconciling the Broken Silence*. Purporting to be a "study resource," the book was an apologetic for homosexual behavior and the "ordination rights" of those who openly engage in it. Contributors to the book constituted a who's who among homosexual activists in the Presbyterian Church (USA). They included Jane Spahr, Chris Glaser, a homosexual author whose writings were frequently published and promoted by denominational agencies, Lisa Larges, a lesbian from Twin Cities Presbytery who was seeking ordination; Daniel Smith, a leader of Presbyterians for Lesbian and Gay Concerns; and Kathryn Poethig, a lesbian who later had her partnership recognized in a "holy union ceremony."

In a telephone interview with *The Presbyterian Layman*, Edward Craxton, associate for Christian education in the Congregational Ministries Division, denied that the book was an apologetic for homosexual behavior. "The intent [of the book] is to address homophobia," he said.[43]

Responding to observations that the book's author and all of its contributors were outspoken advocates of the homosexual lifestyle, Craxton defended it as a "legitimate study" and said that these contributors were chosen in order to acquaint the denomination with "the stories of people who have this perspective."[44]

There Ought to Be a Law!

By 1996, Presbyterians committed to Biblical authority, particularly as it speaks to the issue of human sexuality, realized that their General Assembly victories, undermined by the refusal of staff to implement them, were useless. They were also concerned that an increasingly liberal high court, the Permanent Judicial Commission of the General Assembly (GAPJC), was coming dangerously close to overturning the 1978 ordination standards decision. A minority on the court (soon to be the majority) wrote an opinion that the standard set by the 1978 General Assembly was merely a Gen-

43 *The Presbyterian Layman*, Vol. 27, No. 3, May/June, 1994.

44 Note: The 1978 General Assembly declared that homosexual behavior is contrary to Scripture and that persons who practice it should not be ordained. But it added a statement denouncing "homophobia," the fear of homosexuals that may lead to the denial of their civil rights. National staff members used this "homophobia" portion of the 1978 decision as warrant for programs that undermine the first and primary portion of the 1978 decision with which they did not agree.

eral Assembly opinion, and that it could have the force of law only if it were embedded in the Constitution.

That minority surfaced on October 29, 1995, when the General Assembly Permanent Judicial Commission ruled in favor of Long Island Presbytery's decision not to investigate the acknowledged ordination of homosexual persons by one of its congregations.[45]

In a concurring opinion, seven commission members said, "We believe that the adoption of 1978 and 1979 General Assembly statements on the ordination of such persons ('The 1978 Statement'), and subsequent reaffirmations and judicial decisions, which have been treated as 'authoritative interpretation' (G-13.0103r), were adopted in violation of the *Constitution* for the following reasons: …"[46]

There were two obvious implications in this case's majority and minority opinions. The majority opinion appeared to give presbyteries the discretion to determine whether they will enforce General Assembly policies. The minority opinion showed that liberals on the GAPJC needed only two additional votes to overturn every previous decision by that commission and all General Assembly decisions about the ordination of persons who engage in sexual activity outside of marriage.

In its analysis of the *Central vs. Presbytery of Long Island* case, *The Layman* spelled out its implications and the necessity for a constitutional response: "Seven of the GAPJC's 16 members told this denomination that if it wants to ban the ordination of persons who openly engage in same-gender sexual behavior, then it must say so explicitly in the text of the Constitution.

"If the General Assembly wishes to change or amend the constitutional law of the church, it must do so in accordance with *The Book of Order* through the established process for amendments," said *The Presbyterian Layman*. "A succession of liberal moderators has taken its toll. They have packed the General Assembly Nominating Committee with persons who appear to have little regard for the PCUSA Constitution and who in turn have funneled like-minded judges onto the very court that was designed to defend it. The GAPJC's concurring opinion is wrong. Indeed, for the life of a constitutional church, it is dead wrong, for a Constitution articulates principles, not jots and tittles. If our highest court will not enforce the principles inherent in our Constitution, then we must amend *The Book of Order's*

45 Presbyterian Church (USA), *Minutes of the General Assembly*, 1996, "Central vs. Presbytery of Long Island," pp. 173-175.

46 *Ibid.*, p.175.

ordination standards to state explicitly what Scripture teaches and what General Assemblies since 1978 have affirmed."[47]

An umbrella group called The Presbyterian Coalition was created by Presbyterian renewal organization leaders, expressly for the purpose of drafting and winning approval of the necessary constitutional amendment. Titled G-6.0106(b),[48] the paragraph that Coalition leaders intended to insert into *The Book of Order* stated: "Those who are called to office in the church are to lead a life in obedience to Scripture and in conformity to the historic confessional standards of the church. Among these standards is the requirement to live either in fidelity within the covenant of marriage of a man and a woman (W-4.900), or chastity in singleness. Persons refusing to repent of any self-acknowledged practice which the confessions call sin shall not be ordained and/or installed as deacons, elders or ministers of the Word and Sacrament."

Coalition leaders were confident that Presbyterians in the pews would overwhelmingly support the constitutional change. But the critical challenge was getting it through the General Assembly's gauntlet, a meeting that would be heavily dominated by staff "resource persons" and an infrastructure that was determined to block the legislation. If they could not win passage there, the presbyteries would not have an opportunity to vote on the matter.

'Fidelity and Chastity' Standard Placed in Constitution

The battle was waged in 1996, when the General Assembly met in Albuquerque, NM. The Coalition, aided by the Genevans, a group comprised primarily of a handful of presbytery executives who did not share the dominant ideological convictions of denominational staff, crafted and executed a winning strategy. Having had years of experience within the Presbyterian Church (USA) bureaucracy, the Genevans were experts at General Assembly procedures. Anticipating the hurdles that the amendment would confront, they worked with elected commissioners, drafting motions whose precision could not be ruled out of order by denominational wordsmiths. During late evening sessions, they schooled commissioners in parliamentary procedure, preparing them for tactics that would be employed by oppo-

47 *The Presbyterian Layman*, Vol. 28, No. 6, November/December, 1995.

48 "G" refers to the "Form of Government" section of *The Book of Order*. "6" refers to the chapter titled "The Church and its Officers," that includes a section on ordination standards.

nents of their amendment. Polity experts were assigned to monitor crucial committees, where they made themselves available to commissioners who needed their advice and counsel.

As amendment G-6.0106(b) made its way through the committee process and toward the final plenary vote, it became increasingly clear that its backers had the edge, albeit by an excruciatingly slim majority. General Assembly Moderator John Buchanan, who was strongly opposed to the amendment, saw the handwriting on the wall. He encouraged private negotiations with the Genevans and Coalition leaders, seeking a compromise that would ultimately be known as "local option." Buchanan's idea – patterned on the now deeply entrenched "essential tenets" tradition since 1926 – was that each presbytery be allowed to decide for itself whether it would require sexual behavior standards for those seeking ordination.

Sensing that they had a winning majority among commissioners at this General Assembly meeting, and confident that the amendment would be overwhelmingly ratified when sent to the presbyteries, the Genevans encouraged amendment supporters to hold their ground, winning the day by a vote of 313-236. (The amendment subsequently was ratified by the presbyteries in a 97-74 vote; 86 were required to achieve a majority.)

When the winning vote was displayed on giant video screens in the Albuquerque Convention Center, a hush fell over the room. Buchanan announced that he was exercising his privilege as moderator to grant those who experienced "pain" from the General Assembly's action to express it while the assembly sat in respectful silence.

A solemn march began, led by various gay rights activists. Numerous members of the denomination's national staff, advisory councils, presbytery and synod executives joined the march down the center aisle, carrying above their heads a six-foot cross. When they arrived in front of the podium, they placed the cross on the floor, facing the assembly, and began driving nails into it.

Undermining the Standard

Hailed as a landmark victory by conservatives and evangelicals, G-6.0106(b) was attacked at every level of the denominational infrastructure. Even before the ratification process had run its course, those who manage institutional operations for the denomination and its intermediate governing bodies began efforts to undermine the new standard.

On October 22, 1996, Greater Atlanta Presbytery of the Presbyterian Church (USA) voted that a minister ordained as a man could retain ordination after a sex-change operation. It is believed to be the world's first case of a mainstream church body giving such official recognition to a transsexual.

The matter became an issue for the church when Eric Swenson, a 49-year-old father of two adult daughters, asked for a change of name – to Erin – in church records. Swenson had undergone sex change surgery.

After considering the situation for a year and debating it at a meeting on October 22, the presbytery voted 186 to 161 that Swenson could retain his/her ordination.

The case received national publicity in a *Newsweek* magazine article.[49] Contacted by Ecumenical News International, Swenson confirmed the accuracy of the *Newsweek* account, but declined further comment.

Newsweek quoted Swenson as saying: "I'm no she-male or drag queen, and I don't want to fight society. But I have as much right as anyone to practice my livelihood."[50]

Anne Sayre, the presbytery's associate for justice and women, told Ecumenical News International that the presbytery had a "very hard struggle," but decided it had "no grounds either theologically or morally" for revoking the ordination.[51]

Swenson's initial reticence was short-lived. In numerous General Assembly meetings since 1996, he has appeared as a lobbyist for Presbyterians for Lesbian and Gay Concerns and its successor organization, More Light Presbyterians. He has made speeches at General Assembly events and encouraged commissioners to support proposals designed to undermine the denomination's ordination standards.

In 2003, Swenson led a workshop at a "WOW" (Witness our Welcome) conference, a cross denominational gathering of hundreds of homosexual, bisexual and heterosexual people who are working to liberalize church policies. "Transgender people won't come to your church unless they truly know they are safe there," Swenson warned. Even ostensibly "gay-friendly" congregations are sometimes not prepared for transgender people. "Get your church to be 'trans'-friendly," Swenson urged, including providing bathrooms not marked male or female.

Included among "WOW" conference sponsors were More Light Presbyterians, That All May Freely Serve, and McCormick Theological Seminary, one of the Presbyterian Church (USA)'s officially designated theological institutions.

---

49 *Newsweek*, November 4, 1996.

50 *Ibid.*

51 Ecumenical News International # 96443, November 29, 1996.

'Love – All That and More'

The ink hardly had time to dry on the denomination's "fidelity and chastity standard" before General Assembly agencies began to defy it. In 1997, $100,000 of the Presbyterian Women's Birthday Offering was given to the Center for the Prevention of Sexual and Domestic Violence to create "Love – All That and More," a series of three videotapes on gender roles, sexuality, dating, relationships and love.

The series was released in 2001 and was advertised in *Horizons Magazine*, an official publication of the Presbyterian Church (USA), as an "excellent tool for parents or other educators who would like a well-rounded discussion on dating and love."[52]

Of the "Love" curriculum, *Horizons* said, "The focus is always on the opportunity to grow and learn how to seek and develop a mature, respectful and loving relationship with another person."[53] But in her examination of the curriculum, Mrs. Sylvia Dooling, president of Voices of Orthodox Women, found something quite different. Dooling discovered that the curriculum endorsed "an ethic that legitimizes heterosexual relationships outside of marriage, along with bisexual and homosexual relationships."[54]

Dooling said, "For Presbyterian Women to enthusiastically fund and endorse the 'Love' project – no matter how well intentioned – is to go against what they know to be the clear policies and standards of our church. It is to endorse behaviors that the Bible condemns, that the confessions of our church rebuke and that ignore a morality that has been reaffirmed time and again by our general assemblies and presbyteries."[55]

Seeking 'Common Ground'

On February 27, 1997, when reports from the presbyteries made it clear that G-6.0106(b) would be ratified, General Assembly Moderator John Buchanan and Stated Clerk Clifton Kirkpatrick called a private meeting in Chicago, ostensibly for the purpose of "seeking common ground." As the meeting progressed, it became obvious that its participants had something else in mind. "Common ground" was a euphemism for eviscerating any implementation of the new constitutional standard.

52 *Horizons Magazine*, July-August, 2001.

53 *Ibid.*

54 See archived article: Dooling, Sylvia, "Love – All That and More Observations on A Broken Trust" (www.vow.org/pcusa/pw/financial_accountability/03xxxx-sdooling-broken_trust.html)

55 *Ibid.*

Cynthia Campbell, President of McCormick Theological Seminary and an outspoken participant in the meeting, suggested that if the amendment won the necessary votes for ratification, a plan should be devised so that "it not be enforced." She urged denominational leaders at the meeting to find "non-judicial ways to deal with persons and churches that cannot accept the new constitutional standard."[56]

Predicting that the amendment would pass, Moderator Buchanan told the group that "there will be churches that will have a very difficult time changing their behavior, which in the past has been more inclusive than this amendment will permit them to be. Mine will be one of those churches."[57] Two days later, in Baton Rouge, La., Buchanan said "I'm going to be one of the ones resisting until the lights go out, saying to people who have been baptized in this church and confirmed in this church and called to ministry in this church 'you've got to leave now.' I'm going to resist that."[58]

At the "common ground" meeting, Kirkpatrick also sent signals of his intended resistance. He told the group that the implementation of the new amendment "has the potential to unravel the church." When asked by reporters covering the meeting if he would enforce the Constitution, Kirkpatrick replied that he would deal with others pastorally in love first, but that "we do have a church in which the Constitution must be upheld, and I understand that's the duty of the Office of the Stated Clerk."[59]

Addressing a gathering of "More Light" churches in Portland, Ore. Kirkpatrick told the group that he "never dreamed the constitutional amendment would pass." He said he "intended to be stated clerk to the whole denomination, including its gay community."[60]

Shortly thereafter, however, when incidents of defiance required immediate correction and none was forthcoming, members of the Presbyterian Renewal Network met with Kirkpatrick and called his attention to his duty as the denomination's highest constitutional officer to protect and defend the Constitution. Kirkpatrick told the renewal leaders that it was not his job to enforce the Constitution. This refusal to employ the considerable powers of his office to require constitutional compliance encouraged further defiance.

When it was announced that the ordination standard had won more than

56 *The Presbyterian Layman*, Vol. 30, No. 3, May/June, 1997.

57 Telephone interview with *The Presbyterian Layman*, March 6, 1997.

58 *The Presbyterian Layman*, Vol. 30, No. 3; See also *Presbyterian Outlook*, Vol. 179, No. 8 for discussion of Kirkpatrick's call for 'Common Ground in the Presbyterian Church (USA).'

59 *Ibid*.

60 *Presbyterian Outlook*, Vol. 23, No. 2, 1997.

enough presbytery votes to become part of the Constitution, clusters of homosexual activist organizations in Washington, D.C. and San Francisco, Ca. issued "Covenants of Dissent." The Washington covenant, signed by 14 church sessions, said, "We covenant together to elect, ordain, and install as officers those members with suitable gifts who are called to ministry … without additional requirements or restrictions."[61]

Hudson River Presbytery Encourages Defiance

Sixteen Hudson River Presbytery congregations announced publicly that they would not abide by the denomination's ordination standard. The presbytery created a committee to contact the defiant congregations, but beyond the fact that they conducted conversations on the subject, no disciplinary or remedial action was proposed that would have required the congregations to end their dissent. This willful abandonment of the Constitution was the precipitating factor in a decision by the Presbyterian Church in Circleville, New York to leave the denomination. Leaders of the Circleville congregation said its affiliation with the PCUSA was damaging their church to the extent that separation from the denomination was a matter of survival. The church halted construction on its family life center after it was two-thirds complete because with each report of nearby Presbyterian congregations conducting same-sex weddings and defying constitutional ordination standards it was losing members and contributions.

'Just Do It!'

The Rev. James Collie, executive presbyter of Santa Fe Presbytery, became concerned that these public statements of intent to defy the Constitution might result in an enforcement backlash. He suggested that individuals and sessions that were opposed to the standard simply disobey it without making public statements that could get them in trouble. "I hope that those in National Capital and in San Francisco who are preparing text for sessions to adopt which contain 'will not be bound' implications, will think again whether or not such a strategy really gets them where they wish to go … The kind of disobedience that has real short and long-term effect, the kind that changes systems, and will continue to make a difference in this instance is clearly not to 'announce' disobedience, but to simply 'do it' … Avoid talking about disobedience – just do it."[62]

---

61 *Ibid.*

62 Presbyterian Church (USA), "Presbyterians for Lesbian and Gay Concerns *PresbyNet* Discussion," May, 1997.

Collie's fears that announced intentions to defy the Constitution could backfire apparently were well founded. The Presbytery of Milwaukee adopted a covenant of dissent on May 27, 1997 in which it declared that it would ordain anyone "with suitable gifts ... without additional requirements." That action was subsequently declared "null and void" by the Synod of Lakes and Prairies. The synod said, "Under our Constitution, governing bodies are not free to violate mandatory constitutional provisions ... It is imperative that everyone understand the potential consequences of a failure to do so."[63]

After Collie's advice was made public, Presbyterian Renewal Network representatives asked Stated Clerk Kirkpatrick to cease and desist from his annual practice of appointing Collie to head the "Tracking Office" at General Assembly meetings. All pending business of an assembly passes through the tracking office. Thus, it is a key location in which liberals can spot potential problems for legislation that they favor so they can dispatch influential "resource persons" to the appropriate committees where they can attempt to derail objections. Renewal leaders said that Collie's "just do it" advice constituted defiance of the denomination's Constitution and rendered his General Assembly appointment inappropriate. Their objections to the contrary notwithstanding, Kirkpatrick continued his practice of appointing Collie to this position.

Encouraged by the inaction of the stated clerk, incidents of defiance proliferated, often funded and even orchestrated by agencies of the General Assembly whose officers had promised to uphold the Constitution.

In 1996, the denomination's Stony Point, New York conference center hosted "Caring for Our Soul: An Ingathering of Lesbian, Gay, Bisexual and Transgendered Presbyterians and Our Families and Friends." Homosexual rights activists Jane Spahr and Chris Glaser were leaders for the event, in which participants developed strategies for defeating the recently approved constitutional amendment that limits ordination to persons who practice fidelity in marriage or chastity in singleness. Stony Point is heavily subsidized by the General Assembly Council budget, using mission funds contributed by congregations.

The 1997 Backlash

In 1997, the Coalition, believing that it had accomplished the purpose for which it had been formed, and underestimating the non-compliance initiatives that were being encouraged by denominational leaders, effectively dis-

63 Synod of Lakes and Prairies, *Minutes*, January 18-20, 1998.

banded. Sensing an opportunity to overturn what had been done in Albuquerque, liberal groups and their staff supporters rallied at the 1997 General Assembly in Syracuse, NY, where commissioners adopted an amendment that would throw out the recently ratified constitutional standard. But when that measure went to the presbyteries for ratification, it was defeated, 114 against and 57 for the amendment, a nearly two to one majority.[64]

Stated Clerk Kirkpatrick's public statements during the ratification of the ordination standard in 1996 and 1997 and following the 1997 General Assembly's attempt to remove the standard proved dramatically uneven. After the 1996 General Assembly adopted the standard and during the period when the denomination's presbyteries were debating ratification, Kirkpatrick publicly declared his neutrality on the issue, while privately encouraging Presbyterians not to enforce the standard if it was adopted. But when the 1997 General Assembly voted to remove the standard, and as that action was being circulated among the presbyteries for ratification, Kirkpatrick issued a "Pastoral Letter," calling the assembly's action a marvelous manifestation of "the unity of the Spirit and the bond of peace." Labeling the assembly's attempt to remove the ordination standard merely a "revision," he said, "This revision affirms the high biblical standards required of church officers, but seeks to do so in a way that is inclusive both of faithfulness in marriage as well as faithfulness in other relationships."[65]

Responding to public criticisms of his "Pastoral Letter," Kirkpatrick wrote to *The Presbyterian Layman* that he did not mean to show favoritism toward one side in a church debate, but merely to be a peacemaker who was trying to prevent a religious war in the Presbyterian Church (USA), similar to what he had seen in Croatia and other places.[66]

When his disclaimer failed to quell dissent, Kirkpatrick sent a letter to executives and stated clerks of all presbyteries and synods, alerting them to what he believed to be "an organized campaign" that was working to undermine confidence in the integrity of the General Assembly and to deny funding to its agencies. He said the campaign included a great deal of "misinformation" leading to "confusion and misunderstanding about events and decisions made at the 209th General Assembly."[67]

64 Presbyterian Church (USA), *Minutes of the General Assembly*, 1998 (12.0126), p. 131).

65 "Pastoral Letter" to Presbyterians from the Office of the Stated Clerk, following the conclusion of the 1997 General Assembly in Syracuse, NY.

66 *The Presbyterian Layman*, Vol. 30, No. 6, November/December, 1997.

67 Letter from the Office of the General Assembly, November 10, 1997.

Although Kirkpatrick was not specific regarding the source, composition or identity of the "organized campaign," it appears that he was referring to letters being circulated by several renewal organizations, encouraging presbyteries to vote against the removal of the denomination's constitutional ordination standards.

A Call to Sabbatical

In May, 1998, Kirkpatrick tried a different tactic. He arranged for a clandestine meeting to be held at a private San Diego estate. On his list of invitees were Covenant Network co-moderator the Rev. John Buchanan and Covenant Network board member the Rev. Laird Stuart. Also invited were the Rev. Jack Haberer, moderator of the Presbyterian Coalition, and the Rev. Roberta Hestenes, an evangelical minister who had chaired the assembly commissioners' committee that led to the adoption of G-6.0106(b). The resulting consensus was "A Call to Sabbatical," an agreement in which the liberals promised not to initiate or promote further General Assembly overtures seeking the removal of G-6.0106(b) if the conservatives would refrain from enforcing it via disciplinary action in Presbyterian courts and refrain from "personal attacks, accusations, defamation of character or intrusive exposure of sexual orientation."[68]

"A Call to Sabbatical" was a sweet deal for the Covenant Network. Twice beaten in presbytery referenda – the 1998 experience being a 2-1 defeat – leaders of this organization knew that they could not overturn the denomination's ordination standard any time soon.[69] So in promising that they would refrain from initiating further amendments, they were essentially giving up nothing. But conservatives Haberer and Hestenes made a huge concession. In promising that they would refrain from enforcing the standard, they essentially undermined it, granting the Covenant Network and its allies a three-year lobbying license to prepare for their next assault on the standard.

The Covenant Network issued a public statement of support for "A Call to Sabbatical." In a disingenuous disclaimer, given the fact that its moderator and leading board member were prominent participants among those who forged the "Sabbatical," the Network letter said that "the Sabbatical was not a Covenant Network initiative." Nevertheless, said Network leaders, "we do believe that the church needs to seek "the special grace of civility and

68 "A Call to Sabbatical" May 19, 1998, Presbyterian News Service # 98189, May 20, 1998.

69 When the matter was voted on again in 2001, the margin was indeed greater, almost three to one.

mutual charity when members of the body of Christ differ on what are clearly matters of deep and conscientious conviction for many on all sides."[70]

The board of directors of the Presbyterian Coalition declined to endorse "A Call to Sabbatical" and several of its members expressed their unhappiness over the fact that their moderator had participated in its development without their knowledge or approval. Haberer himself stated that his participation in "A Call to Sabbatical" got him in hot water with his board. "I had already announced my resignation from serving another term as moderator of the Presbyterian Coalition," he said. "Now it became clear that some were ready for me to step aside. Some board members felt betrayed by the Call ... Indeed, feedback over the next several months indicated that some evangelicals wanted to draw a hard line between 'us' and 'them.'"[71]

Although the majority of the Presbyterian Renewal Network was opposed to "A Call to Sabbatical," support for the compromise was expressed by Presbyterians for Renewal's executive, the Rev. Joseph Rightmyer in the Spring, 1998 edition of *Re-News.*

The "Call to Sabbatical" was never legally binding, since it was not a constitutional document. Even if it had been adopted by a General Assembly, it could only have been in force during that meeting, since one assembly cannot bind a future assembly. But the document did carry some moral authority, simply by virtue of the fact that the stated clerk and other denominational leaders often referred to it in recommending that no substantial General Assembly decisions on human sexuality issues be undertaken during the sabbatical period. Thus, the "call" held until the General Assembly of 2001 when the liberals mounted a major assault on G-6.0106(b).

Welcoming 'Angels in our Midst'

In 1999, the Presbyterian Health, Education and Welfare Association, a cluster of groups that are funded by the mission budget of the Presbyterian Church (USA), held its biennial conference in San Diego. Participants in the opening worship service found the worship space decorated by stoles from the "Stoles Project" sponsored by More Light Presbyterians.

In case anyone missed the significance of the colorful strips, Helen Locklear, a member of the denominational staff in Louisville, pointed them out the first evening, saying that they hung there representing gay, lesbian, and bisexual people.

---

70 The Covenant Connection, Vol. 1, No. 4.

71 Haberer, John H. Jr., *GodViews: The Convictions that Drive Us and Divide Us* (Louisville: Geneva Press, 2001), p. 6.

The theme of the conference was "Welcoming Angels in our Midst." Glaucia Vasconcelos Wilkey, the first worship leader, equated angels with anyone "different." Workshop leaders encouraged participants to think of ways that "different Presbyterians" were being denied their ordination rights and to strategize ways to bring justice for angels into the denomination.

Later that year, Hudson River Presbytery adopted a new policy, endorsing same-sex relationships. "Presbytery affirms the freedom of any session to allow its ministers to perform ceremonies of holy union [within or outside the confines of the church's sanctuary] between persons of the same gender, reflecting our understanding at this time that these ceremonies do not constitute marriage as defined in *The Book of Order*." Thus, by substituting "holy union" for "marriage," the presbytery succeeded in permitting activities that were expressly forbidden by General Assembly policy.[72]

Only 'Acknowledged Sins' are Sins

Also in 1999, the Permanent Judicial Commission of the Presbytery of Southern New England ruled that First Presbyterian Church of Stamford, Conn. could install a "gay man" on its session. The candidate, Wayne Osborne, said during his examination that he was "in relationship with another man" but that he would not specify the particulars of that relationship or acknowledge any behavior in which they might be engaged as sinful. "There are many 'sins' mentioned in the confessions that I believe are outdated or out-of-step with current teachings and beliefs," said Osborne. "I find it difficult to say with integrity that I will repent of those particular sins listed when I don't acknowledge them to be sin."

The presbytery's approval of Osborne's ordination was reversed by the Permanent Judicial Commission of the Synod of the Northeast. In an 8-3 ruling, the synod ordered the lower courts to reopen Osborne's examination to determine if he was in compliance with the denomination's ordination standard. It said the session that examined Osborne had an obligation to learn what "sins mentioned in the confessions" he did not believe were sins and what he meant by his expression that he was "chaste in God's eyes."

Following the decision of the synod court, the presbytery instructed the session of First Presbyterian Church, Stamford, to re-examine Osborne, whose term was already half completed during the years of court deliberations. The result of the re-examination, if it occurred, is not known, but

72 In taking this action, Hudson River became the first presbytery officially to endorse the "local option" tactic that would surface at the 2006 General Assembly in a recommendation by the denomination's "Peace, Unity and Purity" task force.

Osborne completed the term of office to which he had been elected.

Meanwhile, *Church & Society*, a magazine published by the National Ministries Division of the Presbyterian Church (USA) dedicated its fall issue to the subject of hate. Included in the issue were articles by several homosexual activists, including one by Chris Glaser suggesting that the Presbyterian Church (USA)'s "anti-gay" policies contributed to the death of Matthew Shepard, a homosexual male who was picked up at a bar and brutally murdered. "In Matthew's final years of high school, as he was developing the normal crushes and contemplating what he would do with his life, the Presbyterian Church was codifying its anti-gay position by an amendment to our *Book of Order* … And the night of Matthew's death, the Presbyterian Church was sleeping on its ecclesiastical sofa, having declared a moratorium on decisions regarding homosexuality."[73]

'Women of Faith' Award

At the 1999 General Assembly, "Lesbian Evangelist" Jane Spahr received the Women of Faith award from the Women's Ministries Program Area of the denomination's National Ministries Division. The selection committee was made up of representatives from Women's Ministries, Presbyterian Women, the Advocacy Committee for Women's Concerns, the National Network of Presbyterian College Women, the National Association of Presbyterian Clergywomen and the Association of Presbyterian Educators.

Spahr's award was briefly held up by a steering committee of the General Assembly Council. "Entities of the General Assembly are obligated to uphold the policies of the Presbyterian Church (USA) and should not be put in the position of appearing to compromise on them in any way," said the steering committee. "The determination of the steering committee was that presenting this award to Dr. Spahr placed the division in conflict with that obligation."[74]

But the steering committee's attempt to uphold denominational standards did not last. In a scathing Internet message, homosexual activist Chris Glaser said, "Kearns [director of the National Ministries Division] should resign or be removed … By his display of bigotry and sexism and an authoritarian management style, he has spiritually humiliated himself and our denomination and has severely diminished any spiritual authority he

73 Glaser, Chris, "If the Church Had Been There, Matthew Shepard Would Not Have Died." *Church & Society* (Louisville: Division of National Ministries), September/October, 1999.

74 *The Presbyterian Layman*, Vol. 32, No. 3, May/June, 1999.

may once have had to serve as a Presbyterian leader."[75]

Glaser called on the denomination's gay/lesbian/bisexual/transgendered lobby to gather at the General Assembly meeting and "interrupt the award breakfast to present Rev. Spahr with the award." He suggested that "supportive national staff members should consider a one-day sick-out during the busiest weeks prior to the upcoming General Assembly to protest Kearns' action, if it is not reversed." He called on "supportive Presbyterians" to launch "a deluge of letters, emails, and phone calls to Kearns and other national church leaders demanding the reversal of this precedent-setting decision."[76]

Adding fuel to Glaser's fire, Gene Huff, an associate pastor in San Francisco Presbytery posted a list of General Assembly Council executive committee members, complete with their home addresses and phone numbers. In an internet message, Huff said, "This episode could well be a watershed moment regardless of which way it finally goes."[77]

Battered by the campaign, the General Assembly Council executive committee met and overrode the steering committee's action, paving the way for Spahr to receive the Woman of Faith Award. Chairman-elect Donetta Wickstrom objected, warning the committee that this decision would not play well in Peoria. Suggesting that the pressure applied to denominational leaders came from a small segment of the Presbyterian population, she said, "I have a concern that there is a silent majority out there who would not be favoring the reinstatement of the award and have not been heard from at this point ... There is going to be damage and there will be collateral damage. I'm concerned how this action will be perceived by the greater church, and how we address that."[78]

Wickstrom's prediction – though it fell unheeded by the executive committee – proved remarkably accurate. Caught between a loud minority that represented national and regional staff and the faith and ethics of the vast majority of Presbyterians, the council voted by secret ballot (41-40) to accede to the minority's demand.[79]

It should have come as no surprise, therefore, that Presbyterians in the pews would begin to find alternative recipients for their benevolent contri-

75 Glaser, Chris, *PresbyNet* May, 1999, quoted in *The Presbyterian Layman*, Vol. 32, No. 3, May/June, 1999.

76 *Ibid.*

77 *Ibid.*

78 *Ibid.*

79 *Presbyterian Outlook*, Vol. 181, No. 24, 1999.

butions. The General Assembly Council's budget crisis corresponds directly to its refusal to reflect the ethos of Presbyterian congregations. That sense of estrangement, so clearly stated in this Sphar award incident, would grow exponentially over the next few years, leading to what many now believe is an inevitable denominational schism.

Demonstration at the 1998 Assembly

On the final night of the 1998 General Assembly a demonstration in the Charlotte Convention Center disrupted what had been one of the most orderly legislative sessions in the denomination's recent history.

The 10:30 p.m. event was led by gay/lesbian activists and choreographed with the help of General Assembly staff and Moderator Douglas Oldenburg, a member of the Covenant Network. In the spectacle that followed, commissioners reconsidered their decision to deny funding to the National Network of Presbyterian College Women (NNPCW), a controversial group that supports lesbian activity on college campuses.[80]

NNPCW was formed by Mary Ann Lundy and her associates at Presbyterian Church (USA) headquarters shortly before Lundy was fired for her role in the 1993 ReImagining God conference. Calling their work "evangelism," NNPCW leaders produced materials for college women that encouraged diversity in sexual behavior. The organization's web site included among its "recommended resources" for college women books and tapes authored by platform speakers at the ReImagining God conference. Also recommended was a link to a lesbian dating service.

NNPCW came to the assembly's attention when it requested $273,000 to underwrite its program for three years. That request opened the door for critics to showcase the group's activities, leading to the assembly's decision not only to deny the requested funds, but to cut off all mission dollars to the organization. Commissioners voted 306-217 to deny continued sponsorship and funding for NNPCW, encouraging the organization to become independent or to become an accountable component of the denomination's campus ministries.

On the eve of adjournment, after two attempts failed to get the assembly to reconsider its action, Moderator Oldenburg announced that he deeply regretted what the assembly had done. Then he told the assembly that he had decided to allow members of NNPCW "a moment of personal privilege." A tearful young woman, Rebecca Morrison, stepped to the microphone and sparked the demonstration. An estimated 200 visitors, many of

80 Presbyterian Church (USA), *General Assembly News*, GA #98129, 1998.

whom donned multi-colored stoles (a symbol for homosexuals who have been denied ordination), cascaded from the bleachers, held hands, and surrounded the commissioners. A small cluster of NNPCW members marched forward holding lit candles and lined up in front of the assembly. The assembly musician, Isaiah Jones, moved to his keyboard on stage and began to play "This Little Light of Mine" as lyrics to the song appeared on giant television screens suspended over commissioners' heads. The song, often used by homosexual demonstrators who call their effort the "More Light Movement," was sung repeatedly as assembly cameras were repositioned to project close-up views of the young women's tear-stained faces.

At the conclusion of the demonstration, Oldenburg again gave the microphone to commissioners who requested a "moment of personal privilege." Commissioners lined up at the microphones, some crying and others expressing anger and dismay that the assembly had "cut these young women adrift." One commissioner said "I deeply grieve … that we send them off without visible support and tell them that their life is over."

After several commissioners had spoken, some asking rhetorically, "What can we do about this?" the moderator suggested that when the assembly returned to business, a motion to reconsider "would be in order." At this point, the Rev. James Mead, vice moderator of the assembly, stepped to the microphone and called for reconsideration. The motion passed, and the assembly recessed for the night.

On the following day, Mead made a motion to continue funding the group for one year and establish a review committee to examine its programs. The motion passed easily. Moderator Oldenburg appointed Mead and himself to the review committee, along with the Rev. Jeffrey Bridgeman, a member of Presbyterians for Renewal who later was named chairman of the General Assembly Council.

At the conclusion of its review, the committee recommended and the succeeding assembly approved not only continuing NNPCW but giving it more money. Its rationale was that NNPCW's excesses were due primarily from the fact that it had not been given sufficient funding and staff support from denominational offices. Missing from the committee's analysis was the fact that denominational officials in the Women's Ministry Unit had organized NNPCW and led it into the very programs that had caused concern.[81]

The NNPCW affair provides a case study on the national staff's role in manipulating a General Assembly. The elected office of General Assembly moderator is primarily a ceremonial role, but there are two areas in which

81 For a brief, corroborating account of the demonstration, see "Emphasis on Pain Rather Than Truth," *Presbyterian Outlook*, Vol. 180, No. 25.

the person who holds that office can make a continuing impact. One is the moderator's opportunity to manipulate decision-making processes during the General Assembly meeting. Moderator Oldenburg probably exceeded his constitutional authority in claiming a period of "personal privilege," just as Moderator Buchanan did when he allowed homosexual activists and their supporters to parade a six-foot cross into the assembly and drive nails into it. But General Assembly commissioners – more than 80 percent of whom have never before served in this role – are unfamiliar with rules of parliamentary debate that could be employed to challenge such excesses by the moderator.

Secondly, the moderator has the power of appointment. Oldenburg's appointment of members to the special investigating committee determined its outcome, as the majority of his appointees were liberals who were committed to the preservation of NNPCW. The few conservatives that he appointed (Mead and Bridgeman) were persons whose desire for denominational unity fueled a propensity toward compromise.

The role of the General Assembly staff in working with homosexual activists to orchestrate the NNPCW demonstration also proved instructive. When Moderator Oldenburg announced his moment of "personal privilege," a series of carefully choreographed events occurred. The flow of demonstrators from the stands, each carrying rainbow ribbons was hardly accidental. The crying young women knew precisely where to stand in order to be within camera range. Isaiah Jones had the musical score at his on-stage keyboard. Camera crews were supplied with directions, and backstage editing determined exactly which images to feed onto the giant convention center screens.

Of course, none of these elaborate preparations by the moderator, demonstrators and General Assembly staff can exempt General Assembly commissioners from responsibility for their gullibility and the resulting unwise decision. But the incident does demonstrate the extent to which the denomination's infrastructure will go to manipulate a decision and its implementation.

Ghost Ranch Welcomes the Goddess

Although it is owned by the Presbyterian Church (USA) and subsidized by its mission budget, the 21,000 acre Ghost Ranch in New Mexico offers little programming that upholds the traditional beliefs of Presbyterians. Most of its offerings promise art and exercise, nothing distinctly Christian. Painting, sculpting, writing, hiking and biking predominate in Ghost Ranch programs.

In a Sept. 30-Oct. 4, 1998 seminar, the conference center offered "The Goddess Returns to Ghost Ranch." Its advertisement included the following text, "The Anasazi Ancient Mothers are calling YOU to celebrate the sacred feminine Goddess in the Land of Enchantment … Honor the Goddess within each woman. Tell YOUR Herstory [sic] with art, voice, dance, ritual …"[82]

Another Ghost Ranch seminar, Oct. 29-Nov. 1, was titled "God's Wildly Inclusive, Extravagant Love: A Retreat for Gay Men, Lesbians, Bisexuals, Transgender Persons, Their Families and Friends." The retreat was led by two of the denomination's leading activists for homosexual causes, Howard Warren and Lisa Larges.[83]

Even Ghost Ranch's announced conferences on "spirituality" suggest a focus that is far removed from Biblical teaching. One, titled "Bio-Spirituality," offered instruction in "bio-spiritual focusing." Another, under the banner of "Fall Hiking," promoted "spiritual movement, time with a Native American healer and lectures and discussions of earth wisdom traditions."[84]

'Coming Out Day' Celebrated

A "National Coming Out Day" service was held Oct. 9, 1998 in the chapel of Columbia Theological Seminary. Following the service, a coffee hour was held in the refectory, where special "Happy Coming Out Day" cookies were served.

Columbia student Karla Fleshman organized the service and preached the sermon, during which she declared, "I didn't magically turn queer on my 21st birthday, I've always been gay."

Fleshman was a non-PCUSA student who, while living in seminary housing, had her same-sex partner's name inserted in the 1996-97 directory where students' spouses are listed.

During a *Layman* interview regarding the service, Dean Hudnut-Beumler, who was serving as acting president of the seminary while President Douglas Oldenburg was serving as moderator of the General Assembly, said that the service was "ecumenical" and that the seminary did not try to control such services. "What a seminary has to do is create space where everybody who calls on Jesus Christ can testify to their experience."[85]

---

82 Presbyterian Church (USA), Ghost Ranch promotional flyer and website advertisement, 1998.

83 *Ibid.*

84 *Ibid.*

85 *The Presbyterian Layman*, Vol. 31, No. 6, November/December, 1998.

Asked if it would be possible, under Columbia Seminary guidelines, for a student to arrange for the worship of the goddess Sophia or, as was the case at San Francisco Seminary's chapel service, the witch Starhawk who prayed prayers to "powers under the earth," Dean Hudnut-Beumler replied, "At a school anything can happen, but at a good school it won't go unremarked."[86]

'The Dawn ... An Epiphany'

In December, 1999, the Presbyterian Church (USA) sponsored a youth event called "The Dawn ... an Epiphany." Included among its seminars was "I'm Absolutely Sure I'm Not Absolutely Sure!" The description read, "We live in a world of religious absolutes. This workshop will focus on Scriptural basis for talking about relativism in our world. Hopefully, we will lose some certainty and gain some faith!"[87]

Another seminar on the subject of human sexuality was titled, "Is There Room for Me at the Table?" The description read, "God has created amazing diversity in people in terms of race, gender, sexual preference, and spiritual life. Is there room for all of us? Come and find out how to be welcoming and welcomed to the table of God."[88]

"The Dawn ... an Epiphany" was planned for a crowd of 30,000 youth and young adults. Only 2,000 showed up, leading to a loss of an estimated $2.1 million, mostly for hotel rooms that were booked and not used. PCUSA official and conference planner Roger Nishioka blamed the disappointing turnout on "Y2K anxiety." He said other religious groups experienced similar setbacks, but he insisted that in youth ministry "we need to be creative and take risks."[89]

By contrast, Urbana 2000, a youth conference sponsored by the evangelical Inter-Varsity Christian Fellowship, Dec. 27-31, 2000 drew more than 20,000 college students and young people. The question before Urbana was "Who is Jesus Christ?" The answer given was unequivocal: Jesus is the Son of God, the Way, the Truth, and the Life.

Speakers and seminar leaders at Urbana challenged contemporary culture and the emergence of a new belief system that depicts all religions as valid paths to God. During the convention, which has been one of the most successful mission-recruiting gatherings in the world, nearly 3,000 students

86 *Ibid.*

87 Presbyterian Church (USA) brochure: "The Dawn ... an Epiphany," 1999.

88 *Ibid.*

89 Presbyterian News Service #00018, January, 2000.

said they will definitely enter mission service and more than 5,500 said they will probably do so.

Horizons: Extramarital Sex is OK

An article appearing in *Horizons*, a magazine published by Presbyterian Women for the Presbyterian Church (USA), declared that sex outside of marriage is not sinful. After writing in glowing terms about her first sexual experience with her boyfriend of two and a half years, author S.L. Walker said, "the church's current policy on ordination requiring 'fidelity in marriage between a man and a woman or chastity in singleness' would require me to repent of this and other sexual experiences should I act on a call from God to seek ordination in the Presbyterian Church (USA)."[90]

Walker continued, "I am highly offended at the insinuation that any and all sex outside marriage between a man and a woman is automatically sinful and incapable of being beautiful and lifegiving. I know this not to be true." She said she based her opinion on opinions affirmed by previous general assemblies.[91]

The timing of Walker's article was noteworthy. It was released immediately following the 2001 General Assembly that had just sent a proposed constitutional amendment to the presbyteries, calling for the removal of sexual behavior standards for ordained leaders.

Session's Confession Troubles the Waters

On May 22, 2001, the Session of First Presbyterian Church, Sebastian, Fla. adopted a resolution, confessing its faith in three Biblical essentials and declaring that it "will not ordain, install or employ in any ministry position any person who will not affirm them." On Feb. 25, 2002, the Permanent Judicial Commission of the Presbytery of Central Florida ordered Sebastian to rescind its confession.

What did Sebastian say in its confession that caused the presbytery judges to take offense? In tandem with more than 1,300 Presbyterian congregations, Sebastian's confession contained three paragraphs:

"Jesus Christ alone is Lord of the Church and the way to salvation for all who will receive him.

"Holy Scripture is the revealed Word of the triune God, and the Church's only infallible rule of faith and life.

"God's people are called to holiness in all areas of life. This includes honoring the sanctity of marriage between a man and a woman, the only rela-

90 Walker, S.L., *Horizons*, July/August, 2001.

91 *Ibid.*

tionship within which sexual activity is appropriate."[92]

The presbytery court ruled that sessions may not establish ordination standards for church officers that are not explicitly stated in *The Book of Order*. At the base of the presbytery's argument was the 1926 General Assembly decision no longer to require candidates for ordination to subscribe to particular beliefs as a condition of their ordination.

Earlier, the court had sent Sebastian a "request" that it recant part of its resolution and rescind its plea that other governing bodies "uphold these historic Christian convictions." The session did not comply with presbytery's request. That triggered an angry response from attorney Alan Pickering, who accused the Sebastian session of "contumacy" – obstinate or contemptuous resistance to authority – for not complying with the court's request.

But in September, the synod court reversed presbytery's order, although it declared that the Sebastian resolution could not be used as a litmus test for examining church officers.

Stated Clerk Lowers the Bar

In 2002, as defiance of the denomination's constitutional standards escalated, Stated Clerk Clifton Kirkpatrick issued public statements purportedly in support of the standards (which his office is obliged to "protect and defend"), but which defenders of those standards – in particular, the executive committee of the Coalition – believed had the opposite effect.

"I am well aware that there is considerable debate about the wisdom of this provision [the fidelity/chastity ordination standard] in our Constitution in light of our historic Presbyterian polity ..." said Kirkpatrick. He reminded his readers that an amendment to remove the standard was being circulated among the presbyteries and said, "until such time when this or a similar amendment is approved, G-6.0106b is the 'law of the church' and should be upheld."[93]

The Coalition Executive Committee responded publicly to Kirkpatrick's letter: "You state mildly that the standards 'should be upheld.' And that no one 'has a right' to ordain someone living outside those standards. Where is the condemnation of such acts as 'unconstitutional?'"[94]

In a "Polity Reflection," a published interpretation of the Constitution by the Office of the Stated Clerk, Kirkpatrick said of G-6.0106(b), "The words ["chastity" and "fidelity"] are not defined. Examining bodies will need to

92 First Presbyterian Church, Sebastian, Florida, *Session Minutes*, May 22, 2001.

93 Kirkpatrick, Clifton, Letter to Middle Governing Body Leaders, January 3, 2002.

94 Coalition Executive Committee, Published Response, January 23, 2002.

consider reasonable definitions and decide which to apply."[95]

This question regarding the definition of key terms in the constitutional ordination standard – reminiscent of a US president's reference to multiple definitions of "is" – would later be employed by the defiant Christ Church of Burlington, Vt., when it produced its own, unique definition of "chastity" and "repentance" in order to declare that it was "in compliance with G-6.0106(b)."

'Train Wreck' Analogy Derailed

At an April, 2002 conference on the Constitution, Kirkpatrick blamed *The Book of Order* for much of the disorder that had erupted in the Presbyterian Church (USA). It contains too many rules, he said, and these rules have become points of disagreement that threaten denominational unity. Kirkpatrick proposed as a solution the creation of an abbreviated *Book of Order* that would reduce the regulatory and disciplinary roles of governing bodies and focus on principles rather than specific rules of behavior.

Kirkpatrick told a story about an "almost train wreck" in Mexico. Two trains were heading toward one another on the same track. Both trains stopped, and their engineers got out and began arguing over which one had the right of way. They looked at the operation manual, but they disagreed about the text, so they resorted to a fist fight. Finally, railroad officers arrived and settled the matter by ordering one train to back up and the other to proceed.

Commenting on the story, Kirkpatrick said that the denomination's *Book of Order* is as fat as the train operator's manual and no more helpful. Appealing to the Constitution, he said, is no way to settle church disputes.

Five of the six panelists who were called on to respond to Kirkpatrick's presentation strongly supported his thesis. But the sixth panelist, the token "evangelical," was the Rev. Jerry Andrews, co-moderator of the Presbyterian Coalition who had been strongly critical of Kirkpatrick's unwillingness "to protect and defend the Constitution." Referring to the stated clerk's train wreck story and looking squarely at Kirkpatrick, Andrews suggested that the dispute was solved, not by throwing out the book, but by the appearance of a railroad official who enforced the book with an order.[96]

---

95 Kirkpatrick, Clifton, "Polity Reflection #19," July 22, 1998.

96 The stated clerk has continued to advocate a revision of the *Book of Order* that would remove much of its mandatory language and focus on principles rather than rules. The 2006 General Assembly accommodated to this request by adopting amendments proposed by its Form of Government Task Force (FOG) and sending them out to the presbyteries for ratification in 2008.

Lesbian's Ordination Sustained on Technicality

Without hearing the facts in the case, the Synod of the Pacific Permanent Judicial Commission dismissed two complaints charging that the Presbytery of Redwoods unconstitutionally ordained the Rev. Kathleen Morrison, a lesbian who said that she was in a sexually active relationship.

The court ruled in its May 17, 2002, order that the complainants failed to state a claim on which relief could be granted because they did not specify when Morrison acknowledged the practice of homosexuality. Morrison made no secret of the fact that she was a lesbian. She stated that in a denomination publication and in the secular media. A former co-chair of the National Network of Presbyterian College Women (NNPCW), Morrison also disclosed her lesbian orientation to the Redwoods Committee on the Preparation for Ministry, but the committee declined to investigate further.[97]

Defiance in Vermont

In 1997, Christ Church of Burlington, Vt. declared publicly that it had not and would not obey G-6.0106(b). In its review of Christ Church's defiance, the Presbytery of Northern New England decided that it was permissible for a session not to comply with that one part of the Constitution. A remedial case was filed against the presbytery for its refusal to require compliance, and the Covenant Network rose to the presbytery's defense. It announced that it would provide "legal and polity advice and expertise pro bono to the Presbytery's Committee of Counsel. Covenant Network will also assist with costs of defending the suit." Covenant Network Co-moderator Robert Bohl called this "a particularly important case … because it challenges the freedom of conscience of a whole presbytery …"[98]

When the case came before the General Assembly Permanent Judicial Commission, the court ruled that a Presbyterian Church governing body does not have the right to defy a selected portion of the Constitution.[99] Despite this decision by the high court, Christ Church left its statement of defiance on its web site for more than two years.

Under the Standing Rules of the General Assembly, Stated Clerk Clifton Kirkpatrick was required to report the Permanent Judicial Commission

97 Presbyterian News Service #02185, May, 2002.

98 "Covenant Network Will Support Challenged Presbytery," *Covenant Connection*, Vol. 2, #1, April, 1999.

99 *Londonderry Presbyterian Church et al. v. The Presbytery of Northern New England*, 2000. See Also Presbyterian News Service #00256, July 13, 2000.

decision and the fact that compliance had occurred to the 2001 General Assembly. He failed to do so, in effect, sweeping Christ Church's refusal to comply under the rug.

As the 2002 General Assembly approached, Kirkpatrick included a year-late report in the pre-assembly packet that was sent to commissioners. But the report simply informed the assembly of the Permanent Judicial Commission's decision and said nothing about the fact that Christ Church remained non-compliant.

Shenango Presbytery sent an overture to the 2002 General Assembly, calling on it to exercise administrative oversight and to require Christ Church to comply with the Constitution. On the eve of the assembly, Christ Church announced that it had "set aside" its declaration of defiance. Several commissioners expressed skepticism, wondering what the words "set aside" meant, but they were assured that this was a step in the right direction, so the General Assembly decided to be gracious and not pursue the matter further.

Redefining the Terms

Meanwhile, Covenant Network strategists returned to the drawing board. The Londonderry decision made it clear that they could not defy the constitutional mandate openly and directly, but could defiance be achieved by another method? At a conference in Minneapolis, two lawyer members of the network, Peter Oddliefson and Doug Nave, came up with a solution. In a plan reminiscent of Clifton Kirkpatrick's Polity Reflection #19, they suggested that church sessions assign their own meaning to the words in G-6.0106(b) so that they could then declare that they are complying with the Constitution by their own definition.[100]

That was the break that Christ Church needed. On November 11, 2002, its session declared that it was now in compliance with the Constitution by virtue of its own, unique definition of "chastity" and "repentance." Christ Church remains in defiance of the Constitution.[101]

20 Cases of Defiance Sidelined

Paul Rolf Jensen, a California trial lawyer was mostly unsuccessful in a series of single-handed attempts to ensure enforcement of the PCUSA Constitution. Having read news reports of Presbyterian leaders who were

100 Adams, John H., "Lawyers Say Ordination Rule Can Be Rendered Meaningless," *The Layman Online*, November 8, 2002.

101 Note: See pages 282-284 for a fuller discussion of Christ Church's defiance.

openly defying the denomination's ordination standards, Jensen filed more than 20 complaints before church courts in several states. In most of these cases, the facts were not at issue. Ministers who performed same-sex weddings in violation of church policy had posted copies of their church bulletins on the Internet. Candidates for ordination who engage in same-sex intimacy had admitted that fact – even boasted of it – in open letters and publications.

Ideally, a judicial complaint is filed by persons who reside in the presbytery where the offense occurs. But Jensen noted that with rare exception, Presbyterians who said they support the Constitution were choosing to look the other way when it was being defied in their own backyard. No stranger to litigation, and aware that *The Book of Order* allows any member of the Presbyterian Church (USA) to file an allegation, Jensen decided to initiate those cases himself.

When an allegation is filed against a minister, his or her presbytery responds by appointing an investigating committee. In a manner similar to a grand jury investigation, the investigating committee determines if there are sufficient grounds for formal charges to be filed against the minister. If it believes the evidence warrants a trial, the investigating committee – not the person who made the original allegation – files charges before the presbytery's permanent judicial commission. If the committee decides not to proceed, the case does not make it to trial.

In four cases, ministers against whom Jensen filed allegations admitted their guilt and either resigned or accepted a plea bargain. A fifth minister admitted the facts but demanded a trial. In several cases, presbyteries appointed investigating committees whose members simply refused to bring charges, even when the evidence of defiance was blatant and uncontested.

Baltimore Presbytery was a case in point. A member of the presbytery, the Rev. Don Stroud, was flagrant in his public claims that he was a homosexual person actively engaged in same-sex behavior. Complaints were brought against Stroud's defiance in 1999 and again in 2000 to no effect. Rather than discipline Stroud, the presbytery honored him by electing him to represent the presbytery as a commissioner to the 2001 General Assembly. During that assembly, he argued vigorously on behalf of proposals to rid the denomination of its sexual behavior standards.

Jensen filed an accusation against Stroud with Baltimore Presbytery, but the presbytery's investigating committee declined to initiate litigation. Considering the committee's staff resource and membership, this attempt to bury Jensen's allegations was not unexpected. The composition of the investigating committee and its staff advisor suggests that several parties had conflicts of interest, an allegation that was later voiced on appeal. The stated clerk of the presbytery, who serves as an official resource person in judicial cases, was a financial contributor to That All May Freely Serve, the homosexual rights organization that employed Stroud as an "evangelist" for same-sex causes. Three members of the investigating committee, Moderator John Kazanjian, Florence Henderson and the Rev. Robert Gench, were also financial contributors to the organization. Baltimore Presbytery shares office space with That All May Freely Serve.

The presbytery's summary dismissal of Jensen's accusations against Stroud was sent to the Synod of Mid-Atlantic for review. Looking only at procedural matters, e.g., "were the proceedings correctly recorded?" and, according to the Rev. Davis Yeuell, chairman of the Synod Council, acting on the advice of Mark Tammen in the Office of the General Assembly, the synod found no procedural fault with Baltimore's action. They acknowledged the fact that Baltimore's stated clerk and three members of the investigating committee were financial supporters of That All May Freely Serve, but they concluded that such support would not prejudice their judgment in the case.

When it was discovered that the synod review committee had not considered all five criteria for review that are mandated by *The Book of Order*, the synod, meeting on Oct. 28, 2005 declared that Baltimore Presbytery was "delinquent in its pastoral and administrative oversight." The synod ordered Baltimore Presbytery to conduct its own review of Stroud's defiance and to issue a written report no later than March 31, 2006.

The mandated review date came and went with no report of compliance on the part of Baltimore Presbytery. An extension was offered and a new date set for the presbytery's report, this time, at the synod meeting scheduled for July 23-25, 2007.

Synod leaders convened the meeting and scheduled consideration of the presbytery's report for fifteen minutes, less than three hours before the mandated adjournment of the three-day meeting. Although presbytery representatives had copies of a 20-page document in their possession at the beginning of the meeting, none were distributed to commissioners before the docketed time for discussion.

When the Baltimore report came up on the docket, several commissioners suggested postponement on grounds that they had not had time to read the report. Some commissioners wanted to ask questions of the presbytery executive, the Rev. Peter Nord, but it was discovered that he had left the meeting on the previous evening. The fifteen minutes scheduled for this matter having transpired, the synod decided to postpone consideration until the synod's October, 2007 meeting.

Baltimore Presbytery had already voted to disapprove a resolution calling on the presbytery to uphold the Constitution and it approved a resolution declaring that it would not accept for disciplinary trial any case arising from allegations of same-sex behavior. This sweeping declaration, coupled with the synod's six-year delay in challenging the presbytery's open defiance, has effectively shut down any enforcement of constitutional ordination standards in Baltimore Presbytery.

The Van Kuiken Case and Mount Auburn

One case that was initiated by Jensen did make it through the gauntlet and to trial. On June 17, 2003, the Presbytery of Cincinnati adopted a resolution declaring that the Rev. Stephen Van Kuiken had renounced the jurisdiction of the PCUSA by virtue of the fact that he continued to perform same-gender "marriages" in defiance of presbytery orders to the contrary.

Van Kuiken's congregation, the Mount Auburn Presbyterian Church, had labeled itself a "More Light" church, declaring that it would not abide by G-6.0106(b). It continued in its public defiance for more than 12 years, with no significant action by the presbytery to stop it. Finally, Jensen, who is not a member of the presbytery, stepped into the picture. He filed accusations against Van Kuiken for his conduct of same-sex weddings, resulting in the presbytery's handing down a "rebuke" and a warning against the defendant, the mildest form of discipline that *The Book of Order* allows. Then Van Kuiken "married" two lesbians in a widely-publicized ceremony. That was the straw the broke the camel's back, forcing Cincinnati Presbytery to remove him from the ministry.[102]

One year later, the Permanent Judicial Commission of the Synod of the Covenant reversed the Presbytery of Cincinnati's ruling. The synod declared that the denomination's Constitution and its highest court do not prohibit Presbyterian ministers from "marrying" same-gender couples. By this time, however, Van Kuiken and a group from the Mount Auburn church had already started a nondenominational congregation called The Gathering, and he decided not to return to the Presbyterian Church (USA).

The synod court based its decision on a semantic loophole in a previous ruling by the General Assembly Permanent Judicial Commission.[103] Referring to that case, the synod said, "While stating that same-sex marriages are

102 *The Cincinnati Enquirer*, June 17, 2003.

103 Presbyterian Church (USA), *Minutes of the General Assembly*, 2000, p. 586 (*Benton et al. v. Presbytery of Hudson River*).

impermissible, it [the General Assembly court] avoids an outright prohibition by using the words 'should' and 'should not' in guidance for sessions and ministers." The synod court ruled that such words are not mandatory, and that if the high court had meant absolutely to prohibit same-sex marriages, it would have used the words "shall" and "shall not."

Thus, the synod court concluded that same-sex marriages are both "impermissible" and "not mandatory," a position that created significant confusion and triggered a dissent from four members of the court. The dissent called the majority opinion "an improper and unjustified attempt to rewrite the clear and unambiguous meaning of W.9001[104] ... to reach a result ... which can only be accomplished by a legislative amendment" to *The Book of Order*.[105]

During the presbytery debate on Van Kuiken's ordination, liberals realized that in the light of his very public, in-your-face defiance, they could no longer protect him. But they were careful to specify his offense was having refused to submit to the presbytery's authority, not the fact that he was violating any ethical standard.

Presbytery Court OKs Gay Marriages

In a controversial two-day trial that drew a crowd of 150 spectators and media from major television networks and newspapers, a PCUSA tribunal vindicated a northern California minister on charges that she violated church law when she married two same-sex couples.

The Permanent Judicial Commission of Redwoods Presbytery ruled that the Rev. Jane Adams Spahr, "evangelist" for lesbian causes, committed "no offense" and acted "within her right of conscience" when she pronounced each lesbian couple "bride and bride and partners in life" in 2004 and 2005. It said that "same-sex marriage has not been shown to be outside of, or contrary to, the essentials of Reformed faith as understood by the Presbytery of the Redwoods."

The ruling was overturned by the Synod of the Pacific Permanent Judicial Commission, which issued a "rebuke" of Spahr, the most lenient punishment that is specified in the *Book of Discipline*. Although bound by the Constitution to censure Spahr's defiance, the court commended her for acts of "conscience and conviction."[106]

104 W.9001 refers to a section of the Directory for Worship, which is a section of the Book of Order, a constitutional document for the Presbyterian Church (USA).

105 PCUSA *News Note* #8217, May 4, 2004.

106 Associated Press, August 24, 2007.

Calling the synod's ruling a "landmark marriage equality case" in the PCUSA, Michael Adee, executive director of More Light Presbyterians said, "For a religious institution to cling to a binary view of gender is a failure of recognizing God's palette of creation."[107]

Spahr's attorney stated that the decision was erroneous because the section of the Constitution that says marriage is a covenant between a man and a woman is "a description, not a directive," and that Spahr is within her rights to conduct same-sex marriages because the denomination's prohibition against the practice "is not essential to Reformed faith." She said that the decision would be appealed to the General Assembly Permanent Judicial Commission.[108]

Louisville Seminary Nuptials

Two lesbian activists were reportedly "married" on Oct. 7, 2006, in Caldwell Chapel of Louisville Presbyterian Theological Seminary.

Dean K. Thompson, president of the seminary, told *The Layman* that he did not know whether the couple was actually married or whether it was a "union" service, a label that has been used to circumvent the denomination's prohibition against same-sex marriage ceremonies. Thompson said that in either event, the seminary forbids discrimination that would limit the use of the chapel.

Undermining the Standard

In 2006, the General Assembly found a way to amend the Constitution without amending the Constitution. Guided by its task force on "Peace, Unity and Purity," the assembly articulated an "authoritative interpretation" of the ordination standard, namely, that although the standard remains in the Constitution, local (sessions) and regional (presbyteries) governing bodies may decide that, in their case, the standard is "not essential." Because the decision was deemed an interpretation of the Constitution rather than a formal amendment to the Constitution, the Advisory Committee on the Constitution ruled that no referendum among the presbyteries was required.

Denominational liberals – and some in the evangelical camp who place a high priority on institutional preservation – claimed that "nothing has changed," citing the fact that no words were removed from the Constitution.

107 Adee, Michael, "Is not love what matters most?" More Light Presbyterians Website, August 25, 2007.

108 Presbyterian News Service #07529, Aug. 27, 2007.

But deep in their hearts, increasing numbers of Presbyterians knew that something very significant had occurred. Deferring to a principle of local autonomy, first established in the 1926 General Assembly, the General Assembly of the Presbyterian Church (USA) eviscerated its Constitution. No longer universally applicable and devoid of any means of enforcement, the Constitution became a book of wishes whose words may mean whatever the reader chooses to have them mean.

Stated Clerk Kirkpatrick, General Assembly Moderator Joan Gray, and General Assembly Council Executive Director Linda Valentine repeatedly stated that the denomination's ordination standards are intact because they remain enshrined in *The Book of Order*. But a book on the shelf, whose text suffers the vicissitudes of multiple and contradictory "authoritative interpretations" hardly fits the definition of a Constitution in any meaningful sense of that word.

Covenant

Holy Scripture

"For thou didst form my inward parts, thou didst knit me together in my mother's womb ... Thy eyes beheld my unformed substance; in thy book were written, every one of them, the days that were formed for me, when as yet there was none of them."

Psalm 139:13, 16

"Suffer the little children to come unto me, and forbid them not, for of such is the kingdom of heaven."

Matthew 19:14

The Constitution

Q. What does God require in the sixth commandment?
A. That I am not to abuse, hate, injure, or kill my neighbor, neither by thought, or by word or gesture, much less by deed, whether by myself or through another ...

The Heidelberg Catechism

Q. What is required in the Sixth Commandment?
A. The Sixth Commandment requireth all lawful endeavors to preserve our own life, and the life of others.

Q. What is forbidden in the Sixth Commandment?
A. The Sixth Commandment forbiddeth the taking away of our own life, or the life of our neighbor unjustly, or whatsoever tendeth thereunto.

The Westminster Shorter Catechism

Broken Covenant

"Women should have full freedom of personal choice concerning the completion or termination of their pregnancies."

General Assembly,
United Presbyterian Church in the U.S.A., 1970

Chapter Seven

The Least of These

Although often categorized as a "health" issue, the subject of abortion was tackled early on by "justice" – oriented denominational agencies. A review of Presbyterian Church debates on abortion provides a graphic example of the tactic already described wherein denominational leaders engage in selective implementation of General Assembly policies.

At the outset, no selectivity was needed. Abortion was placed on the General Assembly's table in the 1960s as a women's entitlement issue. In 1970, the General Assembly declared that women should have full decision-making powers in unwanted pregnancies. It said that women should have "full freedom of personal choice concerning the completion or termination of their pregnancies," and artificial or induced termination of pregnancies should not be restricted by law. The General Assembly's action was sweeping and unqualified: a woman could choose to terminate the life within her womb at any time and for any reason with which she was comfortable.[1]

In 1972, the General Assembly reaffirmed its position, adopting 15 recommendations from a report by the Standing Committee on Women. The recommendations urged development, support and expansion of birth control clinics and favored the establishment of medically sound, easily available, and low-cost abortion services. They called for support of legislation to repeal abortion laws and the development of "theological materials on abortion."[2]

In November 1975, the Advisory Council on Church and Society released a document "designed to assist people in making decisions on

1 United Presbyterian Church in the U.S.A., *Minutes of the General Assembly*, 1970, pp.469-470.

2 United Presbyterian Church in the U.S.A., *Minutes of the General Assembly*, 1972, p. 251.

abortion." Observing that the General Assembly had declared that women should have the legal option of abortion, but that it had not spoken on the morality of abortion itself, the Rev. Kent Organ, chairman, said the council felt such a document could be "helpful." The intent of the study was to address women's needs, not only to feel that an abortion decision was "legal," but that it was "moral" as well.[3]

Alarmed that denominational agencies were advocating abortion at any time and under any circumstances as a moral decision, the Presbyterian pro-life movement was organized on March 19, 1979, in Atlanta, Ga. It declared that its purpose was "the promotion and safeguarding of human life from conception through every stage of life" within the Presbyterian and Reformed family of churches.

On Sept. 27, 1979, seven national agencies of the United Presbyterian Church met with Patricia Gavett, an official of the Religious Coalition on Abortion Rights, to discuss the "legal ramifications of anti-abortionist positions regarding first amendment rights and freedom of religion." At the close of the meeting, synod representatives planned strategies "to maintain pro-choice positions in the courts and to support and develop counseling procedures that would protect a woman's right to choose freely." They agreed to convey their plans to one another through the office of the Presbyterian Council on Women in the Church, located in New York.[4]

In 1980, the General Assembly took "no action" on an overture from the Presbytery of Northeast Florida "to appoint a committee to restudy principles for decisions concerning abortion and recommend ways to discourage abortions as an option."

On June 16, 1981 four religious leaders testifying before a U.S. Senate Judiciary Committee subcommittee rejected the idea of a law banning abortion. "The passage of a bill ... would result in writing into law the most extreme view of one group of religious persons and the denial of views held with equal force by large numbers of other religious persons," said William P. Thompson, a lawyer and stated clerk of the United Presbyterian Church's General Assembly.[5]

Senate Subcommittee Chairman John East then led a 15-minute discussion on the "sanctity of life." The senator attacked the theologians for failing to grant any "right to life" to the unborn. "I don't find any indication that you'll give any right to the unborn under the law ... The ultimate right

3 Religion News Service, November 14, 1975.

4 United Presbyterian Church in the U.S.A., Office of Information, September 27, 1980.

5 Religion News Service, June 16, 1981.

to life is totally absent [from your testimony]. It's a matter of feeling, a matter of privacy, a hunch," he said.[6]

Silencing protests by Thompson and his partner lobbyist, Rosemary Radford Ruether, East accused the group of "defending your political turf" rather than expressing true theological views. Life is a continuum from conception to death, he declared, and Congress must determine at what point on that line life should be protected.[7]

New Abortion Study Commissioned

At the 1988 General Assembly, Presbyterians Pro-Life went all out to move the denomination away from its unrestricted and absolute pro-abortion position. Mrs. Terry Schlossberg, PPL's executive director put together a powerful General Assembly team, topping it with a highly publicized presentation by Mother Teresa of Calcutta, India.

In a Sheraton Hotel ballroom rented by PPL (because the event was "unofficial," convention center facilities that had been reserved by the Office of the General Assembly were unavailable), Mother Teresa appeared, wearing her habit and a threadbare sweater. More than 2,000 commissioners, General Assembly officials, and members of the press gathered to hear this "friend of the poor, the oppressed and the helpless, lover of all God's children."

Surrounded by dignitaries and special guests, including an archbishop, a cardinal and the Mayor of St. Louis, this humble woman accepted a single rosebud from the Rev. Benjamin Sheldon, President of the Presbyterians Pro-Life organization. Then she leaned into a waiting microphone. The softness of her voice forced a hush upon her audience as she wove the words of Scripture through her plea for the life of the unborn. She spoke of the unplanned (insofar as Joseph and Mary were concerned) pregnancy of Mary, mother of Jesus, and referred to Mary's visit to the home of her cousin, Elizabeth. "And something very strange happened when she came there; the little unborn child in Elizabeth's womb 'leaped with joy' at the presence of Jesus. Very strange that God used an unborn child to proclaim the coming of Christ. And we know today that terrible things are happening to that little unborn child: how the mother kills, destroys, murders her own child, created by God Himself for greater things … The mother kills two: the child and her own conscience."

"In Calcutta, we have saved thousands of children from being murdered … and it is something wonderful to see the joy of the young mother as

---

6 *Ibid.*

7 *Ibid.*

somebody wants to help her to protect the child ... For that little one, God has died on the cross, and for us who know what that crucifixion means it should increase in us the desire and determination to save that unborn child ... He says, 'Whatever you do to the least of my brethren, you do it to me. If you give a glass of water in my name, you give it to me! If you receive a little unborn child, you receive me! I was hungry and you gave me to eat. I was naked, and you clothed me. I was homeless, and you took me in. I was sick and imprisoned, and you visited me. I was lonely, and you befriended me. I was unwanted, and you wanted me' ... every little thing."

During a response period following her address, Mother Theresa was told of the Presbyterian Church (USA)'s abortion policy that said, "the decision to terminate a pregnancy may be an affirmation of one's covenant responsibility to accept the limits of human resources" and "Elective abortion is intervention in the process of pregnancy precisely because of the seriousness with which one regards the covenantal responsibility of parenting." The General Assembly's visitor from Calcutta responded to this information with a simple and direct statement: "The child is a gift of God. If they don't want the child, then they can give it to me. I want it."

Stunning in the simplicity and Scriptural integrity of her message, Mother Teresa made a powerful impact on commissioners to the 1988 General Assembly. Denominational leaders struggled to regain the moral high ground, centering their defense of Presbyterian Church (USA) policies on the right of the woman to choose. The Rev. Dana Wilbanks, co-author of the Peacemaking and Resistance paper and an official General Assembly "resource person" argued that abortion was an "entitlement issue" for women. Fredrica Hodges, Executive Director of The Religious Coalition for Abortion Rights, an organization that is funded by the Presbyterian Church (USA) mission budget, argued that the church, especially the pastors, should be more sensitive to the needs of women, and that secular organizations like Planned Parenthood often do a better job than churches in providing "safe space" for women considering abortion.

Presbyterians Pro-Life met this line-up of denominational officials, agencies and "resource persons" with witnesses from medical, psychiatric, legal and other professions. Also among their witnesses were women who testified regarding their traumatic experiences of post-abortion guilt, and women who chose to carry their babies to term in the context of loving Christian congregations.

It was too much to expect that even after such powerful testimony the General Assembly would reverse its well entrenched pro-abortion position. But the PPL team did win a fall-back position, convincing the commissioners to initiate a new study of the issue.

Winning and Losing

In various forms, the "pro-choice" position defended by denominational leaders and the Religious Coalition on Abortion Rights[8] has been reaffirmed by subsequent general assemblies. Shortly after the1988 General Assembly decision to commission a new study of the Presbyterian Church (USA) position, Stated Clerk James Andrews filed an amicus brief with the United States Supreme Court in support of "abortion rights."[9]

Andrews told the General Assembly Council that his office decided to enter the case because "it represents the most intensive effort thus far to change the Constitutional definition of abortion rights in existence since the *Roe v. Wade* decision." Andrews said that he had given "serious consideration" to preparing a separate brief on behalf of the denomination, but he found the document prepared by the Religious Coalition on Abortion Rights "proved to be harmonious with our denominational views."[10]

As the Webster case began to draw increased attention by the media, Mary Ann Lundy, Director of the Women's Ministry Unit of the Presbyterian Church (USA) issued a statement to the national press. Purportedly speaking on behalf of the denomination, Lundy said that its General Assemblies "have continued to affirm that a woman should have the freedom of choice to make her own ethical decisions based on her own faith beliefs, her community of support, her own particular socioeconomic situation and life circumstances which only she had fully known."[11]

Abortion Study Hits Impasse

While denominational leaders argued in court and Congress on behalf of abortion rights, the special committee established by the 1988 General Assembly to revisit the denomination's position on abortion struggled to accomplish its assigned task. Heavily loaded with appointees who were

8 The name of this lobby was subsequently changed to the more benign "Religious Coalition for Reproductive Choice." Its members include three Presbyterian Church (USA) groups that are staffed and funded by the denomination: Presbyterians Reaffirming Reproductive Options, the Women's Ministries Office, and the Washington Office of the Presbyterian Church (USA). The 2006 President and CEO (ex officio) of the organization is the Rev. Carlton Veazey (Presbyterian), and the 2006 Chair of the organization's Council of Governors is the Rev. Eleanora Giddings Ivory, executive director of the Washington Office of the Presbyterian Church (USA).

9 US Supreme Court, *Webster v. Reproductive Health Services*, 1989.

10 *The Presbyterian Layman*, Vol. 22, No. 3, May/June, 1989.

11 Presbyterian Church (USA), Women's Ministry Unit, Press Release, January 23, 1989.

solidly pro-abortion, the committee's outcome was predictable. In 1991, after three years of working to achieve consensus, three minority members of the committee, Dr. Tom Miller, a surgeon from the University of Texas at Houston, Dr. Elizabeth Achtemeier, adjunct professor of Old Testament at Union Theological Seminary in Virginia, and Mrs. Edna Jackson, a health care professional from Dallas, told their associates that they found themselves unable to accept the report which the majority members would likely produce.

Speaking for the dissenting trio, Dr. Miller said, "We believe Scripture has a tremendous amount to say to the issue of abortion which is crystal clear and that these truths of Scripture are being played down in the majority report ... We cannot stand before God and say what is in this document. We have prayed about how to handle this, and we feel we must secede from the group and write a minority report which will express what we believe is an obedient response to the Lordship of Christ and the authority of Scripture."[12]

The majority's draft paper presented a "rainbow" of possible options on abortion, implying that there is no single objective truth. Committee member Mrs. Margie Wentz summed up the majority's approach to Scriptural interpretation by saying, "we don't all hear the text saying the same thing."[13] In essence, the report affirms the right of each individual woman to decide what constitutes sin according to her circumstances and her private interpretation of Scripture.

Dr. Myers Hicks, a member of the group, tried to amend the phrase from "abortion would not seem to be morally acceptable when used casually or repeatedly as a method of conception" to "abortion is not morally acceptable when used casually or repeatedly as a method of conception." The proposed change was rejected.[14]

Despite Andrews' amicus brief and continual lobbying on behalf of "abortion rights" by denominational officials, the Presbyterians Pro-Life group won a tiny victory in 1992. It persuaded the General Assembly to include a modifying clause in the narrative section of its long-awaited report on Abortion and Problem Pregnancies, the study that had been com-

12 *The Presbyterian Layman*, Vol. 25, No. 1, January/February, 1992. Note: The group did file a minority report to the 1992 General Assembly. It did not prevail, but it proved useful to commissioners at that assembly who were able to modify some of the language in the majority report before adopting it.

13 Ms. Wentz made this statement during the January 17-19, 1992 final meeting of the special committee in San Diego, CA.

14 *Ibid.*

missioned by the 1988 General Assembly. The assembly said in its narrative section (a section that functions somewhat like a prologue with no force of law because it merely precedes a recommendation for General Assembly action), "We are disturbed by abortions that seem to be elected only as a convenience or to ease embarrassment. We affirm that abortion should not be used as a method of birth control."[15] The inclusion of these phrases confused but did not change General Assembly's standing policy that granted moral approbation to a woman's choice.

METHERELL CASE RE ABORTION

Dr. Alexander Metherell, a California physician who was deeply troubled by the 204th General Assembly's (1992) refusal to change its policy filed charges against the General Assembly before the Permanent Judicial Commission (GAPJC) on grounds that the General Assembly had violated the teachings of Scripture, its principles of faith, namely, *The Book of Confessions*, and its principles of polity, namely *The Book of Order*. Twelve local church sessions joined Metherell in filing the complaint.

When the GAPJC received *Metherell et al. v. the 204th General Assembly et al.*, it referred the case to its executive committee for advice on whether the matter could be properly addressed by the court. The executive committee recommended that the GAPJC not hear the case, arguing that it had no standing to challenge a decision of the General Assembly since the GAPJC is a part of the General Assembly rather than a separate entity.

In Presbyterian Church (USA) polity, when a governing body creates a commission, it transfers to that body its own authority. It is as if the decision of the commission is the decision of the governing body that created it.

Metherell argued that declaring the GAPJC decision beyond appeal would place the General Assembly above its own Constitution and thereby undercut the essence of what it means to be a constitutional church. If one is unable to challenge the constitutionality of a General Assembly decision – whether it is the decision of a General Assembly or a judicial commission created by a General Assembly – then one must conclude that the Constitution means whatever a particular General Assembly says it means, he said.

In support of his argument, Metherell dug through the annals of Presbyterian Church history. He went to a period when there was no GAPJC and noted that in those days, the General Assembly performed both legislative and judicial functions. The record shows that for many years, the General

15 Presbyterian Church (USA), *Minutes of the General Assembly*, 1992, p. 69.

Assembly met for legislative purposes. Then it declared a recess from its legislative duties, rose, and then sat as a judicatory in order to hear cases of constitutional interpretation.

Metherell noted that in 1836 the General Assembly declared itself a judicatory in order to consider the constitutionality of an action taken by the 1801 General Assembly. The minutes of that meeting record the moderator's instruction to the commissioners that in sitting as a judicatory, they were to perform the function of judges, applying the Presbyterian Church Constitution to the matter at hand. That General Assembly ruled that the General Assembly of 1801 did, in fact, violate the Constitution. It declared the offending act "void, *ab initio*," dead from its very beginning.

Metherell said that as the denomination grew, this two-stage procedure of sitting as a legislature and then as a court became burdensome. Increasingly heavy dockets produced weighty policymaking demands and the complexity of constitutional issues required lengthy judicial sessions. So a Permanent Judicial Commission of the General Assembly (GAPJC) was created to handle the denomination's judicial business while the General Assembly itself continued to meet for policymaking purposes.

Metherell argued that the 1836 case provided a clear precedent for his position that the General Assembly, sitting as a judicial body (the GAPJC), could rule the legislative acts of a previous General Assembly unconstitutional. On those grounds, he called on the GAPJC to rule that the 1992 General Assembly's abortion policy was void, *ab initio* because it violated the denomination's faith and practice as defined by its Constitution.

Although Metherell's case was limited to the General Assembly's abortion policy which he found morally repugnant, it had implications that far exceeded the presenting issue. At question was whether governing bodies of the Presbyterian Church (USA), including its highest governing body, may be held accountable to the Constitution.

Both liberal and conservative camps in the denomination's leadership had problems with Metherell's double-edged sword. If the case prevailed, liberal assemblies might be forced to justify pending actions with reference to the Constitution. While the conservative camp would welcome that outcome, such a win would mean that a small group of politically chosen judges could declare null and void an action by the denomination's highest legislative body. This concentration of power in the hands of a few might temporarily cure the denomination's integrity problem, but at the cost of shifting power centers from legislative to judicial bodies.

Metherell's case was dismissed in 1993 on procedural grounds, namely, that Metherell was an individual, not a governing body, and as such, he had no standing to bring the case.[16] This inability to have Presbyterian courts hold denominational agencies accountable to the Constitution opened the door for more frequent and widespread acts of defiance.

Abortion Advocacy Increases

The fact that the 1992 General Assembly included a clause questioning but not condemning the indiscriminate and unfettered practice of abortion was ignored by General Assembly program agencies and their staff. The Washington Office of the Presbyterian Church (USA) used the home page of its web site in 1994 to summon women to join a political march in Washington, D.C. to oppose any restrictions on abortion. Sponsors of "The March for Women's Lives," including the Religious Coalition for Reproductive Choice and the Presbyterian Church (USA), said their purpose in the march was to advocate absolute choice: "To ensure that all women have the right to choose to have or not to have children, with reproductive health options that are safe, affordable and accessible." Among the marchers' demands was more federal tax money for abortions.

Missing from the denomination's unqualified support for the march was any reference to its 1992 statement that called opposition to abortion "morally justifiable."

In March, 1995, during a meeting of the Presbyterian Church (USA)'s Board of Pensions, staff members Susan Halcomb Craig and Unzu Lee from the Women's Ministries Office and Sally Hinchman and Helena Lee from the Advocacy Committee on Women's Concerns testified on behalf of "abortion rights." At issue was an attempt by the Board of Pensions to alter the denomination's medical plan out of respect for plan members who did not want their contributions to fund abortions. The board was considering an opt-out policy that would honor the consciences of participants who are morally opposed to abortion. Denominational staff members from the two Women's Ministry offices were adamant in their view that medical coverage is "a plan for the whole church, not a plan for a collective of individuals," and that it should not be altered.

The 1996 General Assembly was confronted by two overtures calling for the condemnation of partial birth abortion. The overtures called on the assembly to "affirm that partial birth abortion of a live fetus, except to save

16 Note: The court apparently ignored the fact that 12 church sessions had joined Metherell in filing the complaint. According to the *Book of Order*, sessions are governing bodies, with standing to file judicial actions. Because the General Assembly Permanent Judicial Commission is the denomination's highest court, litigants in this case had no opportunity to appeal its ruling.

the life of a mother, falls short of God's plan for humankind."

The General Assembly rejected the motion, prompting an impassioned comment from Mrs. Terry Schlossberg, director of Presbyterians Pro-Life. She said that observers and many commissioners were shocked by the assembly's failure to take a moral stand against a procedure as abhorrent as this one. "The failure of the General Assembly to seize the opportunity provided and speak a word in defense of the innocent lives destroyed by this barbaric practice, which at least borders on infanticide, places the church in spiritual jeopardy. Jesus said, 'I tell you the truth, whatever you did not do for one of the least of these, you did not do for me.'"[17]

Kirkpatrick Counsels Congress

In May, 1997 Stated Clerk Kirkpatrick jumped into a political debate about partial birth abortion. Overlooking the ambiguities of General Assembly statements regarding late-term abortions, he wrote a letter to the U.S. Congress, urging it to defeat attempts to ban the partial birth procedure. While acknowledging that the General Assembly's position "may not be shared by all Presbyterians," Kirkpatrick cited the then current General Assembly policy: "There is diversity of opinion in the church as to whether or not abortion should be legal and on the extent to which the government should be permitted to regulate or prohibit abortions ... The General Assembly recognizes that if fetal development is no longer the standard by which the government measures the extent of its involvement in abortions, then our lawmakers must find some other acceptable standard by which the rights of the mother to terminate her pregnancy will be balanced against the state's interest in protecting the unborn child."[18]

Among eight "affirmations" that Kirkpatrick said Congress should employ in creating abortion legislation was, "No law should impose criminal penalties against women who choose and physicians who perform abortions."[19]

Two months later, the 1997 General Assembly adopted language that offered a tiny ray of hope toward the protection of unborn children. Under intense lobbying from the Advocacy Committee for Women's Concerns, the Advisory Committee on Social Witness Policy, Presbyterians Affirming Reproductive Options, a network of the Presbyterian Health, Education,

17 *The Presbyterian Layman*, Vol. 29, No. 4, July/August, 1996.

18 Presbyterian News Service #97205, May 13, 1997.

19 *Ibid.*

and Welfare Association that receives most of its funding from denominational offices in Louisville, the assembly maintained its pro-choice stance. But it did at least express "grave moral concern" regarding the practice of partial birth abortion, saying it should be considered only if the mother's life was in danger. This amendment to General Assembly policy marked the Presbyterian Church (USA)'s first clear restriction regarding abortion

In 2006, Presbyterians Pro-Life won another General Assembly victory. It succeeded in getting the assembly to replace the word "fetus" in its abortion policy with the words "unborn babies," and it won approval of a statement that reversed the denomination's previous support for partial birth abortions. Declaring that its new statement "supersedes" its statements of 2002 and 2003, the assembly affirmed "that the lives of viable unborn babies – those well-developed enough to survive outside the womb if delivered – ought to be preserved and cared for and not aborted."[20]

But even after the pro-life group won the inclusion of such wording in a General Assembly policy statement, it was confronted with the intractability of a denominational infrastructure that refuses to implement any change in its radical pro-choice proclivities. Denominational leaders may have conceded that the subjects under discussion are now to be known as "unborn babies," but they continued to insist on the right of their mothers to kill them.

Less than a year after the 2006 General Assembly declared its opposition to partial birth abortion, an *amici curiae* brief was filed in the US Supreme Court by the Religious Coalition for Reproductive Choice, defending the practice.[21] The brief selectively quoted from statements made by the Presbyterian Church (USA) General Assembly in the years prior to 2006, when the assembly supported abortion without any limitation. Reading the language of the brief, one could not know that the 2006 General Assembly had condemned partial birth abortion.

Until 1999, denominational leaders defended such tactics by taking the position that any statement made by a General Assembly in any year was part of the assembly's current policy and could, therefore, be cited as such. This practice allowed staff members to pick the statement that best fit the position that they wished to advocate. Seeking to curtail this practice, the 1999 General Assembly approved Overture 99-43, declaring that the most current statement is the policy in force, and that it supersedes previous statements.

20 Presbyterian Church (USA), *Minutes of the General Assembly*, 2006, p. 905.

21 US Supreme Court, *Gonzales v. Carhart* No. 05-380, Sept. 20, 2006.

Not to be dissuaded by this policy change, the Advisory Committee on Social Witness Policy said that it would respond to policy inquiries by sending the text of the most current policy. "However, past statements shall be included in full response to requests for information." It is this "however" clause that allows staff members to cobble together elements of previous statements, as was done in the *Gonzales v. Carhart* brief.

On April 26, 2007, the US Supreme Court affirmed the government's right to ban partial birth abortion, reversing the rulings of six lower courts that had struck down the ban. The court's *Gonzales v. Carhart* decision constituted a stunning blow to abortion advocates. The Religious Coalition for Reproductive Choice released a 16-page statement condemning "the increasing imposition of sectarian religious beliefs on health care access – especially access to reproductive health and human end-of-life care."[22]

A Presbyterian minister, the Rev. Carlton Veazey, president of the organization, said in a separate statement that the Supreme Court decision "is a serious setback for women's health and for a woman's ability to follow her conscience in medical decisions." He said that in making this decision, the Supreme Court "has taken a step toward valuing a potential person over the woman whose life may be at risk."[23]

Who Is Lord?

The theme that has surfaced in Presbyterian Church (USA) human sexuality debates for more than 40 years is that individuals are entitled to control their own destinies. Missing from that theme is a sense of accountability to anyone other than one's own, autonomous self. Thus, the manner in which denominational leaders have handled the subject of sex – framing it as a "justice" and "human rights" issue – has carried it well beyond the bedroom or the abortionist's procedure room. It has forced parishioners to address the more ultimate question: "Who is Lord?"

This is precisely the way Eden's serpent framed the issue. On the question of ethics – is it right to eat the forbidden fruit? – the serpent turned to theology. Disobey the command, suggested the serpent, and you will "be like God, knowing good and evil."[24] In their disobedience, Adam and Eve set aside divine authority and assumed for themselves the role of God,

22 Religious Coalition for Reproductive Choice, "Supreme Court Decision a Devastating Setback for Women's Health and Freedom of Conscience," April 18, 2007.

23 Religious Coalition for Reproductive Choice, "Statement of Rev. Carlton W. Veazey," April 18, 2007.

24 Genesis 3:5.

determining for themselves, according to their own chosen criteria, what is good and what is evil.[25]

In his beguiling way, the serpent was correct. Questions of ethics – what shall I do? – invariably become questions of authority – whom shall I obey? These are not mere contextual matters, decided by the question how may I find what is the "appropriate" thing to do in my situation? Protecting and defending behavior that Scripture proscribes requires reinventing the faith to square that behavior with the ultimate question of who is Lord.

25 Genesis 3:6.

Covenant

Holy Scripture

"But above all, my brethren, do not swear, either by heaven or by earth or with any other oath, but let your yes be yes and your no be no, that you may not fall under condemnation."

James 5:12

The Constitution

"But if men, under the name of a council, pretend to forge for us new articles of faith, or to make decisions contrary to the Word of God, then we must utterly deny them as the doctrine of devils, drawing our souls from the voice of the one God to follow the doctrines and teachings of men."

The Scots Confession
Chapter XX

"We reject the false doctrine, as though the church in human arrogance could place the Word and work of the Lord in the service of any arbitrarily chosen desires, purposes and plans."

The Theological Declaration of Barmen

Broken Covenant

"Therefore, we believe the church should seek constructive, Christ-like alternatives to the 'yes/no' forms in which questions about sexuality, ordination, and same-gender covenantal relationships have been put to the church in recent decades."

Theological Task Force on Peace, Unity and Purity
Presbyterian Church (USA),
Minutes of the General Assembly, 2006

Chapter Eight

Minority Rule

Viewing with dismay the leadership crisis that has decimated their denomination, many Presbyterians are asking how it came to pass. How did such a small liberal minority manage to gain such control? And how has this minority been able to maintain and even strengthen its control when its policies have resulted in massive losses in money and membership?

These questions are particularly vexatious to Presbyterian laypeople who know how things work in the corporate world. Were they shareholders in a corporation that had lost more than half its market share, decimated its assets and faced repeated and severe budget crises, they would have fired the company's management. But Presbyterian governance makes no provision for shareholder meetings, and the nominal board of directors, which is the General Assembly and its related regional infrastructure, is beyond the people's reach.

Preceding chapters in this book have tracked the long-term, persistent effort by national and regional staff members to retain control. But they could not have accomplished this feat alone. They needed allies. This chapter describes how that alliance came to pass.

The Takeover Strategy

On Nov. 6, 1999, elements of a strategic plan to achieve Presbyterian Church (USA) minority rule were laid out by the Rev. Barbara Wheeler, president of Auburn Seminary and a tactical architect for the Covenant Network of Presbyterians. After the Covenant Network's 1997 attempt to remove ordination standards had suffered a massive defeat, Wheeler addressed the group. She urged them not to abandon ship, but stay committed to their plan for consolidating control of the denomination.[1]

---

1 Wheeler, Barbara G., "Confession: A Presbyterian Dissenter Thinks About the Church," *Covenant Connection*, Vol. 2, #4.

The plan to which Wheeler referred during that speech had been articulated the previous year in an address that she gave to the Auburn/Union Seminary luncheon during the 1998 General Assembly. She called the denomination's constitutional standard that limits ordination to persons who restrict their sexual behavior to the covenant of marriage "not only misguided, but unfaithful to the gospel of Jesus Christ." Presbyterians who are unwilling to abide by the standard now face "a difficult, tragic dilemma," she said. They must choose between openly defying the standard at the cost of possible disciplinary action against them, or quietly defying the standard while lying about it.[2]

Notably, Wheeler did not include the option that Presbyterians obey the standard.

Wheeler said that this situation was identical to the one that was faced by Presbyterians 75 years earlier, when they were burdened by the denomination's requirement that ordained persons subscribe to "essential and necessary" beliefs. She said that Presbyterians today would do well to learn a lesson from strategies employed by those who overturned that restrictive requirement. "I think we can learn a lot from our forebears about strategy," she said. "I derive from this seventy-five-year-old story five operating principles that I think we could profitably consider today."[3]

Wheeler's first principle was "take the offensive." She suggested that Baptist preacher Harry Emerson Fosdick was not acting alone in 1922 when he preached his sermon against fundamentalism. "It appears that Fosdick's sermon was part of a liberal plan to bring things to a head ... Our predecessors in effect named the time, place and their leaders in the confrontation ... It is very likely as well that their choices – Fosdick the Baptist who was hard to sue in Presbyterian court, New York City Presbytery that almost unanimously supported him, and 'Uncle' Henry Sloane Coffin, who was loved by evangelical social gospelers as well as by theological liberals – their choices were deliberate. Those choices proved decisive. If the liberals had waited for the other side to pick the setting and the target, the outcome might have been very different."[4]

Wheeler's second principle was that liberal forces must "be prepared." She reflected on the fact that the Auburn Affirmation group spent almost a year preparing for the confrontation. During that time, assuming that some of their ministers might be disciplined for their refusal to subscribe to

2 Wheeler, Barbara G, "An Auburn Affirmation: Reflections for a 75th Anniversary," *Covenant Connection*, Vol. 2. #1.

3 *Ibid.*

4 *Ibid.*

essential tenets of Christian faith, they "secured the commitment of wealthy laymen to pay the salaries of ministers who might be removed or choose to leave … Thanks to advance planning, the liberals could afford to leave, taking some substantial Presbyterian money with them. This is hardball, and we would do well today, I think, to learn to play it."[5]

"There is safety and power in numbers," Wheeler said in naming her third principle. She pointed out that 1300 ministers, some of whom represented prominent churches, signed the Auburn Affirmation. That substantial list of signatories made a significant impact on the General Assembly, influencing its refusal to remove Fosdick or discipline Affirmation signatories. "The same strategy – several thousand ministers, including a substantial number from larger churches, identified by name in strong support of a statement that tolerance and diversity of views are the nature of the Presbyterian Church – the same strategy could work for us," she said.[6]

Wheeler's fourth and pivotal principle was "convince the moderates." Observing that the liberals comprised a distinct minority that could not win in a face-to-face contest on the issues, Wheeler credited Henry Sloane Coffin, president of Union Theological Seminary in New York with a winning strategy: "What caused the turnaround was Coffin's success in persuading Charles Erdman and his moderately conservative allies that tolerance would promote the evangelical mission of the church and doctrinal fundamentalism would hurt it … This middle-of-the-road position, carefully bolstered by the drafter of the document [the Auburn Affirmation], Robert Hastings Nichols, who was a church historian, won the day with the Commission."[7]

"What was true then remains true today," continued Wheeler. "The winner of the present contest will be the side that convinces the moderate middle to join it. The requirements for accomplishing that are, I think, the same as they were seventy-five years ago. If our side, now in the minority on ordination questions, wants to prevail, we will have to convince the middle, who are moderate conservatives on current ordination issues, that our approach is more Presbyterian and more practical than the alternatives."[8]

Wheeler's final principle, titled "The Gospel has real power," had nothing to do with the gospel as it is revealed in Scripture, but everything to do with politics. Wheeler illustrated "the truth of the gospel" by remembering

5 *Ibid.*

6 *Ibid.*

7 *Ibid.* Note: The commission to which Wheeler referred was the Swearingen Commission that convinced the 1926 General Assembly to drop its requirement that persons standing for ordination subscribe to specified beliefs.

8 *Ibid.*

a 1925 debate between two McCartney brothers, Clarence, the conservative, and Albert, the liberal. Albert said of his bachelor brother Clarence that his position might have been modified had he been married, with "less time to worry over other people's theology." Wheeler quoted Albert's closing argument in what is apparently a definitive "gospel" statement for her: "I believe that there is room for him, and for you and me, to say our prayers in identical language in the Presbyterian Church."[9]

Past Becomes Present

The Wheeler speech became a play book for the Covenant Network. Founded in 1997, following the denomination's adoption of Biblical ordination standards, the organization rallied around a declaration titled, "A Call to Covenant Community." Twenty former General Assembly moderators and eventually some 2500 ministers signed the declaration, thus fulfilling Wheeler's first, second and third principles.

Already in control of the denomination's agencies and staff, leaders of the Covenant Network had the ability to protect or rescue any of their allies who might be disciplined for their defiance of the Constitution. General Assembly staff members could practice defiance with impunity, knowing that if their actions cost them their jobs, alternative opportunities, e.g., Mary Ann Lundy's being "fired up" to a World Council of Churches position, were waiting in the wings. With this system of protection in place, Covenant Network allies could assault denominational standards simultaneously on many fronts and blame the ensuing turmoil on the standards themselves.

But defiance, or, as Wheeler termed it, "taking the offensive," was not enough. Crucial to the liberals' success was her fourth principle, namely, forging an alliance with evangelically inclined moderates, middle-of-the-road Presbyterians whose desire for unity exceeded their commitment to doctrinal purity. Thus, a primary Covenant Network strategy was to drive a wedge into the heart of the Presbyterian Church (USA) renewal network, carving out known evangelicals who might help them legitimize the Covenant Network's agenda.

Targeting Moderates

As we have seen in preceding chapters, from the time that it adopted the Confession of 1967, the denomination's pace toward embedding "progressive theology" in all of its programs and agencies gained rapid momentum.

9 Wheeler was quoting from Longfield, Bradley, *The Presbyterian Controversy: Fundamentalists, Modernists and Moderates* (New York: Oxford University Press, 1991), p. 160.

Simultaneously, numerous renewal organizations were formed in an attempt to stem the tide. Many of these organizations focused on specific manifestations of the liberal agenda. Presbyterians Pro-Life was formed to counter the denomination's endorsement of abortion. Voices of Orthodox Women organized to counter the denomination's radical feminist agenda. Presbyterians for Democracy and Religious Freedom (now Presbyterian Action) was formed to counter the denomination's support for totalitarian leftist regimes. Other organizations, e.g., Presbyterians for Renewal and the Presbyterian Lay Committee, cast a wider net.

Although each renewal organization operated independently, their leaders gathered as the Presbyterian Renewal Network for fellowship, mutual encouragement and support. When it became clear that the denomination's sexual ethic was under a coordinated attack by homosexual lobbyists, that these lobbyists enjoyed the support of national and regional staff members, and that the composition of Presbyterian courts was moving in an increasingly liberal direction, renewal leaders concluded that they must join forces in order to safeguard Biblical ordination standards in the Constitution. Sensing that they needed more coordination than a mere network could supply, Presbyterian renewalists created an umbrella group called the Presbyterian Coalition and asked it to take the lead toward the enactment of a constitutional amendment.

The Coalition did its work in 1995 and 1996, culminating in the passage and ratification of Amendment G-6.0106(b). Then, believing that their purpose had been fulfilled, Coalition leaders let down their guard, refocusing their efforts on their own congregations' ministries. A few months later, the Syracuse General Assembly shocked Coalition members when it adopted Amendment A, an attempt to overturn the newly adopted constitutional standard. A call to arms brought the Coalition back together, and it defeated Amendment A by a two-to-one landslide in the presbyteries.

Union in Christ: A Declaration for the Church

On the heels of their victory in the presbyteries, many Coalition leaders understood that future attacks on the constitutional standard would be unrelenting and that they would face repeated crises unless they could target the centers of liberalism that were now firmly placed in the agencies and structures of the General Assembly.

Responding to this concern, the Coalition formed a 16-member "visioning team" comprised of leaders of renewal organizations, flagship evangelical congregations and seminaries and asked it to draft a strategic plan for the transformation of the Presbyterian Church (USA). For five months, task force members labored on two products, a Barmen-type declaration[10] and a strategy paper consisting of six strategies designed to return the denomination to its confessional integrity.

Called "Union in Christ: A Declaration for the Church," the resulting theological statement included five sections. The first section met the denomination's "Jesus problem" head on. It confessed "Jesus Christ as fully God and fully human, as Savior and Lord," emphasizing the fact that the Presbyterian Church (USA) faces "a crisis of Christology."[11]

The second section introduced the declaration's central theme, "the union of believers with Christ by the power of the Holy Spirit," emphasizing its rejection of "forms of church life that seek their unity in ideologies of pluralism or relativism."[12]

The third section lifted up Christians' participation in Christ's relationship with God the Father, emphasizing that "we turn away from any claim to knowledge of God that is contrary to the full testimony of Scripture as interpreted by the Holy Spirit working in and through the community of faith across time." It also rejected "any supposed love of God that is manifest apart from a continual longing for and striving after that loving obedience which Christ offers to God on our behalf."[13]

The fourth section focused upon the problem of cheap grace and the unredeemed life. It called for the church to turn toward Christ, living lives that participate in his holiness. "In these times of sexual confusion," it declared, "we affirm the consistent teaching of Scripture that calls us to chastity outside of marriage or faithfulness within the covenant of marriage between a man and a woman. We turn away from forms of church life that fail to pray for and strive after a rightly-ordered sexuality as the gracious gift of a loving God, offered to us in the power of the Holy Spirit."[14]

The final section of the declaration emphasized the ecumenical and missional character of the church. "By our union with Christ our lives participate in God's mission to the world: to uphold the value of human life, to

10 The statement was patterned after the Theological Declaration of Barmen, which states not only what the church believes but also what, as a consequence of this belief, it must vigorously oppose. Paragraphs were twinned, one stating an affirmation and the other a rejection. In the words of the Coalition's declaration: "We turn toward … and we turn away from …"

11 Achtemeier, Mark and Purves, Andrew, *Union in Christ: A Declaration for the Church* (Louisville: Witherspoon Press, 1999), I.

12 *Ibid.*, II.

13 *Ibid.*, III.

14 *Ibid.*, IV.

make disciples of all peoples, to establish Christ's justice and peace in all creation, and to secure that visible oneness in Christ that is the promised inheritance of every believer."[15]

Six Strategies for Renewal

The Coalition's visioning team not only crafted its theological declaration, but it produced an action-oriented strategy paper that specified six strategies for renewal in the life of the Presbyterian Church (USA). In a pattern corresponding to the format of the declaration, each strategy included a core value, followed by a specification of "frequently encountered obstacles" that must be overcome if Biblical and confessional integrity is to be restored in the life of the Presbyterian Church (USA).

"The Renewal of Mission" section declared that "the center of the church's mission is a burden for the unreached, and a desire to see persons and cultures transformed to the glory of God."

Frequently encountered obstacles that inhibit the pursuit of that mission were specified: "An incipient universalism that diminishes the urgency of the gospel message; a witness which echoes a particular cultural ideology rather than biblical fidelity; and a limited and biased view of ecumenism which has not allowed us to be in conversation with other evangelical mission enterprises or the rapidly expanding third-world mission organizations."

The statement called on denominational leaders to "evaluate and assess the effectiveness of continuing denominational involvement in mainline ecumenical organizations [The Consultation on Church Union, the National Council of Churches and the World Council of Churches], and explore participating in evangelical ecumenical organizations."

"The Renewal of Worship" section declared that "we must have worship that is Trinitarian, dynamic, and relevant to its cultural setting." Frequently encountered obstacles that inhibit the development of such worship are: "the idolatry of holding that only one worship style is uniquely faithful in expressing the Reformed tradition; nonbiblical and uncompelling preaching; worship services that are manipulated by political and ideological agendas; deep division between proponents of differing styles of worship; and failure to teach our children how to worship."

"The Renewal of Polity" section declared that Presbyterian polity must promote the spiritual objectives of the church, establishing proper lines of accountability, and placing decision-making and mission in the governing body closest to the congregation.

---

15 *Ibid.*, V.

Frequently encountered obstacles that inhibit the pursuit of polity renewal were specified: "an estrangement between the denominational leadership and the church it is called to serve; the ongoing transformation of *The Book of Order* from a constitutional document setting forth the essentials of our faith and governance to a detailed and unwieldy operations manual; and our failure to be knowledgeable, faithful, and responsible presbyters."

"The Renewal of Theological Education" section declared that "we must have theological institutions which support the mission of local congregations in equipping believers to know the scriptures and think theologically within the Trinitarian faith of the Church."

Frequently encountered obstacles that inhibit the achievement of excellence in theological education are: "Theological education that is captive to ideological currents alien to the faith of the Church; theological education that is primarily responsive to the interests and agendas of the academic guilds rather than to the mission of the church; graduates from our theological institutions who are ill-equipped for pastoral ministry."

The document called for strategies that channel support to "seminaries that promote Trinitarian faith, uphold the constitutional standards of the church, and equip candidates for the mission of the local congregation." It included a warning that it would "direct qualified candidates and support to these seminaries and away from those that do not affirm these values." It suggested that alternative approaches to theological education be explored, including the use of "teaching churches."

"The Renewal of Educational Ministries" section declared "we must promote a lifelong process of growth in the knowledge of, love for, and obedience to Christ as revealed in Scripture."

Frequently encountered obstacles include: "the loss of the Christian home as the primary school for faith and life; denominational ministries and programs for high school and college youth which have been ignored by many because of a loss of trust in their faithfulness to our theology and their ineffectiveness in reaching the target populations ... and denominational curricula and materials that are inadequate for teaching biblical faith and frequently defy constitutional standards."

Included in the Coalition's strategic goals were "emphasize biblically faithful, congregationally-based campus ministry as an effective tool for the evangelism and nurture of college students," "encourage, develop, and promote effective ministries which foster healthy marriages," and "develop resources for helping adults integrate Christian faith and professional life, develop biblically faithful curricula for congregational instruction of young people in sexuality that empowers and encourages sexual purity."

"The Renewal of Church Discipline" section declared "If the Presbyterian Church (USA) is to be faithful to Jesus Christ in the 21st century, we must be a disciplined community of faith whose members are accountable to God and to one another for the faithful living out of the gospel in holiness and purity."

Frequently encountered obstacles that inhibit the achievement of Biblical church discipline include: "Refusal to live under the authority of the biblical and constitutional standards of the church; the acceptance of theological and moral pluralism at the expense of biblical and constitutional faithfulness; a distorted understanding of grace which confuses moral permissiveness with biblical compassion; an understanding of personal privacy which undermines practices of self-examination, mutual accountability and encouragement; neglect of denominational procedures for the theological and moral examination of church officers and the disciplining of flagrant violations of constitutional standards."

Colorado Springs, 1998

The visioning team unveiled its theological declaration and strategy paper at a "Y'all come"[16] event in Colorado Springs on May 2, 1998. More than 80 Presbyterian leaders, many of them pastors of the denomination's largest congregations, attended the meeting. Participants heard presentations by the visioning team and then divided into groups corresponding to each of the six proposed strategies in order to discuss them and make editing suggestions.

When the groups re-convened, there was considerable enthusiasm for adopting the declaration and strategy paper on the spot, an action that Coalition moderator, the Rev. Jack Haberer, vigorously opposed. Haberer argued that the "Y'all come" event was merely a listening opportunity, not an official meeting of the Coalition, and that only the Coalition board could act on the visioning team's report. He insisted that the documents, in particular the strategy paper which he believed was unnecessarily strident and unfairly critical of denominational agencies, were merely "drafts," and that they would require substantial modification before the Coalition board would adopt them. He instructed reporters in the room not to publish copies of the visioning team's report, claiming that it was "copyright protected."

But momentum to adopt the documents in the Colorado Springs meeting

16 Although it had a board of directors, the Coalition carried out much of its work through informal gatherings of supporters. These open invitation meetings were labeled by South Carolinian Betty Moore, a founding coordinator of the Coalition as "Y'all come" events in order to distinguish them from the more formal Coalition board meetings.

was strong. Someone made a motion that the gathering declare its approval of the documents in principle, with the understanding that an editorial committee would refine, but not substantially change some portions in the light of editorial suggestions made during the meeting, and that the refined documents be presented to the official Coalition meeting in Dallas, October 8-10. The motion was approved by an overwhelming majority.

Haberer's rationale for attempting to prevent a public affirmation of the documents until they could be substantially modified by his board may not have been understood at the time, but what may have been a clue surfaced later that month when it was learned that he had been engaged in private meetings with denominational officials and leaders of the liberal Covenant Network for the purpose of forging "A Call to Sabbatical." This document called for a period of compromise wherein the liberals promised to forego further attempts to remove the denomination's ordination standards if those representing the conservative side promised not to enforce the standards.[17] Obviously, the Coalition visioning team's strategy paper, particularly its focus on church discipline, was in conflict with this accommodation.

Doctrine Matters

When the Coalition met in Dallas, more than 600 participants unanimously approved the slightly amended declaration and strategy paper. Pittsburgh Theological Seminary professor Andrew Purves, a member of the Coalition's visioning team, called the declaration "a standard lifted high against the confusions of this season in the life of the PCUSA … a clear message of Christian doctrine … a reaffirmation of central doctrinal beliefs – especially Christology – in the light of present circumstances."[18] Purves said, "The mandate we were given spoke of asserting the faith in a church characterized by pluralism and relativism, confusion over sexual ethics, a weakened Christology and a lessened sense of the authority of Scripture."[19]

Alluding to the link between the declaration and the strategy paper, Purves said "We cannot be faithful in serving the mission of the church if we are unfaithful in doctrine. Without doctrine, mission becomes activism without meaning or direction. The image of my cat having a daft turn comes to mind – mission without doctrine is like the silly cat chasing her own tail – much energy going nowhere."[20]

17 See page 208 for a fuller discussion of "A Call to Sabbatical."

18 *The Presbyterian Layman*, Vol. 31, No. 6, November/December, 1998.

19 *Ibid.* See also Presbyterian News Service #98339, Oct. 14, 1998.

20 *Ibid.*

The Dallas gathering not only adopted the declaration and strategy paper, but, in light of the fact that these documents constituted a call to action, it expanded the Coalition board from 11 to 24 members, authorized the employment of a full-time staff coordinator, and approved a $250,000 budget. Representatives of several of the denomination's thirteen renewal organizations pledged to back the Coalition strategies and announced a meeting of the Presbyterian Renewal Leaders' Network for the purpose of organizing that support.

Signs of Struggle

To outside observers, the Coalition's Dallas gathering looked like a launching pad for an evangelical takeover of the denomination. With its declaration and strategy paper, the Coalition seemed to have gotten its act together. It had a mission and a plan, substantial grass roots support, money and indications of cooperation by several independent renewal organizations.

Having been formed in 1995 solely for the purpose of placing sexual behavior standards in the denomination's Constitution, the Coalition had now redefined itself with a much broader scope. It would no longer be content to live in a crisis mode, fighting a steady current of liberalism on the edge of a waterfall. It would go upstream and engage theological issues there.

Reporting on the Coalition's decision, the Rev. Joseph Small, head of the denomination's Theology and Worship office, acknowledged the newfound energy and confrontational turn exhibited by the Coalition. Noting the Barmen-like content of the Coalition's declaration, Small said, "Although speakers emphasized that the declaration is a 'gift' to the church and not a demand, even gifts can be confrontational."[21]

Small called the Coalition's strategy paper "vague," but he noted its significance. "In spite of its many inadequacies, the strategy paper is an important window on conservative-evangelical viewpoints. Moreover, the strategy paper demonstrates that the Coalition's existence is not generated by the politics of sexuality alone. Sexuality issues are the lightening rod that attracts a range of other concerns and expressions of resistance to the PCUSA's official policies and practices."[22]

Small also noted the internal conflict that Coalition leaders had tried hard to mask, but that had been apparent since Haberer stated his objections in the Colorado Springs meeting. "Within the Coalition one detects a

21 Small, Joseph D., "Signs of the post-denominational future – Presbyterian Church U.S.A.," *The Christian Century*, May 5, 1999.

22 *Ibid.*

tension between those who press for more direct challenge of the PCUSA and those who remain open to possibilities for influencing the structures of the church. Although the moderates predominate, their capacity to control radical elements is not limitless. As the Coalition moves toward elaborated structures – an expanded governing board, the employment of a coordinator, a regularized budget and program – internal struggles may intensify. If the moderates prevail, they may force radicals into forms of independent action. Much hinges on whether the moderates' strategies appear to be effective."[23]

Small noted another development among the independent renewal organizations that largely comprised the Coalition, an emerging shadow church. "Whatever the moderates' good feelings about their influence in the denomination, it was evident from the literature tables at Dallas that Coalition members were erecting parallel structures. Information was available on a range of ministries for youth, women, elders and pastors. Evangelism and justice ministries were presented as alternatives to PCUSA programs, and there were signs of a placement system operating outside the PCUSA structures. People were working on a new confirmation curriculum, a theology journal, and a range of church school materials. It is clear that many evangelicals in the church will not invest in the renewal of PCUSA programs, publications and structures, but will continue to develop their own resources and networks."[24]

Small's observations proved prophetic. Presbyterians for Renewal was conducting a summer camp and conference ministry that dwarfed denominational events, attracting more than 10,000 youth annually. Its summer conference at Montreat was consistently one of the largest during the conference season, and it was, in fact, operating a referral service to facilitate connections between evangelical ministers and congregations.

The Presbyterian Layman, the flagship publication of the Presbyterian Lay Committee had reached a circulation of more than 400,000 homes, quadrupling the circulation of the largest denominational publications. Noting that less than ten percent of Presbyterian congregations use the official denominational curriculum, the Lay Committee's Reformation Press joined forces with David C. Cook publications jointly to publish a Sunday School curriculum that is faithful to the Scriptures.

An organization called One by One began a ministry to persons who suffer from gender confusion and a broken sexuality.

---

23 *Ibid.*

24 *Ibid.*

Voices of Orthodox Women published critiques of *Horizons*, a denominational Bible study for women and, during years when it found the *Horizons* material unbiblical and even unchristian, VOW published alternative studies for an ever widening group of readers.

Presbyterian Reformed Ministries International developed a worldwide network of "Dunamis Fellowships" that has given thousands of Presbyterian lay people tools for sharpening Christian discernment in the midst of secular environments.

Knox Fellowship established an international ministry, equipping and training Presbyterian lay people in the field of evangelism.

A Tulsa based ministry called Literacy and Evangelism International published reading primers using Biblical texts and began dispatching teaching missionaries to many countries.

The Outreach Foundation and Presbyterian Frontier Fellowship received millions of mission dollars from evangelicals who no longer trusted denominational agencies.[25]

All of these renewal organization ministries were independent of denominational control, and their combined activities covered every area of ministry that a denomination would normally claim. Thus, the renewal organizations, taken as a group, were in fact already a shadow denomination, attracting millions of dollars annually that might otherwise flow into the Presbyterian Church (USA) treasury.

Louisville Reports

The Christian Century was not the only publication to note a growing tension within the Coalition's leadership and a momentum toward developing shadow church alternatives to the Presbyterian Church (USA). Reporter Jerry Van Marter spotted the same dynamics. A veteran newsman within the denominational bureaucracy, Van Marter couldn't help but notice the fact that denominational leaders were courting Coalition leader Jack Haberer and his allies among the moderates. Haberer was frequently chosen by Stated Clerk Kirkpatrick when he needed a spokesperson for evangelicals at one of his "unity in our diversity" meetings. He was invited to be a featured speaker at a national staff retreat and he participated, at Kirkpatrick's invitation, in several private and public meetings with Covenant Network leaders. The Presbyterian News Service observed and often

25 In 2006, these two independent organizations combined forces to create their own mission sending agency, enabling them to recruit, train and support missionaries separate and apart from denominational agencies.

reported on these developments.

Haberer's book, *GodViews*, was published by the denomination's Geneva Press, and was frequently touted by Stated Clerk Kirkpatrick and Covenant Network founder John Buchanan. "*GodViews* is a book 'for just such a time as this!'" Kirkpatrick wrote in a published endorsement. "I can't imagine a more timely or important book for Presbyterians, indeed for all Christians who seek to deal with the diversity in their churches while seeking the unity that Christ intends." Kirkpatrick said that Haberer "invites the church to move from debate to dialogue so that our respective GodViews may enrich and correct one another and mold us into the vital Christian-community that God intends the Church to be."[26]

Van Marter, who covered the Dallas Coalition meeting for the denominational press, took note of Haberer's discomfort with the confrontational and shadow-church direction that his organization was taking. He quoted Haberer in his report: "We're not interested in tearing down but in building up," Haberer said. "We are not interested in leaving the church."[27]

Van Marter continued his report of Haberer's remarks: "Nor should development of a theological declaration, a strategy for changing the direction of the church and a formalized Coalition structure be interpreted as the establishment of a 'shadow church.'" Haberer told the Presbyterian News Service after the gathering, "The moderates in the Coalition are resolute that it won't become that," he declared. "And the moderates have the votes to resist it."[28]

Coalescing the Moderates

Haberer's identification of "the moderates" within the Coalition and his use of words like "resolute" and "resist" when referring to other voices within the organization indicated his concern that the Coalition's declaration and strategy paper could cause problems. If the Coalition took seriously commitments that were made in these documents, a line of demarcation would be drawn through the denomination. Opposing positions would be hardened. Institutional preservation would be threatened, and Haberer's attempts to achieve accommodation among Presbyterians with different perspectives, as reflected in "A Call to Sabbatical," would be undermined.

Presbyterian Renewal Network leaders had voiced enthusiastic commen-

26 Haberer, John H. Jr., *GodViews: The Convictions that Drive us and Divide us* (Louisville: Geneva Press, 2001).

27 Presbyterian News Service #98339, Oct. 14, 1998.

28 *Ibid.*

dation for the Coalition's documents and announced that they would schedule a meeting in order to develop strategies for implementing them.

Haberer had already caught flak from other renewal leaders and from several members of his own board for his role in "A Call to Sabbatical." He had not cleared his participation in that meeting or approval of the compromise that it produced with the Coalition board, some of whose members were strongly opposed to it. That led to his embarrassment when the Coalition board declined to approve his "A Call to Sabbatical" involvement or endorse the document.[29]

Haberer referred to his fracturing consensus in *GodViews*: "I had already announced my resignation from serving another term as moderator of the Presbyterian Coalition," he said. "Now it became clear that some were ready for me to step aside. Some board members felt betrayed by the Call … Indeed, feedback over the next several months indicated that some evangelicals wanted to draw a hard line between 'us' and 'them.'"[30]

During the sabbatical controversy, the Rev. Joe Rightmyer, executive director of Presbyterians for Renewal, urged Coalition board members and renewal network leaders to stand behind Haberer and his sabbatical involvement as an expression of "loyalty to a brother," and in private communications, he chastised those who criticized Haberer publicly.

PRN Gathers in Kansas City

On July 17, the Presbyterian Renewal Leaders Network (PRN) convened its meeting in Kansas City and proceeded to develop a plan to organize implementation of the Coalition's strategy paper. The renewal leaders analyzed each of the Coalition's six strategies in the light of their renewal organizations' strengths and weaknesses, with the intention of assigning each renewal organization to a particular Coalition strategy. At the close of their six-hour session, renewal leaders had completed their task, signing off on a document that attached implementation specifics to the strategy paper. Subject to the approval of each renewal organization whose leader participated in the meeting, the PRN document that was adopted on the evening of July 17 represented a huge investment into the fulfillment of the Coalition's plan.

The mood of the group that evening was celebrative and hopeful. Partici-

29 During a Coalition board meeting by telephone conference call subsequent to the release of "A Call to Sabbatical," a proposal was made to approve retroactively Haberer's participation and the resulting document. The proposal was not approved.

30 Haberer, p. 6.

pants knew that the Coalition itself, with one part-time staff member and a small budget, would be hard pressed to implement its own strategy paper. On the other hand, the 13 renewal organizations had impressive assets to bring to the table. All of them had staff persons whose coordinated efforts could be significant. All had established donor bases, together representing tens of thousands of Presbyterians, and several administered field operations. If all of this could be brought into focus behind the Coalition's strategy paper, much could be accomplished.

Second Thoughts

But between the PRN's recess on the night of the 17th and its call to order at 8:00 a.m. on the 18th, second thoughts surfaced that threatened to destabilize the project. The next morning, questions were raised regarding the propriety of any renewal group's intervention into an initiative that was "owned by the Coalition." Several renewal leaders expressed concerns that if the "moderate" stance of the Coalition board's leadership continued, any proposed involvement by PRN groups would be spurned and the strategy paper would likely fail for lack of implementation.

This led to a discussion in which PRN members explored what "principles of leadership" must characterize the Coalition if it were to become an effective agent of denominational renewal. The group agreed that the primary principle for the denomination as a whole must be that policies of the PCUSA "are determined by governing bodies composed equally of clergy and lay representatives, seeking the mind of Christ in obedience to God's word, committed to engage one another's ideas through parliamentary debate."[31]

Building on this "first principle," PRN leaders developed a consensus on five corollary principles that, they concluded, must apply not only to the denomination as a whole, but to the independent renewal groups that were working within the denomination:

"(1) We agreed that because our principle insists that Scripture alone is the authority on which we base all our decisions, it is inappropriate to decide on courses of action based on where we think the 'political middle' of the church may be located. Left wing, right wing, and center are political terms that have no place in our discussions. We included the qualifier that in choosing how to express a Scriptural truth to the church we would want to use language that will be most effective in reaching the Presbyterian public, a choice that would be guided by our assessment of where people are,

31 Presbyterian Renewal Network, Minutes, July 18, 1998.

but we affirmed our insistence that it is Scripture, not the 'middle' that must underlie the substance of our decisions."[32]

"(2) We agreed that if we hold to the above principle, decisions should be made by the whole body in open, parliamentary debate, so we must reject any leadership style, for the church at large or for ourselves as renewal groups, no matter how well motivated, that calls for elitist, back room deals among self-selected power brokers."[33]

"(3) We agreed that we will insist on the free flow of information to all parties. We observed that attorneys in secular courts do a better job than we Presbyterians have done in this regard, in that evidence is placed on the table, the results of depositions are made available to all, and there are no 'surprises' with respect to the evidence on which matters are debated. That means we will not parcel out information to privileged parties and withhold it from others in an attempt to win power and influence."[34]

"(4) We agreed that we will insist on a level playing field: no emotional demonstrations, no stacked committees, no position of privilege given to some 'resource people' and not to others.

"(5) We agreed that we will be subject to our brothers and sisters in the Lord, submitting to the will of the majority except in rare moments of high, scriptural principle."[35]

Having concurred that the above principles should apply to the denomination and also to "any sub-group," PRN members proceeded to discuss the appropriate method for recommending them to the Coalition. The group decided to begin with itself by adopting these principles as the manner in which renewal leaders would deal with one another, and "that these guidelines be communicated to the Coalition" with the request that its board adopt them as well.[36]

Coalition Reorganization Proposal

A discussion ensued anticipating how the Coalition's board might respond to suggestions from the PRN that clearly questioned its current composition and operational practices. Joe Rightmyer stated that the Coalition had been closely related to PFR. He pointed out that Betty Moore, PFR's former executive director, served as the Coalition's paid staff, that

32 *Ibid.*

33 *Ibid.*

34 *Ibid.*

35 *Ibid.*

36 *Ibid.*

Jack Haberer, head of PFR's issues committee, served as the Coalition's moderator, and the PFR office staff provided "most of the [Coalition's] day-to-day support."[37]

Reflecting on the Coalition's board and staff composition and the value that could be obtained by broadening it to include greater participation from other renewal organizations, the PRN decided to propose reorganization and an expanded board. PRN minutes report "a general consensus" on three points that were to be suggested to the Coalition in any board reorganization:

"(a) It should be composed of 50% lay people and 50% clergy.

"(b) Leaders should be democratically elected and widely representative of renewal objectives. Only one person per organization on the board.

"(c) A nominating committee be democratically elected and consist of some 'at large' representatives."[38]

Joe Rightmyer expressed his concern that the PRN's discussions the previous evening had made him "uncomfortable" because it appeared to him that the PRN was becoming "a political advocacy group that is seeking to impact the Coalition."[39] But when the proposal was put to a vote on the afternoon of July 18, Rightmyer did not oppose it. Specifically, the PRN authorized a four-person team to meet with the Coalition board to present the PRN's suggestions on the renewal organizations' involvement for implementing the Coalition's strategy paper and to "communicate our concerns and suggestions on the structure and the purpose of the organization providing leadership for the renewal movement for the future."[40]

The PRN also adopted a motion "that each of the member organizations commit to the implementation of the strategies and goals presented to us by the Coalition Visioning Committee to the best of our gifts and abilities and that we affirm the Declaration of Faith as a basis of support."[41] When that vote was taken, Rightmyer stated that the board of Presbyterians for Renewal had not authorized him to act on its behalf at this meeting and that he therefore had abstained from voting on this and all other proposals.

He affirmed that there were some laudable goals in the strategy paper and that his organization was already initiating its own programs to imple-

37 *Ibid.*

38 *Ibid.*

39 *Ibid.*

40 Rightmyer was named as one of the four persons to represent PRN concerns before the Coalition board.

41 Presbyterian Renewal Network, Minutes, July 18, 1998.

ment those portions with which it agreed, but he could not be party to other strategies in the paper, nor did he approve of the tone of the paper as a whole, which he believed was "too confrontational" and constituted attacks on national church staff members whom he knew and loved. In particular, Rightmyer said he was distressed by renewal leaders' public criticisms of Stated Clerk Kirkpatrick, which he regarded as "unwarranted personal attacks" on a friend.

Rightmyer's objections initiated a discussion by the PRN regarding its own composition and role, resulting in the conclusion that the network was not an organization, but a "fellowship of renewal leaders," none of whom had any authority to speak for their own organizations. The meeting ended with a consensus that encouraged each renewal organization to examine the Coalition's strategy paper, and that it identify for support those particular strategies that it believed were compatible with its own goals.

Request Denied

The four-person PRN team contacted Jack Haberer to convey the PRN's request for a discussion between the PRN team and the Coalition board to occur during the Coalition's forthcoming board meeting. Haberer said he would take the matter up with the Coalition's executive committee. He subsequently informed PRN team leader John Boone that the Coalition executive committee had declined PRN's request for a meeting between the PRN delegation and the Coalition board for the purposes proposed by the PRN.[42]

Shortly thereafter, Haberer's term as Coalition moderator ended, and he was not re-elected. He then continued his activities as a board member of Presbyterians for Renewal and chairman of its issues ministry team, and he stood for election as president of PFR during its next election. Rightmyer supported Haberer's candidacy, and he was elected, giving him a new platform from which to promote his plan for working with Covenant Network and denominational leaders.

A Pivotal Moment

The failure of the PRN and Coalition board to achieve – or even formally to discuss – the consensus proposals forged by the PRN in its July meeting proved devastating to the Coalition's new initiative and to the Coalition's future effectiveness as a coordinated voice of renewal in the

42 Coalition minutes do not record any decision by either the full board or the executive committee corresponding to the message that was conveyed by Haberer to Boone.

denomination. The renewal organizations, not the Coalition, were the groups that had large constituencies, staffs, well established funding sources, publishing operations, and significant board leadership. Had their executives made a mutual commitment in their Kansas City meeting to direct the full weight of their ministries into a concentrated campaign to implement the Coalition's declaration and strategy paper, and had the Coalition board agreed to reorganize in a manner that opened the door for focused and coordinated efforts by the renewal organizations toward the implementation of its strategy paper, a major denominational turnaround might have been possible. Lacking that level of involvement, the Coalition's plan was doomed.

In retrospect, it appears that this was a pivotal moment for the Coalition and the renewal movement in the Presbyterian Church (USA). A fragile consensus had been fractured, resulting in disparate, often opposing voices among renewal minded Presbyterians, and wedging a fatal weakness into their ranks.[43] This was, of course, precisely the outcome that Barbara Wheeler called for in her strategy address to the Covenant Network's early meeting.

Strategy Paper Falls by the Wayside

The Coalition board met in October to consider implementing its strategy paper, and it appointed a task force corresponding to each of the six strategies. No funds were allocated to the task forces, some of which never met. The task force on church discipline pulled together some volunteer attorneys who developed encouragement and advice for evangelicals in presbyteries where open defiance of G-6.0106(b) was rampant. Another task force developed a study paper on denominational funding, with particular emphasis on the denomination's per capita budget. Another task force was formed to envision new, less hierarchical ways "to be the church."[44] Senior ministers of several large, evangelically oriented congregations in

43 Remembering this moment in PCUSA history, one is reminded of an observation made by Stated Clerk James E. Andrews on Oct. 17, 1988 during a meeting in Louisville, Ky. with the author. Reflecting on the fact, often documented by the denomination's Office of Research Services, that theologically conservative Presbyterians constitute the largest segment of the PCUSA membership and are its most generous donors, Andrews said, "You conservatives have the numbers and the money. You could take over the denomination if you could ever get your act together."

44 The Coalition board became divided over continuing to support the task force as a part of the Coalition, so task force leaders formed their own freestanding organization, later to become the New Wineskins Association of Churches.

Texas picked up the Coalition's strategy of forming an alternative "mentor church" seminary and discussed it for a couple of years, but with no significant implementation.

In the fall of 1999, with little activity reported from its task forces, the Coalition board concluded that in its attempt to swim upstream, its reach had exceeded its grasp, that its members were not united on any program or purpose beyond the defense of G-6.0106(b), and that it should limit its activities to that purpose, contenting itself with rallying evangelicals and moderates each time the constitutional standard came under attack.

When the 2001 General Assembly adopted an amendment to delete G-6.0106(b) from the Constitution, the Coalition again issued a call to arms. Renewal organizations responded to the call, and a successful campaign in the presbyteries crushed the amendment by an almost three to one majority. But in the aftermath of that victory, support for an organization whose only purpose was to rally the troops when G-6.0106(b) is attacked began to wane. With increasing defiance of the standard at every level of the denomination's infrastructure and no enforcement of the standard by the Office of the General Assembly, many evangelicals wearied of the fight, and some began to consider exit strategies, culminating in discussions by the New Wineskins Association of Churches, that had now spun itself off from the Coalition.

Attendance at the Coalition's annual gatherings declined and contributions to its treasury plummeted. At its 2006 gathering in Atlanta, following the decision by that year's General Assembly that sessions and presbyteries may deem G-6.0106(b) "not essential," the Coalition conducted a straw poll on whether participants wished to continue a "stay, fight and win" strategy or separate from the denomination. The standing vote was not officially counted, and estimates ranged from "slightly more than half" to "slightly less than half" of those present choosing the separation option. Following the poll, the Coalition board adjusted its position, saying that while it would continue seeking to renew the denomination from within, it would also provide support, albeit unspecified, for evangelical congregations that choose to leave.

The Coalition board continues its work, encouraging sessions and presbyteries to declare G-6.0106(b) "essential" within their area of jurisdiction, offering commentary on constitutional amendments that are making their way through the presbytery ratification process, and preparing overtures to the 2008 General Assembly. But the momentum that invigorated this organization when it adopted its declaration and strategy paper is gone. Haberer's prediction to the Presbyterian News Service that the majority of the Coalition board would resist any departure from its moderate stance proved accurate, but it was also deeply damaging to the organization. Since the 2006 General Assembly's evisceration of G-6.0106(b), the Coalition has lost a significant market share among the denomination's evangelicals. In August, 2007, the Coalition "Gathering X" in Houston, an event that had once attracted as many as 1,300 participants in the past, drew an initial crowd of 97 that dwindled to 56 at a scheduled "commitment service" for its new plan to renew the denomination.

Presbyterians for Renewal

Presbyterians for Renewal appears to be in the throes of a transition. After the devastating decisions of the 2006 General Assembly, followed by the resignation of its executive director, the Rev. Michael Walker, the PFR board announced that it would initiate a period of discernment, meet with a consulting firm and assess its future.

Theologically evangelical, the dominant position of this clergy-dominated organization has been based on an abiding belief in the providence of God, whose truth in the short term might be spurned, but who will overcome all resistance to that truth in his own good time. Parallel to that conviction in the sovereignty of God has been PFR's belief that God will not allow the PCUSA to fall into apostasy. It may not be too strong to say that for some of PFR's key leaders, Jesus' promise that the gates of hell would not prevail against his church applies literally to the denomination.[45] Thus, the PFR position has been to model faithfulness to the gospel inside denominational structures, believing that over time that which is false within the denomination will surely pass away.

Michael Walker, who succeeded Joe Rightmyer as PFR's executive director, stated the PFR strategy shortly after he was employed by PFR. Speaking to renewal leaders in Louisville, Walker noted that evangelical congregations are growing, and liberal congregations are dying. Given that trend, he reasoned, evangelicals have only to wait for the ultimate demise of liberalism in the Presbyterian Church (USA), which he predicted would happen within ten years. In the interim, he counseled, renewal organizations should bear faithful witness while resisting the temptation to destabilize denominational structures or separate from the denomination. Rather than engage in

45 This tendency to equate the Church with a particular denomination has been hotly contested by many evangelicals who understand the denomination to be a fallible corporate structure, created by Christians to carry out the work of the church, but which is not in itself the Church that was assured of permanence by Jesus. For an increasing number of evangelicals, a denomination is nothing more than a human institution which is viable only as long as it remains true to its purpose and proclaims the Church's faith with integrity.

win/lose battles with denominational leaders, the PFR approach would be to negotiate with them, behind closed doors if necessary. PFR's focus would be on demonstrating its own theological integrity while doing what it could to ensure the institutional preservation of the PCUSA.

A History of Moderation

PFR's moderate stance did not begin with Walker, Rightmyer, who preceeded Walker, or even Betty Moore, who was the organization's first executive director. It was designed in pre-PFR days by the Rev. Harry Hassall who served as PFR's chief political strategist. Hassall was a southern church leader who served a PFR predecessor organization called the Covenant Fellowship. Charting a course between "extremes" in the southern Presbyterian Church, Hassall's group kept moderate southern evangelicals in the fold during merger talks between northern and southern Presbyterians.

In a self-published chronology of PFR's genesis, Hassall wrote that for much of his career, he and his associates invested their energies in promoting "the third alternative." "Convinced that a third alternative should be laid before the PCUS [Presbyterian Church in The United States, the southern stream predecessor of the Presbyterian Church (USA)], this ad hoc group rejected the impending schism on the Right and the headlong repudiation of our traditions for the liberalism of the Left. A third alternative was hammered out. Many of the Presbyterian leaders in this fellowship covenanted to stand by each other and, thus, the Covenant Fellowship of Presbyterians [the southern forerunner to Presbyterians for Renewal] was born."[46]

When speaking to renewal groups, Hassall often positioned himself before a drawing of a bell-shaped curve. Armed with plenteous statistics from the denomination's presbyteries, he was PFR's revered pre-General Assembly prognosticator, and his bell-shaped curve figured prominently in each presentation.

Although issues and players changed from year to year, Hassall's "curve" was unalterable. Invariably, with magic marker in hand, he drew three orbs on newsprint: a small minority that he called the liberal camp, a larger minority that he called the conservative camp, and a vast, undecided, middle-of-the-road majority. Neither extreme has the votes to win, he often told his conservative colleagues, in an analysis that mirrored Barbara Wheeler's speech to the Covenant Network. The winner must attract more votes from the middle than the other side does. To win those votes, said

46 Hassall, Harry S., *On Jordan's Stormy Banks I Stand* (Dallas: Harry S. Hassall, 1989), p.10.

Hassall, it is important to remember that the middle avoids extremists.

In the early days of his *via media* renewal efforts, Hassall worked with his colleague, the Rev. Andrew Jumper in publishing a newsletter for middle way Presbyterians. An editorial in 1973 expressed their position: "We have spoken often of reconciliation, and we have urged the course of moderation. This has led some of our critics to feel that since we occupy the middle ground, we therefore occupy the position of the mugwumps …

"If we heard only the thunder from the Right, or the rumblings from the Left, then we might be more concerned than we are. But since we are getting considerable flack from both directions, it confirms our conviction that the Moderate Middle, which looks neither to the Left nor to the Right, is where the church at large is, and where the Covenant Fellowship ought to be …

"The Covenant Fellowship of Presbyterians was formed because many of us believed that there is a viable alternative between syncretism and schism, and nothing has happened to make us change our minds. We still believe that between the Far Left and the Far Right there is a real Third Choice, and that this is what the PCUS desperately needs today."[47]

Hassall entertained a unique interpretation of the Protestant Reformation, an event that few historians would describe as a middle of the road occurrence. He called the Presbyterian version of the Reformation the "*via media* of Protestantism" because it was located between the Anglican/Episcopal/Lutheran view and the Anabaptist/Baptist/Church of Christ view.[48]

Hassall expressed admiration for the Rev. Jack Rogers' analogy, relating the "three Reformations" to methods of cleaning out one's sock drawer. The Anglican/Episcopal/Lutheran way, he said, is "to open the sock drawer, perhaps halfway, peek in, pull out those few obvious misfits and wornouts and quickly place them in the rubbish bin."[49]

The Presbyterian/Reformed/Calvinist way completely removes the sock drawer, places new paper liner in the drawer, "and then meticulously selects only the best and most useable socks to return to this 'thoroughly reformed' drawer."[50]

The Anabaptist/Baptist/Church of Christ approach is to "haul the entire

47 *Ibid.*, pp. 50-51.

48 Hassall, Harry S., *Presbyterians: People of the Middle Way* (Franklin, Tenn.: Providence House, 1996), pp. 46-47.

49 *Ibid.*

50 *Ibid.*

chest of drawers out of the house to the alley for city trash pick up, for in that sock drawer there was little to reform and a great deal to discard!"[51]

Hassall urged Presbyterian renewal groups to avoid acting like Anabaptists, wrecking the institution that they were trying to reform. His counsel influenced PFR's mission statement, "our mission is to participate in God's renewing, transforming work in the Presbyterian Church (U.S.A.)" and its goal to be "involved positively in the structure and politics of the PC(USA)," with an emphasis on being positive rather than negative.

Presumably, it was this penchant for improving rather than upending denominational structures that led PFR to locate its offices near Presbyterian Church (USA) headquarters. PFR leaders have often declared that they chose this location in order to be the voice of evangelicals to Louisville. Increasingly, however, critics of their close ties with denominational offices have suggested that PFR leaders may have become the voice of Louisville to evangelicals.

'GodViews'

Jack Haberer subscribes to PFR's theory of seeking a middle course in times of controversy. He says he is ideologically opposed to division. He insists that life is entirely too complex to reduce decisions to true or false, good or evil polarities: "The clearest conclusion that emerged for me was that the church is far too complex – and for most believers it is far too complicated – to continue to allow a simple, two-party theory to summarize the church's divisions. Us-and-them, good-guys-and-bad-guys, liberals-and-conservatives … such categorizations provide a great way to run a war, but they comprise a godawful way to run a church."[52]

In Haberer's thinking, compromise is not merely a political act, but a theological one. In phrases that bring to mind the doctrine of "original sin," he says that "something deep in the human psyche" drives people to separate and go different ways. "Something about independence compellingly attracts us," he says.[53]

For Haberer, the culprit is "binary thinking," a phrase that, not surprisingly, appeared prominently in the denomination's Peace, Unity, and Purity report, that was adopted by the 2006 General Assembly. Haberer was a member of that task force.

"In its simplest form," he says, "such binary thinking boils down to 'us' versus 'them.' Two-party thinking helps organize life clearly, if somewhat

51 *Ibid.*

52 Haberer, p. 8.

53 *Ibid.*, p.22.

simplistically. Binary thinking provides clearly defined choices and simple categorizations, relieving us of the responsibility to deal with uncomfortable issues, undesirable ideas, unattractive options, and unappealing persons.

"Binary thinking also provides a great way to win an argument. Effective salespersons, trial lawyers, and debaters have long understood that one way to try to win an argument is to pose just two options to the person or persons that one is aiming to sell to, persuade, or outdebate. 'The choice is clear,' we say. 'It's either this or that. One or the other. Choose now, or forever hold your peace.'"[54]

Haberer laments the fact that conflict exists between the Presbyterian Coalition and the Covenant Network.[55] "These two organizations are not monolithic," he says. "They are not political parties, comprised of undifferentiated, single-minded allies engaged in groupthink." In an admission that underscores observations made by *Christian Century* and the Presbyterian News Service reporters covering the Coalition, Haberer says, "Speaking from the perspective of a former moderator of one of the organizations, more energy is spent wrestling and juggling the differences within the organization than in combating the flaws of the outsiders."[56]

Haberer suggests that the way out of denominational divisions is for all parties to accept one another's "GodViews," a label he gives to a person's "internalized, passionate conviction." Where do these GodViews come from? Haberer offers not a theological but a psychological/sociological answer: "GodViews arise from many sources. Rooted in our temperaments, they are shaped by our environments, 'converted' by our faith experiences, empowered by our spiritual giftings, reinforced by our affiliations, and magnified by our sense of call."[57]

Carrying his reader through a labyrinth of references to sociologists and psychologists, including Maslow's self-actualization theory, the Taylor-Johnson Temperament Analysis Tests and an explanation of one's "theo-ideological impulses" from the perspective of Psychoanalyst Karen Horney, Haberer concludes that different people have different ideas about God and God's purpose for their life. Those views, according to Haberer, are derived primarily from whatever impulses are bubbling up from one's psyche, and

54 *Ibid.*

55 Note: The assumption that issues dividing the denomination can be sorted into Coalition and Covenant Network categories is revealing, in that it suggests that these two organizations comprise the preferred context for denominational dialogues.

56 *Ibid.*, p. 27.

57 *Ibid.*, p. 35.

then they are formed, shaped and strengthened by influential associations, like the seminaries that people attend and the clubs they join.

Haberer concedes that one's GodViews are also shaped by the direct influence of God, but his discussion of that transaction is cursory, and it is unclear by what authority he concludes that a particular influence is godly. He offers the disclaimer that "the variety of GodViews is not infinite," and that some "perceptions of God" are illegitimate. But he offers his readers no help in discerning true GodViews from false ones, a process that presumably would require "binary thinking," which he opposes.

Believing that human diversity is a reflection of diversity within God's own self – Haberer calls his readers "to embrace ambiguities and complexities akin to those of the character of the godhead."[58/59] Haberer welcomes a variety of GodViews, saying that they "reflect the creative hand of God having formed them."[60]

Although Haberer would certainly object to such a characterization, his GodViews catapults him into religious pluralism, the very theological distortion that Harry Emerson Fosdick proclaimed and J. Gresham Machen condemned almost 80 years ago. Haberer avoids the pluralist label, identifying himself instead as an evangelical.[61]

One is reminded in this regard of Machen's statement about Robert Speer, another self-labeled evangelical who helped facilitate liberalism's control of the denominational power structure in the 1920s: "The plain fact is that in the great issue of the day between Modernism and Christianity in

---

58 *Ibid.*, p. 8.

59 Haberer suggests that the diversity that is evident within The Trinity is reflected in "human diversity." He makes the debatable suggestion that the divine communion of three persons who enjoy mutual relations in perfect symmetry is paralleled by human relationships that encompass mutually exclusive and self-contradictory "truths."

60 *Ibid.*, p. 38.

61 The practice of identifying oneself as "an evangelical" has been frequently employed in recent years. Two demonstrably liberal General Assembly moderators, the Rev. Jack Rogers and the Rev. Susan Andrews appropriated that label for themselves. This underscores the difficulty of saying anything meaningful in a post-modern culture where words are defined not by reference to an objective standard but by the opinion of the person who employs them. In a full-blown post-modern environment, persons of opposite convictions can affirm the same constitution or confession of faith, simply by using their own definitions. This is precisely where the Presbyterian Church (USA) finds itself, and it is this condition that eviscerates the claim made by some that the denomination has not abandoned the faith because it continues to lay claim to *The Book of Confessions*. One can approve a statement made by anyone on any subject if given license to employ one's own definitions.

the Presbyterian Church, Dr. Speer is standing for a palliative, middle-of-the-road, evasive policy, which is in some ways a greater menace to the souls of men than any clear-cut Modernism could be."[62]

'Unity in our Diversity'

Together with the Covenant Network, Stated Clerk Clifton Kirkpatrick made numerous attempts to woo moderate evangelicals into a show of unity with the liberals. In 1996 and 1997, Kirkpatrick invited Mrs. Betty Moore, executive director of PFR, the Rev. John Huffman and the Rev. Craig Barnes, both of whom were members of PFR's board, to enter into "Common Ground Discussions" with members of the Covenant Network and denominational staff members. Although the three evangelicals accepted Kirkpatrick's invitation to participate, they stood their ground and refused to compromise their convictions. These "Common Ground Discussions" revealed little common ground and were not continued once they failed to achieve consensus on denominational issues.

In the spring of 1999, encouraged by his success in facilitating "A Call to Sabbatical," Stated Clerk Clifton Kirkpatrick tried again. He invited Presbyterians to a "Unity in our Diversity" conference in Atlanta, Ga. Promoted for nine months by General Assembly agencies and publications, the conference was designed to forge a bridge between evangelical and revisionist camps, demonstrating that theological and ethical diversity could be encompassed under a broadly inclusive denominational tent. At the urging of denominational headquarters, several presbyteries offered "scholarship assistance," in effect ensuring that anyone who desired to participate could do so on the denomination's tab.

Jack Haberer, Joe Rightmyer and James Mead were invited to participate in the planning committee. Their conference theme lifted up purported denominational achievements in racial and ethnic diversity as a model for building theological and ethical diversity.

Liberals responded enthusiastically. The Covenant Network chose to hold its board meeting simultaneously with the conference in order to ensure maximum participation by its leaders. Sixteen Covenant Network board members signed up for the event. General Assembly staff members and middle governing body executives came, but people from the pews did not. In the final count, this national conference that was designed to showcase thousands of "diverse" Presbyterians in a unity display drew fewer

62 Stonehouse, Ned B., *J. Gresham Machen: A Biographical Memoir* (Grand Rapids: Wm. B. Erdmans, 1954), p. 472.

than 250 participants, many of whom received subsidies to underwrite the cost of their participation.

Haberer had made a concerted effort to woo "conservative evangelical 'headliners'" to the conference. On March 9, 1999, he pleaded with the board of directors of the Presbyterian Coalition to attend, promising to sweeten the deal by arranging a private meeting between Coalition and Covenant Network board members. "On behalf of the 'Sabbatical Six,'" wrote Haberer, "I would like to invite six fellow members of the Presbyterian Coalition Board to a meeting with leaders of the Covenant Network on 28 April at 4:00 till 10:00 PM in Atlanta at a home to be determined … and then to reconvene on Thursday at the conference (in a private room) at the end of the day's meetings … I know you share my conviction that the church's peace, unity and purity are worth fighting for. I hope you will get behind this effort at doing so."[63]

Coalition board members declined Haberer's invitation. Not only was the number of attendees at the conference small, but it demonstrated scant diversity. Other than a handful of moderates recruited by Haberer, Righmyer and Mead, renewal leaders and their evangelical constituencies stayed away in such numbers that former General Assembly Moderator Clinton Marsh asked during a plenary feedback session, "Did conservatives call for a boycott?"[64] Noting the dearth of evangelicals, Jack Haberer told the Presbyterian News Service, "the absence of any conservative evangelical 'headliners' among the plenary speakers probably hampered attendance by those on my end of the spectrum."[65]

The Rev. Stephen Jenks, a liberal interim pastor of Montview Boulevard Presbyterian Church in Denver, said "I am experiencing joy and grief here," he said. "The joy is in the sharing. The grief is that the people I needed to talk to are not here."[66]

The Rev. Craig Hall, the pastor of Opportunity Presbyterian Church in Spokane, Wash., who labeled himself as a moderate, told his fellow conferees that the absence of so many conservative evangelicals caused him grief. "I am living on an ever-shrinking island called the middle," he said. "... Too many who should be here are not."[67]

63 Memo from Jack Haberer to Clayton Bell and the Presbyterian Coalition Board of Directors, March 9, 1999.

64 *The Presbyterian Layman*, Vol. 32, No. 3, May/June, 1999.

65 Presbyterian News Service, #99174.

66 *Ibid.*

67 *Ibid.*

Essentially Diverse

In Atlanta's Unity in our Diversity Conference, keynote speaker Clarice Martin, associate professor of philosophy and religion at Colgate-Rochester University, lifted up diversity as if it were an essential tenet of Christian faith. This proved an interesting development in light of the fact that since 1926, denominational leaders had been vigorous in rejecting subscription to any essential belief.

Martin bolstered her argument with the assertion that the Apostle Paul considered diversity an essential ingredient in the gospel. Recognizing that some of Paul's writings did not support her theme, she solved her problem by declaring that Paul didn't say some of the things that the Bible says he said. She insisted that Paul authored only seven epistles. All the rest, she said, were written by others who used his name.

Like Marcion,[68] Ms. Martin deleted major blocks of Scripture for which she said Paul was not responsible. Then she declared that he affirmed God's acceptance of different behaviors, just as he affirmed persons of different racial/ethnic backgrounds. "Since each person is accountable to God, any warrant for rejecting the cultural or social practices of another is removed," she said.[69]

Other "unity in our diversity" speakers called for greater theological freedom in the Presbyterian Church (USA). The Rev. Jorge Lara-Braud told conference participants that he believed the church tries to draw boundaries "when it feels insecure." He said that Jesus was the kind of person who crossed over boundaries, and that his followers should do so as well.[70]

Cynthia Campbell, president of McCormick Seminary agreed with Lara-Braud. "In what sort of church do I wish to worship and serve?" she asked. "I want a church that concerns itself not by drawing lines but opening doors."[71]

Two persons who represent Biblical theology and ethics were invited to offer brief responses to the deluge of revisionism that came from major platform presentations. The Rev. Catherine Purves argued that Scriptural boundaries are not – as Lara-Braud and Campbell suggested – of human origin, but that they are the gracious gift of God for the good of his people. She pointed out that God established boundaries in the very act of creation

68 Marcion was a second century heretic whose Gnostic beliefs led him radically to excise portions of the New Testament, including writings of the Apostle Paul that did not comport with his views.

69 *The Presbyterian Layman*, Vol. 32, No. 3, May/June, 1999.

70 *Ibid.*

71 *Ibid.*

– creating order in the midst of chaos. God acted again in the life of Israel, said Purves, when he gave Israel the law. It was this law that provided Israel with its identity.

"It was always when Israel's sense of the boundaries became fuzzy and imprecise that they got themselves in trouble," said Purves. "Like healthy adolescents, they turned stretching the boundaries into an art form. Adapting and accommodating the faith to foreign cultures was considered a justifiable survival tactic. All of this resulted in uncertain boundaries and the inevitable incorporation of idolatry and immoral behavior into the life of the faith community."[72]

The Rev. James Logan, Jr., an African American minister and an evangelical, took issue with the conference theme that sought to equate racial/ethnic diversity with diversity in sexual behavior. Logan declared that those who in the name of diversity would "lower the bar to make room for standards of living and practice that do not accord with the words of Scripture need to 'be born again.'"[73]

Joint 'Bible Study' Attempted

Following Haberer's departure from Coalition leadership, members of the Covenant Network approached his successors, Coalition co-moderators Anita Bell and Jerry Andrews, asking for a series of bilateral meetings between the two groups. Coalition leaders responded with a counterproposal. Declaring that they had no interest in continuing conversations on the subject of homosexual behavior, they suggested that the two groups engage in Bible study.

The Covenant Network agreed, named a team of representatives that included a practicing homosexual who was a political organizer for More Light Presbyterians and the leader of PFLAG, Presbyterian Families of Lesbians and Gays. They proposed that the Bible study be limited to the first three chapters of Ephesians (emphasizing our oneness in Christ), and that discussions be "off the record."

The Coalition named a team of renewal organization leaders, agreed to the choice of Ephesians, but insisted that the whole epistle be studied, including chapters four and following, which emphasize the ethical "therefore" that follows from being one in Christ, including admonitions regarding Christian sexual behavior. They rejected the proposal that discussions

72 *Ibid.*

73 *Ibid.*

be private, insisting that reporters from the Presbyterian News Service, *The Presbyterian Layman* and *The Presbyterian Outlook* be invited.

Two discussions were conducted, showcasing dramatically different hermeneutics (the way each group interpreted Scripture). Covenant Network participants typically interpreted the text using external tools, e.g., principles from psychology, philosophy and semantics. Coalition representatives interpreted Scripture with Scripture.

During the second meeting, Covenant Network representatives proposed a "unity in our diversity" statement, suggesting that it be signed by both groups and given to members of the press. Coalition representatives declined to sign the statement, observing that although the discussions demonstrated civility and friendship, they did not reveal unity in any substantial sense. In fact, they proved that in matters of faith and practice, the two groups were dramatically different.

During the period in which the two groups were meeting, 113 presbytery and synod employees who were meeting in San Antonio, Tex. issued an open letter. Lauding the fact that a meeting was occurring between representatives of the Coalition and the Covenant Network they urged participants to come up with a "third way" on issues of same-sex genital behavior. The statement said, "We believe the church we love has a future, but it will not be by determining winners and losers. It will be determined by seeking a third way. We envision a third way which can come only from an openness to the Spirit. We will rely on God's grace and refuse to leave the table until a way is discovered. We believe seeking a third way is critical and is already present among us."[74/75]

Coalition representatives to the bilateral discussions recognized the "third-way" statement as a lobbying effort by denominational executives that was designed to push them into the compromise position that was proffered by Covenant Network representatives. The evangelicals responded with a public statement of their own: "We have not, and we will not engage in any search for an alternative to Scripture's clear and plain teaching, for we believe, as our Preliminary Principles declare, 'Insofar as Christ's will for the church is set forth in Scripture, it is to be obeyed.' Christ's way is about seeking his will

74 Presbyterian News Service, #00464, Dec. 21, 2000.

75 The discerning reader will recognize the similarity of "third way" language in this 1999 statement from presbytery and synod staff members with language voiced in Clifton Kirkpatrick's "Common Ground Discussions," Jack Haberer's "GodViews" theme, and the Atlanta "Unity in our Diversity" conference. This was precursor language that ultimately surfaced in the denomination's "Peace, Unity and Purity Report" that was adopted by the 2006 General Assembly.

by studying his Word and agreeing to obey it in his church."[76]

Shortly thereafter, the discussions broke down, and no further meetings were proposed by either group.

A House Divided

After the 2001 General Assembly declined to make a clear, definitive affirmation of the singular saving lordship of Jesus Christ and adopted yet another assault on the denomination's ordination standards, Jack Haberer dispatched a damage control message to PFR's mailing list: "I find myself wanting to say to all my friends in the denomination, 'Whoa, Nellie.' The battle over the new amendment, coupled with the expanding Confessing Church Movement, all coming on the heels of the Christological controversy – all these points of issue are pushing the PC(USA) headlong into what is looking increasingly like an inevitable division of the church. As appealing as this may feel to some who are battle-weary, I cannot warn loudly enough of the horrifying results that will ensue if such a course is pursued. The severing of friendships and even families always results at such times, and the cause of Christ becomes far more damaged than anything we are experiencing now."[77]

Then Haberer zeroed in on those who, in his judgment, were fomenting division: "Moreover, the present momentum pushing toward division is being fueled by contemptuous judgments being foisted upon one another in the church – most especially by us evangelicals toward our more liberal/progressive counterparts. Our differences do exist, and they are substantial. Our structures deserve to be reworked and revised. But we need to stand down – long before we reach a point of no return, long before we drive ourselves into effectively 'renouncing jurisdiction' due to our maintaining a 'superior' form of the faith."[78]

Interestingly, those whom Haberer singled out were not persons at the assembly who proposed the removal of G-6.0106(b). He expressed no concern about statements from General Assembly commissioners who viewed religions as different pieces of fruit whose diverse flavors should not disqualify them as fruit. Instead, he focused on evangelicals for insisting on their "superior form of the faith."

76 *The Presbyterian Layman*, Vol. 34. No. 1, January/February, 2001.

77 Haberer, Jack, "Rooted and Grounded ... Tossed To and Fro: An Evangelical Perspective on the 213rd General Assembly in Louisville, Ky. June 9-16, 2001." A paper distributed to selected congregations and church leaders by Presbyterians for Renewal.

78 *Ibid.*

Tensions in the Family

After initially opposing the emergence of the Confessing Church Movement, PFR leaders faced the difficulty of seeing the number of signatories soar to more than 1,300 congregations, including many churches that had financially supported PFR. Backing away from a statement that he made prior to the 2001 General Assembly meeting, Haberer said he had been wrong when he told *The Presbyterian Outlook* that the Confessing Church Movement was "an underground movement with a ghetto mentality." Reflecting on the movement's growth, Haberer told *The Presbyterian Layman* that he now believed "the Confessing Church Movement is not the underground movement that I thought it was."[79] Asked why he opposed it earlier, he said that he had been concerned that it might be setting up a schism.

When more than 800 confessing Presbyterians gathered in an Atlanta convention center in 2002 to celebrate the movement, PFR's executive director Joe Rightmyer dispatched an "Open Letter" to the conference. "We celebrate with you the enormous growth of the Confessing Church Movement," it said. Then, addressing the fact that other renewal organizations and movements had surfaced since PFR inaugurated its ministry, it said "In the process, PFR has seemed sometimes to move more ploddingly than some of the other organizations. No doubt that this has been true. To be honest, we too have been distressed over the repeated outbreaks of heterodox teaching in the church, as well as misappropriations of ecclesiastical authority and power. Such errors need to be redressed. We are in a process of restructuring our board of directors in order to help us become more proactive and effective in addressing such issues."[80]

Shortly thereafter, PFR issued a colorful new brochure titled "There's New 'Fire in our Belly!'" While the brochure promised new programs and initiatives, it continued to declare PFR's determination to chart a "middle course" among equally unacceptable alternatives. "A spirit of contentiousness has emerged in our denomination that threatens to undermine our common governance. There is deceitfulness and disregard for our Constitution on one side; legalism and control on the other."[81] Thus PFR continued its practice of defining the plight of the Presbyterian Church (USA) as a struggle between unacceptable polarities – radical liberals on one side and

79 *The Presbyterian Layman*, Vol. 34, No.4, July/August, 2001.

80 Rightmyer, Joseph, "An Open Letter to the Celebration of Confessing Churches," March, 2002.

81 Presbyterians for Renewal, "There's New 'Fire In Our Belly!'" (Louisville: Presbyterians for Renewal, 2002).

radical conservatives on the other – with PFR and the denominational leadership somewhere in the middle.

In February, 2002, a PFR publication for seminarians included an article by the Rev. Robert Henderson, suggesting that the Confessing Church Movement was more ephemeral than substantive. "We're at an interesting juncture in the Presbyterian Church (USA), and one of the resulting phenomena floating around is known as the 'Confessing Church Movement,'" wrote Henderson. "On the surface this appears to be a significant step toward confessional and Biblical orthodoxy, but it may be more appearance than reality ... Simply declaring that one is a 'confessing church' can be a placebo to satisfy one's resistance to the hard work required to actually *refound* a congregation into knowledgeable and faithful discipleship."[82]

In the same issue, Henderson answered what he termed "Seminarians' Question: Where is PFR in the present crisis?" Henderson said "We are frequently approached on the various seminary campuses with some confusion about the various 'renewal' organizations, and where PFR 'fits' into the PC(USA). From its beginning, (1989) PFR positioned itself to be the pro-active advocate, or voice, for the renewal/refounding of the Biblical, confessional, missional heart of the PC(USA). Our desire was also to be a pro-active champion of all the wonderful ministries that take place within this communion, even when chaos seems to dominate the scene. One seminary professor called PFR 'the voice of hope within the PC(USA).' Our headquarters was deliberately placed in Louisville so that we could be in conversation with, and be a ministry to the denominational leadership."[83]

Pursuing a 'Quieter Approach'

In 2002, the Rev. Keith Hill, chairman of PFR's issues ministry team, rose to the defense of his organization after it was criticized for declining to join other renewal groups' condemnation of Stated Clerk Kirkpatrick's refusal to enforce the Constitution. "Since the accused have not joined their accusers either in indicting the Stated Clerk for malfeasance or in declaring a constitutional crisis, the accusers have determined that the accused must lack courage. While I can claim neither great courage nor perfectly pure motives, I can say that there actually is a strategic rationale for a quieter approach."[84]

82 Henderson, Robert, "What Really is a 'Confessing Church?'" Catalyst, February, 2002.

83 *Ibid.*

84 Hill, Keith, "A Quieter Approach," PresbyWeb, November 14, 2002.

Hill continued, "If we evangelicals want to see the Constitution hold, we must be partnered with the broad middle of the church ... This great majority can hold if we seek to apply the Constitution in pastoral ways, but it will not hold if we are perceived as shrill and accusatory. Those in the middle of the church will flee such posturing. They prefer, and wisely so, that disciplinary procedures and necessary enforcement be carried out quietly."[85]

Referring to renewal leaders who openly criticized Stated Clerk Kirkpatrick after Kirkpatrick said it was not his job to enforce the Constitution, Hill said, "Those who choose the way of loud remonstrance have misunderstood the essence of church discipline. However commendable their courage, the actions they are taking are counterproductive for the ends they seek – unless they seek to precipitate division in the church."[86]

Writing for PFR's newsletter in 2003, Hill differentiated PFR from other renewal organizations when calling on his readers to "remain vested in the connectional system of our church."[87] Hill said PFR would avoid the temptation to "lay aside our PFR moniker for a new identity, say maybe PFBE (*Presbyterians For Blaming Someone*), PFBL, (*Presbyterians For Bashing Louisville*), or PFPW (*Presbyterians For Parting Ways*).[88]

Without identifying the radical renewal groups from whom PFR wished to distance itself, Hill continued, "There are plenty in our church whose pursuits would support such names ... When our focus is fixed only upon the sad state of our church and the errors of our opponents, then we are ready candidates for spiritual petrification. Difficult battles and harsh words inevitably harden hearts, even if we're on the 'right' side of the issues." Announcing PFR's intention to expand its issues ministry, Hill said "we will do so not to bash Louisville, nor to part ways. Our hope is to be used by God to foster his renewal in the whole of his church."[89]

Christ Church's Defiance

In chapter five, we discussed the defiance of Christ Church in Burlington, Vt. and the fact that it avoided General Assembly censure by declaring that it was now complying with G-6.0106(b) *according to its own definition* of the words that are contained therein.[90] Among the words for which Christ

85 *Ibid.*

86 *Ibid.*

87 Hill, Keith, "Being True to a Good Name," PFR *ReNews*, September, 2003.

88 *Ibid.*

89 *Ibid.*

90 See page 222.

Church found new definitions were "chastity" and "repentance."

We revisit the Christ Church incident in this chapter in order to examine the role that renewal groups played when the matter came before the 2002 General Assembly. As the time of that assembly meeting approached, Christ Church's violation of the Constitution and its two-year long, public defiance of a court order requiring compliance, were well known to commissioners. Shenango Presbytery had sent an overture to the General Assembly, calling for it to initiate administrative oversight at Christ Church.

On the eve of that General Assembly meeting, when it was clear that the Shenango Overture was gaining momentum and that the majority of commissioners was inclined to take some form of remedial action, Christ Church suddenly announced that it had "set aside" the statement of defiance that it had prominently displayed on its website.

Renewal forces at the General Assembly were divided on how to proceed in light of the Christ Church announcement. Representatives of Shenango Presbytery stood firm, suggesting that Christ Church's language was slippery and that merely taking a statement off the website without explicitly repudiating it left the question of Christ Church's compliance with the Constitution unanswered. Shenango commissioners asked renewal group representatives to stand with them in their insistence that the General Assembly mandate compliance.

But PFR chose to back off. Trusting that Christ Church's "set aside" meant repentance, it encouraged evangelical commissioners to extend "grace" by pressing the matter no further. PFR's withdrawal resulted in a split among evangelical commissioners, depriving Shenango's overture of badly needed votes. The assembly declined to place Christ Church under administrative oversight.

Amazing 'Grace'

Commenting on Christ Church's purported repentance, Jack Haberer, writing on behalf of PFR said, "While some conservatives could parse the words of the retraction, claiming that 'set aside' is not technical language, and accordingly may have no lasting significance, most commissioners readily accepted it as a sincere attempt to turn from their earlier stance. Any proclaimer of grace, any forgiven sinner serving as a commissioner understandably was asking, 'Should we be punishing the penitent?'"[91]

Four months later, the session of Christ Church declared that it was now in

91 Haberer, Jack, "License for Libertines? Or the Wrong Map to the Right Destination? A Shenango Retrospective," Presbyterians for Renewal, June 28, 2002.

compliance with the Constitution by virtue of its own definition of "chastity" and "repentance." Moderates who had been persuaded to grant "grace" to Christ Church during General Assembly deliberations felt betrayed.

PFR issued a statement reflecting its dismay over Christ Church's action: "PFR has read Christ Church's new statement with regret, especially in light of the grace G.A. extended. General Assembly commissioners trusted that Christ Church's withdrawal of their previous statement was done in good faith and for the sake of the larger church. G.A. acted pastorally by demonstrating the gracious heart of God, who delays the exercise of judgment for the sake of those who will receive God's mercy. But note: Just as judgment by God is not curtailed by mercy but will instead be displayed in light of God's mercy, so should it be regarding the General Assembly's mercy and judgment. It is all the more condemning when one has received mercy and ignored it or made a mockery of it. Judgment must follow."[92]

But judgment did not follow. Neither Northern New England Presbytery nor the Synod of the Northeast (that had in 1993 declared itself a "More Light" Synod) was inclined to discipline Christ Church for its violation of the ordination standard. The defiance continues.

The Called Meeting Controversy

When Dr. Alexander Metherell, a commissioner to the 2002 General Assembly learned of Christ Church's deception, he initiated a heretofore unprecedented action. He drafted a petition to be circulated among his fellow commissioners, requesting a special called meeting of the General Assembly to deal with "the constitutional crisis" that had resulted from growing acts of defiance like that of Christ Church and the refusal of denominational officials to enforce compliance.

The Book of Order provided that upon receipt of signatures from 25 ministers and 25 elders who had served as commissioners to the General Assembly, the moderator was required to call the meeting. During his campaign to gain those signatures, Metherell met a solid wall of resistance from the stated clerk and moderator of the General Assembly and from leaders of PFR, some of whom wrote and called evangelical commissioners, urging them not to sign the petition for fear that a called General Assembly might split the church.

PFR issued a statement in the midst of Metherell's petition drive, saying that a called meeting "at this time would be inopportune and perhaps mis-

92 PFR Issues Ministries Team, "Grace Is Not License: PFR Cautions Christ Church," Presbyterians for Renewal, December 21, 2002.

understood." The statement also said that a called meeting would be "largely out of proportion to the problem" and that "several judicial cases are working their way through the system. Yes, some governing bodies have seemingly bungled or distorted various proceedings. But that does not a constitutional crisis make!"[93]

Despite this resistance from denominational officials and PFR, Metherell received more than the required number of signatures (26 pastors and 31 elders from 46 presbyteries and all 16 synods), and he presented the petitions to the Moderator personally during a meeting in Louisville, in the presence of members of the Committee on the Office of the General Assembly, members of the General Assembly Council, and the Office of the Stated Clerk. But instead of calling the meeting, as he was constitutionally required to do, the Moderator wrote to all commissioners who had signed the petition, asking them to reconsider and withdraw their signatures. The stated clerk also wrote to the commissioners, asking them to vote again. Following suit, and presumably at the urging of the stated clerk, some presbytery executives contacted minister commissioners under their jurisdiction, encouraging them with what some ministers reported were veiled threats of unhappy consequences to their careers if they did not comply and withdraw their names.[94]

Noting that the denomination's highest officers were defying the Constitution, the board of directors of the Presbyterian Lay Committee issued an open letter, calling on the moderator and stated clerk to do their constitutional duty. "We have watched with alarm the actions of our denomination's officers and agencies these past several days as they try to thwart a meeting that is guaranteed in our democratic procedures" said the Lay Committee. "It is clear to all fair-minded Presbyterians that the duty of these officials is to perform their responsibilities of office impartially and to execute even-handedly the provisions of our Constitution as they vowed to do when they became officers. Whatever privilege these officers may have had to advocate against such a meeting before the petitions were presented ceased the moment that the requisite petitions from commissioners were handed to them ... We call upon the Moderator and Stated Clerk to fulfill their obligations of office now and to call a timely special meeting of the assembly as required by G-13.0104 of *The Book of Order*."[95]

93 Presbyterians for Renewal, Statement by Board of Directors, Oct. 14, 2002.

94 One such report was made by the Rev. David Long, minister commissioner from Suwannee Presbytery.

95 Presbyterian Lay Committee, "Open Letter to the Members of the Presbyterian Church (USA)," January 17, 2003.

But the Moderator and Stated Clerk continued their attempts to secure petitioner withdrawals. Under intense pressure, several original signatories backed off, pulling the total below the required number. Then the Moderator announced that since he had not received the required number of signatures, he would not call the meeting.

In the ensuing melee, the PFR Issues Ministry tried to calm the waters by issuing a public statement of "gratitude, admonition and hope." PFR affirmed Metherell's right to call for the special meeting, although questioning "the wisdom and efficacy" of it. It assured its readers of its belief that Metherell and the commissioners who joined him were "motivated by a genuine concern for Christ's church," and it cautioned opponents not to "vilify" them or "impugn their motives."[96]

Then PFR directed accolades to denominational officials who had undermined Metherell's called meeting campaign. It stated its gratitude for "the honorable intentions and due diligence of our constitutionally elected officers." It stated that "there is every reason to believe that both the Stated Clerk and the Moderator have been honest and aboveboard in their actions and within the bounds of their constitutional prerogatives." It said they should not be blamed or accused of "underhanded manipulation."

The balance of PFR's statement included a reassurance that Presbyterians could have confidence in their system of government because "the Moderator and Stated Clerk have acted to assure that all is in order," and it called on all parties to extend charity and good will toward one another.

The Covenant Network joined PFR's attempt to defuse the escalating constitutional crisis: "In the controversies of recent weeks, the Moderator of the General Assembly and other church officials have come under unprecedented pressure. The Board of the Covenant Network honors the office of Moderator and affirms its respect for the extraordinary person who now holds that office …"[97]

In his own statement, PFR's president Jack Haberer penned an editorial defending the stated clerk's unwillingness to enforce the Constitution: "The stated clerk has refused to play the role of a monarch, being unwilling to extend his authority into governing bodies beyond the range of his jurisdiction."[98]

96 Presbyterians for Renewal, "PFR Asks: Can We Not Stand Down?" January 27, 2003.

97 The Covenant Network, "Covenant Network Chicago meeting statement," January 28, 2003.

98 Haberer, Jack, *Presbyterian Outlook*, October 14, 2002.

Explanations and Emendations

PFR suffered what it described as "a stampede of responses" from across the denomination, so extensive that it issued a second statement called "Setting the record straight" and a "background paper," assuring its critics that it "hadn't gone soft."

In its question-and-answer background paper, PFR said that its own board was "clearly divided" on the question of whether "our leaders in Louisville followed the procedural rules in regard to the special G.A."

"We have looked at it carefully and have come out with different viewpoints," said the paper. "But PFR is united in believing that (a) the leaders did not act in a reckless or egregious manner, and (b) we shouldn't infer evil intent from their actions."[99]

This statement displays a pattern that often appears in PFR's public opinions regarding the actions of denominational leaders. PFR's focus frequently highlights an assumed good "intent" or "motive" of the denominational leader rather than the content of the action itself.

"Many of us on the PFR Issues Ministry Team," continued the background paper, "are uneasy with the Moderator's letter to commissioners, feeling he moved from moderating to persuading by sending it. But we know Moderator Abu-Akel and consider his error more an over-earnest enthusiasm than a sinister plot. We expressed our uneasiness in our statement."

"We are also able to grant that Stated Clerk Clifton Kirkpatrick's actions were at least defensible, while not actions we can unanimously endorse or would have taken ourselves. If he erred, we aren't ready to condemn his motives that led to the error. If he did not err but did only what was prudent, we're not quite prepared to acclaim it, either."

"Yes, we realize that's an 'on the one hand …, but on the other hand …' kind of answer. Our entire denomination is feeling that ambivalence, which, we contend, is not properly cured by stark pronouncements amid ambiguous circumstances."[100]

Escalating Defiance

Flagrant violations of the ordination standards continued, including a declaration by Baltimore Presbytery that it would not prosecute any minister within its jurisdiction who in conscience determined that he/she must

99 Presbyterians for Renewal, "The Reasoning Behind 'Can We Not Stand Down?'" February 21, 2003.

100 *Ibid.*

defy G-6.0106(b). Evangelicals were incensed by Baltimore Presbytery's action, and even more so when delaying tactics at the synod level ensured that Baltimore would get away with its defiance. Some began calling for the stated clerk's resignation, since he steadfastly declared that it was not his job to enforce the Constitution.

Again, PFR felt constrained to calm the waters. In a statement that found fault both with the defiant Baltimore Presbytery and its critics, PFR said, "There is something amiss in Baltimore, as well as something remiss in some behavior that has resulted."[101]

PFR found "disorder" in three Baltimore actions: "(1) the presbytery has decided to ignore our Constitution, (2) the presbytery's Investigating Committee has turned a blind eye on egregious misbehavior by a pastor, and (3) the presbytery's Permanent Judicial Commission has declined to take up the case on appeal."[102]

But PFR also distanced itself from those who were publicly critical of Baltimore's defiance: "Not everyone has acted decently in response to this presbytery. Some of our co-laborers for constitutional adherence have proposed remedies that are clearly unconstitutional in their own right, or have launched personal attacks toward both church officers and allies not joining their crusades. PFR grieves the indecency of these reactions of the flesh in the same way that it laments the disorder of constitutional defiance and sexual anarchy ... In many ways, this uncharitable and all-too-human response is as bad as the behavior being decried."[103]

Contesting the Lay Committee's statement that the denomination was facing "a constitutional crisis," PFR called on Presbyterians to remain calm and trust the system: "However, PFR wishes to point out that our excellent Presbyterian system of government under our Constitution is working!"[104]

Face to Face in Atlanta

On January 30, 2003, delegations from Presbyterians for Renewal and The Presbyterian Lay Committee met in Atlanta, Ga. to discuss their increasingly public disagreements. During the meeting, representatives prayed for and affirmed one another's commitment to renewal, while challenging their

101 Presbyterians for Renewal, "PFR Calls for Decency and Order Concerning Baltimore Presbytery," November 19, 2002.

102 *Ibid.*

103 *Ibid.*

104 *Ibid.* Note: Although challenged repeatedly, as of August, 2007, Baltimore Presbytery's defiance, enacted on June 27, 2002, has never been rescinded.

different assessments of the condition of the Presbyterian Church (USA) and their different methodologies for addressing that condition.

PFR representatives stated that they did not believe the denomination was currently faced with a constitutional crisis and that "our orderly system, though slow and frustrating at times, is at work." They took umbrage at public criticisms that had been leveled at Stated Clerk Kirkpatrick. Employing language that reflected the theme of Jack Haberer's Oct. 14, 2002 *Presbyterian Outlook* editorial, PFR said, "We believe that our Stated Clerk is being pressured to act beyond the provisions of his position description, and that his character and motives are being unjustly impugned. Therefore, we rise to his defense."[105]

PLC representatives cited the Christ Church case in which the Constitution was being defied by Christ Church's redefinition of its terms, Baltimore Presbytery's declaration that it would not prosecute charges against any minister in the presbytery who chooses openly to defy the Constitution, the fact that dozens of sessions had adopted resolutions saying that they intended to violate church laws on ordinations, membership, communion and same-gender "weddings," and the fact that more than 20 judicial complaints had been filed in several states against ministers and sessions who publicly declared their defiance of the Constitution, most of which had been summarily dismissed by liberal investigating committees and none of which had even made it to trial. Citing these cases, in addition to the fact that General Assembly agencies were flagrantly defying the church's standards, the PLC argued that "the system is not working" and "we are faced with a full-blown constitutional crisis."

Further, PLC representatives insisted that public criticism of the stated clerk regarding documented misfeasance and malfeasance of duty did not constitute a personal attack, but was a legitimate and necessary call to accountability for one who is in the employ of the General Assembly.

PLC representatives summarized their board's position as follows: "The PLC is committed to maintaining the ordination language in *The Book of Order* as a denomination-wide standard for officers. The PLC is committed to adherence to those standards in practice by congregations and presbyteries. This means that the PLC will oppose any efforts to make those standards a local option and will oppose any defiance of the standards or delinquency in enforcement."[106]

The two-day meeting was cordial, prayerful and frank, with each delega-

105 Presbyterians for Renewal, "Statement of Principles," January 10, 2003.

106 Presbyterian Lay Committee, "Position Paper," January 15, 2003.

tion highlighting potential vulnerabilities in the other's position. PFR warned PLC that it was in danger of fomenting schism. PLC warned PFR that it was in danger of accommodating to a non-Christian culture that had overtaken the General Assembly infrastructure. Each side pledged to maintain honest and open lines of communication with the other and to work together on the many issues where the two organizations were in substantial agreement. There was no agreement, however, to terminate the practice of issuing "dueling" assessments of events that were occurring within the denomination.

A Declaration of Conscience

On October 18, 2003, the PLC issued a "Declaration of Conscience," recognizing that a state of "spiritual schism" exists within the Presbyterian Church (USA) "because of a deep and irreconcilable disunion among its members over the person and work of Jesus Christ, the authority of God's Word written, and God's call to a holy life. We are two faiths within one denomination."[107]

The PLC said, "We believe that any compromise with proponents of a false gospel – no matter how laudable the desire for peace and unity that may engender such initiatives – will further erode our denomination's integrity and delay the day of decision that will ultimately come."[108]

Calling on Presbyterians to be "faithful stewards of all that the Lord has entrusted to us," the PLC said "We no longer believe that either the General Assembly per-capita budget or the unrestricted mission budget of the PCUSA is worthy of support."

The PLC encouraged individuals and sessions to engage in prayerful study "as to whether their General Assembly per-capita contribution should be redirected and/or their mission gifts restricted to ministries at home and abroad that are demonstrably faithful to the gospel."[109]

PFR Issues a Response

PFR's counter statement came quickly. Speaking for the board, the PFR Issues Ministry said "the Lay Committee's encouragement to individuals and sessions to prayerfully consider whether their per capita and mission funds ought to be redirected to other causes constitutes an implicit call to

107 Presbyterian Lay Committee, "A Declaration of Conscience," October 18, 2003.

108 *Ibid.*

109 *Ibid.*

others to join in a crusade of withholding funds, which effectively subjects the denomination to power-based methods of coercion that do not bring glory to God."

"Therefore," continued PFR, "along with the Lay Committee, we 'affirm and encourage the efforts of those who remain committed to reform and renewal of the PCUSA' to '... work together for the glory of God and the strengthening of His witness in the world.' But in good conscience, we cannot encourage our fellow Presbyterians to engage in a program of across-the-board withholding of funds, which would cripple much good in the attempt to cure some evil."[110]

The Composition of PUP

When the 2001 General Assembly sent a proposed constitutional amendment to the presbyteries that called for revoking the denomination's ordination standards, liberal strategists knew they faced an uphill battle. Denominational polls had consistently shown that Presbyterians in the pews supported G-6.0106(b) and would oppose any attempt to remove it from the Constitution. Thus, a fallback measure was proposed that could have come straight out of the Covenant Network's play book. The assembly created a Peace, Unity and Purity Task Force, loaded it with a liberal majority and began a search for a token minority of institutionally compliant moderates. If the constitutional amendment failed (which it did, by a smashing 3-1 majority), the task force would be in place to bring the issue back in another form.

For students of Presbyterian Church history, this was 1925-1926 all over again, when the General Assembly created a similarly composed "Swearingen Commission,"[111] whose report led to the liberalization of Princeton Seminary, revocation of the requirement that ordained officers subscribe to essential tenets of Christian faith, and the ultimate defrocking of J. Gresham Machen.

Appointed by the current and two previous General Assembly moderators, a minority group of moderates was selected. Notably, five were chosen from the ranks of PFR. The Rev. Gary Demarest, a former PFR board

110 Presbyterians for Renewal, "Build up or Tear Down? PFR Comments on Presbyterian Lay Committee's 'Declaration of Conscience,'" November 6, 2003.

111 The "Swearingen Commission" was the name given to the General Assembly "peace and unity" group appointed by Moderator Charles Erdman in 1925. The commission recommended that the General Assembly drop its requirement that ordained leaders subscribe to specified essential tenets of Christian faith.

member, was named co-chairman. The Revs. Mark Achtemeier, Jack Haberer, Mike Loudon,[112] and Lonnie Oliver were also drawn from PFR's board, a fact that the Office of the Stated Clerk played up often in order to bolster its contention that the group was "theologically balanced."[113]

During the PUP task force's fall, 2003 meeting, Barbara Wheeler applauded Jack Haberer and PFR, saying that they and the Covenant Network represented "the great middle of the church" as opposed to the "super activists and their sympathizers."[114]

She continued, "With a few exceptions, however, the great middle of the church (including most of us who make up Covenant Network and PFR) has sat silent as a small number of our colleagues siphoned off enormous amounts [sic] of time, energy, and money into judicial proceedings and political grandstanding."[115]

Wheeler made her comments in a paper titled "Turn Back: Hopes and Fears for the Presbyterian Future" that was distributed during the task force meeting. Copies of the paper, which was originally delivered on Jan. 21, 2003 at a conference for Presbyterian pastors at Fuller Theological Seminary in Pasadena, Calif., were also distributed during a presentation that Wheeler and Jack Haberer gave to a gathering of General Assembly attendees in May.

During the period in which the task force was developing its report and recommendations, Haberer and Wheeler made three public appearances in which they affirmed one another as colleagues whose unity outweighed their differences. In their joint presentations, they pointed to their acceptance of one another as a demonstration of the collegiality that they believe must occur if denominational peace is to be achieved.

Haberer said that directors of PFR and the Covenant Network had been talking "informally in informal conversations" about achieving unity in the denomination. "This has not directly involved our boards," he said, indicating that the discussions consisted of clusters of individuals from the organizations rather than formal meetings of the two boards as boards.

---

112 Loudon became a PFR board member in the third quarter of 2005.

113 In a written communication to the author, Rev. Haberer claimed that "evangelicals" comprised "a majority" of the task force membership. This assessment differs from that of Task Force chairman Gary Demarest, who, in a statement at the 2006 West Coast Evangelical Pastors' Conference, defended his having agreed to a compromise position (adopting the task force recommendations with a few modifications) because "we were outnumbered from the start."

114 *The Presbyterian Layman*, Vol. 36, No. 5, September/October, 2003.

115 *Ibid.*

A 'Unanimous' Report

When the task force issued its report in the summer of 2005, many renewal leaders were shocked to learn that it was unanimous, a point that task force members and the Office of the Stated Clerk repeatedly emphasized. This unanimity represented a substantial departure from task forces commissioned by previous general assemblies. Predecessor task forces had also been dominated by ideologically liberal members, but unlike the PUP group, their evangelical minorities remained rooted in their convictions, and when they were unable to persuade majority task force members they filed a minority report. These minority reports flagged flaws in the majority statement and gave evangelical commissioners in the receiving general assemblies a vital point of entry for debate.[116]

PFR's Pre-General Assembly Dilemma

The prominent involvement of PFR board members and the fact that they were unanimous in supporting a task force report that effectively undermined constitutional ordination standards placed the PFR board in a difficult position. How could it oppose the document, several of whose authors were fellow board members and had been so clearly identified with its organization over the years?

After the PUP proposal was released on Oct. 1, 2005, twenty four Presbyterian renewal organization leaders met in Chicago to forge their common response. Although PFR's executive director, the Rev. Michael Walker participated in the meeting, he declined to sign the consensus statement which was strongly critical of the task force document. Walker agreed with other renewal leaders that the PUP report had erred in recommending that governing bodies be allowed to declare the Constitution's ordination standards "non-essential" (Recommendation 5), but he said that he could affirm other sections of the report, including theological and polity sections that served as a basis for PUP's recommendations. Additionally, the representative of Presbyterian Frontier Fellowship stated that he supported the statement personally but could not sign it without explicit authorization from his board. Thus, when the 22 remaining renewal leaders adopted their

116 Examples of the powerful impact made on General Assemblies by minority reports were the 1978 report on ordination of homosexuals, the 1991 Human Sexuality Report, and the 1992 report on abortion. In each case the majority task force report that went to the assembly was contested by a carefully written minority report. This accentuation of theological/ethical differences contributed to lively General Assembly debate and, in the 1978 and 1991 General Assemblies, resulted in decisions that rejected the majority task force recommendations.

Chicago statement on October 1, and released it on October 7, the signatures of PFR and PFF did not appear.

PFR issued its own statement on Oct 7, praising the PUP report as a whole, extolling the motives of its authors, and criticizing only Recommendation 5. This stand-alone position displeased many evangelicals, who publicly entreated PFR to make common cause with the other renewal groups. Letters on numerous websites warned that disunity among the renewal forces would ensure defeat when the 2006 General Assembly met to consider the PUP report. On Nov. 17, PFR issued a statement endorsing the Oct. 1 statement of renewal leaders. "We strongly encourage congregations and governing bodies of the Presbyterian Church (U.S.A.) to use this common statement, along with our own statements, as they consider the Task Force report," it said.[117]

Responding to the 2006 General Assembly

The General Assembly's approval of the PUP report, and in particular, its adoption of Recommendation 5, proved a devastating blow to renewal organizations operating within the denomination. All renewal leaders concurred in their assessment that in issuing the task force's "authoritative interpretation," General Assembly commissioners had found a way effectively to amend the Constitution without submitting that amendment to ratification among the presbyteries.

Following the General Assembly vote, the renewal organizations called a press conference and issued a strongly worded statement:

"Today, in a single vote by 298 commissioners, the Constitution of the Presbyterian Church (U.S.A.) effectively was changed. The mandated requirements of ordination, rooted in Scripture and our Confessions, have been made optional. Sessions and presbyteries have been allowed to treat the Seventh Commandment as 'not essential.' These ordaining bodies have been told that they need not obey the explicit instruction of the apostles: that all Christian believers should 'abstain from ... sexual immorality' (Acts 15:29).

"The consequences of the decision of this General Assembly throw our denomination into crisis. Many individuals and congregations will conclude from this decision that the PC(USA) has abandoned the historic faith of the Church. The decision will be regarded by others in the worldwide body of Christ as profoundly offensive.

117 Presbyterians for Renewal, "PFR Endorses Common Statement on P.U.P. Report," November 17, 2005.

"Yet we do not believe that God has abandoned the members of the PCUSA. We do believe that God's Word, by the power of God's Spirit, is able to convict, transform, and restore. We are thankful for the many Presbyterian congregations and members who testify so boldly to that power – even this week in Birmingham. Faithful commissioners and advisory delegates have stood valiantly and effectively for doctrines such as the Trinity and the sanctity of human life.

"We will redouble our efforts to bear witness to the gospel in this troubled time and place. We reaffirm our ordination vows at the very time when those vows are being cheapened. This recent decision marks a profound deviation from biblical requirements, and we cannot accept, support, or tolerate it. We will take the steps necessary to be faithful to God and to those God calls us to serve.

"Let us all be guided by the passage from which comes, providentially, the theme of this 217th General Assembly:

'Therefore, since we are surrounded by so great a cloud of witnesses, let us also lay aside every weight and the sin that clings so closely, and let us run with perseverance the race that is set before us, looking to Jesus the pioneer and perfecter of our faith, who for the sake of the joy that was set before him endured the cross, disregarding its shame, and has taken his seat at the right hand of the throne of God.'"[118]

Noting the Nuance

The key phrase that generated considerable discussion among renewal leaders when drafting the statement is found in paragraph 3: "Yet we do not believe that God has abandoned *the members* of the PCUSA." (italics added) With the passage of the PUP report, renewal leaders no longer had consensus on the institutional future of the PCUSA. For some, like members of the New Wineskins Initiative (soon to become The New Wineskins Association of Churches), the Presbyterian Lay Committee, Presbyterian Reformed Ministries International, and growing numbers of individuals within other renewal groups, the 2006 General Assembly had crossed the Rubicon.

For other renewalists, like PFR and moderate members of the Coalition board, some hope of renewal – although now deeply wounded – remained alive. Coalition director Mrs. Terry Schlossberg called for volunteers to draft overtures to the 2008 General Assembly to undo damage done to the Constitution by the 2006 General Assembly. Meanwhile, trying to put the best spin on what the assembly had done, she assured members of the

118 Renewal Leaders' Statement, June 20, 2006.

Association for Church Renewal during their post-2006 General Assembly meeting that "the Constitution has not been changed."

This assurance, which was also voiced by the moderator and stated clerk of the General Assembly, may have been technically accurate, but it was also misleading, for the General Assembly's action now allowed governing bodies to declare the Constitution's mandate (albeit unchanged) to be regarded as optional ("non-essential"). Schlossberg's words did little to comfort Presbyterians who knew that a seismic change had just occurred.

Speaking to a PFR event in Montreat, NC, in July, 2006, Michael Walker tried a similar approach. While lamenting what the assembly had done, he suggested that evangelicals not overreact to it, since the result of that action was, as yet, unknown: "The actual 'legal' effect of the assembly's action, in terms of church law, will not be known until we have a couple of precedent-setting decisions by the General Assembly Permanent Judicial Commission. That means we have burdensome and distracting court battles ahead of us."[119]

The essence of Walker's position was that although the 2006 General Assembly did a bad thing by giving governing bodies permission to violate the standard, no practical change can be said to have occurred until some governing body does, in fact, violate the standard, and until the courts of the denomination rule on whether that body can legitimately get away with doing so.

'Free to be Faithful'

Walker emphasized the fact that the General Assembly action was permissive, not coercive. It would now allow governing bodies to ordain persons who will not confine their sexual activity to marriage, but, said Walker, evangelicals can take comfort in the fact that they are not being forced to do so. "We are free to be faithful … We can express our identity locally with confidence and integrity and need not feel defined by the unrepresentative actions of the assembly."[120]

Walker's suggested solution to the problem of living in a post-2006 Presbyterian Church (USA) was to build a network of faithful congregations that will be self consciously separate from but remain structurally within the PCUSA, and encouraging those congregations to re-asses their financial support for the denomination.

This counsel represented a reversal of PFR's previous position, particularly as had been stated in its criticism of the Lay Committee's "Declaration

119 Walker, Michael, "Free to be Faithful: Covenant Community After the 217th General Assembly," July 3, 2006.

120 *Ibid.*

of Conscience." Walker said, "Choosing to emphasize that we as a Presbyterian Church can and should pursue our identity and unity through means not defined by our governing bodies does, in my mind, represent a step further than where PFR and most of the evangelical movement has been in the past. PFR has always been an alternative of sorts, some have even called us a 'shadow denomination.' Whatever we call it, I believe the time has come for the whole evangelical movement to go to the next level: more distinct identity within the PC(USA); reconsidering our stewardship of financial resources and questioning the wisdom of paying per capita and undesignated mission giving – this will vary by presbytery but we do need to ask the questions; and a public, open-ended, theologically informed discussion about where God may be leading us together in the future."[121]

The Presbyterian Global Fellowship

In suggesting this line of thought, Walker signaled the birth of another organization within the denomination called the Presbyterian Global Fellowship (PGF), a group that he served as a consultant during its formation. The PGF would be "missional," supporting missions that are not necessarily tied to denominational structures. In essence, this new group would focus on making connections with the cross-denominational, global church, particularly in the burgeoning Christian communities of the developing world, and it would turn its attention away from doctrinal disputes inside the Presbyterian Church (USA).

Although they present themselves as two separate organizations, the relationship between PGF and PFR is very close. In a fund raising flier mailed in June, 2007 to ministers and elders in Presbyterian Church (USA) congregations, PFR lists PGF as one of its "missional partnerships."[122]

Citing statistical evidence of the Presbyterian Church (USA)'s plight as a precipitating factor in their decision to launch something new, leaders of the PGF called evangelicals to an August 17, 2006, meeting in Atlanta. 800 people accepted the invitation, many of whom came seeking some word of hope in the aftermath of the disastrous 2006 General Assembly.

The Atlanta PGF Gathering

For Presbyterians who believe in the singular saving Lordship of Jesus Christ and honor his call to discipleship, the PGF event proved a thrilling affirmation of the gospel. Its focus was clear: the essence of the church is

121 *Ibid.*

122 Presbyterians for Renewal, "Recovering Gospel Hope," June, 2007.

its mission. Anything less than mission produces institutional religiosity, the petrified relic of a once-vibrant faith.

That Presbyterians who traveled to Atlanta sought an alternative to their dying denomination could hardly be questioned, but PGF leaders had a hard time saying so. In fact, they bent over backwards not to say so. There were veiled references to the fact that all is not well in Zion – references to denominational demographics, losses of missionaries and members – but PGF cast its central focus elsewhere, aiming its vision not toward the church that is, but the church that was meant to be. What happened in Atlanta was a soul-stirring, mission-oriented reach for life. What did not happen was an intentional disengagement from the institution.

Birthing new life in one direction while remaining tethered to a body that is headed the other way created confusion, with some participants wondering how such a contradictory juxtaposition could continue indefinitely. During the Atlanta event, breakout sessions provided opportunities for participant feedback. Here the frustration was repeatedly voiced. During a seminar, after Michael Walker presented his "free to be faithful" message, a participant asked, "Why aren't you angry? I am embarrassed by the way our denomination acts, not just the actions of the 217th General Assembly, but actions that go back more than a decade … 're-imagining God,' killing babies before they are born … I can't associate with that any longer. I won't associate with that!"

Not an 'Ain't It Awful' Time

Despite frequently voiced concerns from participants about being yoked to a theologically corrupt denomination, PGF leaders stayed their "don't jump ship" course. Steering committee leader Rev. Victor Pentz, senior minister of Peachtree Presbyterian, the host church, told the gathering that PGF's role is to create a link between Presbyterian congregations that are committed to evangelical faith and "global Christians around the world," not to criticize the denomination's leaders. "This is not going to be an 'ain't it awful' time," he said.

That appeared to be the initial theme of the emerging PGF, namely, that while its leaders may not agree with the ideology that dominates their denominational infrastructure, they have chosen to ignore rather than contest it. "We are not leaving the PCUSA," said Pentz, "but reforming and redeeming it." Nothing in his comments indicated how the practice of ignoring its policies would result in denominational redemption.

A similar message was given by PGF leader, Stephen Hayner, professor of evangelism at Columbia Theological Seminary: "We dream of a denomination which brings the best of its people, its theology, and its tradition and lays all at the feet of the Lord of the church ... The task before us is NOT getting everyone in the church to agree with our point of view – or to win the war as to who is right. God's call is to become a missional church ... and to extend the love of Christ to a waiting world."

The Rev. Dr. Roberta Hestenes told the PGF gathering that the Presbyterian Church (USA) is "a wonderful work of God that I am grateful to be a part of." She said that the denomination is not the whole picture, for "it is only a part of the richness and diversity and reality of a global church in which the majority of Christians bear a whole bunch of labels," but the denomination was clearly, in her view, a label that PGF Presbyterians should continue to wear.

'Mission Unites; Doctrine Divides'

Thus, the PGF was launched with fanfare, thrilling worship celebrations and a much vaunted focus on Presbyterians becoming "a missional church." The steering committee started a web site, accompanied by a handful of "blogs" from participating ministers, and it sent out a few fund-raising letters. But in its emphasis on promoting "mission that unites" while avoiding "doctrine that divides," the organization may have perpetuated – certainly it has done nothing to correct – the plight of a denomination that purports to have a mission, but cannot agree on its message. Without a clear and unambiguous commitment to the essential tenets of Christian faith, "mission" becomes vacuous. Jesus' question, "Who do you say that I am?" lies at the heart of the Church's mission. A denomination that will not require its leaders to answer that question has no message to proclaim.[123]

Anticipating 'Resurrection'

On April 23, 2007, the PFR Issues Committee issued a public statement, imploring evangelical Presbyterians not to leave the denomination.[124]

123 The 2006 General Assembly's debate over the PUP report included a graphic example of the "mission unites/doctrine divides" philosophy when Marj Carpenter, the "mission" moderator who enjoys almost universal affection from the denomination's evangelicals, was escorted to the microphone by John Buchanan, the "Covenant Network" moderator. Carpenter reminded the assembly of her love for missions, and how she had traveled the world in support of "our missionaries." She said that while she was "personally opposed to ordaining gays," she could see that the controversy was driving people away and undermining the mission budget. She urged commissioners to vote for the PUP report in order to stop the controversy and get on with the mission of the Church.

124 Presbyterians for Renewal, "Why Stay? Twelve Reasons" April 23, 2007.

PFR said that it does not "minimize the problems in the denomination," but "finds compelling reasons to continue gospel ministry within the PCUSA." Included in PFR's rationale was its concern that in leaving the denomination, evangelicals would be "abandoning and weakening" the work of evangelicals who choose to stay. PFR pointed to church history, declaring that "theological and moral problems are not new" and that such problems "took time to be resolved." It described the PCUSA as a "mission field" that is "ripe for harvest." PFR repeated the theme that evangelicals are still "free to be faithful," which includes the freedom to preach an unencumbered gospel and exercise stewardship of financial resources.

The PFR statement pointed to the flight of some of Jesus' disciples prior to Easter morning, who, following the crucifixion of their Lord, "left Jerusalem in despair too soon." Reminding its readers that Jesus' resurrection occurred after those disciples fled, PFR said, "We pray that no one will leave the PCUSA too soon."

PFR's flier that was mailed to all Presbyterian churches two months later underscored its adhesion to denominational structures. "In a season of uncertainty among Presbyterians," it said, "PFR is not going anywhere."[125]

In calling on evangelicals to remain a part of the denomination, PFR repeated themes voiced by Jack Haberer, who having stepped down from its board, had become editor of *The Presbyterian Outlook*. Haberer ran a series of editorials and columns calling for denominational unity. He insisted that in the 2006 General Assembly's decision, "nothing has changed," because no words were taken out of the Constitution. He likened congregational departures from the denomination to a painful divorce in which everyone loses.

In calling on Presbyterians to remain tethered to their institution, being "missional" albeit without a unified message, and avoiding internecine "political" conflicts over the substance of belief, PGF and PFR appear to have adopted the quintessential Erdman role, bringing to mind Machen's critique: "Dr. Erdman does not indeed reject the doctrinal system of our church," he said, "but he is perfectly willing to make common cause with those who reject it, and he is perfectly willing on many occasions to keep it in the background."[126]

The New Wineskins Association of Churches

Commanding center stage among renewal ministries in the Presbyterian Church (USA) since the 2006 General Assembly is the New Wineskins Association of Churches. Initially an informal fellowship of local church

125 Presbyterians for Renewal, "Recovering Gospel Hope," June, 2007.

126 *The Presbyterian*, February 5, 1925.

leaders who prayed together seeking "a new way of being the church," the group crystallized its ideas into a statement of "essential tenets" and "ethical imperatives." Subscription to these standards is required of all who wish to participate. From this initial clarity of belief and morals, participants began to envision accountability networks that place the congregation on the front line of ministry and eschew hierarchical and heavily bureaucratic layers of governance that characterize current denominational structures.

In a manner not unlike other renewal organizations, New Wineskins has become an evangelical home for congregations within the denomination who find themselves estranged from its programs and policies. In this sense, it is acting like a "church within the Church," offering accountability relationships, mutual support, and opportunities for cooperative witness at home and abroad. Increasingly, New Wineskins congregations are re-directing their financial contributions away from denominational agencies and programs and toward transcontinental linkages with the global church.

But the New Wineskins has taken a major step beyond the point that PGF, PFR and the Coalition have been willing to go. They have broadened the perimeters of their fellowship to include not only congregations that choose to remain within the Presbyterian Church (USA) but also those who feel led by conscience to depart from the denomination. In an Orlando, Fl. meeting on Feb. 12, 2007, the New Wineskins Association voted to "further the kingdom" through a "realignment with the Evangelical Presbyterian Church." In June, 2007, the evangelical denomination created a non-geographic presbytery designed to welcome New Wineskins churches.

'A Place to Land'

Thus, the New Wineskins Association has created "a place to land" for congregations that can no longer remain within the PCUSA. Unlike the PCUSA, the Evangelical Presbyterian Church affirms "essential tenets" of Christian faith, and it requires all ordained leaders publicly to subscribe to them. Additionally, it employs a minimal organizational structure, affirming that the congregation is the locus of ministry and that higher governing bodies exist only for the purpose of supporting the congregations. Presentations at the New Wineskins' Orlando event pointed to close parallels between the New Wineskins essential tenets and ethical imperatives and published positions of the Evangelical Presbyterian Church. They also showed that the non-geographic, New Wineskins Presbytery could transfer former PCUSA ministers seamlessly into the EPC's medical and pension plan.

New Wineskins leaders indicate that they plan to conduct the association's ministry on both internal and external tracks. Realizing that it may take many months for some congregational leaders to prepare their people for an exit from the denomination, they say they will maintain a strong network of evangelical congregations within the PCUSA. Some congregational leaders who identify with the New Wineskins' essential tenets and ethical imperatives say they will remain within the PCUSA structure until a precipitating event occurs, presumably when an ordination that violates constitutional standards is upheld by Presbyterian courts. Such congregations are refining their corporate documents in order to strengthen their claim to church property in the event that there should be an eventual parting of the ways.

Cohesion by Coercion

Stated Clerk Clifton Kirkpatrick has predicted publicly that he believes very few congregations will depart from the denomination. Three factors bolster his prediction that, at least initially, the denomination's evangelical horses can be kept in the corral. One is simply the fact of institutional inertia. Having settled under the denominational label, congregational leaders who are risk averse may not be inclined to stir up controversy among their people, especially if they can keep their focus on local ministries and essentially ignore activities of the national bureaucracy that their congregants might find upsetting.

A second factor, namely the Erdman effect, feeds into the first. Kirkpatrick is counting on those who view themselves as "moderate evangelicals" to oil troubled waters among their theological kin. Contemporary Erdmans encourage middle of the road Presbyterians to stay the course in denominational affairs, filling their need for occasional doses of evangelicalism by orchestrating para-church conferences and events where the gospel is passionately embraced and denominational issues are conveniently ignored.

A third factor that will affect congregational defections is Louisville's threat of coercion with respect to ministers' careers and congregations' property. Such tactics may initially prove to be powerful impediments to a congregation's free choice of conscience, but their use will further dismantle an already fragile communion.

Targeting the Clergy

Working on the assumption that cantankerous congregations are being led into denominational disloyalty by their ministers, one of Kirkpatrick's strategies has been to intimidate the clergy. Unable to force local churches to make per capita payments or general mission gifts to Louisville, the stated clerk has warned ministers that although local church resistance to such payments has been deemed constitutional, any minister who advocates such practices may be regarded as having renounced denominational jurisdiction and forfeited her or his ordination.

In a letter to stated clerks of the denomination's 173 presbyteries, Kirkpatrick said, "I am concerned about what appears to be a growing number of ministers and elders who are encouraging congregations to withdraw (or "graciously separate") from the Presbyterian Church (USA) and/or who are advocating the withholding of duly authorized per capita assessments from their governing bodies as a form of protest. Such actions are unconstitutional, and I urge that they stop. It is a violation of our ordination vows to promote schism or the defiance of constitutionally sanctioned governing body directives."[127]

Kirkpatrick's counsel flies in the face of actions by the General Assembly in which it has repeatedly refused to adopt a requirement that local church sessions pay a per capita assessment.[128] It also contradicts several rulings of the General Assembly Permanent Judicial Commission in which that body has overturned presbytery attempts to force local church sessions to pay the fee.[129]

The counsel also runs afoul of *Book of Order* provisions that allow for the orderly departure of Presbyterian Church (USA) congregations that desire to unite with other Reformed bodies. In the stated clerk's view, a congregation may constitutionally choose this course of action, but if a minister or elder encourages the congregation to do so, he or she is guilty of promoting "schism."

Although the General Assembly and its highest judicial body have effectively blocked Kirkpatrick from disciplining local churches for their refusal to pay per capita assessments, his office has issued "warnings" to ministers who counsel their sessions not to make the payment. In an Oct. 14, 1997, email communication, Mark Tammen, legal counsel to the stated clerk, declared that ministers who advocate non payment of per capita may face disciplinary action. Tammen argued that if a minister attends a presbytery meeting where a vote to support per capita payments occurs, that minister

127 Kirkpatrick, Clifton, Letter to Stated Clerks, January 3, 2002.

128 The 2001 General Assembly, for example, rejected Overture 01-01 from the Presbytery of Scioto Valley that would have required congregations to pay per capita.

129 *Westminster United Presbyterian Church v. the Presbytery of Detroit* (1976), *Central Presbyterian v. Presbytery of Long Island* (1991), *Minihan v. the Presbytery of Scioto Valley* (2003), *A. Kirk Johnston, Laurie Johnston, and Session of First United Presbyterian Church, Paola, Kansas v. Heartland Presbytery of the Presbyterian Church (USA)* (2004).

is bound to represent that position in a subsequent meeting of his session. If the minister does not, said Tammen, he or she may be subject to disciplinary charges.[130]

On Oct. 31, Tammen restated his interpretation, saying, "The polity seems clear, at least theoretically." Tammen added that neither he nor the stated clerk had any intention to enforce it by taking any action against anyone urging the withholding of per capita apportionments. He said that his statements to ministers should be received as "pastoral advice to those who are placing themselves at a potential risk ... I'm not using this advice as a threat," he said, "but as a warning."[131]

On January 31, 2004, the Presbytery of Western North Carolina stripped *Presbyterian Layman* Editor Parker T. Williamson of his "validated ministry" status, declaring him a "minister at large" and setting in motion a process that within three years would have resulted in the revocation of his ordination. At issue was the fact that Williamson's employer, the Presbyterian Lay Committee, had published a "Declaration of Conscience," declaring that it could no longer countenance the practice of sending unrestricted gifts, including per capita apportionments, to denominational headquarters. Williamson concurred with the Lay Committee's declaration.

Williamson filed a complaint against the presbytery with the Permanent Judicial Commission of the Synod of Mid-Atlantic, which overturned the presbytery's action against him. On appeal, the General Assembly Permanent Judicial Commission sustained the Synod's action, and Williamson's validation was reinstated.[132]

During depositions taken by Williamson's attorneys in preparation for the Synod trial, the presbytery was required to reveal correspondence and telephone logs showing that the denomination's Office of the Stated Clerk had been advising presbytery officials in their attempt to invalidate Williamson's ministry.

Anecdotal evidence from evangelical ministers across the denomination reveals a widespread experience of intimidation. Ministers understand that presbytery executives and stated clerks can effectively block their call to another congregation. They are also aware of the fact that although there are safeguards in the *Book of Discipline* that grant them the right to hear

130 Tammen, Mark, Letter to the Rev. James Tony, Oct. 14, 1997.

131 *Layman Online* telephone interview with Mark Tammen, October 31, 1997.

132 *Parker T. Williamson, Complainant/Appellee/Cross Appellee v. Presbytery of Western North Carolina, Respondent/Appellant/Cross Appellee,* Permanent Judicial Commission of the Presbyterian Church (U.S.A.) Remedial Case 217-7, April 4, 2005.

charges brought against them and the opportunity to face and cross examine their accusers, presbytery officials often circumvent the *Book of Discipline* by treating ministers administratively rather than by formally filing disciplinary charges against them. By dealing with them administratively, denominational officials assume that they can circumvent rules of fundamental fairness that are mandated by the *Book of Discipline.*

This tactic was employed in the Williamson case. Contesting advice given to the presbytery by the stated clerk's office, the General Assembly Permanent Judicial Commission ruled that if an administrative procedure results in damage to a minister's professional standing, the Constitution requires that the fundamental fairness rules of the *Book of Discipline* be followed, even if the dispute in question is not a disciplinary case. However, *The Book of Order* makes no provision for ministers to be awarded damages, e.g., recovery of attorney fees and court costs, in the event that they should win their case against unjust treatment by their presbytery, a fact which in itself acts as a strong deterrent to any denominational challenge.

Similarly, ministers who contemplate resisting the denominational infrastructure feel threatened by the suggestion that their pensions may be in jeopardy. Responding to inquiries from scores of Presbyterian ministers, the Lay Committee secured the services of a pension law specialist. His opinion, which was published by *The Layman Online* as a service to ministers, was that while the pension plan is not protected under Federal ERISA legislation and can be amended by mere vote of a General Assembly, there are provisions in Pennsylvania law that protect the vested interests of pensioners and to which ministers whose pensions are under threat could appeal.[133] However, regardless of ministers' rights under the law, the cost of legal counsel to defend those rights is an inhibiting factor for many ministers.

Confiscation of Church Property

As an increasing number of congregations engage in conversations over the possibility of leaving the Presbyterian Church (USA), lawyers from the Office of the Stated Clerk are advising presbytery executives and stated clerks on strategies for claiming real property, bank accounts and endowments owned by those congregations. Mark Tammen has met with presbytery leaders in several states, offering advice and counsel on methods of confiscation.

133 The referenced opinion regarding ministers' rights under the Presbyterian Church (USA) pension plan may be found on *The Layman Online* web site (www.layman.org). Pennsylvania law is applicable because the Presbyterian Church (USA) is a Pennsylvania corporation.

During and after September, 2005, Tammen circulated two documents among denominational officials on the subject of church property marked, "Privileged and Confidential Attorney Work Communication" and "This is a legal strategy memorandum. Do not copy or circulate."[134] The statements advised presbytery officials to file affidavits of ownership in civil courts, enter the congregation's property and change the locks, freeze its bank accounts, notify the congregation's insurance company that there is a property dispute, presumably in an attempt to prevent the congregation from funding its defense via insurance claims, direct court cases toward judges whose "hierarchical" religious affiliation might make them inclined to support denominational rather than congregational ownership, find a minority group in the congregation that wishes to remain in the denomination and declare it "the true Church" and the majority members "schismatics."[135]

Tactics suggested in the stated clerk's memoranda have been employed by several presbyteries where officials have suspected that some of their congregations are contemplating a change of denominational affiliation. In some cases, presbytery leaders are taking preemptive actions. In 2006, without citing any provocation for its action, the Presbytery of Eastern Oklahoma filed affidavits of ownership in the courthouse of every county wherein a Presbyterian congregation resides. The 2,700 member Kirk of the Hills Presbyterian Church in Tulsa filed a legal response, disputing the presbytery's claim. Subsequently, Kirk of the Hills renounced the jurisdiction of the Presbyterian Church (USA) and became a member congregation of the Evangelical Presbyterian Church. Kirk of the Hills continues to occupy its property, despite claims by the presbytery that it is no longer the "true Church" and has therefore relinquished ownership.

The basis of the denomination's argument is a trust clause in *The Book of Order*[136] claiming that all local church property, no matter how it is titled, is held in trust for the denomination. The trust clause was added to *The Book of Order* following a 1979 US Supreme Court decision[137] that allows "neutral

134 Despite the fact that the above-cited language was affixed to the face of these documents, the Office of the Stated Clerk issued a statement on April 27, 2007 that the documents "have never been 'secret,' as some have claimed."

135 Presbyterian Church (USA), Office of the General Assembly, "Church Property Disputes: A Resource for those Representing Presbyterian Church (U.S.A.) Presbyteries and True Churches in the Civil Courts" and "Processes for use by presbyteries in responding to congregations seeking to withdraw."

136 Presbyterian Church (USA), *The Book of Order* G-8.0201.

137 US Supreme Court, *Jones v. Wolf,* 443 U.S. 595 (1979).

principles of law" to be used by state courts in resolving church property disputes. Officials argue, however, that the denomination has operated with "an implied trust" from its inception.[138]

This claim is contested by those who point to the fact that Presbyterian congregations existed and owned property for more than one hundred years before a national denomination existed. Further, some congregations cite state laws indicating that a trust can only be made by the owner of a property, not the beneficiary. These congregations claim that they never consented to placing their property in trust.

Another claim employed by the denomination is that the Presbyterian Church (USA) is a "hierarchical church," and therefore that the interests of the national church trump those of a local congregation. Interestingly, the Office of the Stated Clerk admits that the denomination is not a hierarchical church, but it states that when arguing a property case in court, it should refer to itself as such.[139]

'Blest Be The Tie That Binds'

Intimidation of ministers and confiscation of property hardly qualify for a "blest be the tie that binds" award. While such tactics may temporarily retard the migration of Presbyterian congregations toward associations more compatible with their faith and ethics, coercion has never proven itself to be an effective tool for forging human relationships. In fact, the application of such tactics is likely to fracture further whatever is left of denominational unity. History reminds us that coercion often appears as the final stage of a dying institution's existence.

Ecclesiastical exodus rarely begins as a deluge. More often, it appears first as a trickle of congregations whose corporate convictions are so strong that they will make whatever sacrifice is required to separate themselves from what they believe is an apostate denomination. But once the exodus begins, congregations are likely to flow like water down a hillside. Momentarily inhibited by an obstruction, they will find a way over, under or around the impediment.

Ministers who today feel bound by the denomination's medical and pen-

138 For an in-depth analysis of theological, ethical and legal aspects of the property dispute, see Lunceford, Lloyd J., *A Guide to Church Property Law: Theological, Constitutional and Practical Considerations* (Lenoir, NC: Reformation Press, 2006).

139 Presbyterian Church (USA), Office of the General Assembly, "Church Property Disputes: A Resource for those Representing Presbyterian Church (U.S.A.) Presbyteries and True Churches in the Civil Courts," p. 5.

sion benefits package may discover competitive alternatives.[140] They may also find that contributions from current parishioners who desire to depart are more than sufficient to underwrite their pastors' continued salary and benefits in a different venue. Few things galvanize congregational action more effectively than the harsh treatment of their beloved minister by an outside ecclesiastical bureaucracy. And the excitement of launching a new venture often gives impetus to congregational growth heretofore unknown.

Conversely, presbyteries that are strapped for cash may find their legal fees unbearable if they are faced with property claims from a large number of congregations. Their cash flow could also be challenged if congregations with substantial indebtedness simply abandon their heavily mortgaged, single-use and difficult to sell property to the presbytery as they pour their own resources into reorganizing in the same community but in a more promising location.

In the final analysis, congregations whose people are united by theological and ethical conviction and who are vectored by a clear sense of mission are likely to fare well. Thus, while the Office of the General Assembly may employ coercive measures to hold the denomination together physically for a season, the strong likelihood is that these actions will prove self defeating in the end. After all, the church is first and foremost a voluntary organization.

Signs of the End

Some observers will declare the 2006 General Assembly as a defining moment wherein the denomination's 1926 abandonment of theological standards has come full circle and now applies to ethical standards as well. Others defer their judgment, waiting for a General Assembly Permanent Judicial Commission decision that will confirm judicially what the 2006 General Assembly enacted legislatively. Some say they will wait until an openly avowed homosexual has been ordained and installed, ignoring the fact that many have done so without disciplinary repercussions. Still others say the end will be signaled by a definitive schism, manifested in an organized and nationwide walkout of evangelical churches, but after watching the denomination absorb decades of theological and ethical departures, one wonders what event would be sufficiently seismic to cause such an exodus.

140 At the February, 2007 New Wineskins meeting, it was announced that the Evangelical Presbyterian Church medical plan is comparable to that of the Presbyterian Church (USA) and the pension plan is superior because it does not include the Presbyterian Church (USA)'s compulsory leveling provision that takes some of the dues paid by large churches for the benefit of their ministers and subsidizes the pensions of smaller church ministers.

Tectonic shifts in both nature and history occur over many years, often accompanied by conflicting data that proves confusing to real-time participants. The Reformation did not happen in the instant that Martin Luther nailed his 95 theses to the door. Clearly his act was a moment to remember, but it was one of many. Hundreds of sermons, thousands of discussions among the common people, debates in numerous councils and throughout academia all flowed like tributaries converging into a growing and unstoppable stream that we now call the Reformation.

It is after the fact, looking back upon the period from the vantage point of centuries, that one can see what was only partially known by those who traveled through the time.

Renewal movements that began in the mid-1960s with the purpose of restoring the Presbyterian Church (USA) to a life of Biblical integrity have failed in many cases. Prevented by their own disunity from speaking with one voice during a period when they represented the majority of the denomination's membership, renewal organizations have proved themselves unable to dislodge the thoroughgoing liberalism that now dominates the Presbyterian Church (USA) infrastructure. The "stay, fight and win" approach to renewal is being dubbed, albeit cynically, as "stay, fight and lose" by evangelical congregations that are turning greater attention to various exit strategies.

The Gospel According to Politics

This is not to deny that renewal groups have made valiant efforts to achieve a denominational turnaround. A review of their publications and pronouncements between 1966 and 2006 shows numerous occasions in which the denominational drift into liberalism has publicly been challenged. Calls to arms during this period were frequent and the resulting referenda, particularly in the human sexuality arena, were often successful.

But evangelical victories have been short-lived, robbed of their accomplishments by those who resolutely refuse to enact them in denominational policy and programs. Renewalists have proven themselves competent in making declarations, but they have been unable to insist on their implementation.

The fact that liberals could conquer evangelicals in the political arena should come as no surprise. After all, politics is what liberals do. For persons of the "progressive" persuasion, the gospel is politics. In contrast, evangelicals typically have shown little such interest in organizational matters. Devoted to proclaiming the gospel and building vital congregations, they have been inclined to avoid ecclesiastical politics. Time spent in presbytery and committee meetings is regarded as a peripheral obligation, a diversion from their primary purpose and passion.

Serpents and Doves

In their political naiveté, evangelical victors often sabotage their General Assembly successes with generous accommodations to those whom they defeat. Their propensity toward offering the olive branch through a concessionary word or phrase gives a liberal infrastructure license to implement programs that actually defy the policy that was adopted.

In their characteristic emphasis on the affective side of human experience, evangelicals are particularly sensitive to accusations that they are "triumphalistic" in their victories or heavy-handed in their treatment of brothers and sisters in the minority. Thus, they have often gone to great lengths to prove such accusations untrue, even to the extent of declining to discipline those who defy the very standards that they worked so hard to enact.

Political gullibility surfaces among those who label themselves "moderate evangelicals"[141] in their complaint that they are underrepresented in denominational decision making bodies. They bemoan the "injustice" reflected in committee, council and General Assembly compositions, and they plead for "fairness," by which they mean being given a place at the table.

In so doing, evangelicals play right into the liberals' hands. Those who hold the levers of control will gladly offer evangelicals a few token seats in governing bodies, so long as such additions are unlikely to affect desired outcomes. Then they tout the fact that evangelicals were participants in their decisions, suggesting that their presence legitimated the outcome.

The faithful evangelical will protest, not simply that evangelicals are unevenly represented in church councils, but that there are any liberals on that council at all. If, as Machen so clearly demonstrated, liberalism is not Christian, then one liberal on a Christian governing board is one too many. Bargaining for a handful of seats simply accords the appearance of legitimacy. Thus, in pleading for a semblance of representation, evangelicals often work against their own purpose, because their presence masks realities that would otherwise have been unmistakable.

141 The term "moderate evangelicals" or "middle of the road evangelicals" has been placed in quotes because it is essentially an oxymoron. An evangelical Christian is one who has been driven to his or her knees in a painful confession of sin, cried out for mercy to a holy God, come to grips with the fact that Jesus Christ suffered a grueling death on behalf of that very sin, heard the good news of complete and total forgiveness, and knows the peace of God that passes all understanding. No one who has experienced that encounter with Christ can feel neutral, "moderate" or "middle of the road" about it. The word "evangelical" comes from the language of faith. The word "moderate" comes from the language of politics. Although attempts have been made to do so, these words cannot be meaningfully juxtaposed under one label.

Unintended Consequences

A corollary to this error often appears during General Assembly meetings when evangelicals realize that they simply do not have the numbers to win a majority vote on any of their proposals. At this point, their tacticians often seek compromise, either by gaining concessions from advocates of a liberal proposal, or by so watering down their own proposal that some liberals will vote for it. This is the perennial tactic of those who choose to wed themselves to "the middle."

The impetus behind making such concessions is the very human desire to emerge from an assembly with at least a partial victory, something to show for one's efforts, and something to encourage evangelicals to keep on keeping on. Such tactics may be appropriate when the issue is politics, but they are disastrous when a matter of principle is involved.

On matters of principle, the truth is better served by losing. On issues of moment, it is better to fight hard on the floor and go down in defeat than to gain by means of compromise language that files rough edges from an essentially corrupt policy.

There is no shame in honorable defeat. In practical terms, those who refuse to compromise their Biblical principles send a signal to Presbyterians who are not in that assembly hall. When a General Assembly adjourns, there are at least two additional courts that will judge its decision. One is the court of public opinion, which will understand the issue more clearly if it is not sugar coated with compromise language. The second is the throne of Almighty God, the One who discerns good from evil and who knows who has been faithful to his Word.

A Fatal Flaw

Evangelicals are passionate about their personal relationship with Jesus. They are heart Christians who have fallen in love with their savior and are enthralled by the experience of his presence in the Holy Spirit. At their core, it is this personal experience that convicts, moves and motivates them.

While the evangelical's emphasis on personal experience is authentic and beautiful, it is also dangerous. Ironically, personal experience – so central to the evangelical consensus – is precisely the base from which liberals have forged a religion of their own. It was Harry Emerson Fosdick's core conviction in 1922 when he asked "Shall the Fundamentalists Win?" Placing his emphasis on one's personal "spiritual" experience, Fosdick and the Auburn Affirmation supporters eschewed every attempt to identify and require subscription to particular beliefs. For them, the fact that you were a believer was more important than the particularities of your belief. This was the mindset that Machen so eloquently challenged in the 1920s, and it was the ascendancy of this mindset that enabled the Presbyterian Church to oust him from its leadership.

Machen argued that Christian faith must be rooted and grounded in doctrinal truth that is anchored in the Word of God. He knew that, given the propensities of human nature, a heart led Christian will soon drift into error unless he or she practices a disciplined life of the mind that is honed by the Church's historic engagement with Scripture.

A Bridge over Troubled Waters

In Presbyterian Church (USA) conversations, liberals have insisted that their experience of God through "Christ,"[142] however un-Scripturally they choose to define this experience, must be accepted on no other basis than the fact that they have experienced him in their own particular way. By keeping their focus on personal experience, they have found their way into the hearts of some of the denomination's evangelicals, whose lack of discernment glosses over critical differences in defining truths. In such encounters, the evangelical who has experienced Christ assumes that he or she has discovered a connecting bridge with the liberal who has experienced "Christ." Thus, they assume they share something that the stated clerk calls "common ground."

How PUP Became 'Unanimous'

This personal experience emphasis surfaced as an oft-repeated theme from PUP task force members. Having been cloistered for nearly four years, members of the group shared their stories, laughed and cried together, and developed deep and abiding friendships. Critical to this process was the fact that they sought, and the General Assembly granted, an exemption from the denomination's open meeting policy in order to create a "safe space" for their most intimate conversations.

During the period in which the PUP group conducted its work, its members found themselves surrounded by reporters. They were peppered with questions. Profiles of themselves and their fellow members appeared in

142 The use of quotation marks around "Christ" is intentional. Liberal theologians often use the word, but in a manner that is not consonant with the Jesus Christ who is revealed in Scripture. This "Christ" is often a Christ concept or a Christ principle. It is in this sense that speakers at the 9th Assembly of the World Council of Churches referred to "the hidden Christ' whom they say may be found in non-Christian religions. The "hidden Christ" thesis, by logical extension, implies that all religions are "Christian."

print. Speculation abounded. All of this drove them closer toward one another, creating a Stockholm Syndrome effect, a sense in which they had a community "in here" that was different from forces that might divide them "out there."[143] Over time, their common experience became precious to them. Soon each was saying of the other, "I would not want to be a part of a church where other members of this group do not also belong."

The wider church does not know the whole of the PUP task force deliberations because many hours of sensitive discussions were conducted behind closed doors. What we do know is that persons who have professed theological and ethical persuasions that are inherently incompatible found sufficient common cause as to produce a unanimous report. Such a development could not have occurred had they engaged one another from the basis of doctrinal integrity, but it was obviously possible among those for whom personal relationships became a priority.

'Progressive' vs. 'Evangelical' Faith

Parish theologian Mark Patterson has laid bare several defining differences between two faiths that struggle to coexist within the Presbyterian Church (USA). He insists that the differences between them are theological, critical and incompatible.[144]

Patterson employs the word "progressives" instead of "liberals," the word that Machen used to label them and that we have chosen to use in this book, because the progressive label is most often used by today's liberals to categorize themselves.[145]

He makes a sharp distinction between progressive theology and evangelical theology by focusing on their starting points. "Progressive theology is most simply described as 'bottom up' while Evangelical theology may be described as 'top down,'" he says.[146]

Progressives begin with their personal experience of God. In this sense,

143 "Stockholm Syndrome" is the term used to describe personality changes in kidnap victims who, over time, bond with their captors. In 1973, a group of hostages were held for six days in a Stockholm, Sweden bank. Some of the hostages resisted attempts to rescue them and, after they were rescued and their captors were charged with kidnapping, they refused to testify against them.

144 Patterson, Mark R., "Nein! A Response to Progressives" *Theology Matters*, Vol. 13. No. 2, March/April, 2007.

145 The ideology of this group is certainly not progressive, for it is neither new nor forward thinking. Instead, it represents a constellation of historic heresies reverting to ancient violations of the First Commandment.

146 Patterson, p. 6.

progressives are "theocentric," because their focus is entirely on God, whose presence may be experienced everywhere. They acknowledge Jesus Christ as a "window" through whom they see God, but they resist limiting God's revelation to Jesus. In their view, God can be experienced through other, equally valid media. Christ is important, but he is not necessary.

Evangelicals also begin with a personal experience, but theirs is "Christocentric" rather than "theocentric." Their focus is on the Christ to whom the Scriptures attest. In meeting Christ, they understand that they have met God himself. They remember Jesus' statements, "You who have seen me have seen the Father;" "I and my Father are one;" "Believe me that I am in the Father and the Father in me;" "I am the way, the truth and the life. No one comes to the Father except through me."

For evangelicals, Jesus Christ is not merely a window through whom they may see God; he is God. He is not simply an avenue to grace; he is grace. Patterson reminds us that for the evangelical, "not only is grace uniquely bound to the person and work of Jesus, but the message of the Church, if it is to be truly a message of grace, is singularly bound to his incarnation, life, teaching, death, resurrection, and ascension. In contrast to Progressivism, Evangelicalism holds that this message must be told, taught, proclaimed, and received if salvation is to become known and experienced. For God is not known rightly or completely outside of Christ, making the message of his person and work necessary for salvation."[147]

This distinction is of critical importance for our salvation. If Jesus is not divine – if he is simply a window through whom one may see the divine – he can identify with us, love us, offer comforting and therapeutic words to us, morally challenge us and inspire us, but he has no power to save us. Salvation is a divine act. Sinners need someone who can do more than point toward the divine. We need to know the divine person himself.

This distinction explains why progressives are so willing to set Jesus aside if a focus on him proves a stumbling block to fraternal relationships with other faiths. Having no salvific power, the progressives' Jesus is expendable.

It also explains why progressives are so willing to jettison the doctrine of the atonement. Their "Christ" is useful in helping us achieve enlightenment, but he does not in himself remove the burden of our sin, certainly not by appropriating our sin to himself. This fatal flaw was identified by Athanasius during the Nicene controversy of 325 A.D.

To the contrary, authentic evangelicals (in contrast to pseudo evangelicals who employ the label to describe a "feeling of spirituality") focus

147 *Ibid.*, p. 8.

exclusively on the atoning work of Christ. Patterson says, "The Evangelical message, from the preaching of Paul to the preaching of Billy Graham, has had no interest in human religion, spirituality or rituals. Its interest always and only has been on the utterly unique and incomparable sacrifice occurring with the death of Christ … Believing that the Father has demonstrated his grace and love through the death of his Son in our place, has rendered all other philosophies, theologies, religions, and rituals powerless … Thus, grace, within the Evangelical tradition, means the gift of salvation freely given in and through the cross where Christ gave his life as an atoning sacrifice. To define grace apart from this event is to understand nothing of either grace or the cross."[148]

These distinctions lead Patterson to observe that "in spite of shared vocabulary, history, and structure, Evangelicals and Progressives are describing two different realities, two different worldviews, two different methodologies, two different theological perspectives." Therefore, he concludes, "We must say NO! We must no longer tolerate the ambivalent doctrines and immoral ethics that the Progressive wing of the church continues to force upon the church as the only true interpretation of the Christian faith. For we cannot remain Christian when our beliefs reject and deny all the Word means. We cannot remain God's Church when we accept as truth ideas that contradict his Word and work. We cannot call ourselves godly when we take up the ethics and values of the culture and extol these over his command … It is time, in the name of integrity and honesty, for those who have denied and rejected the central tenets of the Reformed faith to graciously separate from the body and leave the church to those who have remained faithful to its standards, doctrine, and traditions."[149]

The progressives whose views Patterson has rightly identified as alien to Christian faith show no signs of voluntarily abandoning their control of the Presbyterian Church (USA), and evangelicals have shown neither the will nor the fortitude to throw them out. It is true that the progressives should leave – certainly logic and integrity require their departure – but the political exigencies of the day do not require it, so they stay.

Patterson's theological analysis offers a helpful insight into the experiential bridge that liberals and some persons who identify themselves as evangelicals have forged among themselves. Yes, each claims a religious experience and proceeds to build a theology on that foundation. But only in the most superficial sense do the religious experiences of the progressive and

148 *Ibid.*

149 *Ibid.*, p. 11.

the evangelical show any signs of similarity. In fact, as Patterson so brilliantly demonstrates, they lead to dramatically different destinations.

THE PCUSA'S CONSTITUTIONAL VS. ITS 'WORKING' THEOLOGY

On June 12, 2007, the two highest ranking officers of the Presbyterian Church (USA), Stated Clerk Clifton Kirkpatrick and General Assembly Council Executive Director Linda Valentine, issued a letter to all executive presbyters and stated clerks. Their stated purpose was to assure middle governing body leaders – and through them, Presbyterians in the pews – that the denomination has not departed from Biblical faith and is, therefore, not apostate.

Arguments employed by Kirkpatrick and Valentine in defense of their thesis are grounded in one proposition: Presbyterian Church (USA) documents, primarily *The Book of Confessions* which affirms Biblical faith, remain intact. A form of this argument was used by the PUP task force in its contention that allowing governing bodies to deem constitutional ordination standards "non-essential," and therefore non-binding did not violate the standards because the words of those standards remain in the text of the Constitution.

The Very Rev. Dr. Philip Turner, former dean of the Berkeley Divinity School at Yale University and a collegial theologian for the Anglican Institute, wrote a commentary for his own denomination in 2005 in which he made a distinction between the "official theology" of the Episcopal Church in the USA and its "working theology."

"How does one both identify and assess the 'working theology' of a church?" asked Turner. "There are theological articles and books of theology. There are liturgies and confessional statements. Nonetheless, the contents of these documents do not necessarily control the working theology of a church … In this day and age, to find the working theology of a church one cannot go to a canon of theological works. One can, however, review the resolutions passed at official gatherings, and listen to what clergy say Sunday by Sunday from the pulpit. One can listen to the conversations that occur at clergy gatherings; and one can listen for the advice they give to troubled parishioners. The working theology of a church is, in short, best determined by becoming what social anthropologists are want to call a 'participant observer.' One can 'be' in the midst of a church, observe its language and practices, and present a descriptive and critical account of what one sees and hears."[150]

150 Turner, Philip W., "ECUSA's GOD, A Descriptive Comment on the 'Working Theology' of the Episcopal Church U.S.A.," Colorado Springs: The Anglican Institute, 2005.

The working theology that Turner discovered in the Episcopal Church (USA) is in every way consonant with that of the Presbyterian Church (USA), their official documents to the contrary notwithstanding. Turner found that the starting point for this theology is "God is love." God loves, accepts and affirms us and all of his creation, just as we are. The corollary to this affirmation is that God wants us to love and accept one another. "Accepting love," observes Turner, "requires a form of justice that is inclusive of all people, particularly those who in some way have been marginalized by oppressive social practice."[151]

Turner calls this working theology "the doctrine of radical inclusion." He points out that with this doctrine one sees "an accompanying reduction in the significance of Christ's death and resurrection; and one can see also the eclipse of participation in Christ's death through growth in holiness of life as a fundamental marker of Christian identity. With the notion of radical inclusion and acceptance comes also the view that one need not come to the Father through the Son. Christ is a way, but not the way. The latter view is exclusionary and thus unacceptable, not being in accord with the open acceptance that has been revealed in the incarnation."[152]

Turner says that the doctrine of radical inclusion that he finds in the Episcopal Church (USA) works itself out in two directions. "In respect to God, it produces a quasi deist theology that posits a benevolent God who favors love and justice as inclusion, but acts neither to save us from our sins nor to raise us to new life after the pattern of Christ. In respect to 'the neighbor' it produces an ethic of tolerant affirmation that carries with it no call to conversion and radical holiness ... [this theology] does not lend itself easily to the sort of meeting with Christ that in traditional Christian terms leads through faith, forgiveness, judgment, repentance, and amendment of life ... Christianity is no longer presented as a religion of salvation."[153]

From the evidence presented in previous chapters of this book, it is clear that the policies, programs, publications and pronouncements of the Presbyterian Church (USA) over a period of four decades reveal a denominational working theology that mirrors Turner's description of the Episcopal Church (USA). In words that apply to both denominations, Turner said, "It will not do in the end, as official spokespersons for ECUSA tend to do, to reply by reference to ECUSA's *Book of Common Prayer* with the comment, 'you see we are orthodox just like you are. We affirm the two testaments as the word of God, we recite the classical creeds in our worship, we celebrate

151 *Ibid.*

152 *Ibid.*

153 *Ibid.*

the dominical sacraments, and we hold to Episcopal order.' The challenge now being put to ECUSA is not about its official documents. It's about its 'working theology' in which most of the Anglican Communion does not recognize the great tradition that gave it birth."

The Hidden Heresy

Why have the denomination's evangelically inclined moderates not thrown the rascals out? Several reasons previously given, i.e., their lack of political acumen, propensity to compromise, uncritical acceptance of the argument that confessional documents remain intact, and penchant for institutional preservation, all have validity. But Patterson's analysis reveals that there is a deeper, more damaging reason for their willingness to accommodate. It relates to the moderates' failure to recognize heresy.

It is important here to understand that there is a difference between heresy and unbelief, the outright denial of Christian faith. That critical distinction was made by nineteenth-century theologian Friedrich Schleiermacher, namely that heresy is that which preserves the appearance of Christianity, yet contradicts its essence, whereas unbelief denies both essence and appearance. The unbeliever, for example, might say "Jesus Christ was only human, certainly not divine." The heretic would say, Jesus Christ is divine," but he would define divinity as an aspect of one's humanity.[154]

Thomas Oden draws a similar distinction: "Heresy is less the assertion of statements directly contrary to faith than the assertion of fragmented pieces of faith in imbalance, so as to lack the cohesion and wholeness of the catholic faith. Heresy is where some legitimate dimension of faith is elevated so asymmetrically and so out of equilibrium as to become a principle of interpretation for all other aspects, so as to deny the unity and balance of the ancient ecumenical consensus."[155]

Because heresy begins as an incremental distortion of a Christian truth its inherent falsehood is easily overlooked. The difference is regarded a matter of "perspective," rather than a difference of essence. "We both affirm Scripture," some argue, "but we just interpret it from different perspectives." Heresy does not bludgeon us into unbelief. We are seduced.[156]

---

154 Schleiermacher, Friedrich, *The Christian Faith* (Edinburgh: T. & T. Clark Ltd., 1928), pp. 95-101.

155 Oden, Thomas C., *Requiem*, (Nashville: Abingdon Press, 1995), p. 147.

156 For an examination of the early church's struggle with the Arian heresy in 325 A.D. and its implications for the contemporary church see Williamson, Parker T., *Standing Firm: Reclaiming Christian Faith in Times of Controversy*, (Lenoir: PLC Publications, 1996).

If one juxtaposes the fact that early stages of heresy appear exceedingly similar to Christian truth and the fact that moderate institutionalists lean toward generosity in order to preserve the peace, one can understand how evangelically inclined moderates fall into the trap of cultural accommodation.

A failure to discern a critical, albeit masked distinction at this early juncture can be as fatal as a railroad engineer's failure to see a switch on the track. At the point of the switch, the tracks appear to be headed in the same direction, but that critical juncture sets the stage for a major divergence.

The evangelically inclined moderate's penchant for institutional preservation may cause him or her to view colleagues who take issue with what appear to be insignificant theological distinctions as alarmists and troublemakers. Thus, they miss the critical switch, set the course for an accommodation to the liberal "perspective," and even oppose those who see a clear and present danger in the denomination's chosen direction.

Jesus observed that "a prophet is not without honor except in his own country." J. Gresham Machen, who rightly saw the course that revisionist Presbyterians were undertaking, was undermined by those who professed to share his faith. Unable and unwilling to see critical distinctions, they welcomed the "inclusive and diverse" church, blurring differences not of perspective but of substance. In that choice, essential tenets of Christian faith were set aside and the denomination embarked on an accelerating course into something far different.

A PCUSA Prognosis

No Christian can deny the possibility that even now the sovereign Lord can intervene and redeem the Presbyterian Church (USA). But it is equally possible that he may declare his divine judgment upon this ecclesiastical institution, punishing it for its unfaithfulness, and allowing it to fall as he did many times when kingdoms that ruled Israel and Judah abandoned his holy Word. Every measurable indication suggests that the Lord's judgment is falling on the Presbyterian Church (USA) and that its end is imminent.[157]

157 On January 9, 2003, John Marcum, director of the department of research services for the Presbyterian Church (USA), made the following projection: "Recently I calculated a simple straight-line projection of membership trends. At the rate of membership decline over the last dozen years, we would cease to have any members by the year 2061." Later, when faced with the fact that denominational losses have accelerated since 2003, Mr. Marcum revised his projection. He now estimates that the last member will be gone by April, 2039. The departure of entire congregations from the PCUSA since 2006 would appear to hasten that date even further.

Already, the denomination's survival depends primarily on consuming accumulated assets bequeathed by former generations. Investments, equities, and properties confiscated from departing congregations may keep it alive for some time to come, but these instruments won't bring God's people back.

Despite their failures to stave off the evil that has befallen their denomination, renewal ministries are to be commended for having beamed the light of truth during a dark period. Like the prophets of old, many renewal leaders have faithfully declared the Word of the Lord to a culture of unbelief, often at no small cost. Although that truth has been largely ignored, its proclamation has been crucial to our time, sowing seed for a more faithful harvest in a time that is yet to come.

Covenant

Holy Scripture

"O Timothy, guard what has been entrusted to you. Avoid the godless chatter and contradictions of what is falsely called knowledge, for by professing it some have missed the mark as regards the faith."

I Timothy 6:20

The Constitution

"So if the interpretation or opinion of any theologian, Kirk or council, is contrary to the plain Word of God written in any other passage of the Scripture, it is most certain that this is not the true understanding and meaning of the Holy Ghost, although councils, realms, and nations have approved and received it."

The Scots Confession
1560

Broken Covenant

"I am concerned about what appears to be a growing number of ministers and elders who are encouraging congregations to withdraw (or 'graciously separate') from the Presbyterian Church (USA) and/or who are advocating the withholding of duly authorized per capita assessments from their governing bodies as a form of protest. Such actions are unconstitutional, and I urge that they stop."

The Rev. Clifton Kirkpatrick
Stated Clerk of the General Assembly
Presbyterian Church (USA)
January 3, 2002

Chapter Nine

New Day Dawning

"The Church's One Foundation" includes a stanza expressing grief over the schism and heresy that have so deeply damaged Christ's Church. But the stanza is not without hope, for it declares that even at times when the church is "rent asunder" there are "saints whose watch are keeping." The Lord will bless their faithful witness, promises this great Wesley hymn, when their "night of weeping shall be the morn of song."[1]

Who are these saints whose watch are keeping? The proclivity of institutional church leaders is to seek those saints in all the wrong places. They assume that heralds of the new dawn will come from the clergy. This will not be so.

It has never been so, for the life of the church historically has bubbled forth not from a professional clergy class but from the presence of the Holy Spirit among the laity, the gathered and scattered people of God. With whom did Jesus Christ surround himself? They were fishermen, farmers, housewives, weavers, carpenters, merchants and even a tax collector. These were the people whose hearts burned within them as they witnessed the Word made flesh and dwelling among them. The women among them were the first evangelists, announcing the empty tomb and telling of their encounter with the risen Lord. From its inception, the Church has been a movement of resurrection faith, traveling from one lay person to another in an unending flow of God's grace.

The Laos

A study of the New Testament church reveals the fact that all of its members – whatever their specific functions in the life of the church may have

1 Wesley, Samuel Sebastian, *The Presbyterian Hymnal* (Louisville, Ky.: Westminster/John Knox Press, 1990), p. 442.

been – were considered laos, the chosen people of God, and that their differentiation was functional, not hierarchical.[2]

Commenting on this New Testament understanding of the Church as the gathered people of God, H. Richard Niebuhr, Daniel D. Williams and James Gustafson said, "Amid the diversity of ministries in the New Testament epoch there was as yet no true priesthood, for Christ was the only high priest and his consummatory and definite sacrifice ended all sacrifices."[3]

Hendrik Kraemer, a Dutch Reformed theologian who directed the Ecumenical Institute at Chateau de Bossey and conducted foundational research on the role of the laity in the life of the church, reminds us that during the church's first three centuries "a number of the great Church Fathers, the first prominent theological thinkers on behalf of the church, were laymen of great ability."[4]

Kraemer continues, "To mention only a few of the very prominent: Tertullian, Cyprian and Augustine. Cyprian and Augustine, having become bishops so to speak by surprise, were essentially, by their whole education and long 'secular' career, laymen. The reason why such an obvious fact has to be stated expressly is that their position as church Fathers has put them so forcefully in the theological, i.e., non-lay category that the simple truth of their being thinking Christian laymen is entirely forgotten or ignored."[5]

Even monasticism, which was eventually dominated by clergy, began as a lay movement. Yves Congar, a Roman Catholic theologian/historian says that monasticism began about the middle of the third century. His study of the period reveals that ordination was not a prerequisite for entry into a monastic order. "The monk as such is not a cleric, though of course he can become one by ordination. His condition is not defined by an office or function but as a state or way of life; in order that he shall not live for the world and in the world's way but rather so much as possible for God and in God's way, this consists in living apart from the world, leading so far as may be a heavenly or angelic life, the life of the Kingdom that is not of this world. In principle, then, clerics and monks were sharply differentiated: 'cleric' indicates a function, 'monk' a state or way of life. A man is a cleric by ordination to the sacred ministry, a monk by personal renouncement of

2 Ephesians 4:1-16.

3 Niebuhr, H. Richard, Williams, Daniel Day, Gustafson, James, *The Ministry in Historical Perspectives* (New York: Harper & Brothers, 1956), p. 27.

4 Kraemer, Hendrik, *A Theology of the Laity* (Vancouver, BC.: Regent College Publishing, 2005), p. 20.

5 *Ibid.*

the world."[6]

During the Dark Ages, when the visible church was driven underground by barbaric invasion, the role of monastic communities in maintaining the Christian tradition and painstakingly hand copying the Scriptures was of inestimable value to the ongoing life and ultimate rebirth of the church. Congar's research reveals that it was the gift of lay people who performed scribal functions, farmed the land, and produced food and income for the monastic community that was instrumental in preserving and propagating the Christian faith for centuries.

Priestly-Hierarchical Domination

Over time, a priestly-hierarchical structure developed in the life of the institutional church, reaching massive power by the Middle Ages. As this clergy class gained its ascendancy, the role of the laity was severely diminished. In fact, the Biblical definition of "laity" was altered. In the Old Testament the word laos was used expressly to designate "the people of God," as distinguished from the Gentiles. In the New Testament, it referred to "the sacred people in opposition to the peoples who were not consecrated …"[7]

As the clergy class increased its dominance over the institutional church, a secularized definition of laos that did not resemble the Biblical definition came into vogue. Classical Greek's word for "layman" meant a private person or an ignorant, uneducated one. Increasingly, clergy leaders replaced the Biblical understanding of laos with the Greek understanding, referring to the laity as an inferior class within the church.

Kraemer comments on this development in the life of the institutional church: "As early as at the end of the 1st century it becomes evident that the significance of 'laos' and 'laikos' is getting a turn, different from its basic significance in the New Testament. The main reason, apart from the profane use of the word in ancient society, is the emergence of an organized, duly ordained clergy as a closed 'status' over against the 'laos,' the people, i.e., the ordinary congregation … The church in fact became a vast body of worship, instruction, piety, activity, consisting of two clearly distinguished bodies, in which the authoritative leadership reposed in the Clergy."[8]

As the priestly-hierarchical class became dominant, the laity receded

6 Congar, Yves, *Jalons Pour un Theologie du Laicat* (London: Cassell Ltd., 1965), p. 7.

7 Congar, p. 3.

8 Kraemer, p. 50-51.

into a passive, observer status. By the time of the Middle Ages, lay people, who could not read Latin, Greek or Hebrew/Aramaic, had no other access to the Bible than that which the priest was willing to share. Further, the Mass was celebrated in Latin by a priest who, when facing the altar, turned his back upon the people. This isolation from the Word of God written and from any meaningful participation in the Sacrament of the Lord's Supper locked the laity into ignorance, made them increasingly dependent on their clergy, and rendered laypeople vulnerable to superstition and heretical distortions of the faith.

Laity and the Reformation

Two major gifts opened the eyes of the laity and sparked a seismic shift in the life of the church. One was the invention of the printing press in 1450, and the other was Martin Luther's translation of the Bible into the language of the people in 1534. With this access to the Word of God, a Biblically informed laity triggered the Protestant Reformation.

Luther's manifesto, *To the Christian Nobility* was a revolutionary document that spoke directly to the laity. It signaled a move that would turn hierarchical church rule upside down. "We see, then, that just as those that we call spiritual, or priests, bishops, or popes, do not differ from other Christians in any other or higher degree but in that they are to be concerned with the word of God and the sacraments – that being their work and office – in the same way the temporal authorities hold the sword and the rod in their hands to punish the wicked and to protect the good. A cobbler, a smith, a peasant, every man, has the office and function of his calling, and yet all alike are consecrated priests and bishops, and every man should by his office or function be useful and beneficial to the rest, so that various kinds of work may all be united for the furtherance of body and soul, just as the members of the body all serve one another."[9]

John Calvin, a Lay Theologian

A pivotal leader of the Reformation, John Calvin was first and foremost a layman. Although he became a member of the clergy later in his career when he was required to be vested with that office in order to continue teaching theology in Geneva, Calvin always understood himself to be a layman. His academic work had been in the humanities, and his vocational

9 Luther, Martin, *Address to the Christian Nobility of the German Nation Respecting the Reformation of the Christian Estate*, The Harvard Classics, Vol. 36, Part 5 (New York: P.F. Collier & Son, 1909-1917).

training was in the field of law. When he wrote his powerfully influential *Institutes of the Christian Religion*, he was a lawyer, not a member of the clergy. It was only in 1535, after the publication of this great theological work, that Calvin became Geneva's ordained lecturer in theology. According to Hendrik Kraemer, Calvin "was introduced to his 'office' without laying on of hands."[10]

Kraemer quotes one of Calvin's letters (*Corpus Ref.* IX. 443), in which Calvin says "I have never been anything else than an ordinary layman as people call it."[11]

With the advent of the Reformation and its concomitant upsurge in lay leadership, Protestant churches experienced a wave of vitality and growth. In the centuries that followed, lay movements stepped to the forefront of church growth and revivalism, especially in a new world called America. Not only did lay initiatives strengthen the ministry of church institutions, but they also sparked many para-church organizations in student work (the YMCA,YWCA, the World Student Federation and InterVarsity Fellowship); evangelism (Dwight L. Moody was a layman and the Billy Graham Evangelistic Association has been primarily a lay organization); Christian education (Presbyterian layperson Henrietta Mears led countless college students into the faith and many into the ministry); missions (World Vision and numerous missionary movements are lay led); and the ecumenical movement (although the World and National Councils of Churches, to their detriment, ultimately came under the control of denominational clergy bureaucrats, they were launched with significant lay leadership).

The Return of the Priestly Hierarchy

The vitality that characterized Protestant denominations in the United States reached its peak in the early 1960s. During this period of the institutional church's prosperity, a priestly-hierarchical class of leaders grew rapidly. By the 21st century, denominations became – much like the medieval church – clergy dominated institutions. Professional clergy cluster at the highest levels of the national church pecking order. Seminary graduates, many of whom have never served a local church, have found their way into the staffs of various boards and agencies. Presbytery resembles a ministerial union hall, where ecclesiastical maintenance issues, like establishing minimum clergy salaries and benefits, impeding the admission of ministers from non-PCUSA seminaries, sharing inside information on

10 Kraemer, p. 25.

11 *Ibid.*

available pulpits and who might be imported to fill them, and other closed shop matters dominate coffee pot conversations.

Even at the level of the local congregation, clergy dominance is the rule rather than the exception. Ministers often assume an administrative role, viewing themselves as CEOs of an organization, and sessions act like corporate boards, granting passive approval and disapproval to ministerial initiatives. Clergy who play the CEO role tend to exhibit a maintenance mindset, keeping peace within the congregation and making sure that the organization runs smoothly. Such orientation tends to be risk averse, and the avoidance of conflict becomes a priority. Thus, many ministers assume gate keeping functions, often shielding their people from wider issues that might disturb the congregation.

In a manner not unlike medieval clergy who stood between the laity and the altar when celebrating the sacrament of the Lord's Supper, clergy professionals often exclude the laity from meaningful involvement in the life of the church. Even at presbytery levels, dissensions over essential Christian beliefs, are often cloistered within clergy ranks, presumably to protect the people from troublesome controversy.

Clergy Renewalists

The dominance of the professional clergy has profoundly damaged the modern church's understanding of itself and the involvement of its people in ministry. Hendrik Kraemer observes that one of the signs of our time is the public view that "church" means the ministry or clergy. "As a consequence of this climate of thinking, the laity in the churches regards itself as of minor and subsidiary significance. Non-church people share this impression. The reasons are obvious. Representatives of the ministry figure, by the nature of the case, as the rulers and administrators of the church, to the public eye. They are, as a rule, the spokesmen of the church, or are considered to be the really authentic spokesmen."[12]

Luder Whitlock, former president of Reformed Theological Seminary and executive director of Trinity Forum, says "In some congregations, all that is expected is for the laity to be present as an audience or to provide support financially and otherwise for approved programs."[13]

Whitlock suggests that one factor contributing to declining lay involvement in the United States has been the growth of large urban churches. "In

12 Kraemer, p.17.

13 Whitlock, Luder, Jr., "The Church and Laity in the Twenty-First Century," January, 1998, p. 2.

several mainline denominations, half the total membership is found in only 13-15 percent of the congregations. In the typical large church, the pastor and staff now run the church and its programs. The larger the church, the more this tends to be the case. Consequently, as churches grow larger, there is usually a decreasingly proportional involvement of lay people in ministry in these churches."[14]

It is noteworthy that in both the Presbyterian Coalition and Presbyterians for Renewal organizations, board members are drawn heavily from among large church pastors, and grants from the congregations they serve comprise their major funding sources.

George Barna on the Future Church

George Barna, founder and president of the Barna Research Group in Oxnard, CA, has conducted demographic and marketing research for secular and religious organizations. His studies of church groups have led him to reflect on mainline denominational decline and the role that today's clergy appear to be playing in it.

Barna characterizes many denominational ministers as "robots," observing that "They operate as if on automatic pilot. They carry out rote tasks, stifle creativity, and set survival as the standard of success. Conflicts are covered up, new ideas tabled, and manners and symbols esteemed above content and impact. The Robot equates predictability with security. Vision is perceived a nuisance; passion is depreciated."[15]

"True Christian leaders," continues Barna, "recognize that ministry is about taking risks, but have the intelligence to manage those risks and the faith to trust God in situations when risks seem warranted."[16] The mainline denominational clergy leader whom Barna seeks but rarely finds is not a manager, but a risk taking entrepreneur. He notes that leaders of this type often gravitate toward independent, nondenominational churches.

Barna says that a "second coming of the church" is possible if it can attract entrepreneurial and revolutionary leaders. This leadership, he says, will not come from the clergy. "Ultimately, the moral and spiritual revolution that will produce the new church will emerge from among the laity. The impetus to change and the creative focus and force reside among the frustrated masses, not among the distracted professionals. Marrying the

---

14 *Ibid.*

15 Barna, George, *The Second Coming of the Church* (Nashville: Word Publishing, 1998), p. 33.

16 *Ibid.*, p. 34.

resources of both the laity and the clergy could introduce an exciting era of Christian renewal. But the catalyst for this new reformation will be the people, not the professionals."[17]

Barna sees the future church growing out of existing local churches that are gifted with strong lay leadership. "Congregations are currently our best organizational resource," he says. "As we develop the church of the future, our best strategy will be to grow the new formations from the resources and assistance provided by these present hubs of strength."[18]

He believes that congregational bodies in the future will be decentralized and multidimensional. The Internet will continue to be developed as a major tool in church ministry. House churches will become increasingly important. "Dialogical forums," similar to Christian coffeehouses, will provide opportunities for Christians to engage their neighbors on matters of faith and ethics. Congregational churches will become "boot camps" for training the laity to carry out their witness in the public square. Another role for the congregational church can be to act as a clearinghouse for service opportunities. Barna envisions the local congregation as being the base for a variety of lay service ministries, but intentionally attracting persons from the broader community into these activities.

"Seminaries could have embraced this role," said Barna, "but have generally chosen to remain professional certification agencies. Thus, teaching churches could fill the gap in teacher training and the absence of leadership development."

Barna believes that denominational headquarters will be "repositioned as resource centers, and denominations themselves will hold a much less significant place on the religious map. There will be fewer full-time, career ministry professionals, since ministry responsibility will be increasingly accepted and executed by lay believers."[19]

'We're Talking Revolution!'

"When a system is radically broken," says Barna, "it is not enough simply to repair the damage; the entire system must be rethought and, perhaps, replaced ... Of course, convincing people that radical change is needed and enlisting them as full and active partners can be extremely difficult. Sometimes it takes a cataclysmic condition to bring about such participation ... The church has got to find a way to sound just such a wake-up call to its

17 *Ibid.*, p 176.

18 *Ibid.*

19 *Ibid.*, p. 184.

workers who are asleep on the job. We're not talking about a little tinkering here and a patch job there; we're talking about a major rehabilitation project. We're talking revolution!"[20]

Dissatisfaction Among the People

Barna says that a revolution cannot occur unless there is significant, widespread dissatisfaction. This must come from the people, not their institutional leaders: "Almost every great movement trickles up, not down. The revolution of faith will not be sparked by the institutions and high-profile leaders who publicly represent the Christian Church today. The role of leaders is to cast a vision for a superior future and provide a means to escape the undesirable present conditions. The movement itself will emerge from the inertia of a groundswell of like-minded people who are willing to act upon their dissatisfaction ... The implication for us is that the second coming of the church will not be a clergy-driven reformation but a lay-driven explosion of spiritual angst and piety."[21]

A second factor that drives revolution is a future focus. "To the revolutionary, all hope lies in the future. The primary goal of every movement is to replace the present reality with a better one. When a group is preoccupied with the present, that is the sign it has become institutionalized. The driving issues become territory and survival, rather than purpose and renewal."[22]

Barna says that revolutionaries are committed to a specific doctrine (e.g., subscribing to "essential tenets") and, far from being anarchical, they demand discipline around well-defined parameters that are tightly controlled. Successful revolutionaries commit themselves to "a transcendent cause," and they are willing to sacrifice for it.

When one reviews Barna's list of revolutionary criteria, it becomes apparent that the early church fulfilled each category: "Jesus came to establish a family, not a multinational corporation," he says. "His ministry was always geared to developing a grassroots outreach that operated in vivid contrast to that of the prevailing religious system. Jesus' focus was to blend present and future together into a startlingly new lifestyle. His doctrinal slant angered every religious group he encountered because it was unique. Jesus recruited people who were willing to sell out to God, with no holds

20 *Ibid.*, p. 197.

21 *Ibid.*, p. 199.

22 *Ibid.*

barred. Early in his ministry, he clearly defined the qualities a Christian should possess to be an effective moral and spiritual revolutionary ..."[23/24]

Toward a Theology of the Laity

What will it take for the laity to assume this revolutionary role? The revolution will not be accomplished by structure-changing tactics, e.g., strategies for taking over a denomination's infrastructure. Doing so would simply repeat the error of liberationists who, as we have seen in earlier chapters of this book, proffered political answers to theological problems. Rather, we must follow the wise counsel of Yves Congar, Hendrik Kraemer and others who have devoted themselves to this matter. We must begin with a Reformed theology of , not merely for, the laity. That invariably implies that we turn to the Word of God.

Incarnation

How did the Lord rescue his world from the hell-bent pursuit of its own destruction? His answer to the world's plight was incarnation. He entered the world in the flesh and blood person of Jesus Christ. It was in and through his immersion in the life and commerce of his people that he demonstrated the holy life, exposed our failure to live it, paid the price for our sin, and set us free to participate joyfully in his earthly kingdom. This was no long-distance transaction, but one in which he became bone of our bone and flesh of our flesh.

Our lay people must know, first and foremost, that "God so loved the world, that he gave his only son." The Lord did not withdraw from the world; he entered it. That entrance was not limited to pristine appearances at holy places, but to seamy streets and cesspools of human sin. He visited power brokers and prostitutes, the weary and those for whom all hope was lost. He entered the brokenness of the human heart.

That is precisely the arena wherein he has dispatched his people. Ours is no retreat from the world, but – following the Lord's command – we are called to penetrate the world, entering every place where his people dwell.

Who is better positioned to pursue that incarnational mission than the

23 *Ibid.*, p. 202.

24 One might challenge Barna's description of Jesus' ministry, considering the degree to which his sociological lenses focus on methodology rather than the dynamism of the gospel itself. But, when his admittedly sociological observations are applied to the life of the church, qua a religious organization, they provide helpful insights into dimensions of today's church.

laity? These are the bricklayers and carpenters, accountants and children's workers, homemakers and health care aides, playwrights and media managers, each one of whom is uniquely skilled to act within a particular place in the world. Just as Jesus was – by his very presence – God's mission to the world, so laypersons who bear the love of Christ assume that missional stance on his behalf.

Christian Vocation

Increasingly, the vaunted vocabulary of a professional priesthood is falling on deaf ears. Meanwhile, university faculty members cluster in coffee shops to share their faith in the Lord Jesus and to explore together the relevance of the Christian faith for academic disciplines in which they have earned expertise. Scholarly papers are being written inquiring into dimensions of discipleship that may be practiced inside the academy. Christian faculty movements are encouraging those who pursue the life of the mind to do so in the service of God. In such contexts, Christian academics are learning to love the Lord their God, not only with all their heart and soul, but with their minds as well.

Medical personnel gather before the Divine Physician, asking how the faith that they share can inform and influence excellence in the practice of medicine. In sacred community they appropriate a humility that challenges the arrogance that often stalks those who deal with life and death. They learn that "the gall bladder in room 200" has a name and they explore how in the name of Jesus they might approach this patient holistically.

Christian attorneys examine the question of representation – what it means to represent someone. Thinking through the implications of the Atonement, they begin to see the sacred significance of one's standing on behalf of others before the judge. Inspired to transcend legalism and loopholes, they bow before Him whose law is a lamp unto their feet and a pathway toward righteous living.

Christian business people pour over the parables of Jesus, appropriating the story of the talents, the lost coin, the last hired worker, and the Good Samaritan into the exchange of goods and services, helping one another discern distinctions between entrepreneurship and exploitation.

Christian retirees reflect on opportunities to grow in areas of life and learning that were unavailable to them during employment years. Inspired by a Lord who gave his life that others might live, they seek avenues of service in which a lifetime of learning can equip them to serve impoverished others without regard for any compensation other than the satisfaction of having been a conduit for Christ's love.

There is, of course, a place for the professional clergy to play in this life of the laity, for the church will always need those who give full-time attention to the study and teaching of God's Word and those who can vector gifts of God's people toward the building of his kingdom. Clergy who are faithful exponents of the Reformed tradition can be particularly helpful in preventing the drift of evangelical lay people toward emotionally appealing but theologically unsound ideas. The principle of parity between clergy and lay people in doing the work of the church is worthy of recovery in modern church life. In this respect, reinstituting the functional differentiation signified in "teaching elder" and "ruling elder" might prove useful.[25]

Technological advances are opening the door to exciting opportunities in the field of lay education and training. Internet communication makes it possible for laypersons in a particular church to take seminary-level courses in Bible and theology under the tutelage of some of the world's brightest Christian minds. Groups can access quality lectures in media equipped rooms at their church and follow up the viewing with guided discussion material. This combination of imported expertise and peer discussions can be an important tool in equipping the laity for the work of the ministry.

The Rule of Vincent of Lerins

A sterling example of consecrated and effective lay leadership can be seen in contributions made by Mrs. Diane Knippers, who before her death in 2005 served as executive director of the Institute for Religion and Democracy and an Episcopal Church (USA) lay leader. Knippers was recognized by *TIME* magazine as one of the country's 25 most influential evangelicals.

Speaking to an American Anglican Council conference in 2003, Knippers recognized the necessity of dealing with legal and financial matters in the church, "temporal matters in the church which are the distinct province of the laity." But she pushed the perimeters of that province significantly by focusing on the laity's particular role and responsibility in the preservation of authentic Christian teaching.

"The first thing I want to emphasize," said Knippers, "is that we [the laity] are the church. One thing of which we laity must repent is our tendency to be cowed by clericalism. Of course we respect our godly leaders, and of course we respect the offices and roles of bishops and priests. But the model that Scripture gives us for the Church of Jesus Christ is not a cor-

25 Presbyterian Church (US) polity identified clergy as "teaching elders" and session members as "ruling elders," designations indicating a difference of function rather than status.

porate flow chart or a military chain of command. It is a body. All the members are necessary. All play a role. All are to be honored. And let's face it; we are a very big part of the body."[26]

In times of theological innovation, when "the faith once and for all given to the saints" is twisted and tested, how does one determine if doctrines being preached are, in fact, authentic expressions of that faith? Knippers concurs with the hallmark principle of the Reformation, namely that Scripture is the benchmark by which every idea must be tested. But she points to the fact that in postmodern times, when words can be made to mean anything, various interpretations of Scripture run rampant. Is there an additional test that can help us to discern truth from error?

Knippers turns to the rule of Vincent of Lerins. She describes Vincent as "an obscure, but well-informed and well-traveled monk who lived in the fifth century" who had observed the church's struggles over heresy and doctrinal truth. Vincent agreed that Scripture is the final authentication of the Church's faith, but in the controversies that he observed, all sides quoted Scripture. The issue, he concluded was not Scriptural authority itself, but how one interprets Scripture. So, in the midst of these controversies, Vincent asked the question, "What has the Church always believed?"

Knippers quoted theologian and patristics scholar Thomas Oden, whom she acknowledges as the person who introduced her to the writings of Vincent of Lerins: "Vincent concludes that the trend of the interpretation of the prophetic and apostolic texts must be understood in accordance with some general rule – a rule plausible cross-culturally to the Church universal as to what constitutes the mind of the believing Church."[27]

The rule that Vincent developed was "a method of consensual recollection: that which has been believed everywhere, always, and by everyone." In her address to the Anglicans, Knippers focused on each key word. "'Everywhere' means worldwide" she said. "Authentic Christianity is universal; it inhabits cross-cultural space. Everywhere means we listen to our fellow Anglicans around the world."[28]

"'Always' means from the beginning – faithful to the teaching of the apostles. This apostolic message is recorded in Scripture. Our bishops have a particular duty to preserve the apostolic teaching of the Church."[29]

26 Knippers, Diane, "The Role of the Laity," American Anglican Council News, October 9, 2003.

27 Oden, Thomas, *The Rebirth of Orthodoxy* (New York: Harper Collins, 2002).

28 Knippers, *op. cit.*

29 *Ibid.*

"By 'everyone' means the consent of the whole body of Christ. That's us – the laity, the people of God. This doesn't mean 100 percent agreement. In fact, it really doesn't mean a majority vote, because this isn't a legislative process – it is a Spirit-driven process. In fact, the heart of consent is within the act of worship. When we gather at the altar, we give assent to the apostolic faith."[30]

Knippers restatement of Vincent's rule is critically important to the modern church, not only in providing a method for assessing proposed theological innovations, but in its emphasis on the role of the laity in preserving the faith.

Worship – Laity's Testing Ground

As professional theologians, clergy are often tempted to treat that which is sacred as a commonplace experience. Scripture study can become an intellectual rather than a devotional exercise. Having been routinely exposed to gospel narratives, it is possible to develop a resistance to them, in the same sense that inoculation can generate antibodies in the bloodstream. In a corollary to the adage that familiarity breeds contempt, those who delve daily into the realm of theology may find innovation preferable to ancient truth.

Thus, professional clergy, exposed to professional theologians in their seminaries and denominational bureaucrats in their professional practice who have never served a local church, never buried a child of the congregation, never struggled with a member's marital or vocational crisis, never shared the joy of a war veteran's homecoming, may be drawn to "outer edge" theologies that push the philosophical envelope. But when bizarre notions are presented to the laity, they subject those ideas to the "sniff test." As a general rule, Christian lay people seek inspiration, not titillation. They thrive on Scriptures that have been handed down over the centuries. Stepping into the sanctuary from their secular pursuits, they welcome the sense of awe that comes from personal encounter with a great tradition that spans the centuries. Bowing before Almighty God, they are nourished by a faith that has stood the test of time. In corporate worship, they experience the fulfillment of Jesus' promise that where they gather in his name, he is present also.

While book club discussions of the latest innovation may draw transitory interest, the laity's long-term passion is for authenticity that they find in worshipping within the communion of the saints. It is here that they live as

30 *Ibid.*

the body of Christ, and it is here that they sense the ring of truth. Armed with Scripture and the great tradition, it is the laity that historically has returned the ship of faith to an on-course heading.

Covenant

Holy Scripture

"Pilate entered the praetorium again and called Jesus, and said to him, 'Are you the King of the Jews?' Jesus answered ... 'My kingship is not of this world ...'"

John 18:33, 36

The Constitution

"The purest churches under heaven are subject both to mixture and error; and some have so degenerated as to become no churches of Christ, but synagogues of Satan. Nevertheless, there shall be always a Church on earth to worship God according to his will."

The Westminster Confession of Faith
Chapter XXV

Broken Covenant

"Christ calls us to help create the political will for a new international economic order."

1978 General Assembly
Presbyterian Church in the US

"We are giving thanks this day for the Nicaraguans who have opened their lives up to us and allowed us to work beside them in this historical experiment known as the Popular Sandinista Revolution."

Presbyterian Church workers in Nicaragua
Nov. 23, 1989

"The Presbyterian Washington Office is the public policy information and advocacy office of the General Assembly of the Presbyterian Church (USA) ... General Assembly policy statements are to be seen as advice and counsel to Presbyterians as we contemplate our action on these issues in an election year."

The Presbyterian Church (USA) Washington Office
July, 2007

Chapter Ten

Thy Kingdom Come

The 2006 General Assembly of the Presbyterian Church (USA) met in Birmingham, Alabama. I found the landscape familiar, remembering some 40 years earlier when Martin Luther King led our entourage just 70 miles from the place where Presbyterians now gathered.

Revisiting that scene, I can see now what was only partially visible to me then. Some marchers shared King's passion for the higher law, a realm of principle that transcends politics, a life of obedience to the Word of God that is the fruit of one's salvation from above. Their commitment was entirely consistent with and, in fact, emanated from a thoroughly Reformed faith.

Other marchers were differently motivated. Driven by a passion for movement politics, they secularized a faith that King held sacred. Among them were leaders of the Presbyterian Church (USA). The same year in which they walked the streets of Alabama, they enacted *The Confession of 1967* and replaced humble obedience to the Word of God with ideological demands for entitlement.

During this period, leaders of the Presbyterian Church (USA) abandoned the one truth that the church has to share with the world, even to the extent that they were willing to diminish the Lord Jesus, if naming his name might offend movement allies. In the final analysis, it was the movement that mattered.

The rest, as we have documented in preceding chapters, is history. Presbyterian Church (USA) policies and the movements that they spawned triggered bloodbaths in Africa, Latin America and Europe. They shielded from ecclesiastical scorn North Korean dictators and a Cuban despot. They endorsed statist economies that have enslaved and impoverished their own people, while condemning an economic system that, albeit blemished by sins that beset any human construct, has produced a higher standard of living for a greater number of people than the world has ever known. They baptized sexual behaviors that Scripture condemns. They approved, and through their medical plan, even underwrote the slaughter of infants in their mothers' wombs. And, finally, having wrought such abominations through the policies and programs of an institution that claims the name "Church," they alienated the faithful, resulting in massive membership departures.

It will not do to say that those whose actions have brought us to this divide meant well. History is replete with disasters that emanated from high minded motives. Romantic visions of bringing in the "Age of Aquarius," of teaching the world "to sing in perfect harmony," of legislating equality, and of forging "unity in the midst of our diversity" are often mistaken for inspiration by those who wander from the Word of God that alone can test the spirit of our time.

An Ancient Procession

History reveals a precedent from which the world – especially the church – could have anticipated the consequences that result from chasing utopias. "Hosanna!" a horde shouted as its king made his way toward Jerusalem. "Look, the world has gone after him," said the Pharisees as multitudes swarmed in the streets and marched into the city. "Silence your disciples," they said, fearing Rome's reaction to the unruly assemblage.

The Pharisees had a point. Caesar did not take kindly to uprisings in his vassal states. Rebels would feel the back of his hand.

But was Jesus leading a revolution against Caesar? For those familiar with the prophet Zechariah, the colt that Jesus rode might have suggested that possibility. "Tell the daughter of Zion, Behold, your king is coming to you, humble, and mounted on an ass, even on a colt, the foal of an ass," said the prophet.[1]

That the people connected Jesus' ride with his kingship was obvious in the words that they shouted: "Hosanna! [literally "save us now!"] Blessed is he who comes in the name of the Lord!"[2] This was the language of royalty, quoting from a messianic psalm that was ritually chanted by the people as they marched around the great altar at the time of festival. It spoke of restoring King David's throne, the resurgence of that golden age when the mighty king of the Jews slew his enemies and signaled the reign of peace and prosperity. Such language was electric and it jolted the crowd into frenzy.

At last, after years of subjugation, this would be the day of liberation. The king would throw off Rome's shackles, cleanse the temple of its defile-

1 Zechariah 9:9.

2 Psalm 118:25-26.

ment and run the tax collectors out of town. Structures of injustice would be overthrown. Liberation was at hand!

Ripping branches off the palms and spreading their garments over the dust, this miserable, ragtag band of would-be revolutionaries greeted their king and anticipated holy war. Already, the city was swarming with Zealots, an armed guerrilla movement that was determined to live and, if necessary, die by the sword.

A Different Kind of King

The crowd rightly extolled Jesus as king, so he would not silence the appellation. The time had come when the truth must be spoken. Had the people been muzzled in that fullness of time, even the rocks would cry out!

But while the people's words proved literally correct, the meaning that they attached to those words tragically missed the mark. The king whom they extolled wore no regal garments. No gilded saddle covered the back of his colt. A crown of thorns would pierce his brow.

In its frenetic street dance, the crowd misread the king who rode in its midst. It failed to see his tears over Jerusalem and the destruction that he knew would surely come when Caesar had enough of its rebellion. Christ was its king, but a very different king than the one it had in mind. "My kingdom," he would say to Pilate, "is not of this world."

What moved the people was a monstrous ideology, not an abiding faith in the King of kings and Lord of lords. They tried to refashion the heavenly King into a secular monarch, to mold a ruler of their own making, to fashion a mascot for the extension of their own sociopolitical ambitions. In that reverse and deadly alchemy that occurs when something secular is substituted for the sacred, they turned the gold of salvation into the dross of liberation, the Word of the Lord into movement politics.

And when Jesus Christ would have none of it, when he refused to play the role that the crowd demanded of him, it turned ugly. The same mob that shouted "Hosanna!" now cried "Crucify Him!"

Theirs was no Christian faith. It was an ideology, one that has appeared many times hence. The world saw it in Hitler's Arian race, in Stalin's extermination of Ukrainian millions, in the suffering and starvation foisted by Kim Il Sung upon his own people, in Robert Mugabe's payments to mercenary thugs, using land stolen from Zimbabwean farmers, in Castro and Guevara's counterinsurgency invasions of Latin American neighbors and in the Presbyterian Church (USA)'s emphasis on liberation rather than salvation. All of these atrocities emanated from grand and glorious "Hosannas," the relentless pursuit of secular utopias.

'Thin Religion'

Mirislov Volf, Professor of Systematic Theology at Yale Divinity School and director of the Yale Center for Faith and Culture, is a native of war-torn Croatia who witnessed firsthand the blood bath that erupted between Croatians and Serbians. He has noted the religious rhetoric that both sides employed to justify their hostilities. Far from being an instrument of peace, said Volf, religion-inspired slogans and symbols exacerbated ethnic animosities.[3]

Volf examined the oratory delivered by murderers, kidnappers, and rapists. He found that while such language included words common to their religious traditions, they were not in themselves authentically religious. He called such rhetoric "thin religion," a term he gave to secular ideologies that are covered with a veneer of religious language. Thus, religion itself was not the cause of the conflict. It was a pale substitute, a counterfeit that gave the appearance of religion but was in fact something entirely different.

Volf attempted to bring Croatian Muslims and Serbian Catholics into dialogue, encouraging each to go deeper into their own religious traditions and to share honestly their most profoundly held beliefs with one another. While going to that deeper level did not bring about conversion from one faith to another he found that those who shared their religious convictions came to a greater acceptance of one another as persons.

In contrast to self-described peacemakers who suggest that religion is the culprit and secularism the antidote, Volf's findings led him to say that the cure for religious zealotry is not less religion but more religion, reflected in stronger and more intelligent practices of faith. This antidote, he suggested would replace "thin religion" with a religious experience that reflects the integrity of its core teachings.[4]

Volf's "thin religion" analysis offers insights into the Presbyterian Church (USA)'s corruption of Reformed theology. Immersed in the passions of a civil rights movement that focused on African American issues in the early sixties and then expanded its reach to include the liberation of "indigenous people," women, homosexuals, youth, the elderly, whales, the spotted owl, and sundry other issues of the moment, denominational leaders surfed the waves of continuous causes, morphing the richness of Reformed faith into the rhetoric of egalitarian ideology.

3 Speaking of Faith: "Religion and Violence," a Krista Tippett interview with Miroslav Volf, Minnesota Public Radio, Aug. 4, 2005.

4 Volf, Miroslav, *Exclusion and Embrace: A Theological Exploration of Identity, Otherness, and Reconciliation* (Nashville: Abingdon Press, 1996).

While many of these issues disclose significant challenges that require correction by competent physical and social scientists, their embrace by ideologues engenders monstrous distortions of both fact and faith, often replacing one inequity with another. In that process the gospel becomes a veneer for a secular agenda, resulting in "thin religion."

'Works Righteousness'

Professor Peter Berger, director of Boston University's Institute for the Study of Economic Culture, has voiced his objection to preacherly incursions into his profession. "While, by definition, [my] insights have no inerrancy and are always open to revision as new empirical evidence comes up, I am reasonably certain that I understand some things about the modern world. Thus, when I go to church or read church publications, I am irritated when I am confronted with statements that I consider to be empirically flawed. I don't go to church in order to hear vulgarized, 'pop' versions of my own field. The irritation deepens when these terrible simplifications are proclaimed to me in tones of utter certitude and moral urgency. Bad analysis obviously makes for bad policy, and here I am not just intellectually irritated, but morally offended."[5]

Berger then specified what he believes is the church's calling. "Faith in the gospel of Christ is constitutive of the Church," he said. "The Church is the community that embodies this faith. Apostasy occurs when any other content is deemed to be constitutive of the Christian community. At that point, the community becomes something other than the Church of Christ. Of all the so-called 'marks of the Church,' the central and indispensable one is that the Church proclaims the gospel, and not any other message of salvation."[6] Berger identified mainline church tendencies to move from the gospel to secular causes as contemporary examples of a theological distortion that the Bible calls "works righteousness."

Increasingly, Presbyterians who love the faith are finding movement politics an unsatisfactory substitution for the gospel. Liberalism's words sound "spiritual," so Christians who do not think deeply about spiritual realities are often unable to specify what is missing. But because those words are not the Word, they are, to use Volf's word, "thin," and they do not satisfy people's hunger for the substance of faith. Presbyterians are falling away, many of them migrating toward evangelical churches where the Word is preached with power and conviction.

5 Berger, Peter, L., *Different Gospels* (London: The C.S. Lewis Centre, Society for Promoting Christian Knowledge, 1993), p. 112.

6 *Ibid.*

Presbyterian Church (USA) leaders are not the first to substitute secular ideals for the faith, and as long as sin remains a part of the human condition, they will not be the last. Like towers of Babel, edifices of self affirmation will rise and fall. Inevitably, they return to the dust from which they came. This is the story of every human institution that chooses lesser gods.

A View from 'Outside'

Philip Turner admits that having been reared in the United States and educated within the context of the Episcopal Church (USA), he was slow to recognize the apostasy that had overtaken his denomination. It was not until he stepped outside his denominational environment, living for ten years among Africa's Baganda people on the North shore of Lake Victoria that he saw it. Looking back upon the Episcopal Church (USA) from afar, he was struck with the truth that changed his life.

Turner describes his wake-up call this way: "It was not until I spent a considerable time outside the confines of my own denomination that I came to realize that its working theology stood miles away from the basic content of 'Nicene Christianity' with its thick description of God as Father, Son, and Holy Spirit, its richly developed Christology, and its compelling account of Christ's call to holiness of life …

"The voice now addressing ECUSA in theological tones that seem not just strange but unacceptable, comes from the Global South, and particularly from people who in the biblical sense are poor. What they are trying to point out is that the working theology of ECUSA does not accord with the great Christian tradition they received from the very people who now seem to be preaching a different gospel. Rather than dismissing this alien voice (as they say, the voice of fundamentalism or the voice of people who have never experienced the Enlightenment) it might be more Christianly apt to adopt a more humble attitude and ask if what this strange voice is saying has any merit. In particular, it might be not only prudent but also charitable to ask if its criticism of ECUSA's working theology has the ring of truth."[7]

Reclaiming the Church's Moral Authority

In *The Reformed Imperative*,[8] John Hadden Leith urged church leaders to remember that the church has a message for the world that no one else can offer. He warned them not to lose sight of the gospel by succumbing to the

7 Turner, Philip W., *op. cit.*

8 Leith, John H., *The Reformed Imperative: What the Church has to say that no one else can say* (Philadelphia: Westminster Press, 1988).

allure of secular pursuits. Acknowledging that psychology can intensify a pastor's awareness of parishioners' emotional states, political science can be useful in assessing the social dimensions of one's ethical presuppositions, and management courses can hone a minister's organizational skills, Leith lamented the growing predilection of clergy to think of themselves as mini-psychologists, politicians and ecclesiastical CEOs.

There is a place for the psychologist, the statesman, and the executive, he said. Each is a worthy vocation, but none can replace those who proclaim the gospel. That, said Leith, is the special province of the Church.

"The Church," said Leith, "is not merely an association of human beings or even an ideal. It is a special kind of community, created by the grace of God. For this reason it is not to be confused with any human enterprise ... The marks by which the Church is identified are not found in its own qualities, but in the divine acts which create and nourish it.[9]

"The premise that the ground of the Church's existence lies outside of itself is basic in John Calvin's doctrine of the Church," said Leith. "The Church obtains the right to existence not by virtue of any quality inherent in itself but solely by virtue of faith in the promise of God, given in Jesus Christ."[10]

The 'Echo' of God

Theologian Colin Gunton says the idea that the Church is merely a human association that bears Christ's name has ancient roots, reaching at least as far back as the Constantinian period. A scriptural view of the Church, he believes, is anchored in the doctrine of the Trinity. "The being of the Church," says Gunton, "should echo the interrelation between the three persons who together constitute the deity. The Church is called to be the kind of reality at a finite level that God is in eternity."[11]

How does this happen? How can a finite institution be the very presence of God on earth? Here Gunton turns to the Reformed dicta of "marks of the Church" (the authentic preaching of the Word and the administration of the sacraments) to which Calvin so often referred. "The concrete means by which the Church becomes an echo of the life of the Godhead are all such as to direct the church away from self-glorification to the source of its life

9 Leith, John H., *John Calvin's Doctrine of the Christian Life* (Louisville, Ky.: Westminster/John Knox Press, 1989), p. 169.

10 *Ibid.*, p. 168.

11 Gunton, Colin E., *On Being the Church: Essays on the Christian Community* (Edinburgh: T. & T. Clark, Ltd., 1989), p. 78.

in the creative and recreative presence of God to the world. The activity of proclamation and the celebration of the gospel sacraments are temporal ways of orienting the community to the being of God. Proclamation turns the community to the Word whose echo it is called to be; baptism and eucharist, the sacraments of incorporation and koinonia, to the love of God the Father towards his world as it is mediated by the Son and Spirit. Thus, there is no timeless Church: only a church then and now and to be, as the Spirit ever and ever again incorporates people into Christ and in the same action brings them into and maintains them in community with each other."[12]

The Locus of the Church's Moral Authority

Here, in its divine commission to be an earthly echo of the Triune God of grace, is the locus of the church's moral authority. It is an authority not granted by human beings, but by the very presence and power of God whom it echoes, albeit imperfectly.

Even those who do not affirm the gospel understand when they see a steeple towering over the village green that the church points to a reality that is beyond itself. Despite the mainstream media's frequent caricatures of effete and irrelevant clergy and the underlying implication that faith is a form of ignorance, the church continues to stand for something crucial to America's heart and mind. Its moral authority is especially visible in times of national crisis.

Seeking the Church's Blessing

It is the church's moral authority that those who dwell outside God's will so desperately seek to appropriate. This is the essence of every campaign to change the theology of the mainline churches. Recognizing but refusing to submit to the church's moral authority, many who choose to live outside God's will still yearn for something that the church alone can give. They entreat, even demand, the church's blessing. Like the Old Testament patriarch Jacob, they cry out, "I will not let you go unless you bless me!"

The Lord did bless Jacob, but he also changed him. Jacob, the "heel grabber," trickster and thief, became Israel. Scripture describes the transformation: "Behold, the old has passed away. The new has come."

Sexuality issues that have consumed our age comprise only one of many battlefields where the world recognizes but also defies the church's author-

12 *Ibid.*, p. 79.